| 83d Congress 2d Session | SENATE | Document No. 164 |

REVIEW OF THE UNITED NATIONS CHARTER

COMPILATION OF STAFF STUDIES PREPARED
FOR THE USE OF THE SUBCOMMITTEE ON
THE UNITED NATIONS CHARTER OF THE
COMMITTEE ON FOREIGN RELATIONS

PURSUANT TO

S. Res. 126
EIGHTY-THIRD CONGRESS

221034

GREENWOOD PRESS, PUBLISHERS
WESTPORT, CONNECTICUT

Originally published in 1955
by The U.S. Government Printing Office, Washington, D.C.

Reprinted from an original copy in the collections
of the University of Illinois Library

First Greenwood Reprinting 1970

Library of Congress Catalogue Card Number 68-55114

SBN 8371-3170-7

Printed in the United States of America

In the Senate of the United States,
August 2 (legislative day, July 2), 1954.

On motion by Mr. Wiley,

Ordered, That a series of staff studies on various aspects of a review of the Charter of the United Nations, together with certain additional studies, to be prepared under the direction of the Special Subcommittee of the United Nations Charter of the Committee on Foreign Relations, be printed as a Senate Document, and that one thousand additional copies be printed for the use of the Committee on Foreign Relations.

COMMITTEE ON FOREIGN RELATIONS

WALTER F. GEORGE, Georgia, *Chairman*

THEODORE FRANCIS GREEN, Rhode Island
J. W. FULBRIGHT, Arkansas
JOHN SPARKMAN, Alabama
HUBERT H. HUMPHREY, Minnesota
MIKE MANSFIELD, Montana
ALBEN W. BARKLEY, Kentucky
WAYNE MORSE, Oregon

ALEXANDER WILEY, Wisconsin
H. ALEXANDER SMITH, New Jersey
BOURKE B. HICKENLOOPER, Iowa
WILLIAM LANGER, North Dakota
WILLIAM F. KNOWLAND, California
GEORGE D. AIKEN, Vermont
HOMER E. CAPEHART, Indiana

CARL MARCY, *Chief of Staff*
PAT M. HOLT, *Consultant*
JULIUS N. CAHN, *Consultant*
ALWYN V. FREEMAN, *Consultant*
C. C. O'DAY, *Chief Clerk*

SUBCOMMITTEE ON THE UNITED NATIONS CHARTER

(Created pursuant to S. Res. 126, 83d Cong., as amended by S. Res. 83, 84th Cong., and continued by S. Res. 193, 83d Cong., and S. Res. 36, 84th Cong.)

Composition during 84th Congress

WALTER F. GEORGE, Georgia, *Chairman*

SPESSARD L. HOLLAND, Florida [1]
JOHN SPARKMAN, Alabama
HUBERT H. HUMPHREY, Minnesota
MIKE MANSFIELD, Montana

ALEXANDER WILEY, Wisconsin
H. ALEXANDER SMITH, New Jersey
WILLIAM F. KNOWLAND, California
GEORGE D. AIKEN, Vermont
—— —— [2]

FRANCIS O. WILCOX, *Chief of Staff*
CARL MARCY, *Consultant*
FRANCIS R. VALEO, *Consultant* [3]
MORELLA HANSEN, *Research Assistant*
JUNE C. PITTS, *Assistant Clerk*
MARY ANN SAMES, *Assistant Clerk*

Composition during 83d Congress

ALEXANDER WILEY, Wisconsin, *Chairman*

HOMER FERGUSON, Michigan
WILLIAM F. KNOWLAND, California
JOHN S. COOPER, [1] Kentucky

SPESSARD L. HOLLAND, [1] Florida
JOHN J. SPARKMAN, Alabama
GUY M. GILLETTE, Iowa
MIKE MANSFIELD, Montana

FRANCIS O. WILCOX, *Chief of Staff*
CARL MARCY, *Consultant*
FRANCIS R. VALEO, *Consultant* [3]
MORELLA HANSEN, *Research Assistant*
JUNE C. PITTS, *Assistant Clerk*
MARY ANN SAMES, *Assistant Clerk*

----

[1] Appointed by the Vice President to serve with the subcommittee.
[2] To be appointed by the Vice President to serve with the subcommittee.
[3] On loan from the Legislative Reference Service, Library of Congress.

PREFACE

By Walter F. George, *Chairman*

This document contains the staff studies prepared for the use of the Subcommittee on the United Nations Charter of the Committee on Foreign Relations. The subcommittee was created by Senate Resolution 126 (83d Cong.) which was introduced by Senator Gillette. It was directed to make a "full and complete study of proposals to amend, revise, or otherwise modify or change existing international peace and security organizations * * *." The purpose of the study was to assist the Senate in discharging its constitutional function of advising the "President with respect to the foreign policy of the United States."

To assist in its work, the subcommittee requested that a series of staff studies be prepared on the various aspects of the United Nations Charter and activities that might be considered in connection with a review conference. These staff studies have been published by the subcommittee as individual committee prints.

In order that these factual background studies may be more readily available, the Senate authorized the publication of these studies as a Senate document.

All the staff studies have now been completed, Staff Studies Nos. 1 to 7 during Senator Wiley's chairmanship of the subcommittee and Staff Studies Nos. 8 to 12 during my own. They have been prepared by members of the subcommittee staff and the Legislative Reference Service of the Library of Congress. All those who have participated in this work deserve credit for the high quality, the objective presentation of issues, and the thoroughness reflected in the staff studies. I should like to pay a special tribute to Francis O. Wilcox, the former chief of staff of the Committee and the Subcommittee on the United Nations Charter, now Assistant Secretary of State for International Organization Affairs, under whose direction these studies were prepared.

In addition to these staff studies, the subcommittee has published a Collection of Documents (S. Doc. 87, 83d Cong.), held hearings in various cities of the United States, which are printed in 13 parts, and made 2 interim reports to the Senate (S. Repts. 14 and 1305, 84th Cong.).

December 1, 1955.

CONTENTS [1]

[1] Each staff study has its individual table of contents.

THE PROBLEM OF THE VETO IN THE UNITED NATIONS SECURITY COUNCIL

STAFF STUDY NO. 1

FEBRUARY 19, 1954

PREFACE

By Alexander Wiley, *Chairman*

Under Senate Resolution 126 (as amended by S. Res. 193), the Foreign Relations Subcommittee on the United Nations Charter is conducting a study of the problems of charter review. It is probable that a conference to review the charter will be called after 1955 and the subcommittee is now preparing for this contingency. In a matter of such major importance to the foreign relations of the United States, the Senate must inform itself fully on the issues involved and the attitudes of the American people thereon.

To assist the subcommittee in its work, I have requested that the staff undertake a series of studies on various aspects of the subject. In January the subcommittee published a collection of basic documents on charter review (S. Doc. No. 87). The present study (staff study No. 1) deals with one of the most complex issues of charter review, the problem of the veto in the Security Council. It was prepared by Mrs. Ellen Collier, Foreign Affairs Division, Legislative Reference Service, the Library of Congress, under the direction of the subcommittee staff.

Almost since the inception of the United Nations, the veto has been criticized as being a kind of monkey wrench in the machinery of the organization. The device has been used 58 times—57 times by the Soviet Union—to block action by the Security Council.

This abuse of the veto has led to demands for its abolition. In seeking to correct an evil, however, care must be taken not to compound it. As this study shows, various methods have already been developed within the framework of the charter which in some degree tend to counterbalance the veto. Moreover, the United States no less than the other great powers insisted upon the veto as a condition for acceptance of the charter. If it were abolished, the way would conceivably be opened for the use of our Armed Forces without our consent and for the loss of other prerogatives which heretofore have been regarded as exclusively national.

Before Americans take a position with respect to abolishing or limiting the veto they must answer some hard questions, including the following:

1. Should the United States be willing to give up the veto over United Nations use of American Armed Forces without our consent?

2. If the veto were abolished in this respect, would a constitutional amendment be necessary to enable us to give effect to a revised charter?

3. Should the United States be willing to relinquish the veto with respect to the admission of new members to the United Nations?

4. If the veto were relinquished with respect to membership, should we still seek its retention with respect to the matter of who should represent China in the United Nations?

3

5. Should the United States be willing to give up the veto with respect to the international control of atomic energy in the event a feasible control plan is devised?

Each of these questions, and many others which will occur to the reader of this study, must be considered by members of this subcommittee if they are to submit constructive suggestions to the Senate. The questions must be answered in terms of what is best for the United States. What course of action with respect to the veto provisions of the United Nations Charter will best assure the security and national interests of the United States?

This study provides a broad framework for a consideration of the veto power and the various proposals which have been made to alter it. Its publication does not indicate either the subcommittee's acceptance or rejection of any of the views which are expressed. Before reaching any conclusions, the subcommittee will want to obtain the thinking of the American people on all the aspects and ramifications of the problem.

FEBRUARY 19, 1954.

CONTENTS

THE PROBLEM OF THE VETO IN THE UNITED NATIONS SECURITY COUNCIL

A. INTRODUCTION

Article 27 of the United Nations Charter, which regulates voting in the Security Council, probably has aroused more controversy and inspired more demands for charter revision than any other provision. For out of the requirement contained in article 27 that certain decisions be made only with the unanimous concurrence of the five permanent members of the Security Council has sprung the issue of the veto. By voting against a resolution, other than on a question deemed procedural, any 1 of the 5 permanent member-states of the Security Council—the United States, the United Kingdom, France, China, or the Soviet Union—can block, or "veto" a decision even though it might be approved by an overwhelming majority of the 11-nation Council. The extensive use of the veto by the Soviet Union has led to the view in some quarters that the United Nations cannot be effective in preserving peace unless some modification is made in the present voting system in the Security Council.

Two major approaches to dealing with the issue of the veto lie beyond the scope of this study. One of these suggests that the solution lies in a general ameliorating of relations between the Soviet Union and the other permanent members of the Security Council so that there will be fewer occasions of disagreement in which the veto is likely to be invoked. Proponents of this solution say that the veto is not the disease which impairs the effectiveness of the United Nations. The veto, it is contended, is merely a symptom of the split between the Soviet block on the one hand and the United States and other great powers on the other. Therefore, all energy should be concentrated on improving relations between the two. It is obvious that the veto would not be as serious a problem as it is if the Soviet Union and the other great powers had harmonious relations, shared common international aims, and agreed on the methods which should be used to attain those aims.

The other major approach to the problem of the veto involves the forming of a new United Nations without the Soviet Union. This course was suggested by former President Hoover in April 1950.

The Kremlin has reduced the United Nations to a propaganda forum for the smearing of free peoples. It has been defeated as a preservative of peace and good will.

*   *   *   *   *   *   *

I suggest that the United Nations should be reorganized without the Communist nations in it. If that is impractical, then a definite New United Front should be organized of those peoples who disavow communism, who stand for morals and religion, and who love freedom. * * * [This] is a proposal to redeem the concept of the United Nations to the high purpose for which it was created.[1]

This proposal would involve such a basic change in the existing situation and system as to reduce the specific issue of the veto to relatively minor importance. As expressed by Gen. Carlos P. Romulo, former President of the General Assembly:

A United Nations reorganized to include only those nations who are prepared to line up with one great power against another would not be a world organization. It would be merely a magnified regional association.[2]

B. THE ORIGIN OF THE VETO

The requirement of five-power unanimity in the Security Council embodies in the charter a concept on which the United Nations was based; that the great powers would continue to cooperate in building the peace as they had cooperated in World War II. It was not easy to devise an effective method for voting in the Security Council. The Council was to be composed of 11 sovereign, juridically equal states. Five of these states, the United States, the United Kingdom, the Soviet Union, France, and China were given permanent seats. The Council was to have authority to take action to keep peace far exceeding that which had been possessed by the Council of the League of Nations.

One problem was to establish a system of voting which would insure that sufficient power lay behind decisions of the Security Council to make these decisions effective. If each state had one vote and a simple majority decided an issue, conceivably the nonpermanent members of the Council representing perhaps only 40 million people and carrying very little political, economic, and military weight could order the United Nations to take action. Obviously a decision made by a majority of this kind could not be forced on the major powers, any one of whom might have greater resources and strength. Nor would such a decision have the requisite prestige to insure that it would be supported by the other members of the United Nations.

Another problem was to make certain that the two most powerful states, the Soviet Union and the United States, would participate in the international organization and actively lend their power to support it. This meant giving assurances that the United Nations would not be able to take action against either or both of these two states contrary to their will, which the organization could hardly do anyway without precipitating a large scale war.

At the same time, it was important that in assigning a special position to the most powerful states, there was not also created a dictatorship of the Big Five which would leave the smaller states without an effective voice.

The response of the old League of Nations to similar problems of voting had been to require that decisions of its Council be unanimous. The unanimity requirement, however, often blocked action. Not only the permanent powers but even temporary members of the Council of the League had used their "veto" to prevent decisions.

A solution for the United Nations was sought in requiring that decisions of the Security Council be taken by a majority which would include all of the permanent members. This approach had the advantage of permitting action by less than unanimous consent. It also insured that a decision would be supported by the prestige and strength needed for its enforcement. It did not, however, provide for a twilight zone; that is, decisions which presumably would have sufficient force behind them to be effective but were opposed by 1 or 2 of the 5 great powers for any one of a multitude of political reasons of their own.

Even in the early stages of planning, the principal powers agreed that the concurrence of the permanent members of the Security Council should be required for all important decisions relating to peace and security. At Dumbarton Oaks in 1944, the need for basic agreement among the big powers was accepted by the United States, the United Kingdom, the Soviet Union and China [3] as a premise for the formation of the organization.

Provisions concerning voting in the Security Council, however, were not incorporated in the Dumbarton Oaks proposals because of disagreement on the questions of size of the majority and the right of a member of the Council to vote in disputes to which the member was a party. The Soviet Union favored a simple majority for substantive decisions (including all the permanent members) whereas the United Kingdom and China preferred a two-thirds majority (including all the permanent members). The United States had expressed a willingness to accept a majority of either size.[4]

The more significant difference of opinion at that time appeared in connection with the question of whether a party to a dispute should be allowed to vote on its own case. On this issue the Russian delegates remained firm in their position that the concurrence of all permanent members should be required for every substantive decision, even if one of them was a party to a dispute. The United Kingdom, the United States, and China, on the other hand, held that no nation should be a judge of its own cause. Hence, a party to a dispute, even a permanent power, should not be allowed to vote. Since agreement on this matter could not be reached at Dumbarton Oaks, a decision on the provisions for voting was postponed until the Yalta Conference.[5]

By that time, the United States had devised a compromise solution. This proposal, known as the Yalta voting formula, provided for a majority of seven, including all of the permanent members, for important decisions. The majority of 7 required 1 vote more than the simple majority which had been advocated by the Soviet Union, and 1 vote less than the two-thirds majority proposed by the United Kingdom and China. It meant, in effect, that a decision on a substantive matter, while requiring unanimity of the great powers, could not be taken without the approval of at least two nonpermanent members. This arrangement offered the smaller states protection against rampant big-power rule, but did not permit any one of them to tie up the operations of the Security Council as had been the case in the League of Nations.

The other unresolved problem, whether a member of the Security Council should be allowed to vote in a dispute to which it was a party, was also met by a compromise. It provided that a party to a dispute, even a permanent power, would be required to abstain from voting in the pacific settlement stage, that is the stage when enforcement measures did not apply. At the stage when enforcement measures

[3] United States. Department of State. Postwar foreign policy preparation, 1939–45. Washington, Government Printing Office, 1949, p. 317
[4] Ibid., p. 658.
[5] Ibid., p. 326.

were being voted upon, however, a party to a dispute would not be required to abstain.

At the Yalta Conference the Soviet Union agreed to this solution of the problem as the United Kingdom had done earlier, and it was incorporated into the earlier Dumbarton Oaks proposals. The Yalta voting formula [6] reads as follows:

1. Each member of the Security Council should have one vote.
2. Decisions of the Security Council on procedural matters should be made by an affirmative vote of seven members.
3. Decisions of the Security Council on all other matters should be made by an affirmative vote of seven members including the concurring votes of the permanent members; provided that, in decisions under chapter VIII, section A and under the second sentence of paragraph 1 of chapter VIII, section C, a party to a dispute should abstain from voting.[7]

At the San Francisco Conference, article 27, dealing with voting in the Security Council, raised more controversy than any other part of the charter. Many of the smaller powers attacked the unanimity requirement as a violation of the principles of democracy and sovereign equality. The sponsoring powers,[8] however, insisted that the permanent members would carry the bulk of responsibility for enforcing decisions of the Security Council and it was unrealistic to assume that they would do so if they were not in accord with such decisions.

Debate at San Francisco did not long center on whether the veto should be abolished or retained.

In general the delegates participating in the discussion were in agreement that the voting provisions, while not perfect in theory, especially with reference to the procedures of pacific settlement, were probably necessary for purposes of enforcement action. The points were raised that the voting procedure was consistent with political realities; that its acceptance in whole or in part was a necessary condition for the creation of the organization.[9]

Attention at San Francisco was primarily devoted to clarifying the limits of the veto power and to an attempt to eliminate the veto in pacific settlement of disputes. In response to the demands for clarification, the sponsoring powers issued a joint statement on June 7, 1945, which was later agreed to by France [10] interpreting article 27.

This statement clarified certain points with respect to the veto. It made clear the dominant view of the permanent powers that a single member of the Security Council could not invoke the veto to prevent bringing to the attention of the Council or the Assembly any situation which might lead to international friction or give rise to a dispute.

In regard to what constitutes procedural matters, for which unanimity of the Big Five was not required, the statement said that the draft charter itself contained an indication of the application of the voting procedures to the various functions of the Council.

The statement said further:

It will be unlikely that there will arise in the future any matters of great importance on which a decision will have to be made as to whether a procedural vote

[6] Later this formula was incorporated in the United Nations Charter. The only changes made were to adjust the citations to the charter, and to change "should" to "shall" in each paragraph.
[7] Postwar Foreign Policy Preparation, 1939–45, p. 665.
[8] China, U. S. S. R., United Kingdom, and the United States.
[9] United Nations Conference on International Organization, Document 417, III/1/19, Summary report on the ninth meeting of Committee III/1, p. 2.
[10] For the full text of the statement, see Senate Foreign Relations Committee Subcommittee on the United Nations Charter, Review of the United Nations Charter, Collection of Documents, U. S. Government Printing Office, 1954, p. 562–564, hereinafter referred to as Collection of Documents.

would apply. Should, however, such a matter arise, the decision regarding the preliminary question as to whether or not such a matter is procedural must be taken by a vote of seven members of the Security Council, including the concurring votes of the permanent members.

The statement pointed out that under the League of Nations every member of the Council had had a veto, so nothing new in the way of authority was being given to the permanent members. Rather, the chance of obstruction was reduced because the veto was being taken away from the nonpermanent members. The statement also included this assurance:

It is not to be assumed * * * that the permanent members, any more than the nonpermanent members, would use their "veto" power willfully to obstruct the operation of the Council.

And in the following terms it made clear that if there was to be a charter at all, it would be necessary for the Conference to accept the Yalta formula:

the four sponsoring governments agreed on the Yalta formula and have presented it to this Conference as essential if an international organization is to be created through which all peace-loving nations can effectively discharge their common responsibilities for the maintenance of international peace and security.

The third paragraph of article 27, which contains the provision for the veto, was adopted by the San Francisco Conference on July 13, 1945, by 30 affirmative votes, and 15 abstentions; Cuba and Colombia voted against the measure.[11]

Article 27 of the United Nations Charter reads as follows:

1. Each member of the Security Council shall have one vote.
2. Decisions of the Security Council on procedural matters shall be made by an affirmative vote of seven members.
3. Decisions of the Security Council on all other matters shall be made by an affirmative vote of seven members including the concurring votes of the permanent members; provided that, in decisions under Chapter VI, and under paragraph 3 of Article 52, a party to a dispute shall abstain from voting.

C. THE UNANIMITY REQUIREMENT IN PRACTICE

The framers of the charter hoped that the unanimity requirement would bind together power and responsibility. They expected that the permanent members of the Security Council would go forward in the same cooperation that they had practiced during the war, using their joint strength to keep the peace of the world. The veto was generally considered to be an open recognition that there would be little prospect for peace if there were serious dissension among the big powers. It was expected that the device would seldom be employed and that by acknowledging the need for unanimity as a precondition of action, unanimity would be encouraged.

Throughout the formative period of the United Nations, the emphasis was placed more on the positive call for cooperation among the permanent members than on the negative possibilities of the veto. The rapporteur's summaries of the proceedings of Committee III/1 of the San Francisco Conference contain the following accounts of statements by representatives of the United States, the U. S. S. R., and the United Kingdom:

[11] Dwight E. Lee. The Genesis of the Veto. International Organization (Boston) vol. 1, February 1947. p. 42. All of these states, however, ratified the charter.

THE UNITED STATES

If the great powers were divided on an issue there was no real hope of a successful peaceful settlement, for disunity would be engendered that might cause a breach of the peace.   When a dispute was brought before the Security Council, after other means of pacific settlement had been exhausted, a solution would have to be found by the united action of the major powers.   The problem which would occupy the best minds of today and tomorrow was to keep the "key oarsmen" pulling together, but it was a problem no greater than had been successfully met by achieving unity in the present war.   The problem of peace must be worked out by a united, not a divided world.[12]

THE U. S. S. R.

* * * the solution [to the voting problem] had been the result of the fundamental desire the feeling of unity among the great powers * * * any change in the Yalta voting formula would be undesirable because if decisions in the Security Council were not unanimous, a cause of friction would occur.[13]

THE UNITED KINGDOM

Peace must rest on the unanimity of the great powers for without it, whatever was built would be built upon shifting sands.   * * *   The unanimity of the great powers was a hard fact but an inescapable one.   The veto power was a means of preserving that unity, and far from being a menace to the small powers, it was their essential safeguard.   Without this unanimity, all countries, large and small, would fall victims to the establishment of gigantic rival blocs which might clash in some future Armageddon.   Cooperation among the great powers was the only escape from this peril; nothing else was of comparable importance.[14]

Use of veto

The San Francisco Conference was scarcely over, however, when relations between the Soviet Union, on the one hand, and the United States, Great Britain, France, and China on the other, began to deteriorate.   Before the United Nations had been in operation a year, the degree of agreement required for consistently effective action by the Security Council had already ceased to exist.   The rule of unanimity, instead of promoting common action of the five great powers, was preventing decisions from being reached; it added to the mistrust and antagonism of which it had already become a symptom.

The sponsoring powers had said in their statement at San Francisco:

It is not to be assumed, however, that the permanent members * * * would use their "veto" power willfully to obstruct the operations of the Council.

Nevertheless, as the Soviet Union voted in the negative on measure after measure, it became apparent that the operations of the Council were being willfully obstructed.   By the end of December 1947, the veto had already been invoked 23 times, almost exclusively by the Soviet Union.

France is the only other great power to have used the device.   On August 25, 1947, a French veto blocked a Soviet resolution proposing that a commission be sent to Indonesia.   Earlier France had joined with the Soviet Union in vetoing a resolution involving the Spanish question.   None of the other great powers has ever cast a negative vote which acted as a veto, that is, on a substantive measure which had attained the affirmative votes of at least seven other members of the Security Council.

---

[12] United Nations Conference on International Organization Documents, vol. 11, summary report of the 19th meeting of Committee III/1.   United Nations Information Organizations, N. Y., 1945.   p. 491.
[13] Ibid.   Summary report of the 10th meeting of Committee III/1.   p. 332.
[14] Ibid.   Summary report of the 18th meeting of Committee III/1.   p. 475.

The Soviet Union cast the first veto on February 16, 1946, and had used eight more before the year was over. As early as December 13, 1946, the General Assembly passed a resolution expressing its concern over the "divergencies which have arisen in regard to the application and interpretation of article 27 of the charter * * *" and requesting the permanent members—

to make every effort, in consultation with one another and with fellow members of the Security Council, to ensure that the use of the special voting privilege of its permanent members does not impede the Security Council in reaching decisions promptly.[15]

By the end of January 1954, the Soviet Union had cast its 57th veto.[16] Forty-three of these occurred in the first 4 years of the Security Council's history, thus having a profound effect on the manner in which the organization has developed.

Of the vetoes, almost half or 28 have been used to block the admission of new members. Fourteen states—Jordan, Ireland, Portugal, Italy, Austria, Finland, Ceylon, South Korea, Nepal, Libya, Japan, Vietnam, Laos, and Cambodia, which would otherwise have had enough votes for a favorable recommendation to the General Assembly have been blocked by the Soviet Union.

The veto was twice used to prevent the selection of a Secretary General. On three occasions, a "double veto" has been employed, that is, a veto to prevent a resolution from being regarded as procedural, and then another when the matter was voted on as a substantive matter.

In less than half of the cases the veto was invoked by the Soviet Union on issues involving the security functions of the Council. Even in these instances most of the vetoes did not pertain to enforcement action but were cast during the process of encouraging pacific settlement.

D. EFFECT OF THE VETO ON THE UNITED NATIONS

At San Francisco the Security Council was established as "an international executive committee representing the whole organization," [16a] and the voting provisions were drawn up to suit this concentration of power and responsibility. The backfiring of the unanimity rule, however, has raised the question of whether the Security Council can act effectively often enough to justify its existence or whether a basic change in organization is required.

Lack of unanimity among the great powers appears already to have impaired the functioning of the Security Council to the point where, at the present time, it scarcely can be said to fulfill the "primary" responsibility for the maintenance of international peace and security. In matters of security members of the United Nations now depend less on the Council than on their national defenses, their regional alliances, and on voluntary action agreed upon in the General Assembly.

The United States, for instance, has been spending far greater sums on national defense in the past few years than at any other time in its peacetime history. Even the organization of collective strength has

---

[15] For full text see Collection of Documents, p. 565.
[16] A table showing the use of the veto by the Soviet Union is published in Collection of Documents, pp. 577-580, with the exception of the 57th veto, cast by the U. S. S. R. on January 22, 1954, on a proposed settlement of the Israeli-Syrian water dispute.
[16a] Dwight E. Lee. Op. cit., p. 34.

taken place to a larger degree outside rather than within the United Nations.   The United States began to buttress the collective-security system of the United Nations as early as 1947 when it took the lead in formulating the Inter-American Treaty of Reciprocal Assistance.[17] This treaty, popularly known as the Rio Treaty, linked all the Republics of Latin America with the United States in a plan for the collective security of the Western Hemisphere.   In 1949, under the North Atlantic Treaty,[18] the nations of the North Atlantic area organized a collective defense system with a view to discouraging aggression.   In 1951 the United States signed a security treaty with New Zealand and Australia,[19] and similar treaties with the Philippines and Japan which provide for cooperative defense in the Pacific.   All of these treaties state that they were formed under article 51 of the charter of the United Nations which acknowledges "the inherent right of individual or collective self-defense."

That member states have taken other measures to fortify their security does not mean that the United Nations or even the Security Council has not made a contribution to maintaining peace and security.   On a number of occasions, the organization has acted to eliminate or lessen international tensions.   At times, it has been the Security Council which has carried the bulk of the responsibility for bringing about a settlement.

For example, fighting between the Netherlands and Indonesia was halted twice by intervention of the Security Council.   The Council also exerted an influence in the settlement of the dispute and in the creation of the United States of Indonesia.   It stopped the large-scale fighting between Israel and the Arab States in 1948, and has retained a Truce Observation Commission in the Middle East to prevent a renewal of the conflict.   The Security Council also negotiated a cease-fire agreement between India and Pakistan in their dispute over Kashmir.

Even when the veto has been used to block decisions in the Security Council, the will of the majority of states has often found expression in some other fashion.   In 1946, for example, despite a Soviet veto of a United States proposal expressing confidence that foreign forces in Syria and Lebanon would be withdrawn "as soon as possible," Great Britain and France did remove their troops.   The Soviet Union vetoed a resolution proposing the lifting of the Berlin blockade, but after the airlift had rendered the blockade ineffectual, informal talks among the representatives of the nations concerned led to its termination. Objectives of other vetoed resolutions such as those on Spain and on border conflicts among the Balkan States were attained by action in the General Assembly.

E. THE DECREASING USE OF THE SECURITY COUNCIL

The frustrating effect of the veto has led to such a decline of activity in the Security Council that the question now frequently posed is whether the Security Council is serving a constructive purpose.   That the volume of work performed by the Security Council is steadily decreasing is indicated by the number of its meetings each year which

[17] For text, see Collection of Documents, p. 682.
[18] Ibid., p. 700.
[19] Ibid., p. 704.

has dropped from a peak of 180 in 1947–48 to a low point of 26 in 1952–53. Certainly the international problems meriting consideration have not decreased to the same degree. Following is a table showing the number of meetings of the Security Council year by year, together with the number of Soviet vetoes.[20]

	Meetings	Vetoes
Jan. 17, 1945 to July 15, 1946	50	5
July 16, 1946 to July 15, 1947	108	5
July 16, 1947 to July 15, 1948	180	16
July 16, 1948 to July 15, 1949	92	4
July 16, 1949 to July 15, 1950	46	13
July 16, 1950 to July 15, 1951	72	4
July 16, 1951 to July 15, 1952	43	3
July 16, 1952 to July 15, 1953	26	6
Total	617	56

Most of the meetings in the 1952–53 period were devoted to discussion of the admission of new members and to the election of a Secretary General while the major threat to peace, Korea, was not even considered; this problem had long since been consigned to the General Assembly. The Security Council, however, continued to be concerned with the situation in Kashmir and Palestine and retained jurisdiction over the Trieste problem.

The record to date has led to a suggestion in some quarters that it is time to consider allowing the Council "to lapse into extinction" and that "there may even be grounds for hastening the process".[21] Included among such grounds were the undesirability of generating antagonism among friendly states in the process of electing nonpermanent members to the Council and the possibility that it would be easier to solve the question of admitting the Chinese Communists to the United Nations if such admission did not also entitle them to membership in a body in which they could wield a veto.

F. THE INCREASING USE OF THE GENERAL ASSEMBLY

Thus far the most fruitful method of obtaining action within the United Nations when the Security Council has been stalemated on an issue has involved transferring the matter to the General Assembly. It has been possible to effect some transfers from the Security Council to the General Assembly by procedural devices. For example, a question may be dropped from the agenda of the Security Council on a procedural vote and subsequently brought up in the General Assembly.

Not only has the General Assembly been able to act on an issue in this manner after a veto, but in several cases the Security Council, in effect, has been bypassed. Questions which perhaps more properly should have been considered by the Council have been referred directly to the General Assembly because of the certainty that differences between the Soviet Union and the other permanent powers would prevent action in the former. Among such questions have been the disposition of certain Italian colonies; the observance of human rights

[20] Compiled from the annual reports of the Security Council to the General Assembly. Published yearly by the United Nations 1946–53. A list of vetoes may be found in Collection of Documents, pp. 577–580.
[21] The Vanishing Security Council. The Economist (London), Sept. 19, 1953, p. 767.

in Bulgaria, Hungary, and Rumania; and the Korean unification question in 1947.[22]

Steps have been taken to formalize the procedures for action through the General Assembly in the event of an impasse in the Security Council. It was apparent at the time of the North Korean aggression in 1950 that the Security Council was able to declare the attack to be a breach of the peace and to call for collective action only because the U. S. S. R. was then boycotting the Council. Realization that the Soviet Union could have prevented these measures had its representative been present stimulated efforts to make action possible in the event of similar crises. It led the United States to propose in the General Assembly on September 20, 1950 certain new principles for maintaining peace. These principles were later incorporated into a draft resolution jointly submitted by Canada, France, the Philippines, Turkey, the United Kingdom, Uruguay, and the United States, with Chile later becoming a cosponsor.

The Uniting for Peace Resolution,[23] as the draft was called, was adopted by the General Assembly on November 3, 1950, by a majority of 52 to 5 (the Soviet bloc), with 2 absentions (Argentina and India). This resolution reaffirmed—

the importance of the exercise by the Security Council of its primary responsibility for the maintenance of international peace and security, and the duty of the permanent members to seek unanimity and to exercise restraint in the use of the veto.

It expressed the belief, however, that—

the failure of the Security Council to discharge its responsibilities on behalf of all the member states * * * does not relieve member states of their obligations or the United Nations of its responsibility under the charter to maintain international peace and security.

Consequently, the Assembly resolved—

that if the Security Council, because of lack of unanimity of the permanent members, fails to exercise its primary responsibility for the maintenance of international peace and security in any case where there appears to be a threat to the peace, breach of the peace, or act of aggression, the General Assembly shall consider the matter immediately with a view to making appropriate recommendations to members for collective measures, including in the case of a breach of the peace or act of aggression the use of armed force when necessary, to maintain or restore international peace and security. If not in session at the time, the General Assembly may meet in emergency special session within 24 hours of the request therefor. Such emergency special session shall be called if requested by the Security Council on the vote of any seven members or by a majority of the members of the United Nations.[24]

In addition, the resolution established a Peace Observation Commission to observe and report on the situation in any area where there existed international tension likely to endanger peace and security. It also urged members to "earmark" units of their Armed Forces for United Nations purposes, and established a Collective Measures Committee to report on methods which might be used to maintain and strengthen international peace and security.

Thus the Uniting for Peace Resolution established machinery whereby the General Assembly could recommend collective action to maintain peace if the Security Council were blocked by the veto. Some delegates expressed the opinion that the letter of the charter

---

[22] William M. Jordan. Annual Review of United Nations Affairs. New York, New York University Press, 1951, p. 79.
[23] The full text is published in the Collection of Documents, p. 557.
[24] Ibid., p. 558.

has been exceeded by this resolution because of the manner in which it extended the competence of the General Assembly. Nevertheless, they voted in favor of the resolution as necessary if the United Nations were to carry out its basic purposes.

Simultaneously, the General Assembly adopted two other resolutions. One was a Soviet-sponsored measure recommending to the Security Council that it take the—

necessary steps to ensure that the action provided for under the Charter is taken with respect to threats to the peace * * * [and] that it should devise measures for the earliest application of Articles 43, 45, 46, and 47 of the Charter of the United Nations regarding the placing of armed forces at the disposal of the Security Council by the States Members of the United Nations and the effective functioning of the Military Staff Committee.[25]

However, this resolution had been amended by the French delegation to say that it should in no manner prevent the General Assembly from fulfilling its functions under the Uniting for Peace Resolution.

Along the same lines was an Iraqi-Syrian resolution recommending to the—

permanent members of the Security Council that they meet and discuss * * * all problems which are likely to threaten international peace and hamper the activities of the United Nations, with a view to their resolving fundamental differences and reaching agreement in accordance with the spirit and letter of the Charter.

Although the Uniting for Peace Resolution provides a way around the veto, it is by no means a substitute for the Council's function, as originally conceived, in situations involving threats to the peace. The Council was intended to have enforcement powers and the unanimity of the five permanent members in that body was provided for in part because they were to have the bulk of responsibility for carrying out decisions on enforcement. In the General Assembly there is no way to insure that the two-thirds majority required for action under the Uniting for Peace Resolution will represent sufficient power to carry out a recommendation. In addition, the Assembly can only recommend action and hence is dependent on voluntary cooperation of members. Under the Security Council an element of command is possible. Under the Uniting for Peace Resolution, in short, decisions do not have precisely the same teeth as was intended by the founders for action by the Security Council.

G. POSSIBILITIES OF FORMAL AMENDMENT

It was the dissatisfaction with article 27 on the part of a number of the smaller states which furnished much of the impetus for making provision for the possible revision of the charter by conference.[26] The Dumbarton Oaks proposals had not contained a clause similar to article 109 of the charter. This article, which permits a general conference to review the present charter to be called at any time by a vote of two-thirds of the General Assembly and any seven members of the Security Council was a concession to the smaller states. Under article 109, consideration of a review conference will automatically be placed on the agenda of the 10th annual session of the General Assembly, if such a conference has not already been convened by that time, and

[25] Ibid. p. 561.
[26] See Wellington Koo, Jr., Voting Procedures in International Political Organizations. New York, Columbia University Press, 1947, pp. 213-224.

the conference can be called by a simple majority of the Assembly and any seven members of the Security Council.

A veto cannot prevent amendments to the charter approved by two-thirds of the members from being adopted by the conference. Such amendments or revisions, like any others, however, will not take effect unless ratified by two-thirds of the members of the United Nations "including all the permanent members of the Security Council."

Whether the Soviet Union would ratify any changes whatsoever in the charter is not known with certainty. The attitude of the Russians on the veto, however, has been made clear both by action and word. Not only have they used the device extensively, but they have tried to enlarge, rather than narrow, its scope. Their position was made explicit in April 1949, during consideration of the Interim Committee's proposals for changes in voting procedures in the Security Council. At that time the Soviet delegate, Andrei A. Gromyko, called the principle of unanimity—

one of the vital provisions of the United Nations Charter, one of the most important pillars of this Organization, the very cornerstone of its existence. * * * Should the principle of unanimity be abolished or weakened, the Security Council would be transformed into a blind instrument in the hands of the Anglo-American bloc. All decisions would be taken only under United States dictation. Therefore, can anyone seriously believe that the Soviet Union would agree with the opponents of the "veto"? [27]

In view of Soviet intransigeance on this issue, it would appear questionable whether, at the present time, the Russians would ratify any revisions of article 27 which had the effect of modifying the veto. However, there is little doubt that if the review conference is held, the veto will be one of the chief topics for discussion. Several nations already have called for a special conference specifically to amend article 27. In fact, Cuba submitted such a proposal during the first session of the General Assembly.

The changes which have been proposed range from complete abolition of the veto or restrictions on its use through a variety of new voting combinations in the Security Council. These proposed combinations usually represent what their originators believe is necessary to ensure that a decision will be supported by sufficient power to be effective while at the same time depriving a single permanent member of the power to veto action. For example, the Philippines at one time suggested that the present majority of 7 on substantive questions ought to be retained with the proviso that it need include only 3 of the permanent members. New Zealand proposed that the affirmative votes of 4 of the permanent members should be required in the 7-vote majority.

Even if the Soviet Union objects to changes, it will still be possible for a review conference to adopt amendments to the voting procedure. While such amendments could not take effect unless ratified by the Soviet Union, they would make clear the position of other members of the United Nations and possibly exert some pressure for moderation in the use of the veto.

The probability of a movement among the smaller states for abolition of the veto makes it necessary to determine how far the United States would be willing to go in accepting changes. Although

[27] General Assembly, Verbatim Records. April 14, 1949. A/PV 192, 1948–49, pp. 33–50.

this country has never cast a veto, our delegates have hinted, on at least two occasions, that they might.[28] On other occasions the United States has voted in the minority but its vote did not act as a veto because enough other representatives abstained to prevent the resolution from reaching the necessary majority of seven.

Whenever the United States finds itself at variance with the views of the Council's majority, the veto, whether utilized or not, offers a safeguard to the American position. Abolition of the veto would mean giving up that safeguard in matters which heretofor have generally been considered the exclusive concern of the nation. The Security Council, for example, could order the armed forces of member nations into action provided the military agreements envisioned in article 43 were concluded. If the veto were abolished, United States troops might conceivably be called upon to support a United Nations decision which the United States opposed.

The fact that the veto ensures that our Armed Forces will not be used without the approval of the United States was emphasized when the charter was presented to the Senate for its approval. The report of the Senate Foreign Relations Committee on the charter stated:

The special position of the United States as 1 of the 5 permanent members of the Security Council whose approval is needed for any enforcement action needs to be emphasized once again * * *. No United States forces can be employed, no enforcement action of any kind against a nation breaking the peace can be taken, without the full concurrence of the United States acting through its delegate on the Security Council.[29]

Proposed modifications in the power of the Security Council

One method of eliminating the veto which has been suggested recognizes the above fact when it proposes deliberately to "extract the teeth" of the Security Council which are provided in chapter VII of the charter.[30] Instead of "command" powers, the Security Council would have only "recommending" powers. Proponents of this suggestion point out that, if the Security Council had power only to recommend, not to command, the Permanent Powers could safely give up the veto because they would then in no way be compelled to follow decrees of a majority of the Council to which they were not a part. It is maintained, moreover, that compulsory power is a fiction anyway, that no sovereign state can be compelled to do something against its will, not, at least, without risk of war. They point to Korea as proof that action can be taken merely on the strength of a recommendation backed by a majority of the United Nations and the Security Council.

One advantage of this plan over the Uniting for Peace Resolution might be that the Council at least would continue as a small and workable executive committee. Certainly 60 states cannot reach agreement and take action as quickly as a majority of a Council of eleven members. In the event of a major crisis the time element might be a decisive factor in determining whether collective action

[28] In October 1950, Warren Austin threatened to use the first United States veto in order to retain Trygve Lie as Secretary General. The New York Times of July 29, 1953, reported that on the previous day Secretary of State Dulles "implied, but would not say categorically, that the United States would use its veto power to block Communist China's admission [to the United Nations]." Mr. Dulles said that, although the United States in the past had taken the position that admissions [credentials] should not be subject to the veto, the United States would be free to invoke the veto because other countries had not agreed to limit the use of the veto in this respect.
[29] Collection of Documents, p. 62.
[30] Clement Davies, MP, Revised Charter to Safeguard Peace, New Commonwealth (London), v. 25. March 16, 1953, p. 264, and Dr. Gilbert Murray, Buttressing an Agency for Building World Peace, New Commonwealth (London), v. 25, March 30, 1953, pp. 320–321.

was to be successful. Nor would the smaller body be likely to prove as unwieldy as the General Assembly during the execution of recommendations.

Either the Security Council without enforcement powers and without the veto, as suggested above, or the General Assembly under the Uniting for Peace Resolution, could move against any aggressor, even a major power. By contrast, the United Nations was not originally set up to act against an aggressor if the aggressor were a permanent member of the Security Council, because it was felt that this would in effect mean war anyway. The alternatives discussed above suggest that if there were a third world war, it might be conducted under the aegis and with the machinery of the United Nations.

Restriction on the use of the veto

The United States could support restrictions on the use of the veto without supporting complete abolition. This country has already expressed a willingness to eliminate the veto from the pacific settlement of disputes and the admission of new members. Other nations have proposed narrowing the list of decisions subject to the veto by spelling out, in the charter, a number of questions which might be deemed procedural. Even these modifications, however, might entail a surrendering of the safeguards for our national policies which are provided by the veto greater than many Americans would be prepared to allow. For example, if the veto were eliminated in the question of admission of new member states it would be difficult to justify its use on the subordinate, more clearly procedural, question of what government shall represent a member state.

H. CHANGES WITHOUT FORMAL AMENDMENT

Modification in the veto power does not necessarily require revision of the charter. During the past 8 years this country has participated in efforts to reduce the use of the veto by agreement among the permanent members or other methods which did not involve revision.

Article 27 provides only a bare framework for regulating voting in the Security Council and opens wide avenues for interpretation. Through interpretation, embodied in the practice of the Security Council, the number of decisions which are subject to the veto can be considerably enlarged or narrowed.

The process of interpretation began at the San Francisco Conference with the joint statement of the sponsoring powers previously mentioned. This statement was described by the chairman of the United States Delegation as an effort to "interpret the [voting] formula officially," insofar as it was possible at that time.[31]

There is disagreement on the extent of the binding force of the San Francisco statement. The Soviet Union has insisted that it is binding on the Big Five. As early as 1946, the United States, Great Britain, France, and China proposed that the General Assembly ask the permanent members to reconsider the statement in the light of the experience of the first 10 months.[32] However, the Soviet Union opposed any modification of voting procedures at that time, as it has ever since.

---

[31] United Nations Conference on International Organization, Documents v. 11, p. 710.
[32] Yearbook of the United Nations, 1946–47, p. 132.

The position of the United States was expressed by John Foster Dulles before the First Committee of the General Assembly on November 17, 1947:

That statement by its terms was a "statement of general attitude." It did not purport to be an agreement, much less an agreement binding in perpetuity. The views therein expressed were only partly made explicit in the charter and to the extent that they were not so made explicit, the views were never accepted by the San Francisco conference as a whole. The statement was based on certain assumptions which in the light of developments have proved incorrect. Thus the statement said that "It is not to be assumed, however, that the permanent members * * * would use their 'veto' power willfully to obstruct the operation of the [Council] * * *." Also it was assumed that it would be "unlikely that there will arise in the future any matters of great importance on which a decision will have to be made as to whether a procedural vote would apply." None of these assumptions has been borne out by events.

In view of all of these considerations, we believe that the parties to the San Francisco statement are free to explore the question of whether, and if so, how, better voting procedures can be put into operation. We feel that, if better procedures can be found, the United States would not be prevented from seeking to achieve them merely because that might involve an attitude not in all respects identical with the attitude taken by the United States on June 7, 1945. We do not, however, abandon that earlier attitude until the matter has been further explored and until we are satisfied as to precisely what is the better attitude to be taken.[33]

Following a thorough analysis of the problem in 1948, the General Assembly by a vote of 43 to 6, with 2 abstentions, adopted a resolution recommending the following:

(1) That 35 types of decisions be deemed procedural. (These included, for example, the transmission to the General Assembly of any questions relating to the maintenance of international peace and security, the approval of credentials of representatives of members of the Security Council, and the establishment of subsidiary organs which the Security Council might deem necessary for the performance of its functions. [34])

(2) That the permanent members of the Security Council seek agreement on types of decisions on which they might forebear to exercise their veto right. (Among the types proposed were those which were listed as not necessarily procedural but nevertheless of a kind that should require only the concurrence of any seven members, such as the admission of new members, the preliminary question of whether a matter is procedural, and major aspects of pacific settlement of disputes.[35])

(3) That the permanent members consult together whenever feasible before a vote is taken, and if there is not unanimity, "to exercise the veto only when they consider the question of vital importance, taking into account the interest of the United Nations as a whole, and to state upon what ground they consider this condition to be present."

(4) That in conferring additional functions on the Security Council, members provide conditions of voting "as would to the greatest extent feasible exclude the application of the rule of unanimity of the permanent members." [36]

[33] Collection of Documents, p. 568.
[34] For full text of the resolution and list of decisions deemed procedural, see Collection of Documents, pp. 572–575.
[35] For full list, see Collection of Documents, p. 573.
[36] This fourth recommendation is illustrated by the United States proposals in 1946 for control of atomic energy. The proposals would have conferred functions on the Security Council not provided for in the Charter and they contained the proviso that in the execution of these functions the veto would not be applicable. See Collection of Documents, p. 432.

Practice of abstention

Thus far, however, the Soviet Union has opposed such resolutions of the General Assembly on the grounds that they are an attempt to abrogate the charter, and has refused to be considered bound by any of them. Nevertheless certain modifications of the voting procedures have come about through practice with the tacit consent of the Russians.

For instance, abstentions and absences are not regarded as vetoes, although the charter requires substantive decisions to include "the concurring votes of the permanent members." Even at San Francisco, the permanent members interpreted this clause to mean that they must be present and voting.[37]

It was the Soviet Union which first voluntarily abstained from voting so as not to cast a veto.[38] This occurred on May 2, 1946, on a resolution to appoint a subcommittee to study and report on the Spanish question. Although the Soviet delegate was dissatisfied ~~with~~ with the resolution, he said:

bearing in mind in this connection that my voting against the Australian draft resolution would make its adoption impossible, I abstain from voting. * * * My abstention from voting on this matter may in no way be regarded as a precedent capable of influencing in any way the question of the abstention of permanent members of the Security Council.

The practice, nevertheless, quickly became popular because representatives often found themselves unable to vote for a resolution yet unwilling to thwart the will of the majority of the Council. At least 40 substantive resolutions had been passed by the end of 1949 in which a permanent member had abstained. These decisions represented four-fifths of the substantive decisions taken by the Security Council up to that time. No substantive proposal has ever been declared defeated because a permanent member has abstained.

Although the legality of a resolution passed during the absence of a permanent member has aroused more controversy than when the member though present, has abstained, the practice in the Security Council has also been to count the absence of a permanent member as an abstention.[39] The problem arose first when the Soviet delegate withdrew during discussion of the Iranian case in 1946 and a second time in 1950 on the Korean question when the Soviet Union was again absent. Although the resolutions passed during the first absence may not have been clearly substantive, during the 1950 absence several such resolutions were adopted including the decision on action in response to the North Korean aggression.

In the case of the Security Council's resolution of June 27, 1950, concerning the complaint of aggression in Korea, the Soviet Union contended that

* * * This resolution was adopted by 6 votes, the seventh vote being that of the Kuomintang representative Dr. Tingfu F. Tsiang who has no legal right to represent China. * * * As is known, moreover, the above resolution was passed in the absence of 2 permanent members of the Security Council, the Union of Soviet Socialist Republics and China, whereas under the United Nations Charter a decision of the Security Council on an important matter can only be made with

---

[37] Wellington Koo, Jr. Op. cit., p. 156.
[38] Yuen-Li Liang, S. J. D. The Settlement of Disputes in the Security Council: The Yalta Voting Formula. British Yearbook of International Law, 1947, p. 358.
[39] Myres S. McDougal and Richard N. Gardner. The Veto and the Charter: An Interpretation for Survival. Yale Law Journal (New Haven), vol. 60, February 1951, p. 279. This also applies to nonpermanent members. When the Ukrainian delegate was absent during the 392d meeting of the Security Council he was counted as having abstained on a resolution passed during his absence.

the concurring votes of all 5 permanent members of the Council. * * * In view of the foregoing it is quite clear that the said resolution of the Security Council on the Korean question has no legal force.[40]

The Soviet contention was not accepted by the majority of the United Nations. In a statement issued by the Department of State on June 30, 1950, the United States took the following position:

* * * By a long series of precedents * * * dating back to 1946, the practice has been established whereby abstention by permanent members of the Council does not constitute a veto.

In short, prior to the Soviet allegations, every member of the United Nations, including the U. S. S. R., accepted as legal and binding decisions of the Security Council made without the concurrence, as expressed through an affirmative vote of all permanent members of the Council.[41]

After listing several important decisions of the Security Council on which the Soviet Union had abstained and others in which some other permanent member of the Security Council had abstained, the Department of State contended that—

in none of these instances has the Soviet Union challenged the legality of the action taken by the Security Council.

The Department further pointed out that the voluntary absence of a permanent member was "clearly analogous to abstention" and that article 28, providing that the Security Council be organized so as to function continuously, would be defeated if the absence of a representative of a permanent member prevented action by the Council.[42]

Broadening of procedural matter

A difficulty in relying on practice and interpretation to modify the veto is that it is sometimes difficult to determine the prevailing practice on procedural questions. Since decisions on such questions can be made by an affirmative vote of any 7 members of the Security Council, while on "all other matters" the 7 votes must include those of all permanent members, one of the earliest attempts to minimize the effect of the veto was through broadening the concept of procedural matters.

The statement of the sponsoring powers at San Francisco clarified their interpretation of "procedural." It made explicit that included within their understanding of this term were not only decisions affecting the machinery for the conduct of the business of the Security Council but also some decisions in connection with settlement of disputes which did not involve taking direct measures. In this regard the statement said:

1. The Yalta voting formula recognizes that the Security Council, in discharging its responsibilities for the maintenance of international peace and security, will have two broad groups of functions. Under chapter VIII, the Council will have to make decisions which involve its taking direct measures in connection with settlement of disputes, adjustment of situations likely to lead to disputes, determination of threats to the peace, removal of threats to the peace, and suppression of breaches of the peace. It will also have to make decisions which do not involve the taking of such measures. The Yalta formula provides that the second of these 2 groups of decisions will be governed by a procedural vote—that is, the vote of any 7 members. The first groups of decisions will be governed by a qualified vote—that is, the vote of 7 members, including the concurring votes of the 5 permanent members, subject to the proviso that in decisions under section A and a part of section C of chapter VIII parties to a dispute shall abstain from voting.

[40] Collection of Documents, p. 575.
[41] Ibid., p. 576.
[42] Ibid., p. 577.

2. For example, under the Yalta formula a procedural vote will govern the decisions made under the entire section D of chapter VI. This means that the Council will, by a vote of any seven of its members adopt or alter its rules of procedure; determine the method of selecting its President; organize itself in such a way as to be able to function continuously; select the times and places of its regular and special meetings; establish such bodies or agencies as it may deem necessary for the performance of its functions; invite a member of the Organization not represented on the Council to participate in its discussion when that member's interests are specially affected; and invite any state when it is a party to a dispute being considered by the Council to participate in the discussion relating to that dispute.

3. Further, no individual member of the Council can alone prevent consideration and discussion by the Council of a dispute or situation brought to its attention under paragraph 2, section A, chapter VIII. Nor can parties to such dispute be prevented by these means from being heard by the Council. * * * [43]

The statement of sponsoring powers also left a great deal to future interpretation, stating that—

the draft charter itself contains an indication of the application of the voting procedures to the various functions of the Council.

In the "unlikely" event, however, that a decision would have to be made on whether a question were procedural or substantive that decision, the statement made clear, would require the concurring votes of the permanent members.

The double veto

Actually, differences of opinion on whether a matter is procedural or substantive have arisen many times and have led on occasion to what has come to be termed the "double veto"; that is, one veto is used to prevent a question from being considered procedural and another is used to defeat the resolution as a substantive question. The Soviet Union has used the double veto three times, on June 26, 1946, against a resolution to keep the Spanish question on the agenda "without prejudice to the rights of the General Assembly"; on September 15, 1947, against a resolution requesting the General Assembly to consider a dispute between Greece and Albania, Yugoslavia, and Bulgaria; and on May 24, 1948, on a resolution to set up a subcommittee to hear evidence in connection with the Communist coup in Czechoslovakia. The effect of the tactic has been to narrow the list of nonvetoable subjects.

Since May 24, 1948, the double veto has not been invoked. There has been one case since then, when despite a negative vote of a permanent member against the majority, the member was unable to prevent a resolution from being considered procedural and hence was unable to veto it. It occurred on September 30, 1950, in connection with a resolution to postpone consideration of the Chinese Communist charge of armed invasion of Formosa and to ask a representative of the Peking government to attend the Security Council during the discussion. There were 7 votes in favor, 3 against (China, the United States, and Cuba), and 1 abstention. The President of the Council announced that the resolution had been adopted. The delegate of Nationalist China then insisted that his negative vote be counted as a veto and invoked the pertinent provision of the San Francisco statement and precedents set by the Soviet Union. In the discussion which followed the other delegates stressed that if the vote of Nationalist China was allowed to count as a veto, a matter which was clearly procedural would be changed into a matter of substance. Another

[43] Collection of Documents, p. 562.

vote was taken to deem the preceding resolution procedural. Nationalist China alone voted in the negative. The delegate of the United Kingdom, Sir Gladwyn Jebb, who was serving as the President of the Council at the time, ruled, nevertheless, that the resolution had been deemed procedural.

Although the Chinese delegate protested and suggested that an advisory opinion of the International Court of Justice be sought, when the President called for a vote on whether his opinion should be overruled, nobody voted and the President declared his ruling stood.[44]

Cited by the President of the Council as a basis for refusing to consider the Chinese negative vote as a veto was the resolution of the General Assembly on April 14, 1949. This resolution, previously referred to, had listed invitations to States to sit in on the Council meetings as 1 of 35 types of decisions which should be considered procedural.

The position of the United States on the issue was that—

Part II, paragraph 2 of the San Francisco statement was never intended, and cannot properly be construed, to give the five permanent members of the Security Council the right to use the device of the double veto to determine unilaterally to be nonprocedural, matters which the charter provides, or which were agreed in part I of the San Francisco statement, as procedural. * * * In the present state of the world, it is not difficult to see that the unlimited power of the veto and the double veto in the Security Council would be dangerous to security.[45]

The Formosa case has sometimes been interpreted as constituting a precedent for requiring that the double veto be used only with the approval of the majority of the Council.[46] Needless to say acceptance of such as interpretation would go far toward minimizing the power of the veto. However, there are some who disagree with this analysis and hold that the double veto is not only still possible but even necessary. As one commentator points out:

The far-reaching conclusions drawn from the Formosa case are unwarranted because the point at issue was settled in the statement (of the sponsoring powers at San Francisco) as one subject to a procedural vote, and there was no more reason to start a series of votes on this point than there would have been on a motion of adjournment. * * * Such unwarranted deductions, as already pointed out, might also lead to attempts, in contravention of the charter, to eliminate the use of the veto even from decisions where at least until now, there has been no doubt that the principle of the unanimity of the permanent members applied. * * *

The Formosa incident, rather than inspiring far-flung ideas about exorcising the veto from the charter, should convince all members of the United Nations and particularly those represented on the Security Council of the usefulness of the statement as a means of facilitating the functioning of the Security Council. * * * The double veto is a logical and, in a sense, inevitable consequence of the voting rule embodied in article 27 of the charter just as it was the logical and inevitable consequence of article 5 of the Covenant of the League of Nations.[47]

I. THE VETO AND MEMBERSHIP

There has been considerable effort to eliminate the veto on the question of admission of new members. Of the 57 vetoes invoked by the Soviet Union to date, 28 have been used to bar candidate states which had received the endorsement of a majority of 7 in the Security Council. Fourteen states have been prevented from joining

[44] Alexander W. Rudzinski. The so-called double veto. American Journal of International Law (Washington) July 1951, v. 45, pp. 454–455.
[45] Ibid., p. 456.
[46] Ibid., p. 457.
[47] Leo Gross. The Double Veto and the Four Power Statement on Voting in the Security Council. Harvard Law Review (Boston) v. 67 December 1953, pp. 276–277.

the United Nations by these vetoes. They are Jordan, Ireland, Portugal, Italy, Austria, Finland, Ceylon, Republic of Korea, Nepal, Libya, Japan, Vietnam, Laos, and Cambodia. Of 28 applicants for membership since the United Nations came into existence, only 9 have been admitted; the last of these was Indonesia in September 1950. Five Soviet-supported candidates, Albania, Bulgaria, Hungary, the Mongolian People's Republic, and Rumania have never received a majority of seven votes in the Security Council.

The problem of the veto in connection with membership arose when it became apparent that applicant states were being excluded, not because they lacked the qualifications listed under article 4 of the Charter but for other reasons. The Soviet Union in effect has admitted that 9 of the 14 vetoed states were qualified for admission by proposing that Jordan, Ireland, Portugal, Italy, Austria, Finland, Ceylon, Nepal, and Libya be admitted simultaneously in a "package" with the five Soviet-sponsored states. Nevertheless, when these states have been voted on individually, they have been consistently vetoed. Jordan, Ireland, Portugal, and Ceylon have been vetoed 3 times, and Italy has been vetoed 5 times.

In November 1947 in the First Committee of the General Assembly, the United States and the United Kingdom stated they were prepared to waive the veto in applications for membership and France announced that it would not veto any of the pending applications.[48] On June 11, 1948, the United States Senate supported this policy in the Vandenberg resolution.[49] Some weeks later the Interim Committee of the General Assembly was requested to consider the problem of voting in the Security Council. The committee did not agree on whether the matter of membership should or should not be regarded as procedural but concluded that in either case a decision of the Security Council to recommend admission of a state should be taken by the vote of any seven members.

A recommendation to this effect was adopted by the General Assembly on April 14, 1949. It was ignored by the Soviet Union, however, which has continued to use the veto in connection with applications for membership.

On two occasions, aspects of the problem of the veto and membership have been referred by the General Assembly to the International Court of Justice for an advisory opinion. In 1947 the question posed was whether a member of the Council or Assembly could condition its vote on membership on factors not provided for in the Charter. The Court replied that a member was not juridically entitled to make consent to admission of a state dependent on conditions not expressly provided for in article 4 paragraph 1, of the charter.

In 1950 the Assembly asked the Court whether the General Assembly could admit a state which had not received a recommendation from the Security Council because of a veto. The Court merely held that an affirmative recommendation of the Council was required before the Assembly could admit an applicant. This limited opinion still left open the question of whether an "affirmative" recommendation necessarily included the unanimous consent of the permanent members. Even if the Court said it did not, there would be no assurance that the Soviet Union would follow an advisory opinion.

[48] Before the Yalta conference the United States had taken the position that the admission of new members was an area in which the unanimity of the permanent members of the Security Council should be required. Postwar Foreign Policy Preparation, 1939–45. p. 659.
[49] See Collection of Documents, p. 140.

Unless the Soviet Union alters its present stand, it would appear that revision of the charter would be necessary to eliminate the veto in questions involving the admission of new members. The United States has already indicated on several occasions that it would be ready to consider revision in this connection.

James F. Byrnes, a United States Representative to the last session of the General Assembly, stated:

* * * we should bear in mind, as we look ahead to the future, the prospect of a charter review conference as envisaged in article 109. Every proposed amendment should receive most careful consideration. If, by the time such a conference is held, a solution of the membership problem has not been found, there will be proposals to deal with it by an amendment of the charter. In the meantime, we should study the possibilities which a review conference may offer.[50]

Charter revision in this field would not necessarily have to involve a change in the voting procedure of the Security Council as provided for in article 27. The problem could conceivably be dealt with through a more liberal interpretation of article 4 relating to member-ship. The latter approach would involve curbing the veto power in only one area and hence, might be more generally acceptable.

J. THE VETO AND PACIFIC SETTLEMENT OF DISPUTES

Pacific settlement of disputes constitutes a major function of the Security Council in which consistent efforts have been made to eliminate the veto. Even before a veto had actually been used in this connection, there was widespread feeling that decisions relating to pacific settlement should not require the unanimous consent of the permanent members.

At San Francisco, much of the sentiment against the veto was channeled into an effort to eliminate the unanimity rule in procedures for pacific settlement. Although there was acquiescence in the view that the permanent members should have the veto in decisions which might require them to make material sacrifices, those relating to pacific settlement did not require sacrifices from anyone except perhaps the parties to the dispute.

The Yalta formula had recognized that pacific settlement was the single stage at which even a permanent power, if a party to a dispute, would be required to abstain from voting. To this extent at least the veto was curbed. Efforts to eliminate the veto entirely from pacific settlement, however, were in vain.

A large part of the San Francisco statement on voting was devoted to explaining why the veto was necessary in pacific settlement as well as in enforcement.[51] The statement sustained the view first advanced by the Soviet Union that a decision in the stage of pacific settlement might inaugurate a "chain of events" which could, in the end, require enforcement action by the Council. Consideration or discussion of a situation was not included in the "chain of events," according to the statement, and hence not vetoable. The chain, it was held, began when the—

Council decided to make an investigation, or determines that the time has come to call upon States to settle their differences, or makes recommendations to the parties. It is to such decisions and actions that unanimity of the permanent members applies, with the important proviso, referred to above, for abstention from voting by parties to a dispute.

[50] Department of State Bulletin, v. XXIX, November 1953, p. 607.
[51] Collection of Documents, p. 562.

Delegates of many other states at San Francisco expressed their disapproval of the position taken by the Big Five. Mr. Evatt, delegate from Australia, said the interpretation given in the statement was even more limited than had been indicated in debate. In his view the statement meant that—

without veto, the Council can only discuss whether a dispute can be discussed, and can only investigate whether it should be investigated.[52]

In practice, the Security Council has established a list of questions under pacific settlement which are regarded as procedural. The list includes placing questions on the agenda, inviting interested states to be heard, general and full discussion of disputes, and inauguration of fact-finding studies. For instance, the establishment of the Corfu Channel Subcommittee was determined to be a procedural matter because its purpose was to clarify facts presented, not to discover whether it was a situation which was likely to endanger the maintenance of international peace and security. The Security Council has also treated the calling of witnesses as a procedural matter. In considering the question of the Czechoslovakian coup, the former Czech representative to the United Nations was invited to make a factual statement before the Council despite the adverse vote of the Soviet Union.[53] This was in accord with the Council's rules of procedure which provide that—

The Security Council may invite members of the Secretariat or other persons whom it considers competent for the purpose, to supply it with information or to give other assistance in examining matters within its competence.

In spite of the number of matters established as procedural in this field, the Soviet Union has used the veto at least nine times in connection with pacific settlement.[54] The United States has expressed its willingness to eliminate the veto during the pacific settlement stage. This position was endorsed by the Senate in the Vandenberg resolution of 1948.[55] As pointed out previously, the same view has long been held by many of the smaller states.

K. CONCLUDING COMMENTS

In a discussion of the problems of voting in the Security Council, the frustration which has resulted from use of the veto tends to over-shadow the less apparent advantages which have accrued from the requirement for unanimity among the permanent members. It is pertinent to point out, therefore, that support of decisions of the Security Council by all five permanent members adds greatly to their prestige and value. An affirmative decision which includes these states signifies that the combined weight of the great powers lies behind the will of the world community. With such support, it has been possible to cope, for example, with the problems in Kashmir, and Palestine, where decisions with less powerful support might have been ignored.

Furthermore, the veto has not necessarily been the insurmountable obstacle which it conceivably could be. The determination of the majority of the United Nations to make the international organiza-

[52] United Nations Conference on International Organization. Documents, XI, pp. 230-235.
[53] Eduardo de Arechaga Jimenez. Voting and the Handling of Disputes in the Security Council. New York, Carnegie Endowment for International Peace, 1950, p. 82.
[54] Bernard G. Bechhoefer. Voting in the Security Council. U. S. Department of State Bulletin, July 4, 1948, p. 7.
[55] Collection of Documents, p. 140.

tion operate in spite of frequent use of the device has inspired ingenious methods to keep the peace and the Soviet Union, however reluctantly, has more or less acquiesced in these developments.

Nevertheless, the veto remains a very real problem. It has contributed to the undermining of public faith in the United Nations. As a manifestation of basic international disagreement, it has become symbolic of the difficulty of developing international cooperation. It has impaired the ability of the Security Council to exercise "primary responsibility for the maintenance of international peace and security." In spite of the numerous ways which have been devised to "get around the veto," it has not yet proved possible to provide a fully satisfactory substitute for action of the Security Council in matters of aggression and threats to international peace.

The major approaches to meeting the problem of the veto which have been advanced include the following:

1. Abolish the veto completely and accord equality in voting to all members of the Security Council.

2. Substitute a voting formula which would preclude a veto by any single permanent member but would require the support of enough of the permanent members, perhaps 3 or 4, for a decision to command adequate prestige and power.

3. Restrict the use of the veto to clearly defined areas and eliminate it entirely from the admission of new members and the pacific settlement of disputes.

4. Alter the fundamental nature of the Security Council by substituting recommendatory powers for its present enforcement powers.

5. Strengthen further the role of the General Assembly, by authorizing that body to act on matters which remain deadlocked in the Security Council by reason of the veto.

Revision of the United Nations Charter offers some possibility, however meager, of limiting the use of the veto or otherwise reconstructing the machinery of the United Nations to meet the needs of the present situation. Since the matter of the veto is almost certain to be presented if a conference to review the charter is held, the United States needs to determine how far it is willing to go in altering the veto regardless of the Soviet position.

The United States is already on record as favoring removal of pacific settlement of disputes and admission of new members from the province of the veto. To go much beyond this point raises fundamental questions of the degree to which we are willing to entrust to collective decision matters which heretofore, for the most part, we have dealt with alone.

HOW THE UNITED NATIONS CHARTER HAS DEVELOPED

STAFF STUDY NO. 2

MAY 18, 1954

PREFACE

By Alexander Wiley, *Chairman*

Senate Resolution 126 (as amended by S. Res. 193) authorized a subcommittee of the Committee on Foreign Relations to make a study of the United Nations Charter, bearing in mind the likelihood that a charter-review conference will be held after 1955.

The present study (staff study No. 2) discusses the ways in which the charter has grown and the methods by which it can be amended. It is important for Members of the Senate, and for Americans concerned with the possibility of changes in the charter, to have an understanding of the instrument as it has developed in practice and the methods by which it may be changed.

This study describes the formal methods by which the charter can be amended. Principal attention is given to the ways in which the charter has changed by a process that can best be described as "informal amendment." For example, some provisions of the charter, such as those dealing with putting armed forces at the disposal of the Security Council, have not been given effect. Other articles have been expanded in scope by action spelling out the details of United Nations operations. In addition, important changes have been wrought in the United Nations system by means of agreements, such as the North Atlantic Treaty, which supplement charter provisions regarding collective security.

The United Nations Charter, as is true with many organic instruments, has been adapted to meet the requirements of the day. Thus, extensive use of the veto by the Soviet Union has required the development of other methods to enable the organization to discharge its basic functions in the field of peaceful settlement of disputes and the protection of states from aggression. It would not have been possible in view of the Soviet veto, for example, for the United Nations to find the Chinese Communists guilty of aggression by the device of a Security Council vote. It was necessary therefore to carry this issue to the General Assembly for recommendatory action.

It is my hope that this study will enable members of the Senate and the public to which the Government must look for support, understanding, and guidance, to give attention and thought to the problems we face in considering the subject of charter review.

This staff study was prepared by Francis O. Wilcox, chief of staff of the Committee on Foreign Relations. He has been intimately concerned with the United Nations since its inception, having served as an adviser to the American delegation to the San Francisco Conference and having participated in most sessions of the General Assembly during the past 8 years.

The views expressed in this study are not necessarily the views of the subcommittee.

May 18, 1954.

CONTENTS

HOW THE UNITED NATIONS CHARTER HAS DEVELOPED

I. INTRODUCTORY COMMENT

Chief Justice Marshall once said of the Constitution of the United States that—

it was intended to endure for ages to come, and, consequently, to be adapted to the various crises of human affairs.

To that end the framers of the Constitution built better than they realized. They succeeded in bringing into harmony to a remarkable degree the concepts of stability and permanence on the one hand and the ideas of flexibility and change on the other. As a result the Constitution has kept in tune with the times. It has grown and developed over the last century and a half so as to keep pace with the growth of our Nation—through its infancy, its adolescence, and now its difficult position of world leadership.

This process of constitutional growth and amendment has gone on unceasingly. The striking thing, of course, is the fact that, for the most part, these changes have not been formal in character. The formal amending process has been invoked in only a few instances and, indeed, in the last two decades of dynamic change, it has been invoked only once.

Far more important have been the "informal amendments" that have been added from time to time. These changes—largely in the form of constitutional customs and practices, basic legislation passed by Congress, and interpretation of the Constitution by the courts— have done much to keep the Constitution a living document.

What we have in the United States today, therefore, is a Constitution which has undergone remarkably little textual change but which has developed over the years into a vast and intricate complex of rules for the conduct of our Government.

In some respects the Charter of the United Nations is much like the Constitution. Both are written in form and both would be classified by political scientists as fairly "rigid" in character because they contain rather difficult amendment procedures. The charter, like the Constitution, was designed to lay a broad base for an institution which might develop to meet changing needs. And the charter, like the Constitution, has proven flexible enough to be adapted to many new situations without the need for formal amendment.

It is important to keep this fact in mind when the problem of charter revision is under consideration. In the 8 years of U. N. existence not a single formal amendment has even so much as reached the final voting stage in the General Assembly. Even so, many far-reaching changes have taken place within the U. N. system. Some important articles of the charter have already fallen into disuse. Others have been applied in a way that the San Francisco drafters did not contemplate.

We are by no means examining the charter that was drafted in San Francisco in 1945. We are examining the charter of 1954 as it has been amplified by custom and usage, resolutions of the various U. N. organs, and treaties, like the Atlantic Pact, which are consistent with the charter and have a heavy impact on the U. N. system. If we should proceed now to consider amendments to the old charter rather than the new, it would be very much like a surgeon planning a major operation on the basis of a diagnosis made 9 years ago.

It is the purpose of this study to examine briefly the growth of the United Nations Charter. First it reviews the provisions of the charter relating to the formal amending process. Then it surveys the informal means by which the charter has developed since 1945.[1]

II. FORMAL AMENDMENTS TO THE CHARTER

At the San Francisco Conference the formal amending process, which was inextricably bound up with the veto problem, became the subject of prolonged and heated debate. The question before the Conference may be simply put: How was it possible to inject sufficient flexibility into the charter in order to provide room for adaptation without, at the same time, making it possible for member states to upset, through the amendment procedure, the delicate balance of power that had been so carefully worked out?

Those who favored a rigid charter presented convincing arguments to support their case. Many of the provisions of the charter—particularly those relating to the privileged position of the great powers—were the result of uneasy compromises. They had been agreed upon only after long and painful negotiations. Any premature tinkering with the charter, therefore, would only reopen a Pandora's box of difficult issues and hamper the functioning of the new organization.

Moreover, from the point of view of the five permanent members, no amendment procedure was either logical or acceptable unless it incorporated the principle of the great power veto. For what protection would the veto offer them if it could later be removed from the charter by an amendment which might be adopted without their unanimous consent?

On the other hand, some delegates, who bitterly opposed the veto, agreed to ease up on their opposition if they could get some kind of assurance that the amending process might be liberalized. Basically they objected to any arrangement that would freeze the status quo and permit any great power, through the exercise of the veto, to

[1] On this question of charter amendment and charter growth see the following: L. M. Goodrich and E. Hambro, Charter of the United Nations, Commentary and Documents, ch. 18; Hans Kelsen, The Law of the United Nations, 1950, pp. 816-824; A. Vandenbosch and W. N. Hogan, The United Nations, Background, Organization, Functions, Activities, 1952, ch. 20; S. Engle, The Changing Charter of the United Nations, The Yearbook of World Affairs, 1953; E. P. Chase, The United Nations in Action, 1950, ch. 18; E. Gross, Revising the Charter: Is It Possible? Is It Wise?, Foreign Affairs, January 1954. See also Committee on Foreign Relations, S. Doc. No. 87, 1954, Review of the United Nations Charter: A Collection of Documents; Report to the President On the Results of the San Francisco Conference, ch. XVIII; Department of State Publication 2349, June 26, 1945; N. L. Hill, International Organization, ch. XVII, 1952; S. Engle, De facto Revision of the Charter of the United Nations, Journal of Politics, February 1952; H. Shawcross, The Constitutional Structure of the United Nations, Nebraska Law Review, November 1950; N. de M. Bentwich and A. Martin, A Commentary on the Charter of the United Nations . . . With An Appendix On the Developments of the Charter Between May 1949 and March 1951, 1951; the United Nations, the United Nations Yearbook, vols. 1946-47, 1947-48, 1948-49, 1950, and 1951; C. Eagleton and R. N. Swift, editors, Annual Review of United Nations Affairs, 1949, 1950, 1951, and 1952; A. H. Feller, United Nations and World Community, 1952; H. Morgenthau, The United Nations and the Revision of the Charter, The Review of Politics, January 1954; and J. F. Dulles, War or Peace, 1950.

prevent needed charter changes. The veto in itself was bad enough they felt. But the veto irrevocably imbedded in a rigid charter was doubly bad.

A. ARTICLE 108

As a result of this verbal tug of war two different methods of amending the charter were finally agreed upon. The ordinary procedure is set forth in article 108.

Amendments to the present Charter shall come into force for all Members of the United Nations when they have been adopted by a vote of two-thirds of the members of the General Assembly and ratified in accordance with their respective constitutional processes by two-thirds of the Members of the United Nations, including all the permanent members of the Security Council.

Article 108 thus outlines two distinct steps that are to be followed in the normal amending process: (1) Adoption of the proposal by a two-thirds vote of the General Assembly; and (2) ratification by two-thirds of the members of the United Nations, including the permanent members of the Security Council. Four important points should be noted in connection with these steps.

First.—Proposed amendments may be adopted by the General Assembly without any action on the part of the Security Council. In the initial stages, at least, the will of a majority of two-thirds of the members prevails. No single state or small group of states can prevent an amendment from being approved and sent on to the member nations for further consideration and possible ratification.

Article 108 expressly provides that amendments must be approved by a vote of two-thirds of the members of the General Assembly. This undoubtedly means two-thirds of the total membership of the U. N. and not the two-thirds majority of the members present and voting which is required for other so-called "important questions" according to the language of article 18. The two-thirds requirement has the effect of discouraging frivolous attempts at charter revision. At the same time it guarantees that only those proposals which have strong enough support in the U. N. to make ratification by two-thirds of the members probable, will be forwarded to the states for final action.

Second.—Article 108 reiterates the predominant position of the great powers in the U. N. The requirement that amendments must be ratified by two-thirds of the U. N. members, including the five permanent members, simply means that no amendment can become effective if it meets with the disapproval of any of the permanent members. By failing to take positive action on an amendment adopted by the General Assembly any 1 of the 5 great powers can prevent its entry into force even though it may be ratified by all the other members of the United Nations.

Third.—Once an amendment receives the required number of ratifications, including those of the five permanent members, it becomes effective with respect to all members, even those who voted against it or failed to ratify it. This is an interesting example of the impact of the charter upon the traditional concept of state sovereignty. For, apart from the permanent members, the entire membership of the U. N. have committed themselves in advance to accept any new obligations that charter changes might bring in their wake.

Suppose, however, that a state vigorously opposes an amendment and does not wish to be bound by its provisions after its entry into force? In that event, it has the option of withdrawing from the U. N. While the charter itself contains no express provision for withdrawal, a declaration of interpretation adopted by the San Francisco Conference leaves no doubt on this point.

Nor would a Member be bound—

reads the declaration—

to remain in the Organization if its rights and obligations as such were changed by Charter amendment in which it has not concurred and which it finds itself unable to accept, or if an amendment duly accepted by the necessary majority in the Assembly or in a general conference fails to secure the ratifications necessary to bring such amendment into effect.[2]

While an avenue of withdrawal is thus left open to dissatisfied states, presumably the right would not be exercised except in very rare instances. Such a step would be a serious one and any state, about to lose the benefits that accrue to it from U. N. membership, probably would hesitate a long time before taking it.

Fourth.—No reference is made in article 108 to any time period within which amendments proposed by the General Assembly must be ratified. This might give rise to some interesting consequences. States may consider it a legitimate reason for withdrawal from the United Nations if an amendment approved by the General Assembly fails to secure the requisite number of ratifications to go into effect. Yet without any specific dateline, one may ask when a state is justified in assuming that an amendment has failed to secure the necessary number of ratifications.

It should also be noted that amendments must be ratified by member states "in accordance with their respective constitutional processes." While this proviso is a bow in the direction of popular government, it is not altogether clear what practical effect it has. In a few countries the chief executive, acting on his own authority under the constitution, would have power to approve amendments. In most states, however, positive action by the legislative branch would be called for.

In the United States there is little doubt that our Government would follow the regular treaty procedure outlined in the Constitution and secure the advice and consent of the Senate before ratifying a proposed amendment since any other course would be a subversion of the treatymaking process. Certainly it would be illogical if the President, after securing a two-thirds vote of the Senate approving the ratification of the original charter, could then proceed to alter drastically the nature of our commitments in the United Nations by accepting amendments without referring them to the Senate for approval.

In one sense, even with the great power veto, the amending process set forth in the charter is a comparatively liberal one. Many multilateral treaties cannot be amended without the consent of all the signatories. The North Atlantic Treaty is a good case in point. No change, however slight, in the text of that agreement could be accomplished without the specific approval of each one of the 14 treaty members.

---

[2] Report to the President on the results of the San Francisco Conference, June 26, 1945, pp. 48–49.

Theoretically, at least, the charter is much more flexible. If 40 U. N. members agree, it would be possible to bring about far-reaching changes in the charter even against the opposition of as many as 20 nations, excluding the Big Five.

The League of Nations experience

In this connection it is interesting to recall the experience of the League of Nations. Article 26 of the covenant provided that amendments would take effect when ratified by all the states represented on the Council and by a majority of those represented in the Assembly. Thus not only the great powers but every other member of the Council possessed a veto. Since the membership of the Council changed from time to time this requirement proved to be an almost insuperable hurdle. Of the numerous amendments approved by the Assembly only a few technical ones ever received the requisite number of ratifications.

One example will suffice. In 1923 the ratifications of only two states represented on the Council—Uruguay and Spain—were necessary to bring a particular amendment into force. These ratifications were obtained in 1924 and 1930, respectively. Meanwhile, however, the composition of the Council changed from year to year so that by 1935 the ratifications of Argentina, Germany, Mexico, Russia, and Turkey still had to be secured before the amendment could come into effect.

In practice, this "transitory" veto exercised by the nonpermanent members of the League Council proved almost as baffling—and certainly far more bewildering—than the veto power of the permanent members of the U. N. Security Council.

B. ARTICLE 109

As has been pointed out above, the normal amending procedure outlined in article 108 was not enough to satisfy the demands of many delegations who were displeased with the charter as it emerged at San Francisco. Some delegates argued that they would be unable to secure ratification of the instrument in their states unless assurances could be given that, within a reasonable period of time, there would be an opportunity to review the charter and strengthen its provisions in the light of experience. For this reason article 109 was developed. Basically it is the residue of an attempt to set up a second method of charter amendment different from and easier than that found in article 108. The attempt fell short of its mark. A reading of the text shows that while article 109 establishes a somewhat different procedure, it is certainly no easier than that envisaged in article 108.

1. A General Conference of the Members of the United Nations for the purpose of reviewing the present Charter may be held at a date and place to be fixed by a two-thirds vote of the members of the General Assembly and by a vote of any seven members of the Security Council. Each Member of the United Nations shall have one vote in the conference.

2. Any alteration of the present Charter recommended by a two-thirds vote of the conference shall take effect when ratified in accordance with their respective constitutional processes by two-thirds of the Members of the United Nations including all the permanent members of the Security Council.

3. If such a conference has not been held before the tenth annual session of the General Assembly following the coming into force of the present Charter, the proposal to call such a conference shall be placed on the agenda of that session of

the General Assembly, and the conference shall be held if so decided by a majority vote of the members of the General Assembly and by a vote of any seven members of the Security Council.

It may be useful to recall the history of article 109.   Even before the San Francisco Conference convened the United States delegation agreed that the opportunity offered by article 108 for the piecemeal amendment of the charter would not suffice.   The charter was forged in the crucible of war and it seemed desirable to provide an opportunity to take a look at the entire organization at some future date.   The delegation was opposed to any provision that would make the United Nations seem temporary or transitory in character.   At the same time it recognized the value of setting up procedures for a more general review than would be possible under the hit-and-miss system of having the General Assembly consider isolated amendments from time to time.[3]

The idea of a Review Conference

On the opening day of the Conference the United States delegation agreed upon the text of an article to be inserted in the charter.   This new article provided that a General Conference to review the charter might be called whenever three-quarters of the General Assembly and any seven members of the Security Council so voted.   It also provided that any amendments recommended by such a Conference by a two-thirds vote would take effect when ratified by two-thirds of the members of the organization, including the five permanent members of the Security Council.   This is essentially the language of paragraphs 1 and 2 of article 109, as they were accepted by the Conference.

But many delegations wished to go even further.   Specifically they argued that (1) the convening of the General Conference should be made easier and (2) a date for the Conference should be indicated. Some insisted that a fixed date be set, preferably 5 or 7 years after the establishment of the new organization.   Others, following the lead of Brazil and Canada, suggested that the Conference might be made mandatory at some undesignated time within a 5- to 10-year period.

The first proposition was agreed to.   The language of article 109 was liberalized so as to make possible the calling of a Review Conference by a two-thirds (instead of the original three-fourths) vote of the General Assembly.

The second proposition, however, met with considerable opposition. Who could say in advance when it would be wise to hold a Review Conference?   Suppose the date selected should by chance fall during a period of world crisis, thus making such an enterprise inadvisable? Would it not be more logical to await events and permit the members of the organization to determine whether such a Conference might serve a useful purpose?

These conflicting issues were straddled in the compromise incorporated in paragraph 3 of article 109.   While the final compromise is based upon a time limit of a kind, it does not guarantee that a Review Conference will be convened on any fixed date.   The only guaranty involved is that the question of calling the Conference will be placed on the agenda of the General Assembly after 10 years have elapsed. This in itself is not a concession of any great moment since any member has the right to request that an item be placed on the agenda and the General Assembly approves its agenda by a simple majority vote.

---

[3] Ibid., ch. XVIII.   See also the works of Goodrich and Hambro, and Kelsen cited above.

One significant concession however, should be noted. If 10 years elapse and the question of calling a Review Conference is automatically placed on the General Assembly's agenda, the decision to call the Conference may be taken by a majority vote of its members instead of the two-thirds vote required under paragraph 1. This decision must be concurred in by an affirmative vote of any 7 members of the Security Council. Thus no great power, by its negative vote, can prevent the convening of a Review Conference. It can, under the terms of paragraph 2, prevent a charter amendment from coming into force by failing to ratify it.

Differences between articles 108 and 109

Basically there is little difference between article 108 and article 109. Actually, the General Conference contemplated in article 109 has the same composition as the General Assembly referred to in article 108. In both cases each member of the U. N. would be represented and would have 1 vote. Likewise any amendment approved by either the General Assembly or the General Conference would require a two-thirds vote of the entire U. N. membership. Moreover, whether one thinks in terms of "alterations" or "amendments" to the charter, they would come into force under exactly the same circumstances— namely, through ratification, in accordance with their constitutional processes, by two-thirds of the members of the United Nations including the five permanent members of the Security Council.[4]

Thus article 109 as it was finally adopted, is no easier from a legal point of view than is article 108. The gamut an amendment has to run is just as long and just as difficult under one article as the other. There is no reason to suppose that a fundamental change in the charter that has been rejected by the General Assembly would muster any more support in a General Conference called under article 109.

In some respects it might prove simpler to secure action through the General Assembly since that is an established organ of the U. N. and meets at least once every year. It is regularly available. No special effort, no positive vote, is required to bring it into being as is the case with the General Conference.

On the other hand, there are practical difficulties involved in attempting to divert the attention of the General Assembly to such a controversial matter as the amending process. Confronted each fall with an overflowing agenda, most delegates have been inclined to postpone any serious discussion of charter amendments pending the convening of the first General Conference under article 109.

The atmosphere in a General Conference should be much more conducive to a balanced appraisal of the various arguments relating to charter revision and review. That will be the task of the Conference. It will be convened for that specific purpose. Delegations will be briefed on the issues involved and will have instructions from their governments.

The question of whether to hold a General Conference for Charter Review will, therefore, be on the agenda of the 10th annual session of the General Assembly in 1955 and it is likely that the Conference, if agreed to by a majority vote, will be held the following year. Secretary of State Dulles, as early as August 1953, announced that the United States would vote in favor of convening such a General Conference.

---

[4] See Kelsen, op. cit., pp. 817-818.

III. INFORMAL CHARTER CHANGES

It is likely that when the formal amending procedures set forth in a constitution are too rigid to permit necessary changes, then other ways and means will be found to achieve the desired ends.

The charter has been subjected to what one might call informal amendments in a variety of ways: (1) Through the nonimplementation or nonapplication of certain provisions of the charter; (2) through the interpretation of the charter by various organs and members of the U. N.; (3) through the conclusion of supplementary treaties or agreements, such as the Headquarters Agreement of 1947, and the North Atlantic Pact; and (4) through the creation of special organs and agencies.

These informal amendments substantially affect the provisions of the charter although they leave its text intact. In some cases they create gaping holes in the document as it was drafted at San Francisco. In other cases they merely fill in the interstices. In still other cases they chart fundamentally new paths of progress for the U. N.

It is outside the scope of this study to examine in detail the growth of the charter since 1945. But it does seem desirable to take a quick look at the process in general terms, for without a knowledge of what has been happening during the past 8 years one cannot tackle intelligently the broader problem of charter revision.[5]

A. NONIMPLEMENTATION OR NONAPPLICATION OF CHARTER PROVISIONS

In a number of instances organs or members of the U. N. have disregarded or have failed to implement certain charter provisions. As a result several articles, which the framers believed were highly important in making the U. N. an effective instrumentality for world peace, have already fallen into disuse.

Perhaps the best example is article 43. That article was designed to put teeth into the United Nations system. Under its terms the members of the U. N. agreed to make available to the Security Council the armed forces, assistance, and the facilities necessary for the purpose of maintaining international peace and security. But after 8 years of fruitless negotiations the great powers remain deadlocked over such questions as the numbers and types of forces each country shall make available, their locations, their degree of readiness, etc. Consequently, the agreements referred to in article 43 have never come into existence and that provision of the charter remains a dead letter.

Much the same situation exists with respect to articles 44, 45, 46, 48, and most of article 47, which relate to the use of armed forces by the Security Council. These provisions of the charter are largely contingent upon the entry into force of article 43. Taken together they constitute the heart of the U. N. collective security system as it was envisaged by the framers at San Francisco.

Article 106 offers still another striking example. Briefly put this article provides that prior to the time the Security Council is ready to begin its peace-keeping functions under articles 42 and 43, the five permanent members should consult with one another with a view to such joint action as may be necessary to maintain world peace. The

---

[5] On this problem of informal charter change see the articles by S. Engle cited above. Portions of this section are based on these articles.

great powers, in other words, were given the joint responsibility for maintaining peace, on a transitional basis, until the new organization was properly equipped to perform its functions in an effective manner.

But the split between the East and West has not only hamstrung the Security Council, it has prevented giving effect to the transitional arrangement which was supposed to hold the line until the full organization could swing into action.

Mention might also be made of article 23, paragraph 1. This article specifically provides that the General Assembly in electing the six nonpermanent members of the Security Council shall pay special regard, in the first instance, to the contribution of U. N. members to the maintenance of peace and security and to the other purposes of the organization, and also to equitable geographical distribution. In actual practice the General Assembly has pretty largely disregarded the first two criteria, placing most of its emphasis on equitable geographical distribution. Normally 2 members have been elected from Latin America, 1 from Western Europe, 1 from the British Commonwealth, 1 from the Middle East, and, during the first few years at least, 1 from the Soviet satellite bloc.

Of course it can be argued that these criteria are in no way legally binding upon the General Assembly. Certainly if they are disregarded there is no method provided for appealing the action of the General Assembly. Yet when the guideposts are ignored it simply means that, in effect, article 23, paragraph 1, has been dropped, at least temporarily, from the charter.

B. INTERPRETATION OF THE CHARTER

It is a confusing fact that the charter makes no provision for its interpretation. The International Court of Justice hands down advisory opinions, on request, from time to time but these have no binding legal effect. In practice the organs and members of the U. N. are left free to interpret the various articles of the charter in accordance with their own discretion. Consequently, any meaning which a provision of the charter might reasonably have can prevail in any particular instance. This flexibility has led to a number of interesting developments.

Voting in the Security Council

One of the most significant of these developments relates to the all-important question of voting in the Security Council. The language of article 27, paragraph 3, seems quite clear. It provides specifically that for other than procedural matters, decisions of the Security Council are to be made "by an affirmative vote of seven members including the concurring votes of the permanent members."

Does this mean that action cannot be taken by the Security Council unless it is concurred in by all five of the great powers? Does it mean when a permanent member abstains or is absent at the time the vote is taken that no decision can be reached? Certainly any strict construction of the charter might lead to that conclusion.

Early in its history the Security Council took the position that an abstention or an absence of a permanent member did not constitute a negative vote. It was this liberal interpretation of the charter, coupled with the absence of the Soviet representative from the meetings at the time, which paved the way for swift Security Council decisions when the Republic of South Korea was attacked in June 1950. With only 4 permanent members present the Security Council brushed aside a number of neat legal problems and approved 3 resolutions which made possible U. N. decisions against the aggressor in a way not contemplated by the charter.[7]

Before leaving article 27 it might be well to point out that that article, perhaps more than any other, illustrates how differently the charter may be interpreted by certain members on the one hand and by an organ of the U. N. on the other. At San Francisco the great powers agreed upon a very narrow interpretation of "procedural" questions. For the most part these were the organizational matters referred to in articles 28–32 of the charter; the adoption of the rules of procedure of the Council, the selection of the President, the time and place of meetings, the establishment of subsidiary organs, etc. Beyond this point, argued the sponsoring governments in their statement of June 7, 1945, decisions of the Security Council might have "major political consequences," and accordingly would require the unanimous vote of the permanent members.[8]

Since that time the General Assembly—in an attempt to narrow the area within which the veto applies—has been inclined to define procedural questions very broadly. On April 14, 1949, the General Assembly recommended to the Security Council that a long list of some 31 decisions be considered procedural and that the Council conduct its business accordingly. Included in the list were a number of decisions—such as the admission of states to U. N. membership—which had heretofore been considered substantive in character.[9]

The distance between the narrow interpretation of the sponsoring governments at San Francisco and the liberal interpretation of the General Assembly is great. Since the charter itself does not spell out the distinctions between procedural and substantive questions, either of these two interpretations could apply. Clearly there is great elasticity in this part of the charter if the members wish to use it.

The Secretary-General

There has also proved to be considerable elasticity in the charter provisions relating to the role of the Secretary-General in the United Nations. Articles 97–100 might leave the impression that his political functions were to be quite limited in scope. As chief administrative officer of the U. N. (art. 97) with authority to appoint his staff (art. 101) and submit an annual report to the General Assembly on the work of the U. N. (art. 98), the post naturally carries with it a certain amount of prestige and influence. But only in article 99, under which he may bring to the attention of the Security Council matters which in his opinion may threaten world peace, is there any real grant of political initiative.

Yet, in fact, influence exercised by the Secretary-General has been one of the significant developments within the United Nations.

---

[7] For a fuller discussion of the practice of abstention, see, United States Senate Committee on Foreign Relations, Subcommittee on the United Nations Charter Staff Study No. 1, The Problem of the Veto in the United Nations Security Council.

[8] United States Senate Committee on Foreign Relations, Subcommittee on the United Nations S. Doc. 87, Review of the United Nations Charter: A Collection of Documents (hereinafter referred to as Collection of Documents), p. 562.

[9] Collection of Documents, p. 572.

Both the General Assembly and the Security Council—and still more important the Secretary-General himself—have taken a broad view of his functions. He has made statements before both bodies on a variety of questions, and he has undisputed authority to place any item he considers necessary on the General Assembly's provisional agenda. One has only to recall his vigorous role in the Korean crisis (which the Soviet Union bitterly resented), his proposal for a U. N. guard force, and his attempts to bring about a rapprochement between the Soviet bloc and the free world, to understand the expanding nature of his political activities.

Non-self-governing territories

Still another demonstration of what custom and usage can do is reflected in the General Assembly's interpretation of article 73 (e) regarding non-self-governing territories as distinguished from trust territories. According to the provisions of that article the member states are obligated to submit to the Secretary-General "for information purposes," data of a technical nature relating to the economic, social, and educational conditions in the non-self-governing territories for which they are responsible. Presumably this language does not grant to any U. N. organ the authority to deal with the information furnished or to make recommendations about it. The General Assembly, however, in the face of rather vigorous opposition from some of the colonial powers, has gone considerably beyond the letter of article 73. In 1949 it created a special committee to examine the information transmitted and to submit reports thereon to the General Assembly—

with such procedural recommendations as it may deem fit, and with such substantive recommendations as it may deem desirable relating to functional fields generally but not with respect to individual territories.[10]

With this as a starting point, the General Assembly has gradually expanded its influence. It has approved a standardized form for governments to use in submitting information. It has requested additional information from member states. It has debated at considerable length the reports submitted to it on the information received. If the present trend continues, the time may come when world opinion would expect the colonial powers to account to the U. N. for the efficient administration of their non-self-governing territories.[11]

The General Assembly

Finally, perhaps the most significant informal change in the charter has taken place as a result of the sharp shift in the balance of power between the Security Council and the General Assembly. During the past 5 years the Security Council, meeting less and less frequently, has faded into the background. The General Assembly, on the other hand, has played a much more important role than the framers of the charter anticipated.

At San Francisco much emphasis was placed upon the Security Council's primary responsibility for the maintenance of world peace. It was to meet in continuous session. Armed forces were to be placed at its disposal. It could make decisions binding on all U. N. members.

[10] Collection of Documents, p. 727
[11] Ibid., pt. C (X), pp. 749–779.

It was to be a small body capable of acting with vigor and dispatch in order to keep the peace.

The General Assembly was designed to be a much less powerful organ. It was scheduled to meet in regular annual sessions. It was to have no armed forces at its disposal. It could not make decisions— only recommendations. Its main weapon was discussion and debate.

As the Security Council has fallen into disuse, largely because of dissension among the great powers, the General Assembly has become a stronger and more vigorous organ. By various devices, including the creation in 1947 of the Interim Committee, or the so-called Little Assembly, ways and means have been found to keep the General Assembly in virtually continuous session. Moreover, the Uniting for Peace Resolution, which was approved in 1950 after the attack on Korea, geared the General Assembly to take quick action against an aggressor in the event the Security Council failed to exercise its responsibility for the maintenance of peace.[12]

Today, the General Assembly may be convened in emergency session in 24 hours. It may make appropriate recommendations to the members for collective measures, including the use of armed forces. It has created two important subsidiary organs: (1) A Collective Measures Committee of 14 members to report on the methods which might be used to strengthen international peace and security; and (2) a Peace Observation Commission, likewise made up of 14 members, to observe and report on any situation which might endanger international peace and security. Finally, member states have been asked to earmark certain of their armed forces so organized, trained, and equipped that they could be made available promptly for service as United Nations units.[13]

In filling this new role the General Assembly has already demonstrated that it can make far-reaching recommendations. Thus, on February 1, 1951, it approved a resolution finding that Communist China had engaged in aggression in Korea.[14] This was followed on May 18, 1951, by a second resolution calling for an embargo on the shipment of war materials to Communist China and North Korea.[15] It can be argued, of course, that resolutions of this kind are only recommendations to the member states, and as such have no binding effect. But in fact, the strategic materials embargo has been put into operation by some 45 countries and has considerably limited strategic trade with aggressor nations.

C. THE CONCLUSION OF AGREEMENTS WHICH SUPPLEMENT THE CHARTER

The character of the charter has also been changed as a result of numerous treaties and agreements which have been entered into by various member states. These agreements define in greater detail the general provisions of the charter. They usually spell out in more specific form the rights and duties of member states and the powers and functions of U. N. organs. In some instances they lay down obligations and commitments which go beyond those contained in the charter. In all such cases the text of the charter has remained

[12] Ibid., pt. C (V), pp. 494-556.
[13] Ibid., p. 557.
[14] Ibid., p. 596.
[15] Ibid., p. 597.

unchanged.   A few examples may be helpful to show the nature of this development.

Convention on Privileges and Immunities and Headquarters Agreement

The charter itself, for example, sets forth in only the broadest of terms the basic principles relating to the legal capacity of the U. N. and the privileges and immunities to be enjoyed by representatives of the member states and by U. N. officials.   (See arts. 104–105.)   At San Francisco it was assumed that these were matters which could be worked out more properly at a later date.   Indeed, article 105, paragraph 3, specifically calls upon the General Assembly to make recommendations with a view to determining the details of the application of the principles regarding privileges and immunities or to propose conventions to the members for this purpose.

Under the Convention on the Privileges and Immunities of the United Nations of February 13, 1946, what was once 2 short articles of the charter—some 9 lines—has grown into a document of 36 sections, setting forth in some detail the juridical personality of the U. N., the immunity of U. N. property, funds and assets, the right of the U. N. to use communication facilities, the privileges and immunities of officials accredited to the U. N., and so on.   As of October 1953, 42 nations—the United States not among them—had ratified the convention.[16]

In the same category is the Headquarters Agreement between the United States and the United Nations signed on June 26, 1947.   This agreement defines the headquarters district in New York and clarifies the rights of the U. N. with respect to postal and radio facilities, the use of an airport, the inviolability of the headquarters, police protection, and related matters.   Like the Convention on Privileges and Immunities it gives substance to the general provisions of the charter.[17]

Of a somewhat different character are the declarations which some 44 nations have made voluntarily accepting the compulsory jurisdiction of the International Court of Justice.   It is true, of course, that all members of the U. N. are obligated to settle their differences by peaceful means.[18]   But the charter does not impose any particular method of solution upon the parties to a dispute.   Consequently, when U. N. members accede to the so-called optional clause of the Court statute (art. 36) and agree in advance to submit their legal disputes to the Court for settlement, they not only enlarge the competence of that body but they accept obligations over and above those already embodied in the charter.

Regional collective security agreements

Most important, from the point of view of the future development of the U. N., are the changes which have taken place as a result of the conclusion of such agreements as the Brussels Treaty, the Rio Treaty, and the North Atlantic Pact.[19]   The United Nations Charter was designed to tackle the problem of collective security on a worldwide basis, vesting primary responsibility for the maintenance of peace in the Security Council.   That grand design soon proved inadequate. As a consequence, U. N. members, who feared the threat of Soviet

[16] Ibid., p. 191.
[17] Ibid., p. 197.
[18] Ibid., p. 2 (art. 2 (3)) of the charter.
[19] Ibid., pt. C (VIII).

aggression, were compelled to continue their quest for security in other directions. In such agreements as the Rio Treaty and the North Atlantic Treaty they shifted their emphasis from universal collective security to security based on regional pacts and the idea of collective self-defense as expressed in article 51.

Thus the United Nations is a much different organization than it was 8 years ago. Then it stressed the essential unity of all members against aggression anywhere. Now it is an organization within which groups of states are seeking to preserve the peace by uniting their strength in order to deter aggression from Communist sources.

There are, to be sure, some critics who still argue that the Atlantic Pact is not a regional arrangement and that it violates the spirit if not the letter of the United Nations Charter. Whether the Atlantic Pact is based upon the regional chapter (arts. 52–54) of the charter, or whether it derives its existence from article 51, is beside the point. The real point is that these agreements have added new wings to the U. N. structure. In developing, as they do, new techniques for joint action against armed attack they give new meaning and new vitality to articles 51–54.

In this connection mention should also be made of the bilateral mutual defense treaties which the United States has concluded with the Philippines, Japan, and Korea, and the tripartite pact with Australia and New Zealand. These treaties, which also spring from article 51, outline a somewhat different approach to the security problem in an area of the world which is not quite ready for the kind of commitments contained in the Atlantic Pact. The words in article VIII of the treaty with Australia and New Zealand, "Pending the development of a more comprehensive system of regional security in the Pacific area," leave the implication, however, that the treaties are only the first step in the building of a more effective security system for the Pacific.

The Senate Foreign Relations Committee has expressed its belief that a regional pact for the Pacific area "is a desirable ultimate objective" of United States policy (Ex. Rept. 2, 82d Cong., 2d sess., p. 25; see also Ex. Rept. 1, 83d Cong., 2d sess., p. 8). Since the executive branch seems to concur generally in this view it is probable that eventually there will be further evolution of the collective security concept in that area. Suggestions from various quarters relating to the desirability of a similar security pact for middle eastern countries merely serve to underline the flexible character of the charter.

The Soviet Union has also concluded a system of regional alliances which give lipservice to the provisions of the United Nations Charter. While it cannot be said that they contribute to the growth of the United Nations, they do effect a change in the United Nations system.

It has been suggested with respect to the development of regional security organizations that they do not—

supplement but rather express distrust in the peace machinery of the United Nations—

and that while they may contribute to peace and security—

they are doing so not in the charter's spirit of cooperative, collective effort toward mutual restraint but instead by the precarious balancing of mutually opposed groupings.[20]

---

[20] Werner Levi, Political and Military Agreements in the Far East, Eighth Report, Commission To Study the Organization of the Peace.

Mr. Dulles, however, in commenting on the development of regional organizations, has said that they are—

actually a demonstration of the basic principle of the United Nations, and a realization of that principle in the ways which perhaps are at the moment the most practical, having regard to the exercise of the veto power by the Soviet Union.[21]

D. THE CREATION OF SUBSIDIARY ORGANS

Somewhat akin to the conclusion of supplementary agreements, although of less constitutional significance, has been the creation of special organs within the U. N. system. While both these devices were anticipated by the charter, they have helped to round out that document in a way that probably was not foreseen a decade ago.

The charter provides that both the General Assembly and the Security Council may establish such subsidiary organs as are deemed necessary for the performance of their respective functions. (See arts. 22, 29.) A good many standing committees have been set up under the Rules of Procedure of the two bodies. Among these are the six main committees of the General Assembly, the Advisory Committee on Administrative and Budgetary Questions, the Committee on Contributions of the General Assembly, and the Committee on Admission of New Members of the Security Council. These standing committees are largely designed to facilitate the proceedings of the two principal organs of the U. N.

In addition, a large number of committees and commissions have been established by resolution of the two parent organs to perform certain specific functions. Some of these are of a semipermanent nature, like the Interim Committee of the General Assembly, the International Law Commission, and the Disarmament Commission. Still others are ad hoc bodies, like the U. N. Commission for India and Pakistan, the U. N. Special Committee on the Balkans, the Palestine Conciliation Commission, the U. N. Commission for the Unification and Rehabilitation of Korea, and the Committee on the Question of Defining Aggression. The titles of these bodies give some indication of their diversity. As of March 1953 there were at least 32 subsidiary organs of the General Assembly and 3 of the Security Council.[22]

The Interim Committee

The Interim Committee, or the Little Assembly, is perhaps the best example of this type of constitutional development. It was established by a resolution of the General Assembly in 1947 for a 1-year term, continued in 1948 for another year, and reestablished indefinitely by a General Assembly resolution on November 21, 1949.[23] Since it was created to strengthen the General Assembly and thus to offset the veto-ridden Security Council, it was given broad competence to deal with questions within the jurisdiction of the General Assembly when the latter was not in session. Its jurisdiction includes (1) matters referred to it by the General Assembly; (2) important disputes or situations proposed for inclusion in the agenda of the General Assembly or referred to the General Assembly by the Security Council;

[21] Remarks of Secretary Dulles, March 1, 1953, before the American Association for the United Nations. Department of State Press Release No. 116.
[22] United Nations, Department of Public Information. Structure of the United Nations (Sixth Revision) May 1953. U. N. Document ST/DPI/7*.
[23] Collection of Documents, pp. 499–505.

and (3) methods of implementing article 11 (1) and article 13 (1) (a) of the charter. For the proper exercise of these functions the Interim Committee was given the power to conduct investigations, to appoint commissions of inquiry, to adopt additional rules of procedure not inconsistent with those of the General Assembly, and to advise on the calling of special sessions of the General Assembly.

Soviet opposition to Interim Committee

The resolution creating the Interim Committee underlined its character as a subsidiary organ of the General Assembly in accordance with the terms of article 22. Nevertheless, the Soviet Union and its satellites challenged the constitutionality of the Committee. They charged that it was designed to circumvent and weaken the Security Council which had primary responsibility for the maintenance of peace and security under the charter. They insisted, too, that the Committee possessed such broad powers that it was equal in rank with the General Assembly and consequently did not constitute a "subsidiary organ" within the meaning of article 22.

These arguments were not accepted by the General Assembly. At the same time the terms of reference of the Interim Committee were narrowed somewhat so as to meet the criticisms launched against it. Its authority to conduct investigations was circumscribed and its power to advise on the calling of special sessions of the General Assembly was limited to questions actually under discussion by the Committee. In addition, it was made clear that the Committee was not to trespass on the sphere of activity of any other organ of the United Nations.

Despite these assurances the Soviet Union and its satellite states continued to regard the Interim Committee as unconstitutional and refused to participate in its work. The Committee has not met since 1952.

The Soviet bloc has vigorously opposed the creation of a number of other subsidiary organs on constitutional grounds. They attacked the U. N. Commission for the Unification and Rehabilitation of Korea, insisting that it constituted illegal intervention in a civil war and interference in the internal affairs of another state. Similarly they held that the terms of reference of the U. N. Special Committee on the Balkans were incompatible with the charter and the principle of the sovereign equality of states. But these organs were established and discharged their responsibilities.

Out of U. N. experience with subsidiary organs to date the following principles emerge:

1. The authority of the General Assembly and the Security Council to establish subsidiary organs to perform a wide variety of functions has been established. Without this kind of assistance they could not effectively discharge their responsibilities under the charter.

2. The authority which these agencies exercise cannot go beyond the authority possessed by the parent organ under the United Nations Charter.

3. Most of the subsidiary organs exercise their mandates within a definite time period, the length of which depends upon the nature of the task to be performed.

4. The subsidiary organs are strictly accountable to the General Assembly or the Security Council and must submit reports on their activities at regular intervals.

The subsidiary organs by no means have a free rein; rather they are carefully hedged about by restrictions and limitations. They do not amend the charter in any substantive way. Yet they do constitute a significant part of the charter structure.

IV. Concluding Comments

As the time for the review of the United Nations Charter approaches, those who are interested in determining whether the United Nations can become a more effective instrumentality for world peace will want to examine carefully the alternatives open to them. Should an effort be made to bring the charter up to date through the formal amending process? Or would it be more prudent to wait upon the normal development of the charter through informal adaptation and change? This is a fundamental question that must be faced before the Charter Review Conference is convened.

In his book, entitled "War or Peace," published in 1950, Secretary of State John Foster Dulles commented as follows:

I have never seen any proposal made for collective security with "teeth" in it, or for "world government" or for "world federation," which could not be carried out either by the United Nations or under the United Nations Charter.

If the principal members of the United Nations, including the Soviet Union, are willing to take part in a proposed new world organization, then the United Nations itself could quickly be made into that organization.

If, as is the fact, the Soviet Union and others would not take part in the projected organization, then those who want to go ahead without them can form a collective security association under article 51.[24]

Mr. Dulles' suggestion that there is still a great deal of room for the development of the U. N. system within the four corners of the charter, reflects the experience of the organization to date. As the examples outlined above illustrate, U. N. members have inclined toward a liberal rather than a strict or narrow interpretation of the charter. As the late legal counsel to the U. N. wrote in 1952:

Few, if any, national constitutions have undergone such dramatic and such rapid developments in usage.[25]

Many of the imperfections in the U. N. system could be remedied without the change of a word in the charter. Certainly the impact of the veto could be softened quietly and quickly if the permanent members would informally agree to refrain from using it. Likewise, many nations now awaiting admission to the U. N. could be admitted without any formal charter change.

A. LIMITATIONS ON INFORMAL CHARTER CHANGES

While the charter is gradually being developed by these informal methods, certain disadvantages stem from relying on them instead of amendments of a more formal nature. For one thing, they are much less permanent in character. A formal amendment is firmly imbedded in the charter for all to see for years to come. But an informal charter change can be relatively easily modified or abrogated;

---

[24] John Foster Dulles, War or Peace, p. 204.
[25] A. H. Feller, United Nations and World Community, 1952, p. 31.

it may be here today and gone tomorrow depending upon the will of certain states or the action taken by a particular organ of the U. N.

More important still, informal changes may be much more limited in scope because they apply only to those States responsible for them.

The Atlantic Pact, for example, binds only the 14 nations members of NATO.   And a particular interpretation of the charter agreed upon by the five great powers has no legal validity beyond this limited group. On the other hand, a formal amendment, once in effect, is binding upon all the members of the U. N. whether they vote for it or not.

Some people, also, are inclined to question the constitutionality of informal amendments.   In practice, however, there is no satisfactory way in which the constitutionality of an informal amendment can be effectively challenged.   To be sure, the International Court of Justice may hand down advisory opinions, but such opinions are purely advisory in nature and have no binding effect either upon the members or upon the organs of the U. N.   There is no power of judicial review within the U. N. system.

The members and the various organs of the United Nations are alone competent to pass upon the constitutionality of their actions.   This being the case, changes brought about through the informal amendment processes must be considered constitutional so long as the states involved remain within their obligations under the charter.

On the other hand, charter growth through interpretation can only proceed within well-defined constitutional limits.   The United Nations is not a superstate.   It is based squarely upon the principle of the sovereign equality of all its members as article 2 constantly reminds us, and it must function within the specific limitations laid down in the charter.   However broad an interpretation one might place upon the charter, the United Nations—under the limiting language found in article 2, paragraph 7—is not authorized to intervene in matters essentially within the domestic jurisdiction of any state.   Likewise the authority of the General Assembly cannot be increased beyond a certain point for, under the express provisions of the charter, it can only recommend; it cannot make decisions binding on U. N. members.

The foregoing paragraphs indicate that many changes in the United Nations have been brought about by informal methods and by agreements made outside, but at the same time collateral to, the charter. Some changes which have been proposed, however, could only come about by formal amendment.   Thus, a change in the permanent membership of the Security Council, a change in the formal amending process, or a grant of authority to enable the General Assembly to make decisions instead of recommendations would undoubtedly require formal amendment before they could be made effective.   In fact, it has been argued (by the Soviet Union) that some of the informal changes mentioned in preceding paragraphs, many of which were developed as the result of American leadership, are of the type which should have been submitted for approval by the formal amendment procedures provided in the charter.

B. THE SOVIET ATTITUDE TOWARD CHARTER REVIEW

Up to this point the flexibility of the charter has been a bone of contention in the clash of ideologies between the Communist states and the non-Communist world.   With few exceptions the Soviet

Union has doggedly insisted upon a very strict construction of the charter. There seems little likelihood that there will be any substantial change in this approach toward the U. N. unless, of course, the Kremlin's attitude toward world affairs generally undergoes a marked and unexpected transformation.

Soviet opposition to formal charter amendments has been persistent. Those who urge the revision of the charter, the Soviets argue, are bent upon weakening the Security Council and destroying the fundamental principle upon which the U. N. is based—the unanimity of the five permanent members. Mr. Andrei Vyshinsky, of the U. S. S. R., reiterated this charge last September when he attacked Secretary Dulles' suggestion that a charter review conference "can be of major importance." Said Mr. Vyshinsky:

All information indicates that the campaign for the revision of the charter is to be transformed into one of true cold war in order to stimulate reactionary trends and to use them to intensify international tension.[26]

This attitude is generally in harmony with the Soviet desire to do what they can to prevent the U. N. from becoming a more effective agency for world peace. A strong U. N. would obviously run counter to the grand design of international communism for eventual world domination.

Today exponents of charter review are confronted with the hard fact that any amendment, no matter how commendable, will require the consent of the Soviet Union.

C. OTHER CONSIDERATIONS

Two years hence, when the debate on the problem of revision takes place, this obstacle may not prove insurmountable. Even if it does, 9 years of experience have shown that much progress can still be made in improving the U. N. within the elastic framework of the present charter without resorting to formal amendments.

While the Soviet Union may be counted upon to do more than its share of objecting, it would be erroneous to assume that the Russians and their satellites are the only obstacles in the way of charter revision. The small states, for example, would bitterly resent any proposal to change the system of voting in the General Assembly in such a way as radically to alter their position of equality with the great powers. Likewise, Great Britain, France, and other countries with colonial possessions, no doubt would oppose amendments conferring upon the U. N. greater authority with respect to non-self-governing territories. And certainly our Government, among others, would vigorously object to any charter change which would empower the U. N. to use our troops for enforcement action without our consent.

Our Government has indicated that when the question arises in 1955, the United States will favor calling a Review Conference. The existence of the veto does not mean that such a Conference would be a waste of time. The only logical course of action now is to proceed with a careful study of the entire problem and the formulation of proposals which we may find in our national interest, on the assumption that no single nation will willfully block approval of any desirable amendments.

---

[26] Ibid., p. 781.

This assumption may prove wrong.   If it does, supporters of the U. N. may well conclude that their objective of developing an organization that can better serve the cause of world peace, can still be attained without invoking the formal amendment process.   Since its inception the charter has demonstrated a remarkable facility for adapting itself to changing needs and circumstances.   This flexibility may provide the way in which the United Nations can be made more effective in protecting the interests of the United States and preserving peace.[27]

[27] On the desirability of calling a review conference, see article by Ernest A. Gross cited above.

THE PROBLEM OF MEMBERSHIP IN THE UNITED NATIONS

STAFF STUDY NO. 3

MAY 21, 1954

PREFACE

By Alexander Wiley, *Chairman*

One of the most important problems confronting the United Nations concerns the admission of new states to the organization. Although the charter contemplated "universality" of membership as an eventual objective, the fact is that only 9 states have been admitted since the United Nations was established while some 20 applicants have been denied membership. A few of the pending applicants, such as Hungary, Albania, and Rumania, have never been deemed qualified under the terms of the charter by a majority of the present members. Others, such as Ireland, Portugal, Italy, Japan, and Finland, have had overwhelming support, but the door to admission remains shut by the Soviet use of the veto.

States like the latter undoubtedly could make a significant contribution to the effectiveness of the organization. It seems clear, however, that they are not likely to gain admission so long as the Soviet Union persists in the abuse of the veto power.

In an effort to break the deadlock on membership, there have been proposals to abolish or to curb the veto with respect to membership. There have also been suggestions of a "package deal," whereby states favored by a majority of the present members could be admitted simultaneously with states supported by the Soviet Union. Whatever solution is found, it is likely to have important repercussions with respect to the two principal functions of the United Nations; that is, peaceful settlement of disputes and collective security.

As far as the United States Senate is concerned, this body endorsed the Vandenberg resolution in 1948, favoring the conclusion of an agreement whereby the Big Five would refrain from use of the veto on the admission of new member states. This position raises problems, however, with respect to the similar question of what government is to represent a state that is already a member.

This study was prepared under the direction of the subcommittee staff by Ellen C. Collier, Foreign Affairs Division, Legislative Reference Service, Library of Congress, and Bradford Westerfield, who served with the subcommittee while on leave from the Harvard University faculty. It provides a background for the study of the problem of admission of new members and proposals which have been made for dealing with it. Its publication does not indicate either the subcommittee's acceptance or rejection of any of the views which are expressed.

May 21, 1954.

CONTENTS

THE PROBLEM OF MEMBERSHIP IN THE UNITED NATIONS

A. Charter Provisions on Membership

The United Nations was designed to be a worldwide organization, but membership is not open to every State regardless of character. Nor is membership irrevocable.

Most of the states presently in the United Nations are original members which are defined in chapter II, article 3, of the charter as—

the states which, having participated in the United Nations Conference on International Organization at San Francisco, or having previously signed the Declaration by United Nations of January 1, 1942, sign the present Charter and ratify it in accordance with Article 110.

States other than original members may also be admitted. The manner in which they are to be admitted and the question of qualifications for admission were debated at considerable length during the formative period of the organization. At the San Francisco Conference in 1945 there was some sentiment in favor of encouraging the quick achievement of universality. Led by Uruguay, several participating states even went so far as to propose that—

All communities should be members of the Organization and * * * their participation is obligatory, that is to say that it will not be left to the choice of *any nation* whether to become a member of the organization or to withdraw from it * * * [1]

Although there was general agreement that absolute universality was "an idea toward which it was proper to aim," most of the participants at the San Francisco Conference favored some sort of selectivity in the admission of new members. This selectivity was achieved by establishing the following qualifications and procedures for admission under article 4 of the charter:

1. Membership in the United Nations is open to all other peace-loving states which accept the obligations contained in the present Charter and, in the judgment of the Organization, are able and willing to carry out these obligations.
2. The admission of any such state to membership in the United Nations will be effected by a decision of the General Assembly upon the recommendation of the Security Council.

The Committee which dealt with the membership problem at San Francisco acknowledged that article 4 left much to the discretion of states already members of the United Nations in determining the qualifications of applicants. It did not feel, however, that it—

should recommend the enumeration of the elements which were to be taken into consideration. It considered the difficulties which would arise in evaluating the political institutions of States and feared that the mention in the Charter of [such considerations] would be a breach of the principle of nonintervention, or, if, preferred, of noninterference. This does not imply, however, that in passing upon the admission of a new member, considerations of all kinds cannot be brought into account.[2]

---

[1] Documents of the United Nations Conference on International Organization. New York, United Nations Information Organizations, 1945, vol. VII, p. 325.
[2] Quoted in Leland M. Goodrich and Edward Hambro, Charter of the United Nations (revised edition). Boston, World Peace Foundation, 1949, p. 126.

With respect to procedure for admission the United States at one stage in the formation of the organization considered giving authority to act to the General Assembly exclusively, by a two-thirds or three-fourths majority.[3]   At Dumbarton Oaks in 1944, however, it was agreed that the Security Council should make a recommendation on applicants after which the General Assembly would reach the final decision on admission, by a two-thirds vote.   This procedure was accepted at San Francisco in spite of an attempt by several of the smaller states to increase the authority of the General Assembly as against that of the Security Council.

Provision is also made in the charter for the suspension or expulsion of members.   Article 5 permits the rights and privileges of membership to be suspended in the case of a member against which the Security Council has taken preventive or enforcement action.[4]   Under article 6 members repeatedly violating the principles of the charter may be expelled.[5]

There was considerable opposition at the San Francisco Conference to the provision for expulsion on the grounds that it was incompatible with the ultimate aim of universality.   It was contended, moreover, that expulsion would weaken the United Nations because an expelled member would not be bound by the obligations of the charter.   As an alternative some participants favored broadening the suspension provisions of article 5.   The latter approach, however, was strongly opposed, particularly by the Soviet Union.

Both suspension and expulsion are subject to the veto.[

Specific provision is not made in the charter for the voluntary withdrawal of members from the United Nations.   At San Francisco it was recognized that it would be difficult to prohibit a sovereign state from severing its ties with the Organization, yet there was no desire to make withdrawal easy.   The Conference approved a declaration which said in part:

* * * The highest duty of the nations which will become Members is to continue their cooperation within the Organization for the preservation of international peace and security.   If, however, a Member because of exceptional circumstances feels constrained to withdraw, and leave the burden of maintaining international peace and security on the other Members, it is not the purpose of the Organization to compel that Member to continue its cooperation in the organization.

It is obvious * * * that withdrawal or some other forms of dissolution of the Organization would become inevitable if, deceiving the hopes of humanity, the Organization was revealed to be unable to maintain peace or could do so only at the expense of law and justice.

Nor would it be the purpose of the Organization to compel a Member to remain in the Organization if its rights and obligations as such were changed by Charter amendment in which it has not concurred and which it finds itself unable to accept, or if an amendment duly accepted by the necessary majority in the Assembly or in a general conference fails to secure the ratification necessary to bring such amendment into effect.[6]

---

[3] Admission to the League of Nations had been decided by a two-thirds vote of the Assembly, without the concurrence of the League Council.

[4] "A Member of the United Nations against which preventive or enforcement action has been taken by the Security Council may be suspended from the exercise of the rights and privileges of membership by the General Assembly upon the recommendation of the Security Council.   The exercise of these rights and privileges may be restored by the Security Council."

[5] "A Member of the United Nations which has persistently violated the Principles contained in the present Charter may be expelled from the Organization by the General Assembly upon the recommendation of the Security Council."

[6] Leland M. Goodrich and Edvard Hambro.   Op. cit., pp. 143–144.

B. MEMBERSHIP PROVISIONS IN PRACTICE

PRESENT MEMBERSHIP

Upon ratification of the charter, the following nations became original members of the United Nations in accordance with article 3:[7]

Argentine Republic	Ethiopia	Paraguay
Australia	France	Peru
Belgium	Greece	Philippine Republic
Bolivia	Guatamala	Poland
Brazil	Haiti	Saudi Arabia
Byelorussian S. S. R.	Honduras	Syria
Canada	India	Turkey
Chile	Iran	Ukrainian S. S. R.
China	Iraq	Union of South Africa
Colombia	Lebanon	U. S. S. R.
Costa Rica	Liberia	United Kingdom
Cuba	Luxembourg	United States
Czechoslovakia	Mexico	Uruguay
Denmark	Netherlands	Venezuela
Dominican Republic	New Zealand	Yugoslavia
Ecuador	Nicaragua	
Egypt	Norway	
El Salvador	Panama	

Nine other states have since been admitted:

Afghanistan	Thailand	Burma
Iceland	Pakistan	Israel
Sweden	Yemen	Indonesia

These additions bring the total membership of the organization to 60.[8]

No member has been either suspended or expelled since the founding of the organization. Nor has any member withdrawn from membership.

ACTION ON MEMBERSHIP APPLICATIONS

In the first few months after the United Nations was established, the Security Council received applications for membership from eight countries: Albania, Mongolian People's Republic, Jordan, Afghanistan, Ireland, Portugal, Iceland, and Sweden.[9] Initially, the United States, waiving its misgivings about the qualifications of Albania and the Mongolian People's Republic, proposed that the Security Council vote to recommend the admission of all eight applicants, "to accelerate advancement of the universality of membership." [10] The Soviet Union refused to agree to en bloc admission and insisted that each application be considered individually. When so considered, only Iceland, Sweden, and Afghanistan received a majority of 7 votes, including the concurrence of the 5 permanent members, needed for a favorable recommendation to the General Assembly. Albania and the Mongolian People's Republic obtained only 5 and 6 affirmative votes, respectively.

---

[7] 50 nations had signed the charter at San Francisco on June 26, 1945. Poland signed on October 15, 1945.
[8] Once admitted, the status of new members is not different in any way from that of the original members.
[9] An application received from Siam (Thailand) on August 5, 1946, was not voted on when the Council considered the first report of the Committee on the Admission of New Members. Siam had requested on August 28 that consideration of its application be adjourned until a territorial dispute with France had been settled.
[10] Yearbook of the United Nations, 1946–47, p. 414.

Although the United States had earlier supported the admission of all eight applicants—

when * * * it became evident that exercise of the veto would prevent the admission of certain states which we believed better qualified for membership than Albania and Outer Mongolia, the United States voted against those two States * * * [11]

Jordan, Ireland, and Portugal each secured more than seven affirmative votes. They did not receive a recommendation for admission, however, because the Soviet Union cast a negative vote against each and its vote acted as a veto.

The General Assembly voted to admit Afghanistan, Iceland, and Sweden, the states which had received a recommendation from the Security Council. In addition, the Assembly requested the Security Council to reconsider the other five applications—

on their respective merits as measured by the yardstick of the charter, in accordance with article 4.[12]

These applications have been reconsidered more than once, and additional reasons for and against admission have been introduced, but they have yet to gain a favorable recommendation either because of the Soviet veto or failure to obtain a majority of seven in the Security Council.

PRESENT STATUS OF APPLICATIONS

The action on the first 8 applicants seems to have set the pattern for future developments with respect to the admission of new members. Six additional states [13] subsequently received affirmative recommendations from the Security Council and were admitted to membership by the General Assembly. Most of the applicants since 1946, however, have failed to clear the Security Council.

In 1953 the United Nations listed 21 applications for membership which had not received the recommendation of the Security Council.[14] Of these, 14 had received at least 7 votes on one or more occasions but were consistently vetoed by the Soviet Union. Five applicants had failed to obtain a majority of 7 because the majority did not believe that they met the qualifications of "peaceloving states" which were "able and willing" to carry out the charter obligations. The majority of the Security Council has refused to refer the application of the North Korean regime to the Committee on the Admission of New Members or to regard the application of the Vietminh regime of Ho Chi Minh as coming from a state.[15] The General Assembly has repeatedly urged the Security Council to clear for admission the 14 states which the majority support as qualified but the Soviet Union has continued to ignore all such requests.

[11] Report by the President on the United Nations, 1946, p. 40. In doing so, the United States pointed out that this country did not have diplomatic relations with the Albanian Government and expressed doubt that it met the qualifications set forth in art. 4. As for Outer Mongolia, objections were based on the absence of sufficient available information to show whether it was capable of fulfilling the obligations of the charter.
[12] Resolution 35 (I) of November 19, 1946. Yearbook of the United Nations, 1946–47, p. 125.
[13] Thailand later in 1946, Yemen and Pakistan in 1947, Burma in 1948, Israel in 1949, and Indonesia in 1950.
[14] Senate Foreign Relations Committee, Subcommittee on the United Nations Charter, Review of the United Nations Charter, A Collection of Documents, Washington, U. S. Government Printing Office, 1954, p. 385, hereinafter referred to as Collection of Documents.
[15] The United States does not consider as valid applications the communications requesting admission by the North Korean and Vietminh regimes, and therefore considers that there are only 19 pending applications. Report by the President to the Congress for the year 1952, p. 89.

Summary of action on membership applications, 1946–53

Country [1] (in order of application)	Year of application	Year admitted	Blocked in Security Council		Year of 1st endorsement by General Assembly
			Insufficient votes	Vetoed	
Albania	1946		X		
Mongolia, People's Republic of	1946		X		
Jordan	1946			X	1947
Afghanistan	1946	1946			
Ireland	1946			X	1947
Portugal	1946			X	1947
Iceland	1946	1946			
Thailand	1946	1946			
Sweden	1946	1946			
Hungary	1947		X		
Italy	1947			X	1947
Austria	1947			X	1947
Rumania	1947		X		
Yemen	1947	1947			
Bulgaria	1947		X		
Pakistan	1947	1947			
Finland	1947			X	1948
Burma	1948	1948			
Ceylon	1948			X	1948
Israel	1948	1949			
Korea, Republic of	1949			X	1949
Korea (North), Democratic People's Republic of [2]	1949		X		
Nepal	1949			X	1949
Indonesia	1950	1950			
Viet-Nam	1951			X	1952
Libya	1951			X	1952
Viet-Nam (Ho Chi Minh), Democratic Republic of [2]	1951		X		
Cambodia	1952			X	1952
Japan	1952			X	1952
Laos	1952			X	1952

[1] Italicized states have been admitted.
[2] The United States does not consider these applications valid.

SOVIET "PACKAGE PROPOSALS"

The Soviet Union proposed a package admission of five applicants in September 1947, after the peace treaties with Italy, Finland, Hungary, Rumania, and Bulgaria had come into force. The Russians held that "all or none" of these states must be admitted to the United Nations.[16] The United Kingdom and the United States objected to consideration en bloc of the five applicants [17] and held that each application should be judged individually according to whether it fulfilled the qualifications expressed in article 4 of the charter.

When voted on individually, Hungary obtained only 5 affirmative votes, Rumania 4, and Bulgaria 1. Italy and Finland each received 9 affirmative votes, but were vetoed by the Soviet Union on the grounds that their applications were in the same category as the other 3 states and should not have been considered separately.

In 1949 the Soviet Union broadened its "package" proposal to include 13 states. In 1952 Libya was added to the list. The proposal now includes Albania, Outer Mongolia, Jordan, Ireland, Portugal, Hungary, Italy, Austria, Rumania, Bulgaria, Finland, Ceylon, Nepal, and Libya.

[16] The Soviet Union argued that the language of the treaties and the Potsdam agreement bound the United States, Great Britain, and the Soviet Union to support all 5 applicants.
[17] They contended that these treaties did not bind them to support the applications. They pointed out that the treaties had not been carried out by the Balkan countries in a manner which could form the basis of friendly relations and that the human rights provisions of the treaties had been violated by these 3 states.

Applicants which the Soviet Union does not include in this proposal are the Republic of Korea, Vietnam, Laos, Cambodia, and Japan, already endorsed by the General Assembly, and two Soviet-sponsored candidates, North Korea and the Vietnam of Ho Chi Minh.

None of the various package proposals has received seven favorable votes in the Security Council. A majority of the Council, including the United States, has held that they are contrary to the principles of the charter, reaffirmed by the International Court. The majority further contends that these proposals include candidates which are not qualified while excluding others which are, and that each application should be considered separately on its own merits.

C. Interpretation of the Membership Provisions of the Charter

The backlog of applications for membership has inspired attempts to ease entry by reinterpreting the procedures on admission now in use. As previously mentioned, article 4 provides that admission is effected—

by a decision of the General Assembly upon the recommendation of the Security Council.

Thus far this provision has been interpreted to mean that the Assembly can approve an applicant only following a favorable recommendation from the Security Council. The Council, in turn, has held that a favorable recommendation is made only when an applicant receives a majority of 7 affirmative votes including those of the 5 permanent members. All attempts to modify this interpretation have failed.[18]

The General Assembly has never officially held that the question of membership be considered a procedural rather than a substantive matter and hence not subject to the veto. However, the Assembly did recommend to the permanent members of the Security Council on April 14, 1949, that they seek agreement to forbear to exercise the veto on certain issues, including admission to membership. China, France, the United Kingdom, and the United States supported this proposal but the Soviet Union denounced it and continued to prevent admissions by the use of the device.

Several proposals have been advanced in the General Assembly calling for interpretations of the charter which would, in effect, give greater authority to that body in the admission of new members or at least bypass the veto on this question. Australia began efforts along this line in 1946, when it was a member of the Security Council. The Australian delegate argued that the initiative for the admission of new members rested with the General Assembly and the Security Council's recommendation should only concern matters relating to security. For this reason he abstained from voting throughout the year on membership applications before the Council. A resolution containing

---

[18] In 1945 the United States had included the admission of new members (as well as suspension and expulsion of members) in a list of decisions which would require the concurrence of all the permanent members under the proposed Yalta voting formula, later incorporated into the charter as article 27. The position has since been maintained by all the permanent members of the Security Council that the right of veto exists in the case of recommendations for membership as long as the permanent members choose to exercise it. United States, Department of State, Postwar Foreign Policy Preparation, 1939–45 p. 659.

the Australian viewpoint, however, was not accepted by either the Security Council or the General Assembly.

Several Central American states and others have proposed that the General Assembly should consider an application as having received a favorable recommendation if approved by any seven members of the Security Council. They based their proposal on the San Francisco statement on voting [19] which, in their opinion, excluded the admission of new members from the area of the veto. Argentina has held that since the General Assembly is responsible for the final decision on new members it could accept or reject an unfavorable as well as a favorable recommendation from the Security Council.

In support of the view that the veto should not be allowed to defeat a Security Council recommendation on an application, it was argued by the Cuban representative that the Uniting for Peace Resolution, by which the General Assembly could recommend collective action when the Security Council was stymied by the veto, provided a precedent for coping with the membership problem in a similar fashion.

The Peruvian delegation proposed that the General Assembly consider any application to have fulfilled the requirement for a favorable recommendation from the Security Council if seven members of that body, including the permanent members, had ever recognized by word or act that an applicant fulfilled the qualifications for membership whether or not the application had been vetoed when voted upon individually. Under this proposal the General Assembly, in effect, would be entitled to admit any of the non-Soviet applicants which the Soviet Union would approve under its package proposal.

The above proposals, among others, for solution of the problem by interpretation of the charter, were considered by a special committee of 19 states established by the General Assembly on December 21, 1952. The Committee concluded that—

Generally speaking, the proposals and suggestions * * * envisaged a solution of the problem along the line of interpretation of the Charter based on the views that the voting procedures of Article 27, paragraph 3, of the Charter [the veto] did not apply to the admission of new members and that under Article 4, paragraph 2, it was for the Council to make recommendations but for the General Assembly to decide. The discussion of that * * * group of proposals and suggestions made it apparent, however, that such an approach was not generally acceptable, principally on the grounds that the unanimity rule in the Security Council applied to the admission of new Members and that the provisions of Article 4 did not allow the General Assembly to admit new Members in the absence of a favourable recommendation by the Council.[20]

Secretary Dulles has recently suggested that the General Assembly might establish a type of "associate membership" which would allow applicants barred by the veto to take part in the Assembly's activities. Already nonmembers may become associate members of some of the subsidiary organs such as the regional economic commissions and in some instances have even been elevated to full membership.

[19] Collection of Documents, p. 562. In response to this argument, the United States representative has pointed out that the San Francisco statement was made in answer to a questionnaire primarily concerned with the use of the veto on the pacific settlement of disputes. The questionnaire had not even mentioned the admission of new members. Collection of Documents, pp. 399–400.
[20] Collection of Documents, p. 415.

ADVISORY OPINIONS OF THE INTERNATIONAL COURT

The General Assembly has requested two advisory opinions from the International Court of Justice in an attempt to discover whether the membership provisions of the charter were being properly interpreted in current procedures. On November 17, 1947, the opinion of the Court was sought on whether a member of the Security Council voting on an application for membership was—

juridically entitled to make its consent to the admission dependent on conditions not expressly provided by [Article 4]. In particular, can such a Member, while it recognizes the conditions set forth in that provision to be fulfilled by the State concerned, subject its affirmative vote to the additional condition that other States be admitted to membership in the United Nations together with that State? [21]

The Court's opinion was sought after the Soviet Union had vetoed the membership applications of Italy and Finland. The Soviet Union did not deny that these two states were qualified for membership, but it refused to vote for their admission unless Bulgaria, Hungary, and Rumania were admitted simultaneously. When it became apparent that the latter three states would not receive the seven-vote majority necessary for admission, the U. S. S. R. vetoed the admission of Italy and Finland. In the opinion of many members of the General Assembly this was a violation of the charter.

In an advisory opinion rendered May 28, 1948, by a majority of 9–6, the Court's answer was that a member of the Security Council could not subject its vote on admission of an applicant to the additional condition that other states also be admitted if it considered that the applicant, on its own merits, met the requirements.[22] The Court held that article 4 did—

not forbid the taking into account of any factor which it is possible reasonably and in good faith to connect with the conditions laid down in that article.

But, in the opinion of the Court, a member was not juridically entitled to state that its opposition was based on grounds not included in relevant provisions of the charter.

The six dissenting judges regarded such a treatment of the problem as an invitation to hypocrisy. They believed a member should be free to be frank about the reasons for its vote upon an applicant.[23]

Subsequent to the opinion, the General Assembly asked the Security Council to reconsider the applications which had been vetoed by the Soviet Union "on grounds not included in article 4." The Soviet Union expressed itself in agreement with the views of the dissenting judges and, since the opinion of the Court was only advisory, no new admissions were obtained.

In 1950 the General Assembly sought an advisory opinion of the Court on the procedure for admission of new members. It asked:

Can the admission of a State to membership in the United Nations be effected by a decision of the General Assembly when the Security Council has made no recommendation for admission by reason of the candidate failing to obtain the requisite majority or of the negative vote of a permanent Member * * *?[24]

The Court did not accept this as an invitation to rule on the use of the veto in connection with the admission of members. It stated that

[21] Ibid., p. 373.
[22] Collection of Documents, pp. 373–379.
[23] International Court of Justice, Reports of Judgments, Advisory Opinions and Orders, 1948, p. 83.
[24] Collection of Documents, p. 380

the question assumed that the negative vote of a permanent member defeated a recommendation which had otherwise received seven votes. The Court expressed the view that it was impossible for the General Assembly to attribute to a vote of the Security Council the effect of a recommendation when the Security Council itself did not consider that such a recommendation had been made.   The Court held, by a vote of 12 to 2, that—

admission of a State to membership in the United Nations * * * cannot be effected by a decision of the General Assembly when the Security Council has made no recommendation for admission, by reason of the candidate failing to obtain the requisite majority or of the negative vote of a permanent Member * * * [25]

It has been suggested that an additional advisory opinion could be sought from the International Court on the precise question of whether the veto of a permanent member defeats a membership application which has otherwise obtained seven or more votes in the Security Council.[26]   That is, Is the Security Council correct in its present view that admission to membership is a nonprocedural decision and therefore subject to the veto?

D. Political Solution

Unless it is possible to secure an interpretation of article 4 along the lines of the above proposals which would be acceptable to the five permanent powers, the only other possibility of breaking the membership deadlock short of charter revision would appear to lie in securing their agreement to the admission of at least some applicants.   There have been efforts to facilitate a solution along this line on several occasions.

In 1947, for example, the General Assembly adopted a resolution proposing that the permanent members of the Security Council—

consult with a view to reaching agreement on the admission to membership of the applicants which have not been recommended hitherto, and to submit their conclusions to the Security Council.[27]

Possibilities of agreement along these lines were discussed by a Special Committee which the General Assembly established in 1952. However, none of the proposals secured general acceptance, either on the grounds they were not in accord with article 4 or that they would not lead to practical results.

For instance, Egypt and the Philippines suggested that the Security Council reconsider the Soviet "package" with the understanding that if the Security Council recommended all 14 states, then the General Assembly could accept all or only part of the recommended states, depending on their qualifications.   They argued that as a general practice a state should be considered peace-loving unless actually found guilty by an appropriate United Nations organ of a threat to the peace, a breach of the peace, or an act of aggression.   And, similarly, an applicant should be deemed willing and able to carry out the obligations of the charter "unless clear evidence, which goes beyond mere suspicion or accusation, is presented to the contrary." [28] Those states unqualified according to these standards would not have

[25] Collection of Documents, pp. 380–384.
[26] Such a course was proposed in 1951 by Costa Rica, El Salvador, Guatemala, Honduras, and Nicaragua but was not put to the vote.   Yearbook of the United Nations, 1951, p. 200.
[27] Yearbook of the United Nations, 1947–48, p. 44.
[28] United Nations Document A/2400, p. 20.

to be admitted by the General Assembly but the door would be opened for others which were deemed qualified by the Assembly. The Philippine delegate stated that this proposal could be used as a basis of a compromise or a counterproposal of an enlarged package.

Several states, however objected to a political bargain on the admission of states simultaneously instead of considering each on its individual merits according to article 4. In addition, there was the legal question of whether the Assembly could accept only part of the states if the Security Council had recommended them in a "package" form. Some states felt that the package proposal would not offer a solution to the problem because even if it were to include all present applicants, it would still leave uncertain the fate of other states, such as Western Germany, which might seek admission in the future.

The United States and other permanent powers, except the Soviet Union, have officially declined for several years to consider the matter in these terms at all. They have insisted that every applicant be truly qualified and be considered separately on its merits.

There appears to be, nevertheless, considerable sentiment in the United Nations in favor of a political solution. Some states place responsibility for the deadlock not only on the Soviet Union but at least in part on the other permanent powers. A rapporteur's summary of the Special Committee of the General Assembly established to study the admission of new members, for example, reported that—

The representative of Egypt stated that * * * the unfortunate current situation was certainly the result of a regrettable display of power politics, a clash over spheres of influence of great Powers. It was not entirely due to the obstructionism of only one of the Permanent Members of the Security Council but was also due to the fact that other permanent members pursued a policy of discrimination against some applicants and of favouritism towards others.[29]

A number of states outside the Soviet bloc have supported recommendations that the Security Council reconsider the applications of the 14 states included in the Soviet package proposal with a view to recommending their simultaneous admission. In 1951 a Soviet resolution to this effect, amended by Argentina to make clear that the purpose was a greater degree of universality, received 22 votes in favor and 21 against, with 16 abstentions. However, it was not adopted because the Assembly had decided that the question required a two-thirds majority.[30]

On October 23, 1953, the General Assembly adopted a Peruvian resolution to establish a Committee of Good Offices. The Committee, consisting of representatives of Egypt, the Netherlands, and Peru, is to consult with members of the Security Council—

with the object of exploring the possibilities of reaching an understanding which would facilitate the admission of new Members in accordance with article 4 of the charter.[31]

[29] Collection of Documents, p. 408.
[30] Yearbook of the United Nations, 1951, p. 202.
[31] Collection of Documents, p. 419.

E. Possible Amendment of the Charter

ELIMINATION OF THE VETO

The Soviet Union's veto has been the only barrier to the admission of 14 applicant states, Austria, Cambodia, Ceylon, Finland, Ireland, Italy, Japan, Jordan, the Republic of Korea, Laos, Libya, Nepal, Portugal, and Viet-Nam. All have received a majority of at least 7 in the Security Council and resolutions of the General Assembly have urged their admission.

Of these countries, Italy has been vetoed 5 times; Jordan, Ireland, Portugal, and Ceylon have been vetoed 3 times; and Austria and Finland twice.

None of the permanent members of the Security Council other than the Soviet Union has ever vetoed a membership application. Although they have in some cases voted against the admission of certain states, their negative votes did not constitute a veto because the states had not attained the necessary seven-vote majority. The United States, British, and French delegations have on occasion abstained from voting on applications when their negative vote might have had the effect of vetoing an application.

As early as 1947 the United States expressed a willingness to eliminate the veto on admission to membership. The United States representative told the General Assembly:

* * * The United States will not exercise its right of veto in the Security Council to exclude from the United Nations any of the present applicants which the Assembly deems qualified for membership, and we would go further and would be willing to accept complete elimination of the veto in the Security Council in reference to the admission of applicants in the future.[32]

The United States Senate endorsed this position in the Vandenberg resolution approved on June 11, 1948, by a vote of 64–4. This resolution called for voluntary agreement among the permanent powers to remove the veto from the admission of new members and questions concerning the pacific settlement of international disputes. On October 5, 1953, the United States delegate, James F. Byrnes, stated that if a solution to the membership problem had not been found in the interim, there would be proposals to deal with it by an amendment at a future conference to review the charter.[33]

The Soviet Union has consistently refused to accept any modification of the use of the veto on the question. What the position of the other permanent members would be on proposals to eliminate the veto in questions of membership is uncertain. Although all the permanent members of the Security Council except the Soviet Union supported a General Assembly recommendation that the permanent members agree to forego use of the veto on admission of new members, statements on the subject by France and China have not made clear a readiness to abolish it completely. China has continued to vote against the admission of Outer Mongolia. France has implied that its agreement to forego the use of the veto on applications applies only to those pending as of 1948.[34]

From the point of view of the United States total elimination of the veto in this matter could mean membership for many states

---

[32] General Assembly. Verbatim record, November 17, 1947. A/P. V 118, p 57.
[33] Collection of Documents, p. 419.
[34] Collection of Documents, p. 403.

whose admission this country has favored, such as Italy, Portugal, and Japan. At the same time, however, such a change carries the prospect of admission of states whose membership we have opposed. This prospect, in some cases, may be long-range rather than immediate since such states have so far been unable to command a majority in the Security Council. It is, however, none the less real.[35]

MODIFICATION OF QUALIFICATIONS

Still another possibility of amendment, more limited in scope than abolition of the veto in membership questions, lies in modification of paragraph 1 of article 4, which deals with qualifications of new members. As phrased by the International Court, the qualifications provide that—

an applicant must (1) be a State; (2) be peace-loving; (3) accept the obligations of the Charter; (4) be able to carry out these obligations; and (5) be willing to do so.[36]

These criteria presumably might be spelled out more precisely by charter amendment or tests could be established by which the qualifications of an applicant could be judged on a more objective basis.[37]

As pointed out earlier, however, such a course was rejected at the San Francisco Conference and more flexible qualifications were established, leaving greater discretion in interpretation to the states already members. While it might be desirable to delineate qualifications in greater detail so that it would be more difficult to use political factors to keep out applicants which were qualified, such an attempt might prove impractical. As long as the organization remains selective to any significant degree, each member will retain the right under existing practice to judge for itself whether or not an applicant meets the qualifications, regardless of how specifically they might be defined.

Some states at San Francisco advocated a United Nations based on the principle of absolute universality. To pursue this course, in effect, would mean a sweeping abandonment of the qualifications now stipulated in article 4. Even acceptance of this extreme view, however, would not solve all the problems of admission for it would still be necessary to determine what constitutes a State. The membership of the Ukrainian S. S. R. and the Byelorussian S. S. R.,[38] for example, might be considered a precedent for the admission of territorial entities of questionable sovereignty.

The abandonment of all qualifications, furthermore, would still not necessarily bring about universality because a few nations have not applied for membership, notably the Federal Republic of Germany and Spain, although these states might if there were greater assurance they would be admitted. Thus far Switzerland, however, has never applied for membership in the belief that fulfillment of the obligations of the charter might jeopardize its traditional neutrality.

[35] Elimination of the veto on membership if it could conceivably be obtained might be brought about through a change in art. 27, which regulates voting in the Security Council or in art. 4 concerning admission of new members.
[36] Collection of Documents, p. 376.
[37] Something along this line was attempted in February 1952 when the General Assembly passed a resolution in which it expressed the view that the judgment of the organization on the qualifications of applicant states should be based on "facts such as: the maintenance of friendly relations with other states, the fulfillment of international obligations, and the record of a state's willingness and present disposition to submit international claims or controversies to pacific means of settlement established by international law "
[38] This was agreed to at Yalta and San Francisco Conferences as a concession to the Soviet Union which wanted all 16 constituent republics to be full members.

F. Representation of Member States

Distinct from the question of admission of new member states, although sometimes confused with it, is the question of seating the representatives of a state already in the United Nations. Under present practice, membership in the organization accrues to a country; representation involves seating the delegation of a member country.

The charter does not make provision for determining the representation of a member country. This matter is handled independently in each organ or subsidiary body of the United Nations. The government of each member state issues credentials to its representatives. The rules of procedure of each organ normally stipulate that credentials are to be examined by a Credentials Committee whose report is passed upon by the parent body.[39]

If there is a clear-cut succession of governments in a member country which reflects itself in changes in the country's delegations at the United Nations, no problem is normally involved. The old delegation may be withdrawn by the new government and a new delegation accredited by each organ in which the member country participates.

The case of China, however, is unique in that the Chinese Government has continued to function on Formosa as the Government of all China while the Communists have established a rival regime in Peiping. There are two claimants for the seat of a single member state of the United Nations.

This situation suggests problems which could arise repeatedly in the future. For instance, since each organ can decide questions of representation for itself, it would be possible, in cases of rival claimant governments, for one to represent a member state in the General Assembly and another in the Security Council.[40] Furthermore, there are implications in this issue which go beyond the immediate question.

---

[39] Following are the rules of procedures concerning this question in the General Assembly and the Security Council.

"A. GENERAL ASSEMBLY

"Rule 27. The credentials of representatives, and the names of members of a delegation shall be submitted to the Secretary-General if possible not less than one week before the date fixed for the opening of the session. The credentials shall be either by the Head of the State or Government or by the Minister for Foreign Affairs.

"Rule 28. A Credentials Committee shall be appointed at the beginning of each session. It shall consist of nine members, who shall be appointed by the General Assembly on the proposal of the President. The Committee shall elect its own officers. It shall examine the credentials of representatives and report without delay.

"Rule 29. Any representative to whose admission a Member has made objection shall be seated provisionally with the same rights as other representatives, until the Credentials Committee has reported and the General Assembly has given its decision.

[Rules of Procedure of the General Assembly. A/520/Rev. 2. 5 June 1951, p. 6.]

"B. SECURITY COUNCIL

"Rule 15. The credentials of representatives on the Security Council and of any representative appointed in accordance with Rule 14 shall be examined by the Secretary-General who shall submit a report to the Security Council for approval.

"Rule 16. Pending the approval of the credentials of a representative on the Security Council in accordance with Rule 15, such representative shall be seated provisionally with the same rights as other representatives.

"Rule 17. Any representative on the Security Council, to whose credentials objection has been made within the Security Council, shall continue to sit with the same rights as other representatives until the Security Council has decided the matter."

[Yearbook of the United Nations, 1946–47, p. 456.]

[40] In the case of China, all of the organs have acted in like manner and refused to seat the representative of Communist China. The issue has normally been dealt with at the parliamentary point at which it was raised. Communist Chinese representation has been voted on about 150 times in some 50 organs or bodies. In only one minor body, the Executive and Liaison Committee of the Universal Postal Union, was a Communist delegate seated even provisionally, and this decision was later reversed.

Secretary Dulles, for instance, has intimated that the method of handling representation offered a means to prevent a government from participating in the General Assembly, if it had violated the principles of the charter, when the member state itself could not be expelled because of the veto.

The General Assembly discussed the problem of "Recognition of the representation of a member state" in 1950. There were two principal approaches to the question. One was to limit the concern of the United Nations to the effectiveness of the claimant government in its national territory. For example, the United Kingdom delegate proposed:

> The right of a government to represent the Member State concerned in the United Nations should be recognized if that Government exercised effective control and authority over all or nearly all the national territory, and had the obedience of the bulk of the population of that territory, in such a way that this control, authority and obedience appeared to be of a permanent character.[41]

On the other hand many delegates, including the United States representative, felt that effectiveness was not an adequate test, but that other criteria should also be established, that the willingness to carry out the obligations of the charter which is a qualification required for admission of a state should also be required of a government for accreditation.

A Cuban draft resolution suggested the following criteria for accrediting a government:

> a. effective authority over the national territory;
> b. the general consent of the population;
> c. ability and willingness to achieve the Purpose of the Charter, to observe its Principles and fulfill the international obligations of the State; and
> d. respect for human rights and fundamental freedoms.[42]

Various other criteria were suggested at that time. For instance, the United States wished also to include the extent to which a new authority had been established through "internal processes" in the member state. However it was not possible to reach agreement on specific criteria. After debate the resolution finally approved by the General Assembly (including the United States) on December 14, 1950, recommended only that—

> Whenever more than one authority claims to be the government entitled to represent a Member State in the United Nations and this question becomes the subject of controversy in the United Nations, the question should be considered in the light of the Purposes and Principles of the Charter and the circumstances of each case.[43]

The resolution recommended that, whenever any such question arose—

> It should be considered by the General Assembly, or by the Interim Committee if the General Assembly is not in session; * * * [and] that the attitude adopted by the General Assembly or its Interim Committee concerning any such question should be taken into account in other organs of the United Nations and in the specialized agencies.

There are also differences of opinion on the linking of the question of representation in the United Nations with recognition by member governments.

---

[41] Yearbook of the United Nations, 1950, p. 431. To go beyond these criteria, some supporters felt, would be to interfere in the domestic concerns of a member. Some proponents of these criteria believe that participation in the United Nations would help lead to acceptance of the general principles of the United Nations by the recognized government.
[42] Yearbook of the United Nations, 1950, p. 430.
[43] Collection of Documents, p. 425.

On March 8, 1950, the then Secretary-General, Trygve Lie, circulated a memorandum in which he contended:

The recognition of a new State, or of a new government of an existing State, is a unilateral act which the recognizing government can grant or withhold * * * while States may regard it as desirable to follow certain legal principles in according or withholding recognition, the practice of States shows that the act of recognition is still regarded as essentially a political decision, which each state decides in accordance with its own free appreciation of the actuation. * * *

* * * [The] United Nations does not possess any authority to recognize either a new State or a new government of an existing State. To establish the rule of collective recognition by the United Nations would require either an amendment of the Charter or a treaty to which all Members would adhere.

On the other hand *membership* of a State in the United Nations and representation of a State in the organ is clearly determined by a collective act of the appropriate organs; in the case of membership by vote of the General Assembly on recommendation of the Security Council, in the case of representation, by vote of each competent organ on the credentials of the representatives. Since, therefore, recognition of either State or government is an individual act, and either admission to membership or acceptance of representation in the Organization are collective acts, it would appear to be legally inadmissible to condition the latter acts by a requirement that they be preceded by individual recognition.[44]

Mr. Lie pointed to several instances where states, for example Yemen and Burma, had been admitted to membership in the United Nations even though they were not recognized by all other members.

The Secretary-General's memorandum was protested by the Chinese representative as a violation of the proper functions of the Secretary-General and a "deliberate attack on China's U. N. front." [45] In a letter of protest the Chinese delegate stated:

On the technical side your memorandum asserts that it is wrong to link the question of representation with the question of recognition by Member Governments. International law has nothing direct to say for or against this linkage. As practised in the League of Nations as well as in the United Nations, this linkage is the general rule; the few cases of nonoperation of linkage which your memorandum cited, have been the exceptions. The Soviet delegation, in voting on admission of new Members, specifically stressed the linkage between admission and recognition. In spite of the advisory opinion of the International Court of Justice, the Soviet veto on a number of applications for membership holds today. The deputy representative of the United States to the United Nations, in his press statement of 8 March, made it clear that the American Government would continue to support my delegation and to vote against admission of a Communist delegation for the specific reason that the United States continued to recognize the National Government of China.

* * * In fact, recognition and representation are based on similar considerations. The linkage between recognition and representation is only natural and inevitable.[45]

In the Security Council the question has been raised as to whether representation of member states in the Council is a substantive decision and hence subject to the veto, or a procedural question to be settled by the vote of any seven members. The issue arose in connection with the case of representation of China, but has not been settled because a move to unseat the Nationalist delegate and seat a Communist delegate has not received the seven votes necessary to carry even a procedural question. In January 1950, the Soviet Union introduced a resolution which, had it been adopted, would have invalidated the credentials of the Chinese representative, Dr. T. F. Tsiang. Six members, including three permanent members, the United States, France, and China, voted against the resolution. The representative of the United States stated:

---

[44] Collection of Documents, p. 421.
[45] Collection of Documents, p. 423.

The resolution submitted by the representative of the Soviet Union is directed at unseating Dr. Tsiang on the ground that his credentials are no longer valid because they emanate from a government which the Soviet Union no longer recognizes. Each member of the Council is of course free to vote on this proposal in accordance with its own views concerning the question of recognition. The United States Government recognizes as the Government of China the government which has accredited Dr. Tsiang to the Security Council. My Government therefore considers that Dr. Tsiang's credentials remain valid and will vote against the Soviet Union draft resolution.

I should like to make it clear that the United States Government considers that the Soviet Union draft resolution presents to the Council a procedural question involving the credentials of a representative of a member. Accordingly, a vote against the motion by my Government could not be considered as a veto, even assuming that seven members of the Council vote in favor of the resolution. I wish to make it clear that my Government will accept the decision of the Security Council on this matter when made by an affirmative vote of seven members.[46]

A similar position was taken by France.

Mr. Tsiang, the representative of Nationalist China, held that the problem was not merely the procedural question of accreditation of a delegate but the basic question of the right of his Government to be represented, and that his Government would treat it as a substantive question.

Since late in 1950 the problem has been overshadowed by the participation of the Chinese Communists in the Korean conflict. Not only have their troops fought forces under the United Nations command, but the Peiping regime has been labeled an aggressor by the General Assembly. Such conduct by a member is the kind probably envisioned under articles 5 and 6 as punishable by suspension or expulsion from the United Nations.

The United States position appears to have since shifted from its earlier willingness to consider representation as a procedural question. In June 1951 the Secretary of State suggested that if the United States ever found itself in the minority on the Chinese representation question, the United States would seek an advisory opinion from the International Court of Justice on the question of whether the matter could be vetoed. Both the House and Senate have voted unanimously that—

"the Communist Chinese Government should not be admitted to the United Nations as the representative of China." [47]

On July 29, 1953, the New York Times reported that on the previous day Secretary of State Dulles had—

implied, but would not say categorically, that the United States would use its veto power to block Communist China's admission. He said he felt this country's influence and the like-mindedness of friendly nations in respect to Communist China would be enough to forestall that nation's admission.[48]

The charter offers no guidance for handling problems of representation. In April 1949, however, the General Assembly expressed the view that the approval of credentials of representatives to the Security Council was a procedural decision. The Assembly did not specify that this expression of view necessarily applied to cases where there was more than one claimant for the seat of a member state.[49]

The United States favors the elimination of the veto on admission of states to membership. However, United States Ambassador

[46] United Nations, Security Council. Verbatim record. S/P. V. 460, 1950, pp. 7–8.
[47] Collection of Documents, pp. 177 and 185.
[48] New York Times, July 29, 1953, p. 1.
[49] Collection of Documents, pp. 572–575.

Henry Cabot Lodge, delegate to the United Nations, has made clear that this position does not bear on the question of Chinese representation since the matters are regarded as "legally quite distinct." [50]

G. UNIVERSALITY OR SELECTIVITY

Underlying the various problems concerning membership is the fundamental question of whether the United Nations is to move toward a universality of membership, which would encompass practically every state in the world regardless of character and international aim, or toward greater selectivity, with membership restricted to states clearly sharing certain concepts of the United Nations. Any significant changes which might be made in the membership provisions of chapter II will have a bearing on this question. They will act as an impetus either toward universality or greater selectivity. If changes are made in qualifications or procedures of admission, or both, which aim at greater selectivity, it is conceivable that they might go so far as to lead to an organization limited strictly to states which not only are willing to abide by the principles of the charter, but can agree among themselves on the meaning of those principles in every significant situation. Such changes could even have the effect of excluding from the organization certain of the present members. From the United States point of view this would mean the Communist nations, at the very least. However, since suspension, expulsion, and charter amendment are all subject to the Soviet veto, the only way to attain such a degree of selectivity might very well be the formation of a new organization.

Herbert Hoover expressed this view in 1950:

I suggest that the United Nations should be reorganized without the Communist nations in it. If that is impractical, then a definite New United Front should be organized of those peoples who disavow communism, who stand for morals and religion, and who love freedom.

This is specifically not a proposed extension of a military alliance or any color of it. It is a proposal based solely upon moral, spiritual, and defense foundations. It is a proposal to redeem the concept of the United Nations to the high purpose for which it was created. It is a proposal for moral and spiritual cooperation of God-fearing free nations.

If the free nations join together, they have many potent moral, spiritual, and even economic weapons at their disposal. They would unlikely ever need such weapons. Such a phalanx of free nations could come far nearer to making a workable relation with the other half of the two worlds than the United States can ever do alone.[51]

By contrast, if changes are made in chapter II, which seek to bring about a relaxation of the present procedures and qualifications for the admission of new states, they could conceivably lead toward a universality which ultimately might result in the automatic inclusion of practically every state in the world. Clark Eichelberger, National Director of the American Association for the United Nations, has suggested this course:

* * * Membership in the United Nations must be synonymous with membership in the family of nations * * * there should be no such thing as admission or the right of withdrawal. Each state is a member of the family of nations and, therefore, a member of the United Nations. * * *

To my thinking, automatic membership is the most important principle that must be adopted if the United Nations is to advance on the road to world government. * * *

[50] Testimony before the Subcommittee on the United Nations Charter, March 3, 1954.
[51] Speech before American Newspaper Publishers Association, April 27, 1950. New York Times, April 28, 1950, p. 13.

And the argument is made that it is better to have governments that we do not like in the community of nations and bound by its law, than outside.[52]

The current position of the United States on this fundamental question lies somewhere between strict selectivity and universality or, so to speak, at a point of "approximate universality."

On January 18, 1954, Secretary of State John Foster Dulles stated:

It is useful that there be an organization which is, generally speaking, universal and whose processes run throughout the world. Otherwise the association takes on the character of an alliance. Of course, universality inevitably means bringing together nations whose governments may strongly disagree. This has disadvantages. But such an organization maintains contacts between potential enemies and, as President Eisenhower said in his state of the union message on January 7, 1954, it provides "the only real world forum where we have the opportunity for international presentation and rebuttal." This process tends, though slowly, to bring about conformity to a common standard. It is, of course, unlikely that there will be universality in the complete and literal sense of that word. Unfortunately there are governments or rulers who do not respect the elemental decencies of international conduct, so that they can properly be brought into the organized family of nations. That is illustrated by the regime which now rules the China mainland.

Even approximate universality does, of course, carry certain disadvantages. There are bound to be differences of opinion which limit effectiveness of action.

It seems at the present time that most of the members of the United Nations feel that it is better to have even discordant members in the organization rather than to attempt to confine membership to those who hold the same views.[53]

The choice between universality and selectivity is intimately related to what the primary function of the United Nations is deemed to be. The two principal functions of the organization, collective security and pacific settlement, are both dedicated to keeping the peace. While few would suggest at this time that the organization completely abandon either of these functions, there is considerable controversy as to which function—collective security or pacific settlement—should be given primary emphasis. Each may require a different type of membership for maximum effectiveness.[54]

The former representative of the United Kingdom to the United Nations, Sir Gladwyn Jebb, is one of the leading exponents of the view that the function of pacific settlement should be given chief emphasis:

* * * [As] we all know, the United Nations has another quite distinct role [from collective security], namely "pacific settlement." Had there been no cold war this would no doubt have been less important than the other function of organizing genuine "collective security." As things are, though one may admit that collective resistance to aggression remains a "primary" function, pacific settlement seems to me, at any rate, to have become the more important from a practical point of view. For, after all, if World War III actually does break out, nobody can pretend that what the United Nations does or says, however useful it may be, will be an element of the first importance in the winning of the war. Whereas if we are to avoid World War III there must be a long period of co-existence with the Soviet world during which the United Nations might be of the greatest value. Always supposing an absence of general hostilities, it

---

[52] Senate Foreign Relations Committee. Hearing on Revision of the United Nations Charter, 1950, pp. 355–6.

Actually, states which are not members of the United Nations may nonetheless be bound by United Nations action.

For instance, art. 2, par. 6, prescribes that—

"The Organization shall insure that states which are not Members of the United Nations act in accordance with [its] principles so far as may be necessary for the maintenance of international peace and security."

In addition to these general obligations on all nonmembers, Italy has been given specific responsibilities as an Administering Authority for the Trust Territory of Somaliland. Furthermore, it sent a field ambulance unit to support the United Nations forces in Korea. Similarly, Japan assumed certain charter obligations in its peace treaty.

[53] See Senate Foreign Relations Subcommittee on the United Nations Charter. Review of the United Nations Charter hearings, p. 6.

[54] See Alexander W. Rudzinski, Admission of New Members, the United Nations and the League of Nations, International Conciliation, April 1952, pp. 188–196.

will, as I see it, be in the United Nations that negotiated settlements between the West and the Stalinist world may eventually be reached.[55]

Collective security, it is argued by those who hold the above or similar views, can best be organized in the main against specific threats under regional alliances such as the North Atlantic Treaty.

It is further contended that the uncommitted or neutral nations, although their sympathies lie more with the West than with the Soviet Union, are not willing to join in preparations specifically against Soviet aggression. Attempts to get these states to make definite commitments in advance within the United Nations against Soviet aggression, it is held, might shake their faith in the United Nations and the Western powers.

Obviously, if the function of pacific settlement is to be effectively pursued within the United Nations, the organization must contain at least a minimum of the opposing points of view which are to be conciliated. Moreover, the more inclusive the membership, the more complete will be the world forum in which problems can be considered. The presence of the Soviet Union and other "unlike minded" nations, according to this school of thought, is not only necessary but desirable. Defense against possible aggression by such nations presumably would be provided not primarily by the United Nations but by the regional organizations.

Another view objects to minimizing the functions of collective security of the United Nations in order to concentrate upon pacific settlement. Instead, proponents of this view would favor strengthening the United Nations as an organization to enforce peace. Regional organizations, it is contended, do not provide an adequate substitute for collective security under the United Nations, primarily because they do not include all members, even those whom the United States might feel called upon to defend. It is the opinion of Hamilton Fish Armstrong, editor of Foreign Affairs, that—

* * * [The] general acceptance of the idea that the United Nations is simply a "town meeting of the world," with unlimited power to talk but little responsibility for action, soon would result in making even its talk of little account; and if it tries to settle disputes without feeling that it has any duty to enforce its decisions its efforts at conciliation will be very much less effective than they would be if the ultimate sanction of force against an aggressor remained intact * * *
* * * And the final danger in playing down the role of the United Nations as a security organization and extolling it as a forum for discussion is that in the process it will little by little be turned into an agency of appeasement. * * * If the idea spread that this might be the eventual function of the United Nations in a moment of crisis between the Soviet Union and the United States the days of American participation in it would be numbered and therewith no doubt the days of the organization itself.[56]

If the United Nations is to be the central force, however, for collective security against the threat of aggressive communism, it can fulfill this role only by continuing to bypass the veto in the Security Council and by mobilizing large non-Communist majorities in the General Assembly able and willing to follow the enforcement recommendations of that body. It is conceivable that this role may best be played without the participation of the Soviet Union and some other nations now members in the organization. If the latter extremity is reached, however, it will circumscribe the capacity of the United Nations to discharge its functions of peaceful settlement.

[55] Sir Gladwyn Jebb. The Free World and the United Nations. Foreign Affairs, April 1953, p. 387.
[56] Hamilton Fish Armstrong. The World is Round, Foreign Affairs, January 1953, pp. 195–196.

Within the extremes there is a spectrum of opinion with respect to the membership question. The differences tend to coincide with opinion as to what relative weight should be assigned to the principal functions of the United Nation and the direction in which they should develop. They appear to be, more often than not, differences of emphasis rather than sharply opposed convictions.

H. Concluding Comments

There now exists a backlog of a score of applications for admission to the United Nations. The bulk of these applications comes from states believed by most present members of the organization to merit admission. They have not been admitted largely because of the use of the veto by the Soviet Union.

Various efforts and proposals have been made to break the deadlock on membership. Advisory opinions of the World Court have failed to influence the Soviet to refrain from use of the veto in membership cases. Recommendations of the General Assembly to obtain voluntary abstention from employment of the veto have been ignored. "Package proposals" to admit a number of Soviet-sponsored applicants—applicants lacking majority support—as a quid pro quo for the admission of some applicants favored by a majority of the members have been repeatedly rejected.

In the event of a charter review conference, the issue of membership will no doubt be given careful consideration, especially if a solution is not found in the interim. All of the permanent powers as well as most of the smaller nations have manifested a continuing interest in this matter. Of the latter, a number of nations have indicated their dissatisfaction with the qualifications and procedures for admission established under the charter or, at least, with the manner in which they have been interpreted by the permanent members of the Security Council.

From the consideration which has been given to the subject in the United Nations and elsewhere, it seems clear that amendments could be devised which should have the effect of opening membership to some or all of the present applicants. The acceptability of such amendments to the permanent powers, especially the Soviet Union, however, is another matter.

From the point of view of the United States, our policy with respect to the membership issue cannot easily be separated from our interest in the question of what government should represent states already members of the United Nations, in the event there are two claimants to this prerogative, as in the case of China. Certainly, who represents as well as what countries are represented has a profound bearing on the character of the organization.

Nor is it likely that an effective policy on membership can be determined except in the context of the two principal functions of the United Nations: peaceful settlement and enforcement measures against aggression. The relative importance which is assigned to each of these functions has significance with respect to the approach to be taken to the membership question.

In any event it is inconceivable that such important states as Japan, Italy, Portugal, Finland, and Ireland—and eventually Germany—should remain for long outside the United Nations. Some way will have to be found to admit them if the organization is to make its most effective contribution to world peace.

REPRESENTATION AND VOTING IN THE UNITED NATIONS GENERAL ASSEMBLY

STAFF STUDY NO. 4
SEPTEMBER 1954

PREFACE

By Alexander Wiley, *Chairman*

In considering the review of the United Nations Charter two problems relating to voting ought to be carefully studied: (1) the veto in the Security Council; and (2) the voting procedures in the General Assembly.

The veto, in some ways, gives the big states too much power. In the General Assembly, where each state has one vote, the little nations have too much power. This study deals with the latter problem.

The General Assembly is based upon the idea of sovereign equality of states and the principle of one-state-one-vote prevails. The only exception to this principle is the Soviet Union which, under the agreement reached at Yalta, obtained the admission of Byelorussia and the Ukraine as full members of the United Nations. This concession not only gave the Soviet Union three times the voting power she deserves; what is even worse, it tripled her speaking power in the General Assembly.

Like many other delegates to the General Assembly, I have had to sit by the hour and listen to the repetitive tirades of the Soviet Union, Byelorussia, and the Ukraine. When the time comes to consider the revision of the charter we should protest this arrangement. Byelorussia and the Ukraine are constituent states of the Soviet Union— somewhat like Texas and New York are constituent States of our own Federal Republic. If they deserve separate representation, then we should seek additional votes for Texas, New York, Wisconsin, and the other States of the Union.

Inherent in the one-state-one-vote system are some strange theoretical possibilities. This report shows that it is possible, for example, for a majority to be obtained in the General Assembly by states representing about 5 percent of the population of the members of the organization. States containing only 2.3 percent of the total population of United Nations members—if the smaller countries stood together—could block decisions on important questions. These and similar anomalies of the present voting system, of course, have not presented themselves in this extreme form and may never do so. The possibilities, nevertheless, are there and give cause to pause and consider this question.

So far, the one-state-one-vote formula has not been a serious problem insofar as United States policies are concerned. We have normally had a comfortable majority of the member states following our leadership on issues of importance to us. On the very critical issues, such as the Uniting For Peace Resolution in 1950, and the resolutions relating to Korea, the Soviet bloc of five votes has been isolated and the great majority of the members have voted with us.

While the present voting system has worked well for us, we cannot ignore the fact that alinements of nations change from time to time. Furthermore, if any substantial number of the 19 or so present applicants for membership are admitted to the United Nations their votes could have a drastic effect on the situation.

Apart from these very practical considerations, a question of equity is also involved in this issue. Should a state which subscribes 30 percent of the budget of the United Nations have no greater control over the apportionment than one which pays less than 1 percent? Should states with vast populations and power wield the same influence as the very small countries? Should Great Britain and Luxembourg, for example, stand on an equal footing in the Assembly?

A great many people think the veto is undemocratic because it gives the big states too much power in the Security Council. But can it not be argued just as effectively that the principle of State equality is undemocratic besause it gives the little countries voting strength in the General Assembly far out of proportion to their real influence in the world?

The Secretary of State, when he appeared before the Subcommittee on United Nations Charter on January 18, 1954, posed the question in this fashion:

If the General Assembly is to assume greater responsibilities, then should there not be some form of weighted voting so that nations which are themselves unable to assume serious military or financial responsibilities cannot put these responsibilities on other nations?

I asked the staff of the Foreign Relations Committee to examine this question. I instructed the staff to find out what the possibilities were for devising a voting system that would protect the principle of sovereign equality of member states but at the same time safeguard the larger states, particularly the United States, from irresponsible decisions on the part of the smaller nations in the General Assembly.

This study, which was prepared by Francis O. Wilcox, chief of staff of the committee, presents an analysis of the voting systems already in use or proposed. It then sets forth for purposes of study and consideration an illustrative system of dual voting for the General Assembly.

Mr. Wilcox's fresh analysis of this problem deserves the most careful consideration of those interested in the United Nations. It reveals not only the advantages but the difficulties and disadvantages which may be involved in the adoption of weighted voting in the General Assembly. This document is released in order to stimulate study and discussion of an important issue. The views presented therein do not necessarily represent those of the subcommittee or any of its members.

SEPTEMBER 1954.

CONTENTS

REPRESENTATION AND VOTING IN THE UNITED NATIONS GENERAL ASSEMBLY

I. INTRODUCTORY COMMENTS

It is a curious fact that while public opinion in the United States has been deeply disturbed over the veto and the problem of voting in the U. N. Security Council, there has been relatively little interest in the problem of voting in the General Assembly. This remains true in spite of the fact that the prestige and influence of the Security Council have been on the wane and the star of the General Assembly has been rising.

As the charter was drafted, voting power in the Security Council, where decisions on all substantive questions require the concurring votes of the five permanent members, is heavily weighted in favor of the great powers. In the General Assembly, where all states have an equal voice, the scales are balanced in favor of the smaller nations. The great powers were willing to accept such an arrangement at the San Francisco Conference because they believed their interests would be adequately protected by their right of veto in the Security Council. At the time this seemed a reasonable assumption. The Security Council was charged with the primary responsibility for the maintenance of peace and it was in that body that the really important decisions of the U. N. were to be taken. The General Assembly, which possessed only the power of recommendation, was destined, they believed, to be an organ of lesser political significance.

This estimate of the situation proved wrong. Gradually, as the tension between the Soviet bloc and the free world has increased, the importance of the Security Council—when compared with that of the General Assembly—has declined. During the past few years that organ has been greatly handicapped by the excessive use of the veto on the part of the Soviet Union.

The table below shows in a quantitative way, the extent to which the General Assembly has displaced the Security Council as a forum for the handling of international political issues. During the early years of the U. N., as the framers of the charter intended, the Security Council functioned as the principal political organ of the U. N. Beginning in 1948, however, its importance has steadily declined. By July 1951, Security Council activity reached a disturbingly low point and has continued on the decline since that time.

Political issues considered by General Assembly and Security Council—Jan. 1, 1946, to June 30, 1953[1]

Period	General Assembly	Security Council
Jan. 1–June 30, 1946	2	8
July 1, 1946–June 30, 1947	6	8
July 1, 1947–June 30, 1948	9	14
July 1, 1948–June 30, 1949	15	10
July 1, 1949–June 30, 1950	13	12
July 1, 1950–June 30, 1951	24	12
July 1, 1951–June 30, 1952	17	9
July 1, 1952–June 30, 1953	18	5
Total	104	78

[1] Table from H. J. Morgenthau, The United Nations and the Revision of the Charter, The Review of Politics, January 1954, p. 4.

Over the years there has been a comparable reduction in the number of meetings of the Security Council. In 1946, 88 meetings were held; in 1947, 137; in 1948, 168; in 1949, 62; in 1950, 73; in 1951, 39; in 1952, 42. In 1953, the Council met only 43 times. During the first 7 months of the year it dealt primarily with one subject, the election of a Secretary-General.

Given this shift of power within the U. N. structure, the importance of a reconsideration of the voting procedures in the General Assembly becomes apparent. Thus far relatively few suggestions for changes in the existing system have been made. In any event, it will be helpful to examine briefly present voting practices in the General Assembly and then turn to the proposals that have been advanced to amend the charter in this regard.

II. Present Voting Practices in the General Assembly

In the past, international organizations ordinarily have been based on two fundamental principles: the legal equality of states and unanimity in voting. In practice this has meant that nations like Luxembourg and Iceland, with very small populations, have participated in international assemblies on a basis of legal equality with large nations like the United States, China, and India. "Russia and Geneva have equal rights," declared Chief Justice Marshall in 1825, and this principle of state equality applied to international conferences (as well as to international commerce).

It has meant, too, that whenever the decision stage has been reached at an international conference, any small state, as well as any large one, has been in a position to block action on substantive questions by casting a negative vote. Sometimes little countries have responded to the pressure of other states and have abandoned their opposition; at other times they have prevented conferences from arriving at decisions which, but for their opposition, might have been unanimously approved.

ARTICLE 18

At the San Francisco Conference the framers of the U. N. Charter accepted the first of these principles but rejected the second. Article 18, which lays down the procedure for voting in the General Assembly, reads as follows:

1. Each member of the General Assembly shall have one vote.
2. Decisions of the General Assembly on important questions shall be made by a two-thirds majority of the members present and voting. These questions shall include: recommendations with respect to the maintenance of international peace and security, the election of the nonpermanent members of the Security Council, the election of the members of the Economic and Social Council, the election of members of the Trusteeship Council in accordance with paragraph 1 (c) of Article 86, the admission of new Members to the United Nations, the suspension of the rights and privileges of membership, the expulsion of Members, questions relating to the operation of the trusteeship system, and budgetary questions.
3. Decisions on other questions, including the determination of additional categories of questions to be decided by a two-thirds majority, shall be made by a majority of the members present and voting.

The fundamental proposition, expressed in article 2, that the U. N. is based on the sovereign equality of all its members is reiterated in article 18. Each member is given one vote. Theoretically, at least, it would have been possible to devise a system of weighted voting which would accord member nations a number of votes more commensurate with their relative importance in world affairs. But the practical difficulties involved in building a formula that would take account of the various factors that need to be measured were so great, and traditional concepts of sovereign equality of states so strong, that the matter was not given serious consideration either at Dumbarton Oaks or San Francisco. The time-honored doctrine of one-state-one-vote became part and parcel of the U. N. system.[2]

The only exception to this principle is to be found in the privileged position of the Soviet Union. At the San Francisco Conference, in accordance with an arrangement made at the Yalta Conference, Byelorussia and the Ukraine—which are constituent republics of the U. S. S. R. and do not qualify as "states" in the strict sense of that term—were admitted as U. N. members. They each have 1 vote which, combined with that of the Soviet Union, make a total of 3 votes for 1 country.

Actually, this arrangement involves far more than two additional votes for the Soviet Union. She is also entitled to two additional delegations. This not only triples her voting power, it triples her speaking power as well.

With respect to the principle of unanimity, the charter turns its back upon the past. No doubt the experience of the League of Nations was, in large part, responsible for this departure. Article 5 of the League Covenant, in effect, gave every member of the League a veto by providing that, with certain exceptions, "decisions at any meeting of the Assembly or of the Council shall require the agreement of all the members of the League represented at the meeting." This requirement by no means paralyzed the League Assembly. It did, however, hamper its activity and on some occasions prevented it from reaching important decisions strongly advocated by a majority of the members.

Article 18 of the charter provides for votes on two types of questions. The first category includes the so-called important questions which require a two-thirds majority. The second category includes all other questions and these call for a simple majority. It will be noted that the majority required under the article is a majority of the members

[2] Goodrich and Hambro, Charter of the United Nations: Commentary and Documents, 1949, p. 188.

"present and voting." Members abstaining from the vote are considered as not voting.

By a simple majority the General Assembly may decide that further categories of questions—in addition to those enumerated in article 18—are of sufficient importance to require a two-thirds vote. It can also modify or abolish these additional categories by a majority of the members present and voting.

The two-thirds majority for the handling of important questions seems to have worked fairly well in practice. No doubt it has served as a deterrent to hasty and ill-considered action by the General Assembly. On the other hand, it has not prevented action on any measure desired by a large majority of U. N. members. During the first 6 years of the United Nations, there were some 18 instances in which draft resolutions (or portions of resolutions), received a simple majority in the committees of the General Assembly but were not adopted because they failed to secure the necessary two-thirds vote in the Assembly itself.

The principal effect of article 18 is to reject the veto with respect to General Assembly votes. This is a move in the direction of democracy in world affairs in that it decreases the negative power of individual states. At the same time it increases the positive power of groups of states which may wish to band together to accomplish their objectives within the U. N. system.

THE POWER OF THE GENERAL ASSEMBLY

At this point it may be helpful to keep in mind the fact that the General Assembly does not possess international legislative authority. It can study, it can debate, it can recommend but it cannot legislate. In general, it cannot make decisions that are binding upon the members of the United Nations.

Within its limitations, however, the scope of activity of the General Assembly is far broader than that of the Security Council. It may discuss and make recommendations on any matter within the scope of the charter or relating to the functions and powers of any U. N. organs (art. 10). Similarly, it may make recommendations concerning the general principles of cooperation in the maintenance of peace and security, including the problem of disarmament (art. 11). It may promote international cooperation in the economic, social, cultural, education, and health fields (art. 13). And it may recommend measures for the peaceful adjustment of any situation likely to impair the general welfare or friendly relations among nations (art. 14).

It is true that General Assembly votes on these matters do not carry compulsion in their wake. But there can be little doubt that many General Assembly resolutions such as those relating to Spain, Korea, Palestine, Communist China, and atomic energy, have had a fateful impact upon the course of world events. Recommendations with wide support may be more effective than half-hearted decisions, supposedly binding on member states.

INEQUALITIES RESULTING FROM ONE-STATE-ONE-VOTE CONCEPT

The principle of one-state-one-vote results in glaring inequalities in the General Assembly. Only 9 states can boast a population of 40 million or more. Some 26 states have a population of 5 million or under, including Iceland with 146,000 and Luxembourg with 300,000. Three countries—China, India and the Soviet Union—contain more than half the total U. N. population of roughly 1,800 million.

Under the circumstances, it is theoretically possible to secure a majority of 31 votes which represent only a little over 5 percent of the population of U. N. members. A vote of the 21 smallest countries—representing only about 2.3 percent of the U. N. population—could prevent the two-thirds majority needed for the approval of "important" resolutions. On the other hand, if a contest should arise between the large and small states, a two-thirds majority could be rolled up by 40 of the smallest nations with a population of only about 11 percent.[3]

Clearly, this is a hypothetical danger which probably will never arise in practice in the extreme form referred to above. U. N. members are unlikely ever to divide on important issues merely because of population differences. Even so, these figures illustrate the lack of balance which exists between population and voting strength; a very small minority of the U. N. population is in a position to control decisive votes and to frustrate the will of the majority.

Similar inequalities exist with respect to national wealth, productivity, national territory, and other factors. The U. S. S. R., for example, has a total area of 8,700,000 square miles. This is more than 1,000 times the area of El Salvador. An even greater margin of difference exists with respect to the gross national product. According to the best estimates available some 6 U. N. members had a gross national product of less than $200 million in 1952 or 1953. In contrast, the gross national product of the United States is estimated at $363 billion for 1953. The comparable figure for the Soviet Union is $100 billion, for the United Kingdom, $45 billion, and for France, $39 billion.

BLOC VOTING IN THE GENERAL ASSEMBLY

The situation has been complicated further by the development of what has come to be known as bloc voting in the General Assembly. By pooling or combining their voting strength on particular issues groups of small states are able to exert an influence far out of proportion to either their population or their political importance.

While this tendency toward bloc voting has developed considerably since 1945, the lineup in the General Assembly varies a great deal depending upon the issue. The five Communist states will invariably be found on the same side. The seven Arab countries often vote as a unit particularly with respect to Israeli-Arab problems and resolutions having to do with dependent areas. In most cases two-thirds of the 20 Latin American states will be found in the same camp.[4]

On the other hand, there is no predictable solidarity among the countries of Western Europe. The Benelux states (Luxembourg, Belgium, and the Netherlands) vote together on some issues as do the Scandinavian countries. The seven British Commonwealth nations rarely vote as a unit. Nevertheless, during the past few years, the free world countries have demonstrated a remarkable unity whenever

[3] See Vandenbosch and Hogan, The United Nations: Background, Organization, Functions, Activities, 1952, p. 116.
[4] On this subject see Margaret Ball, Bloc Voting in the General Assembly, International Organization, February 1951.

the most vital issues are up for a vote.   The 52 to 5 vote on the Uniting for Peace Resolution in 1950 is a case in point.

An interesting example of what the small states can do when they are effectively organized emerged during the third session of the General Assembly when the resolution providing for the use of Spanish as one of the working languages of the U. N. was approved by a vote of 32–20 with 5 abstentions.   In that case, the small states successfully opposed the permanent members.   Latin America and the Arab countries, with a few supporting votes, outvoted the United States, China, three of the British Commonwealth nations, and all of Europe, including the United Kingdom.

Sir Carl Berendsen of New Zealand called attention to this problem in the plenary session of the General Assembly in 1947.   "Another analogous source of irresponsibility," he said:

is the system of bloc voting that has grown up.   Let no one tell me that what we have seen at this session and on many occasions, of groups of powers voting as one, is a good system.   Some of these blocs are large; indeed, they can become so large as, in effect, to constitute a veto with regard to any question of importance requiring a two-thirds majority.   That is not a proper exercise of responsibility.[5]

Thus far, this problem has not proved serious so far as the United States is concerned.   There has been some "bloc" voting, just as there has been some "huckstering of votes in the market place," as Sir Carl pointed out.   But generally—with some few exceptions—the democratic processes in the General Assembly have worked fairly well and the United States has received the kind of cooperation that has enabled us to achieve our policy objectives in the United Nations, especially in the political field.

On the other hand, we should keep in mind the fact that the U. N. by no means has reached its outer limits with respect to membership. There are now pending 19 applications for membership including 14 countries approved by the General Assembly as qualified under the charter.   If the organization continues to expand, and particularly if a number of small states are admitted, a reconsideration of the voting procedures in the General Assembly might become a more pressing issue.

III. Attempts in Past to Change Methods of Voting and Representation

For a long time the states of the international community have been groping for a satisfactory voting formula that will prove more workable in practice and still be compatible with the principle of state sovereignty.   The real need is to find a measuring stick which will reflect in terms of voting power the glaring inequalities in power and importance which now exist among the nations of the world.   A brief review of experience to date may be helpful in determining whether a more effective formula can now be developed.[6]

In a number of international organizations extra voting power has been given to states with colonial possessions.   This practice was adopted early in the life of the Universal Postal Union and persists today.   Thus for voting purposes Portuguese colonies in West Africa form a separate country as do the Portuguese colonies in East Africa,

[5] GA. II.   1947.   Official Records Plenary, pp. 694–695.
[6] On this general question see the articles in Louis B. Sohn, Cases and Other Materials on World Law, 1950, pp. 316–347.

Asia, and Oceania.[7] Such an arrangement may have its commendable features in granting some voting power to people who have not yet attained their independence. No one would argue, however, that a formula which gives more votes to Portugal than to India and China together is a very good index of the relative importance of the members.

In some cases, also, attempts have been made to relate the financial contributions of members to their voting power. This was true of the former International Institute of Agriculture established in Rome in 1905. The convention setting up the Institute created five classes of membership with the number of votes allotted to states in each category increasing in arithmetical progression. The contributions of states in the various categories increased in geometric progression. Article 10 established the various categories as follows: [8]

Groups of nations	Number of votes	Units of assessment
I	5	16
II	4	8
III	3	4
IV	2	2
V	1	1

More successful perhaps are the attempts which have been made to relate voting power to the varying interests of states in a particular problem. The International Sugar Council [9] and the International Wheat Council [10] are cases in point. The new International Sugar Agreement (1953), for example, provides that a total of 2,000 votes are to be apportioned among the Council members, divided equally between the exporting and importing countries. In general, the number of votes assigned to each importing state is related to that state's average imports. Countries like Saudi Arabia and Jordan, with relatively small imports, have 15 votes. The largest importing countries, the United Kingdom and the United States, have 245 votes each. The 1,000 votes allocated to the exporting countries are assigned in much the same fashion.

Decisions of the Sugar Council, in general, are taken by a majority of the votes cast by the exporting states and a majority of the votes cast by the importing states. In all voting, decisions taken by a majority of the importing countries must include the votes of at least one-third of the importing states present and voting. This special proviso results in increasing the voting power of the smaller importing nations whose total votes are only slightly larger than the combined total assigned to the United States and the United Kingdom.

Of a somewhat similar character are the complicated voting procedures used by the International Bank for Reconstruction and Development [11] and the International Monetary Fund.[12] In these organizations, the voting power of each member reflects its proportion-

[7] See U. S. Senate, Committee on Foreign Relations. A Decade of American Foreign Policy. S. Doc. 123, 81st Cong., 1st sess., p. 201. In the International Telecommunications Union (1932) the International Wine Office (1924), and the International Office of Chemistry, votes were awarded for colonial possessions.
[8] Malloy, compiler. Treaties, Conventions, International Acts, Protocols and Agreements between the United States of America and other powers. S. Doc. 357, 61st Cong., 2d sess., vol. II, p. 2143.
[9] See S. Ex. B, 83d Cong., 2d sess., pp. 28–29.
[10] See S. Ex. H, 83d Cong., 1st sess., pp. 20–24.
[11] U. S. Senate, Committee on Foreign Relations, op. cit., pp. 251–272.
[12] Ibid, pp. 273–304.

ate share of the total capital to which the members as a whole have subscribed. As of June 30, 1953, for example, Panama had subscribed to less than 0.005 percent of the bank's capital and was entitled to 252 votes out of a total of 103,865. The United States, on the other end of the spectrum, having subscribed to 35.13 percent of the capital was assigned 32,000 votes, or approximately one-third of the total.

Up to the present time, population has been rarely used in international organizations as a factor in determining voting strength. The new European Consultative Assembly, which is the deliberative organ of the Council of Europe, appears to be one of the few current exceptions to the rule. Article 26 of the Statute of the Council of Europe [13] provides that member states shall be entitled to the number of representatives given below:

Belgium	6	Netherlands	6
Denmark	4	Norway	4
France	18	Sweden	6
Irish Republic	4	United Kingdom	18
Italy	18		
Luxembourg	3	Total	87

It will be seen that while voting strength in the Consultative Assembly is based roughly on population, the scale nevertheless remains weighted in favor of the small states. Thus, Luxembourg with population of less than one one-hundredth that of France nevertheless has one-sixth the number of votes. Moreover, a two-thirds vote is required for all resolutions approved by the Assembly. This means that even if the three largest states—France, Italy, and the United Kingdom—supported a proposal, their combined votes (54) would still be short of the total of 58 necessary for approval.

On the whole it has not been easy to induce states to depart from the principle of one-state-one-vote. It has been done in a few cases where international organizations have been set up to deal with special problems. It remains for the future, however, to develop a satisfactory voting formula that will be workable in the General Assembly and at the same time acceptable to the members of the U. N.

IV. Mr. Dulles' Proposal for Weighted Voting

In 1950, in his book entitled War or Peace, John Foster Dulles set forth a proposal for weighted voting in the General Assembly. While his suggestions were general in character they merit careful study, first because they embrace some interesting possibilities, and second because his is the only proposal of its kind which has emerged from official or semiofficial sources.

Mr. Dulles points out that in the Congress we have two ways of voting. In the Senate each State, regardless of size, has two votes. New York with its 15 million people, and Nevada with its 150,000, have equal voting strength. In the House of Representatives, however, where representation is based on population, New York has 45 votes to Nevada's 1.

"I would not abolish in the United Nations," he writes,

an Assembly vote which, like that of our Senate, reflects the sovereign equality of all nations and gives them all an equal vote. But there might be introduced, in addition, a system of "weighted" voting so that the result would indicate,

[13] Published by the Council of Europe, May 5, 1949, p. 8. See also the Statute for the European Community (articles 16–17) which provide for a 2-house parliament with representation based, in part, on population.

roughly, a verdict in terms also of ability to play a part in world affairs. Then it should be provided that decisions on important matters would require a simple majority, rather than two-thirds, under each of the two voting procedures." [14]

Mr. Dulles apparently has in mind other factors in addition to population. The weight of the General Assembly's recommendations, he contends, would be far greater than they are at present if votes reflected "not merely numbers but also ability to contribute to the maintenance of international peace and security."

This point he stressed again on January 18, 1954, in his statement before the Senate Foreign Relations Committee's special subcommittee on the U. N. Charter. "If the General Assembly is to assume greater responsibilities," he said,

then should there not be some form of weighted voting, so that nations which are themselves unable to assume serious military or financial responsibilities cannot put those responsibilities on other nations? Should there be, in some matters, a combination vote whereby affirmative action requires both a majority of all the members, on the basis of sovereign equality, and also a majority vote, on some weighted basis, which takes into account population, resources, and so forth? [15]

Mr. Dulles' proposal has a great deal of merit. In the first place, it would not disturb existing machinery. It is designed to fit into the present organization without any major alterations or adjustments. Mr. Dulles does not suggest the creation of a second Assembly, nor even the need for additional delegates. He merely proposes that each vote in the General Assembly be tallied twice; the first tally would correspond to the present sovereign-state arrangement with each state casting one vote; in the second tally additional votes would be awarded to states depending upon their ability— because of population, productive capacity, armed strength, etc.— to contribute to the maintenance of world peace. A simple majority under each of the two procedures would be necessary for the General Assembly to reach a decision.

This double-barreled vote would have a double-barreled effect. It would not take away from the small nations their ability to protect their vital interests in the United Nations. So long as they could command a simple majority of the votes—and the large majority of U. N. members are relatively small nations—they could prevent decisions which might prove inimical to them. At the same time it would place in the hands of the larger states a potential veto which they could exercise in order to block what they might consider irresponsible action on the part of the smaller countries.

Moreover, if this kind of balanced-weighted voting were introduced, it would equip the General Assembly to assume full responsibility for such organizational matters as the selection of the Secretary General and the admission of new members to the U. N. As things stand now, this responsibility is shared with the Security Council where the negative vote of a permanent member has often blocked action for long periods of time.

Few people would question the logic of bestowing upon the permanent members added weight in connection with important organizational decisions. But it is certainly not logical to permit any single state, by the use of the veto, to tie the hands of the United Nations with respect to such issues. This dilemma could be resolved if the

[14] John Foster Dulles, War or Peace, 1950, pp. 191–194.
[15] U. S. Senate Committee on Foreign Relations, Subcommittee on the United Nations. Review of the United Nations Charter. Hearings pt. I, 1954, p. 7.

interests of the great powers were reflected by an appropriate system of weighted voting in the General Assembly. In such an event the responsibility of the Security Council with respect to such matters might well be brought to an end.

As ingenious as Mr. Dulles' plan is, it raises certain extremely difficult questions. Would the smaller nations agree to any proposal which reduces the relative importance of their role in the General Assembly? At the San Francisco Conference they bitterly resented the privileged position given to the great powers in the United Nations. By the same token would they not now resist any adverse readjustment in the balance of power that was so carefully worked out at San Francisco?

More important still, what criteria would be used in computing the voting strength of the different members? Population? Literacy? Territorial possessions? National wealth? Productive capacity? Financial contribution to the U. N.? World trade? Military strength? Willingness to contribute to the maintenance of world peace? And if several of these factors should be used, how much importance should be attached to each?

It is here that we encounter the crux of the problem of weighted voting. From a mathematical point of view, it would be far simpler to use a single criterion, such as population, and apportion the votes accordingly. But the differences between the states are so vast that any single factor would result in a false picture of the relative importance of various countries in the world and would concentrate voting power in the hands of a few states in an unrealistic way.

If, for example, an attempt is made to award votes directly in proportion to total population then we find that two states, India and China, would be entitled to nearly one-half the voting power in the General Assembly, and Burma would have six times as many votes as Norway. If military strength is our standard, considerably more than half the votes would go to the United States and the Soviet Union. On the other hand, if world trade is the measuring stick, Great Britain would receive a relatively large number of votes and the Soviet Union would be rather far down the scale.

The problem of weighted voting must be approached realistically. Clearly the small countries, which have been used to the principle of legal equality, are not going to underwrite any system of voting which gives the great powers 50 or 100 votes to their 1. They might, however, agree to a system which is far less discriminatory from their point of view.

The problem then, would seem to be one of agreeing upon two or three criteria—such as population, national production and contribution to the U. N.—and balancing them in such a way as to reflect, on a considerably reduced scale, the relative importance of the various countries in the organization. It might then be possible to set up 4 or 5 categories of states, as in the case of the International Institute of Agriculture, with each state receiving from 1 to 5 votes, depending upon its importance.

Any proposal for weighted voting in the General Assembly should also take into consideration the unique position of the Soviet Union which, together with its two constituent republics, Byelorussia and the Ukraine, already possesses three votes. The difficulty of removing voting power which has already been granted is apparent. Nevertheless, before any new formula is fixed, it would seem desirable to offset, insofar as that is possible, the initial advantage given to the Soviet Union at San Francisco.

At present, the chief weakness of Mr. Dulles' proposal is at once its greatest strength. If it were spelled out in detail it might stir up a hornet's nest of opposition. So long as it remains couched in general terms, it will probably command the support of a great many people.

V. United Nations Contributions and Voting Power

It has been suggested by at least one delegation that voting power should be directly related to a state's contribution to the U. N. budget. In 1950, the New Zealand delegate to the First Committee of the General Assembly (Mr. Doidge) called attention to the "obvious elements of absurdity" that are involved in according to a small nation the same voting power accorded a country with a population of 200 million.

Equally—

he said—

there is much unreality in giving to a member without armed forces and one without any desire or willingness to supply armed forces even for common defense the same voting power as to those which do possess armed forces and have from time to time, by the devotion of the lives of their citizens, proved their willingess to undertake those international duties which are correlative to all international rights.

Mr. Doidge then went on to point up the complexity of the problem, suggesting that "voting must be based on many considerations and not on population alone." "Perhaps," he remarked—

a voting power to each member roughly equal to the proportion which its financial contribution to the funds of the United Nations bears to the total contribution would provide a system of rough justice and efficiency.[16]

Since the United Nations is based upon the principle of sovereign equality—which implies equal obligations as well as equal rights—there would seem to be some logic in Mr. Doidge's suggestion. In some organizations with small expenditures, members contribute to the budget on an equal or nearly equal basis. No member of the International Telecommunications Union, for example, pays more than 5 percent of the budget, and the highest contribution in the Universal Postal Union is approximately 8 percent.

But the United Nations, with a much larger budget than any other international organization, constitutes a special case. In 1954 only 16 states contributed more than 1 percent each of the budget. Nine countries contributed as little as 0.04 percent each. The 5 permanent members contributed nearly 70 percent of the total with the United States assessed for 33.33 percent, the Soviet Union roughly 14 percent, the United Kingdom 10 percent, France and China approximately 5.5 percent each.[17]

If these figures were translated into proportional voting terms, they would mean that the United States, with one-third of the votes, would be in a position to block any important resolution proposed in the

[16] Statement made on October 11, 1950, during the Fifth General Assembly.
[17] U. S. Senate, Committee on Foreign Relations, Subcommittee on the United Nations Charter. Review of the United Nations Charter. S. Doc. 87, 83d Cong., 2d sess. p. 719-720.

General Assembly. They would mean that the five permanent members—assuming they were in agreement to do so—could always command a two-thirds majority. They would mean that the United States, the United Kingdom, and France would have a simple majority of the votes in their pockets before any voting began.

Such an arrangement would be open to serious objection. It would draw an invidious distinction between rich and poor countries. Even more important, as the United States delegation to the U. N. has repeatedly pointed out, it would be most unfortunate if any single state were to be placed in a position where it could exert undue influence over the organization. Given the tremendous differences that exist among U. N. members with respect to their capacity to pay, the contributions scale would seem to be an even less reliable criterion than population for determining voting strength.

On the other hand, from the point of view of the United States, if any reshuffling of voting power is contemplated, the financial angle certainly should not be ignored. It is a well-known fact that some of the loudest advocates of state equality show much less enthusiasm for that principle when it comes to the question of apportioning the expenses of an international organization. The Latin American countries, for example, are strong supporters of the principle of the legal equality of all states. Yet the United States, which has only 1 vote out of 21 in the inter-American system, bears more than half the expenses of the Organization of American States.

Perhaps the relationship between legal equality and financial responsibility has not been stressed enough in the United Nations. It is suggested that if an arrangement can be worked out to give some additional voting strength to states which do their best to meet their financial responsibilities it might have at least one salutary effect; it might encourage some states to increase their contributions and thus make possible a revision of the contributions scale.

In this connection consideration should also be given to certain special U. N. programs, like those dealing with Korean reconstruction and Palestine refugees, which are financed by voluntary contributions. In such instances, even more than in the regular U. N. budget, the main burden has fallen upon the United States. While the figures vary somewhat from year to year, our Government has contributed over 65 percent of the total for the U. N. Children's Fund, some 60 percent of the funds for the U. N. technical assistance program, 61 percent of the Palestine refugee program, and more than 65 percent of the funds going to the Korean Reconstruction Agency.

If it is not possible to work out a general voting formula that would take into account the contribution of members to the regular U. N. budget, it might still be feasible to accord additional voting power of an ad hoc nature to states contributing heavily to these special programs. This could be done by devising a weighted voting formula for the Executive Board of the Children's Fund, for example, which is charged with the general supervision of that particular program. It would seem logical that those governments which volunteer heavy contributions to extracurricular activities should be• given additional control over the expenditure of the funds.

VI. Population and Voting Strength

In addition to the suggestions outlined above, a number of proposals have been advanced relating to representation and voting by organizations that advocate the establishment of some kind of supranational agency endowed with additional authority to meet present-day world problems. For the most part, these proposals would make drastic inroads upon the concept of national sovereignty. They would either subject the United Nations to a thorough overhaul or else replace it altogether.

Many people feel that, under present circumstances, these far-reaching proposals have no chance whatsoever of receiving the necessary support in U. N. circles to put them into effect. Nevertheless, most of these proposals represent the thinking of a substantial number of people and it may be worthwhile to review them briefly for whatever light they may shed upon the problem under consideration.

In the General Assembly, in line with the principle of sovereign equality, each state is represented by 5 delegates and 5 alternates and each delegation has 1 vote. The supranational proposals, for the most part, would abandon the principle of state sovereignty by suggesting fundamental changes in the size and character of the representation to which each country is entitled. Most of them advocate some form of weighted or proportionate representation the net effect of which would be a system of weighted voting.

THE CLARK-SOHN PROPOSALS

The most fully developed of these plans are the so-called Clark-Sohn proposals.[18] These proposals call for the creation of a United Nations peace force and would delegate to the General Assembly certain legislative authority particularly with respect to the enforcement of universal disarmament and the control of atomic energy.

Representation in the General Assembly, under the Clark-Sohn plans would be based solely on population. Each member of the U. N. would be entitled to 1 representative for each 5 million population or major fraction thereof. Small states with a population of more than 100,000 and not more than 2,500,000 would be entitled to 1 representative and members with large populations would be limited to 30 representatives. Nations with a population of 100,000 or less—such as San Marino and Monaco—would be entitled to a delegate with the right to participate in the discussion but without the right to vote. The formula would be adjusted from time to time, taking account of world population increases, in order to insure that the number of representatives should never exceed 400. The net effect of the plan would be to create a General Assembly of 382 representatives and 3 delegates to represent a world population of 2,400 million.

The authors specifically reject any system of weighted representation based on economic resources, productive capacity, literacy, trade, national income, or related factors.

[18] Grenville Clark and Louis B. Sohn. Peace Through Disarmament and Charter Revision. July 1953

They believe that all such plans, which necessarily give weight to wealth and other economic factors that are largely the result of geography and history, involve an anachronistic discrimination. Such a discrimination would run counter to the inherent equality of all individuals, which in the modern world should not and cannot be denied. They have, therefore, come to the conclusion that the true solution lies in an apportionment based fundamentally on population. It is for reasons of workability only that in the foregoing proposal upper and lower limits have been placed on the representation of any nation.[19]

By limiting to 30 the maximum number of representatives the largest countries may have, and by counting the people of the non-self-governing territories for purposes of representation, the authors of the plan would keep fairly even the voting strength of the great powers. China, the U. S. S. R., the United States, and India would be given 30 representatives, the United Kingdom 25, and France 19. On the other hand, Germany would be entitled to only 14, Italy to 9, Japan to 17, and Indonesia and Pakistan to 15 each. Some 40 nations would have only 1 representative.

With such a wide spread in voting power, the more populous nations would be given a dominant position in the General Assembly. As a practical matter, it is extremely doubtful, at best, that the smaller countries would be willing to accept any system in which India or China would be allotted almost as many votes as the 20 Latin American States combined.

In one other important respect, the Clark-Sohn proposal departs from the principle of state sovereignty. The authors suggest that representatives to the General Assembly be chosen in national elections or by vote of the national legislatures. This, they argue, would "stress the desirability that the representatives shall receive their mandate directly from the peoples of the respective nations." [20]

Since the idea is advanced by other proponents of supranational government, and since it would drastically alter the role of national governments in the organization, it will be discussed in some detail in a later section of this study.

BRITISH PARLIAMENTARY GROUP FOR WORLD GOVERNMENT

Somewhat similar to the Clark-Sohn proposals are the recommendations of the British Parliamentary Group for World Government. In their so-called plan A [21] they call for the creation of a world legislative body made up of two chambers, the upper chamber consisting of "one representative of each nation state appointed in a manner to be determined by that state." The intention here apparently is to provide for some continuity with the present General Assembly. The group also argues that such an arrangement would "tend to secure the representation of some valuable men and women who were not willing to submit themselves to popular suffrages." [22]

In contrast to the upper house, the lower chamber would consist of representatives of member states "in numbers proportionate to population." This would reflect in some degree the balance achieved by the Senate and the House in the Congress of the United States. While the British Parliamentary Group does not spell out their plan in any detail, they evidently contemplate placing an upper limit upon the

[19] Ibid., p. 21.
[20] Ibid., p. 23.
[21] Report of the Second London Parliamentary Conference on World Government, pp. 101-107.
[22] Ibid., p. 105.

number of representatives from any state. In a note dealing with the lower chamber they point out that—

the reason for weighting the representation is to avoid the overwhelming preponderance of the nations with the largest population, and thus make it more attractive to join.

In suggesting a double-vote system based on the sovereign equality of states and some form of weighted representation, the British Parliamentary Group approach somewhat the proposal of Mr. Dulles. The principal difference would seem to be that Mr. Dulles does not suggest changing the simple unicameral character of, or the method of representation in, the present General Assembly. He would secure his double vote by mathematical rather than physical changes.

FEDERAL UNION AND ATLANTIC UNION

Supporters of the Federal Union and Atlantic Union movements have advocated a two-house Union legislature comparable, with some variations, to our House and Senate. As Clarence Streit put it in his book Union Now,[23] the lower house would be "based completely on the population and the other modifying this principle of equal men in favor of equal states." This body would exercise the legislative authority granted to it, within a limited geographical area, for the 15 democracies first suggested for membership in the Union.

According to the formula for representation presented in Union Now—which was for illustrative purposes only—one representative would be allotted in the House for every million inhabitants. On this basis the United States would have received 129 of the 280 seats, in accordance with the population statistics then available. In the Senate, where it was proposed that each self-governing nation with less than 25 million inhabitants should be given 2 senators, with 2 additional senators for every population increment of 25 million or major portion thereof up to 100 million, the United States would have been allotted 8 of the 40 seats.

Under this plan the three largest countries (France, 42; Great Britain, 47; the United States, 129) would have 218 out of 280 representatives in the House and 16 out of 40 in the Senate. Thus, an equitable balance would be achieved, with the small states holding a substantial majority in the Senate and the large states commanding a majority in the House. No one member could possibly control either house, and the voting strength of each member would diminish relatively as other states entered the Union.

Since the suggested membership of the Union has varied somewhat, the supporters of Federal Union and Atlantic Union have deliberately refrained from developing their formula for representation in any detail. The exact number and distribution of seats would depend upon the list of participating states. Under their proposal, however, representatives in the Union legislature would be elected by popular vote, would vote as individuals, and would be responsible to the people rather than to their governments.

With respect to voting, the Atlantic Union Committee has this to say:

It is likely * * * that the constitution of an Atlantic Union would provide for a two-thirds or even three-fourths vote on questions of particular concern to its

---

[23] Clarence Streit, Union Now, 1940, p. 142

constituent peoples. This, together with provision for two houses in the Union's legislature, would afford protection to minority interests. Such protection, which could be carried as far as the people forming the Union believed desirable, would have to satisfy the American people in order to secure their ratification of the Union's constitution.[24]

VII. Regionalism and Voting Strength

Still another approach to the problem emerged in 1948 from the Committee to Frame a World Constitution. This committee, which conducted its studies at the University of Chicago, used the concept of regionalism as a basis for representation in a world assembly. The formula which they devised was designed to accomplish two major objectives: (1) To deemphasize national boundary lines and minimize the importance of the nation state; and (2) to develop a method of representation based on population, yet weighted in favor of those countries with the richest experience in democratic government.[25]

Under the committee's proposal a Federal convention would be convened consisting of delegates elected directly by the member states, one delegate for each million of population or major fraction thereof. This body would then subdivide into 9 electoral colleges, corresponding to 9 regions of the world, for the purpose of nominating and electing a President and the members of the world council or legislature. The council would be made up of 9 members from each region with 18 elected at large, or a total of 99. Representatives would vote as individuals rather than as members of instructed delegations.

The nine regions are delineated in the draft constitution as follows: [26]

(1) The continent of Europe and its islands outside the Russian area, together with the United Kingdom if the latter so decides, and with such overseas English- or French- or Cape Dutch-speaking communities of the British Commonwealth of Nations or the French Union as decide to associate (this whole area here tentatively denominated "Europa");

(2) The United States of America, with the United Kingdom if the latter so decides, and such kindred communities of British, or Franco-British, or Dutch-British or Irish civilization and lineage as decide to associate (Atlantis);

(3) Russia, European and Asiatic, with such east Baltic or Slavic or south Danubian nations as associate with Russia (Eurasia);

(4) The Near and Middle East, with the states of north Africa, and Pakistan if the latter so decides (Afrasia);

(5) Africa, south of the Sahara, with or without the South African Union as the latter may decide;

(6) India, with Pakistan if the latter so decides;

(7) China, Korea, Japan, with the associate archipelagoes of the north- and mid-Pacific (Asia Major);

(8) Indochina and Indonesia, with Pakistan if the latter so decides, and with such other mid- and south-Pacific lands and islands as decide to associate (Austrasia);

(9) The Western Hemisphere south of the United States (Columbia).

[24] Atlantic Union Committee, 20 Questions on Atlantic Union, pp. 14–15.
[25] Preliminary draft of a World Constitution, University of Chicago, 1948.
[26] Ibid. art. V.

It will be noted that some of these regions would have a greater representation in proportion to population than others. Thus Asia Major (China, Japan, Korea), with about 25 percent of the world's population, would receive 11 percent of the total representation, while Columbia (Latin America) would have the same number of representatives with only about 7 percent of the population. The three regions of the Western World—Europa, Atlantis, and Columbia—with about a fifth of the world's population, would be given one-third of the representation.

Admittedly, this device of grouping kindred nations or cultures together into regions for representation and voting purposes would have certain theoretical advantages which some of the other proposals would not have. Certainly no single region, and no bloc of 2 or 3 regions, could dominate the world assembly or prevent the approval of desirable measures. Moreover, the formula provides a basis for representation other than mere population statistics without undue discrimination against any area of the world.

Space will not permit an analysis of the plan's weak points. Obviously it is a very complex proposal which assumes that people and governments are willing to move much further in the direction of world government and regionalism than is probably the case. There is little in the experience of the United Nations to date that would indicate that states are ready to pool their voting power with their neighbors on a purely regional basis. Proximity does not necessarily result in compatibility between states.

VIII. Other Proposals

Certain groups have also suggested that representation and voting be weighted on the basis of population and other factors. For the most part, they do not explain in any detail the procedure by which this might be accomplished.

The United World Federalists have long favored a system of "balanced representation" in their projected world legislative assembly. In 1949, Alan Cranston, speaking for the UWF stated:

It is unlikely that a system of representation based solely upon population, with no upper or lower limits, would be more acceptable or desirable, for then India and China, with their vast millions, would receive a voting power out of proportion to their present role in the world.

Again, we do not seek to provide a precise formula, but we suggest that in addition to population other factors might be taken into account, such as economic development and education.[27]

In 1950, in his testimony before the Senate Foreign Relations Committee, Mr. Cranston suggested that such factors as population, industrial capacity, monetary contribution and regional formulas ought to be taken into account. Other representatives of UWF have expressed, in general terms, the same point of view.[28]

In their so-called plan B, which is designed to remove what they regard as certain imperfections in the U. N. Charter, the British Parliamentary Group for World Government arrive at the same con-

---

[27] U. S. House of Representatives, Committee on Foreign Affairs, To Seek Development of the United Nations into a World Federation, hearings on H. Con Res. 64, 1949, p. 163.
[28] U. S. Senate, Committee on Foreign Relations, Revision of the United Nations Charter, hearings, 1950, pp. 523 and 127.

clusion. Plan B recommends that the governments of member states of the U. N. take action—

to improve the representative character of the Assembly, by, for example, introducing the principle of weighted voting possibly by establishing a bicameral Assembly and relating representation in one of the chambers to economic and/or population factors.[29]

The means for implementing the proposal are not indicated in the plan.

IX. REPRESENTATIVES VOTING AS INDIVIDUALS

One common feature of the so-called supranational proposals is the proposition that representatives to a world assembly should be popularly elected and should cast their votes as individuals. While such a recommendation might be considered essential in any scheme of world government where state sovereignty is relegated to the background, if it were transplanted to the General Assembly, as suggested in the Clark-Sohn proposals, it would involve a fundamental change in the character of the United Nations.

If some kind of weighted representation should be considered for the General Assembly, it will be particularly important to keep the problem of responsibility in mind. At present our delegation to the General Assembly is appointed by the Government, is responsible to the Government, and votes in accordance with instructions issued by the Government. The lines of responsibility are clear and direct. Any other arrangement might well result in an unmanageable dispersal of power that would prove embarrassing both to the member states and to the U. N.

Advocates of world government pointed out that in the beginning elected delegates probably would vote in national blocs but as time goes on this tendency would be overcome. "It is true," state the Clark-Sohn proposals:

that the representatives of a particular nation would tend to vote the same way on issues of great importance to that nation * * *. It can, however, be expected that there would develop in the course of time a spirit of representing the interests of the world as a whole rather than those of individual nations; and that the representatives would more and more tend to vote in accordance with their judgment as to the best interests of all the peoples as in the case of national parliaments where the interests of the whole nation have become of no less importance than the interests of a particular section or group.[30]

The arguments against such an arrangement in an organization of sovereign states are apparent. The first has to do with the relations between democratic countries and totalitarian systems. Democratic delegates might possibly vote as individuals but it is inconceivable that the representatives of totalitarian states would ever be in a position to do so.

In the second place, the lack of discipline would be harmful to United Nations programs. What good would come from our delegation voting for a General Assembly resolution if, after it was passed, our Government refused to support it?

Finally, with the conduct of diplomacy as complicated as it is, states find it extremely difficult to develop a unified, cohesive foreign

[29] Report of the Second London Parliamentary Conference on World Government, p. 108.
[30] Clark and Sohn, op. cit., pp. 47–48.

policy even under the best of conditions. It would seem unlikely that most governments and the people they represent would want to abdicate their responsibility for the conduct of foreign relations to persons voting as "individuals" and thus beyond their control in an international organization.

X. Concluding Comments

In spite of the growing importance of voting in the General Assembly, this remains one of the great unexplored areas of the charter. Very little research has been done on this problem; very few practical suggestions have been made for improving the present situation. Nor does the experience of international organizations in the past shed much helpful light on the subject. It is apparent that the whole question needs very careful analysis before our Government can be in a position to consider seriously any specific proposals for changing the present charter provisions.

Summarizing what has been said above, however, two conclusions seem inescapable. In the first place, there are striking inequalities among the 60 U. N. members with respect to population, armed strength, national income, territory, contribution to the U. N. and other factors. The present system of awarding one vote to each state thus confers upon the smaller countries a voting strength far out of proportion to their influence in world affairs.

In the second place, if any departure is made from the principle of one-state-one-vote it will have to be a modest one with a relatively low ceiling placed on the voting power of the great nations. For the small states, having been in a favorable voting position for many years, can be expected to put up a vigorous fight to block any proposal which would seriously alter what is in effect their privileged status in the General Assembly.

This does not mean that a satisfactory quid pro quo could not be arranged. It would appear that the problem of weighted voting is closely related to the further revision of the charter. The small states, in other words, might be persuaded to make significant concessions in this respect if the General Assembly is given sufficient authority to take vigorous and effective action on behalf of world peace.

There is presented below, by way of illustration, an approach to the problem of weighted voting which is based, in part, on past experience and which does not constitute a drastic departure from present procedures. The idea is not final in form; rather it is presented as a tentative suggestion in order to stimulate further discussion of an important issue.

It is suggested in this illustration, in line with Mr. Dulles' proposal outlined above, that the vote of each state in the General Assembly be counted twice; once on the basis of one vote for each state and the second time on the basis of a weighted formula. A majority of each of the votes would be required for the General Assembly to reach a decision.

ILLUSTRATIVE WEIGHTED VOTING FORMULA—UNITED NATIONS GENERAL ASSEMBLY VOTING STRENGTH IN ORDER OF POPULATION, FINANCIAL CONTRIBUTION, AND COMBINED WEIGHTED VOTES

Population vote

Rank	Country	Population [31] (thousands)	Vote	Per-cent of population vote
1	China	463,493	5	
2	India	367,000	5	
3	United States	156,981	5	2.87
4	U. S. S. R.	151,663	5	
5	United Kingdom	[33]122,537	5	
6	France	[33]91,128	5	
7	Indonesia	78,163	4	
8	Pakistan	75,842	4	
9	Brazil	54,477	4	
10	Ukraine	30,960	4	2.30
11	Mexico	26,922	4	
12	Poland	24,977	4	
13	Egypt	21,425	4	
14	Turkey	20,934	4	
15	Philippines	20,631	4	
16	Iran	19,798	3	
17	Thailand	19,193	3	
18	Burma	18,859	3	
19	Argentina	18,054	3	
20	Yugoslavia	16,729	3	
21	Ethiopia	15,000	3	
22	Canada	14,430	3	
23	Union of South Africa	12,912	3	
24	Czechoslovakia	12,340	3	1.73
25	Afghanistan	12,000	3	
26	Colombia	11,768	3	
27	Netherlands	10,377	3	
28	Peru	8,864	3	
29	Belgium	8,706	3	
30	Australia	8,649	3	
31	Greece	7,761	3	
32	Sweden	7,125	3	
33	Saudi Arabia	7,000	3	
34	Cuba	5,832	3	
35	Byelorussia	5,927	3	
36	Venezuela	5,568	3	
37		5,280	3	
38	Iraq	5,100	3	

Contribution vote

Rank	Country	Contribution [32] (dollars)	Vote	Percent of contribution vote
1	United States	13,765,290	5	
2	U. S. S. R.	5,843,950	5	
3	United Kingdom	4,047,400	5	3.05
4	France	2,374,750	5	
5	China	2,321,060	5	
6	India	1,404,200	4	
7	Canada	1,362,900	4	
8	Ukraine	776,440	4	
9	Australia	722,750	4	
10	Poland	714,490	4	2.44
11	Sweden	681,450	4	
12	Brazil	578,200	4	
13	Argentina	578,200	4	
14	Belgium	569,940	4	
15	Netherlands	516,250	4	
16	Czechoslovakia	433,650	3	
17	Denmark	322,140	3	
18	Union of South Africa	322,140	3	
19	Mexico	309,750	3	
20	Pakistan	309,750	3	
21	Turkey	268,450	3	
22	Indonesia	247,800	3	
23	Byelorussia	206,500	3	
24	Norway	206,500	3	1.83
25	New Zealand	198,240	3	
26	Egypt	194,110	3	
27	Philippines	185,850	3	
28	Yugoslavia	181,720	3	
29	Colombia	169,330	3	
30	Venezuela	161,070	3	
31	Cuba	140,420	3	
32	Chile	136,290	3	
33	Iran	115,640	3	
34	Greece	86,730	2	
35	Peru	74,340	2	
36	Thailand	74,340	2	
37	Uruguay	74,340	2	

Combined vote

Rank	Country	Vote	Per-cent of combined vote
1	China	10	
	U. S. S. R.	10	
	United Kingdom	10	2.96
	United States	10	
	France	10	
2	India	9	2.66
3	Brazil	8	
	Poland	8	2.37
	Ukraine	8	
4	Argentina	7	
	Australia	7	
	Belgium	7	
	Canada	7	
	Egypt	7	
	Indonesia	7	2.07
	Mexico	7	
	Netherlands	7	
	Pakistan	7	
	Philippines	7	
	Sweden	7	
	Turkey	7	
5	Byelorussia	6	
	Chile	6	
	Colombia	6	
	Cuba	6	
	Czechoslovakia	6	1.78
	Iran	6	
	Union of South Africa	6	
	Venezuela	6	
	Yugoslavia	6	
	Afghanistan	5	
	Burma	5	
	Denmark	5	
	Ethiopia	5	
	Greece	5	

No.	Country	Population[31]	Votes	%
39	Yemen	4,500	2	
40	Denmark	4,334	2	
41	Syria	3,381	2	
42	Ecuador	3,350	2	
43	Norway	3,327	2	
44	Haiti	3,200	2	
45	Bolivia	3,089	2	
46	Guatemala	2,938	2	
47	Uruguay	2,365	2	1.15
48	Dominican Republic	2,236	2	
49	New Zealand	1,995	2	
50	El Salvador	1,986	2	
51	Liberia	1,648	2	
52	Israel	1,607	2	
53	Honduras	1,513	2	
54	Paraguay	1,464	2	
55	Lebanon	1,320	2	
56	Nicaragua	1,128	2	
57	Costa Rica	850	1	.57
58	Panama	841	1	
59	Luxembourg	301	1	
60	Iceland	148	1	
	Total	2,012,026	175	

No.	Country	Population	Votes	%
38	Israel	70,210	2	
39	Burma	53,690	2	
40	Iraq	49,560	2	
41	Ethiopia	41,300	2	
42	Afghanistan	33,040	2	1.22
43	Syria	33,040	2	
44	Saudi Arabia	28,910	2	
45	Guatemala	28,910	2	
46	Bolivia	24,780	2	
47	El Salvador	24,780	2	
48	Luxembourg	24,780	2	
49	Dominican Republic	20,650	2	
50	Lebanon	20,650	2	
51	Panama	20,650	2	
52	Costa Rica	16,520	1	.61
53	Ecuador	16,520	1	
54	Haiti	16,520	1	
55	Honduras	16,520	1	
56	Iceland	16,520	1	
57	Liberia	16,520	1	
58	Paraguay	16,520	1	
59	Nicaragua	16,520	1	
60	Yemen	16,520	1	
	Total	41,300,000	164	

Cat.	Country	Votes	%
6	Iraq	5	1.48
	New Zealand	5	
	Norway	5	
	Peru	5	
	Saudi Arabia	5	
	Thailand	5	
7	Bolivia	4	1.18
	Dominican Republic	4	
	El Salvador	4	
	Guatemala	4	
	Israel	4	
	Lebanon	4	
	Syria	4	
	Uruguay	4	
8	Ecuador	3	.89
	Haiti	3	
	Honduras	3	
	Liberia	3	
	Luxembourg	3	
	Nicaragua	3	
	Panama	3	
	Paraguay	3	
	Yemen	3	
9	Costa Rica	2	.59
	Iceland	2	
	Total	339	

[31] Statistical Office of the U. N., Population and Vital Statistics Reports, Series A, vol. VI, No. 2, New York, April 1954.

[32] U. S. Senate Subcommittee on the United Nations, Review of the United Nations Charter, 83d Cong., 2d sess., Doc. No. 87, Washington, 1954, pp. 719-720.

[33] Aggregate figure, including non-self-governing territories and dependencies. In this illustrative formula, France, a permanent member of the Security Council is awarded 5 votes even though her total population falls below the 100 million suggested for the first category of states.

In the weighted voting formula here presented, only two criteria are taken into account; a state's population and its contribution to the United Nations. Each state would be awarded from 2 to 10 votes with the scale running from 1 to 5 for each criterion. Votes would be awarded for population in accordance with the following scale: States under 1 million would receive 1 vote; 1 to 5 million, 2 votes; 5 to 20 million, 3 votes; 20 to 100 million, 4 votes; and over 100 million, 5 votes. For U. N. contributions the scale would be: States contributing less than $20,000 to the regular U. N. budget would receive 1 vote; $20,000 to $100,000, 2 votes; $100,000 to $500,000, 3 votes; $500,000 to $2 million, 4 votes; and all over $2 million, 5 votes.

Several observations may be made about this kind of illustrative weighted voting system.

1. It would increase the relative voting strength of certain countries—particularly the great nations—but it would not materially alter the balance of power in the General Assembly.

2. The Latin American and the Arab States would lose somewhat, as indeed they would in almost any system of weighted voting that could be devised. Thus, the 20 Latin American states, with a total of 91 out of the 338 votes in the General Assembly, would command only 27 percent of the votes instead of the strategic one-third they now control. The 6 Arab States would drop from 10 percent to roughly 8 percent.

3. Unless the votes of the Ukraine and Byelorussia were discounted somewhat, as suggested earlier in this study, the Soviet bloc would pick up voting strength. The 5 Communist states now control 8 percent of the votes; under the illustrative schedule they would claim 11 percent. The so-called neutralist states of India, Indonesia, and Burma would also add slightly to their voting power.

4. Two other groups of states, generally inclined to support American policy, would either hold their own or else gain voting strength. The 12 NATO states in the U. N. would continue to hold roughly one-fifth of the votes. The seven British Commonwealth countries would increase their total from 11.6 percent to 15 percent.

5. If other criteria, such as national income, productivity and foreign trade, are taken into account, the states of Western Europe and the British Commonwealth countries would improve their relative standings somewhat. The more complicated the formula, however, the more opposition it is likely to encounter.

6. In this chart the votes are calculated on the basis of the contribution of each member to the *regular* U. N. budget. Clearly, this is not the most satisfactory measuring stick. It would be far better—though perhaps not very practical—if a schedule could be devised that would reflect the ability and the willingness of U. N. members to contribute manpower, military equipment and supplies, as well as bases and other facilities toward the maintenance of world peace.

Thus far there has been little congressional comment on the concept of weighted voting. Two Senators, however, have declared themselves in opposition. Senator Guy M. Gillette, a member of the Special Subcommittee on the U. N. Charter, told the American Society of International Law in April 1954 that he was strongly against it. Senator John Bricker of Ohio in a speech before the Iowa Bar Association in Des Moines on June 4, 1954, said he would oppose weighted voting because it "paves the way for vesting the General Assembly with legislative authority" and is a move in the direction of transforming the U. N. "into a limited or full world government." Additional comment can be expected as the issue becomes sharper in the public mind.

Voting in the General Assembly is grimly serious business. Any significant realinement of votes might have an adverse impact upon our policy—either now or at some time in the unpredictable future.

Before we urge the principle of weighted voting, therefore, we must make certain, through a careful analysis of the facts, that such a move is in our national interest. We must make sure that we are not opening a Pandora's box from which a host of unpleasant results might flow to plague us in the years to come.

Clearly, any formula that would result in a substantial decrease in voting power for the 20 Latin American countries would be open to grave objections on our part. Generally speaking, these nations have been the most consistent supporters of our policy in the United Nations and we hope they will remain so.

Our national position on this issue must also be conditioned by the probability that a number of states—including the relatively great powers of Germany, Japan, and Italy—may be admitted to the U. N. within the next few years. With a possible increase in membership that may run as high as 30 percent, Assembly voting patterns could undergo drastic changes.

Up to the present time, the United States has been able to retain its position of leadership in the General Assembly through the logic of its argument and the justice of its cause. In a political organization where each state has one vote, we have been able to rally the small countries to the cause of the free world.

Theoretically, there may be logical reasons for supporting a system of weighted voting for the General Assembly. From a practical point of view, however, it might be better to let well enough alone.

PACIFIC SETTLEMENT OF DISPUTES IN THE UNITED NATIONS

STAFF STUDY NO. 5

OCTOBER 17, 1954

PREFACE

By Alexander Wiley, *Chairman*

This study raises some fundamental questions as to what the principal function of the United Nations should be. In some cases, the organization has played an important part in stopping fires before they could flame into conflagrations of worldwide proportions. The cases of Indonesia, Kashmir, and Palestine come to mind in this connection. In these situations, the United Nations was able to get the disputants, to a large extent, to leave their guns outside, to sit down at a table and try to talk out their differences instead of shooting them out. In Korea, on the other hand, the United Nations was unable to prevent a major conflict but it did act—as effectively as could be expected in the opinion of some, inadequately in the opinion of others—to mobilize certain member nations against the Communist aggressor.

If the United Nations is an instrument capable of stopping aggression and preventing war, then it offers hope for mankind. If it is incapable of getting states to settle their disputes peacefully and is incapable of preventing aggression, the sooner we know that, the better.

In any event, the holocaust of world war III has not descended on us and that is good. We are trying, on this subcommittee, to find out what part the United Nations has played and can play in preventing such a catastrophe.

After 8 years of experience, it has become clear that there are two principal ways in which the United Nations may help to maintain peace. On the one hand, it may act as a kind of crossroads of the world where representatives of all nations meet to talk over their problems and settle them by peaceful means—a town meeting of the world, as the late Senator Vandenberg used to say. If the organization works successfully in all disputes in this fashion, then there would be no need for enforcement functions and no wars. If it does not, on the other hand, the United Nations might still help to preserve peace by serving not simply as a crossroads, but as the policeman at the crossroads—able to enforce order.

As indicated in this staff study, there are some who believe that the United Nations should confine its activity primarily to debate, discussion, and conciliation. It should try to help nations to settle their problems without war. Some who hold this view believe that to conceive of the United Nations as an instrument able to bring effective force to bear against a Soviet, or Soviet-sponsored, aggressor is like expecting the minister and the policeman to be one and the same entity. Others regard it as a futile effort to try to prevent crime when criminals are on the police force. Those who take the latter position often believe that nations which want to preserve peace and oppose aggression must rely on their own strength or on regional defense

115

organizations made up of those with like standards of morality and with a fairly close community of interest.

If all the nations members of the U. N. were to live up to their undertaking in the charter to "settle their international disputes by peaceful means" there would be no problem. Unfortunately there are nations in the world which still view treaties as scraps of paper if it suits their convenience. It is the attitudes and actions of such states which make it essential for nations of good will constantly to seek ways to develop reliable and effective methods to promote the peaceful settlement of disputes which might lead to war.

One of the jobs of this subcommittee is to examine the record of the United Nations with respect to pacific settlement and to determine whether or not any charter changes would be in the interests of the United States.

This study was prepared by Charles R. Gellner of the Legislative Reference Service of the Library of Congress, under the direction of the staff of the subcommittee. The study is for the background use of the subcommittee and does not necessarily represent the views of any of its members.

OCTOBER 17, 1954.

CONTENTS

PACIFIC SETTLEMENT OF DISPUTES IN THE UNITED NATIONS

I. INTRODUCTION

The charter makes clear that a principal purpose of the United Nations is to contribute to the maintenance of peace. Yet 8 years after the end of World War II there is little evidence that permanent peace has been achieved. It is true that in some situations the United Nations has been a major instrument in bringing quarreling countries together and possibly in preventing little wars from erupting into major catastrophes. The Organization's record in contributing to the peaceful settlement of disputes shows that it has exerted a major influence in such key areas of potential world conflict as Greece, Palestine, Indonesia, and Kashmir. It is possible that without the intercession of the United Nations, any one of these local conflicts might have erupted into a devasting conflict with worldwide implications.

Nevertheless, largely because of the continuing tension between the Soviet bloc and the free nations some of the initial expectation—that the United Nations held, at last, the answer to the hope for permanent peace—has been shaken by events of the past 8 years. There is in some quarters a tendency to believe that since peace is still ephemeral, the United Nations has failed.

It is the purpose of this study to examine the ways in which the Organization has tried to promote peace, to record briefly its activity in this respect, and to survey the proposals that have been made with regard to United Nations activities in the field of peaceful settlement.

The United Nations is designed to contribute to the maintenance of peace in two principal ways. First, it is to serve as a center of conciliation where the nations of the world may work out differences in accordance with orderly procedures for pacific settlement. Second, the United Nations is expected to act as an agency for mobilizing collective force—whether moral, economic, or military—against a nation or group of nations which threatens or breaks the peace.

During the brief period of its existence, the United Nations has exercised both of the above functions, that is, pacific settlement and enforcement action. The first has been brought into play in connection with numerous disputes and tensions since the end of World War II. In the Korean aggression in 1950, military enforcement was employed for the first time.

The manner in which the United Nations has discharged these two functions has differed sharply from what was expected at the time the organization was established. As adopted in 1945, the charter reflected the belief that substantial cooperation would prevail among the principal victors after World War II. The appearance, instead, of conflict between the Soviet Union and the other great powers has had an impact on practically every activity of the United Nations.

Those activities related to pacific settlement are no exception. In this function, as in others, the split manifests itself in the abuse of the veto, in the rapid evolution of some organs and procedures for dealing with disputes and in the declining effectiveness of other organs and procedures.

If an international review of the charter should take place after 1955, it is likely that the function of peaceful settlement will undergo close scrutiny. Even at the San Francisco Conference in 1945, there was dissatisfaction on the part of the smaller nations with some aspects of the charter relative to the handling of disputes. The General Assembly has since expressed the view that the veto should not be employed, as it has often been, in questions of pacific settlement. So too has the Senate of the United States. In other quarters, proposals have been advanced for establishing new procedures of conciliation, some of which would enhance the powers of the United Nations in this field.

Pacific settlement in the United Nations gives rise to problems that are complex and technical. Many parts of the charter are directly involved in this function and others are closely related. Are the articles adopted in 1945 and the procedures which have grown up under them still valid today? Does the relationship between peaceful settlement and other functions of the U. N., notably enforcement action, require clarification? Should changes be considered in the veto power with respect to peaceful settlement? What of the role of the General Assembly in this function, a role which has evolved in a considerably different fashion than originally, expected?

Such questions are clearly pertinent to any review of peaceful settlement. Beyond them, moreover, are other, fundamental issues: What, for example, is the scope of pacific settlement in an organization of sovereign states, and in a sharply divided world?

II. THE PROVISIONS OF THE CHARTER

BACKGROUND

While World War II was being fought, preparations went on simultaneously in many countries looking toward the establishment of an organization which could maintain peace. Much of this preparation was based on the experience of the League of Nations. There was relatively little sentiment, however, in favor of a revival of the League. Instead wartime preparations were directed for the most part to the creation of a new international organization.

The basic approach followed in the preparations for the United Nations, however, was not unlike that suggested by the experience of the old League. Mechanisms were sought which on the one hand would permit joint action to stop armed conflict and aggression and, on the other hand, would encourage a solution of disputes or a relaxation of tensions among nations before they reached the stage of violence. These mechanisms, moreover, had to be of a kind that would be acceptable to a conglomeration of sovereign nations, great and small alike.

At the Dumbarton Oaks Conference in 1944, the United States delegates advanced proposals for an international organization which were generally supported by the British and Chinese delegations. In broad outline, the American approach called for an executive council of the great powers with some representation for the small states in this body. The Council would have primary responsibility for international peace and security. In addition there would be a General Assembly composed of all the member nations of the Organization. The Assembly would be authorized to make recommendations on disputes which did not endanger the peace and on the general principles of international cooperation.

Such evidence as is available indicates that the Soviet Union favored an international organization in which an executive committee of the United States, the U. S. S. R., and Great Britain would be all powerful.[1] This committee would hold all other countries in check and thus keep the peace. Under the Soviet concept the three powers would have to agree among themselves and could take no enforcement action against each other. Each great power, moreover, would have its own geographical sphere of influence and together they would serve as the international executive committee only with respect to worldwide questions. The Soviet proposals also provided for a general assembly of all member states, but the smaller powers were to have little or no authority in matters of security.

Both the American and Soviet approaches appear to have coincided at least to this extent: Since their influence and strength made them predominant in the world, the great powers should have a preeminent position in the proposed Organization. Such differences as existed were reconciled to a great extent at Dumbarton Oaks and subsequently at Yalta in 1945. The great powers reserved to themselves permanent and special positions within the Security Council which was to be established, and endowed the Council with primary responsibility for maintaining peace and security.

THE CHARTER AND THE SECURITY COUNCIL

The proposals for the Security Council agreed upon at Dumbarton Oaks and Yalta were incorporated with few changes in the United Nations Charter at the San Francisco Conference in 1945. The charter places "primary responsibility" for maintaining international peace and security on the Security Council. Special functions are assigned to the Council in this connection and these are divided into two groups. The first group, embodied in chapter VI of the charter, concerns pacific settlement of disputes. The second group, which deals with enforcement action to maintain or restore peace, is described in chapter VII.

Underlying the functions of chapters VI and VII is a fundamental obligation assumed by all members of the United Nations. They pledge in chapter I of the charter to settle any international dispute in which they may become involved "in such a manner that international peace and security, and justice, are not endangered," and to "refrain in their international relations from the threat or use of force" in a manner inconsistent with the charter.

[1] Leland M. Goodrich, Development of the General Assembly, International Conciliation, No. 471, May 1951, pp. 236–240.

PACIFIC SETTLEMENT FUNCTIONS UNDER CHAPTER VI

Nations involved in a serious international dispute have an obligation under the charter to try to work out a settlement themselves. They are required to seek a solution first of all "by negotiation, enquiry, mediation, conciliation, arbitration, judicial settlement, resort to regional agencies or arrangements, or other peaceful means of their own choice." If the dispute persists, then the charter provides for consideration of the matter by the Security Council.[2]

For purposes of pacific settlement, the Council is assigned a number of recommendatory powers. The Council may call upon the disputants to resort to one of the methods of settlement mentioned above. It may itself propose procedures for adjusting the dispute. Or the Council may enter into the substance of the dispute and recommend actual terms of settlement; in other words, act itself as the agent of conciliation.

Functioning in these ways under chapter VI, the Security Council may exercise considerable influence with respect to a situation that endangers the peace. This influence, however, is persuasive only. Under chapter VI, the Council may make recommendations to the disputants; it cannot order them to settle their differences.

THE VETO AND PACIFIC SETTLEMENT

The principal types of decisions that the Security Council may reach under chapter VI—to "investigate" a dispute to see if it is likely to endanger the peace, to "call upon" the parties to settle their dispute, to propose "procedures * * * of adjustment," and to recommend "terms of settlement"—are subject to the veto. Any 1 of the 5 permanent powers, therefore, is in a position to prevent the Council from taking measures for the peaceful settlement of a dispute. There is only one exception to this provision: a permanent power must abstain from voting if it is a party to the dispute under consideration.

At the San Francisco Conference this arrangement was opposed by a number of smaller nations.[3] They argued that it was unreasonable for one country to be able to block the Council when it was engaged in the purely recommendatory function of pacific settlement. The great powers, on the other hand, insisted at the time that even recommendations under chapter VI might by a "chain of events" lead to enforcement action under chapter VII. In the latter case, there was

[2] The charter provides that disputes may be brought before the Security Council by the disputants themselves or in other ways. The Security Council itself may investigate "any dispute, or any situation which might lead to international friction or give rise to a dispute." A member of the United Nations, even if not directly involved, may bring a dispute or situation to the attention of either the Security Council or General Assembly. The Secretary General also may call to the attention of the Security Council any matter which in his opinion may threaten the maintenance of international peace and security. The General Assembly is also authorized to "call the attention of the Security Council to situations which are likely to endanger international peace and security." Even a nonmember may bring to the attention of either the Council or Assembly a dispute, "to which it is a party if it accepts in advance, for the purposes of the dispute, the obligations of pacific settlement provided in the present charter." A nonmember, however, may not bring before the United Nations a "situation" or "dispute" to which it is not a party, even though its interests may be affected.

[3] Dr. Herbert V. Evatt, of Australia, told Commission III (Security Council) of the San Francisco Conference on June 20, 1945:

"It is our view, however, and we hold it strongly * * * that the veto should not be applicable to any of the processes of peaceful settlement, that is, of conciliation. That is not only the view of the Australian Delegation but of many other delegations which supported it either by voting against the formula or by abstaining from voting. It is perfectly obvious from this document which contains the detailed account of the voting that the majority of the members of this conference do not approve of the veto being applicable to the processes of conciliation." (United Nations Conference on International Organization, San Francisco 1945, Documents, New York, United Nations Information Organization, 1945, vol. 11, p. 124.)

general agreement at the Conference that the veto should apply since forces to be supplied principally by the five great powers might be necessary to enforce a Council decision.[4] The views of the great powers prevailed and the Conference voted against a proposed amendment which would have forbidden the use of the veto in pacific settlement.[5]

PACIFIC SETTLEMENT AND THE GENERAL ASSEMBLY

The Dumbarton Oaks proposals with respect to the role of the General Assembly in the settlement of disputes were approved by the San Francisco Conference and embodied in the charter. These proposals assigned to the Assembly the right to consider general principles of cooperation among nations. On referral from the Council or from any member country, the Assembly could also make recommendations on more specific questions relating to peace and security.

Although the Dumbarton Oaks proposals were included in the charter, there was dissatisfaction with them, especially among the smaller nations. Some opposed the special powers assigned to the Big Five. They maintained that the authority of the General Assembly, in which they had a large majority, should be expanded. With this end in view, many of the smaller states at the San Francisco Conference supported proposals to broaden the functions of the Assembly.

One result of their initiative was the adoption of article 10. This article authorizes the Assembly to discuss any matter within the scope of the charter. It also permits the Assembly to make recommendations to the members of the United Nations or to the Security Council on any questions, except when the latter is exercising its functions with respect to them. According to one author [6] the significant contribution of this article—

was the change it wrought in the spirit of the Dumbarton Oaks plan, proclaiming explicitly that the boundaries of the Assembly's authority to discuss and recommend should be as extensive as those of the entire Charter.

Another major expansion of the powers of the Assembly resulted largely from the efforts of Senator Arthur H. Vandenberg of the United States delegation. Largely on his insistence it was decided to grant the Assembly, under article 14, overall authority to—

recommend measures for the peaceful adjustment of any situation, regardless of origin, which it deems likely to impair the general welfare or friendly relations among nations * * *.

The inclusion of articles 10 and 14 in the charter has been a major factor in the expansion of the influence of the General Assembly that has taken place in recent years. Most of the cases dealing with peace and security coming before that body have been brought up on the basis of article 10, or articles 10 and 14 together.[7]

---

[4] The "chain of events" argument is described in greater detail in sec. IV below. The Soviet Union at San Francisco for a time held that even discussion of a dispute by the Council should be subject to the veto, but eventually receded from this position and agreed that discussion should be regarded as a procedural matter and, hence, not subject to veto.

[5] The amendment was proposed by Australia. Twenty nations voted against the amendment. Ten voted in favor of it and 15 abstained from voting.

[6] H. Field Haviland, Jr., The Political Role of the General Assembly, New York, Carnegie Endowment for International Peace, 1951, p. 13.

[7] For example, the Palestine, Spanish, and South African cases. Art. 14 was invoked to justify the Assembly's consideration of the Korean independence case in 1947. Leland M. Goodrich and Edvard Hambro, Charter of the United Nations: Commentary and Documents, Boston, World Peace Foundation, 1949, p. 180.

III. Pacific Settlement in Practice

During 8 years of operation the Security Council and the General Assembly have employed a variety of methods in an attempt to bring about solutions of disputes and to ease situations of tension. Some of the questions with which these bodies have dealt have involved hostilities; some have not. In those cases where actual fighting had broken out, for example, Korea, Indonesia, and Palestine, the United Nations took measures to end it. These measures included, in the case of Indonesia, "calls" upon the parties to cease military operations; in the case of Palestine, a threat to use enforcement action against "any" government or authority continuing hostilities; and in the case of Korea, a recommendation of the use of collective force against the Communist aggressors of North Korea.

The open discussion of disputes in both the General Assembly and the Security Council has served to clarify them and to focus the influence of public opinion upon the issues. Many observers believe that this "goldfish bowl" treatment which the organization gives to international controversies exercises a sobering and restraining influence on the disputants.

On the other hand, it is often contended that once international attention has been centered on a dispute, the national honor and prestige of the disputants become involved. Consequently, their positions tend to harden and they become less amenable to compromise and conciliation.

The ability of the Security Council to act in the field of pacific settlement has undoubtedly been hampered by the Soviet Union's use of the veto. By invoking this device in the Greek question, for example, the Soviet Union blocked measures for ending Communist-supported guerrilla hostilities in Greece. In the Berlin question the U. S. S. R. used the veto to forestall adoption of a plan, backed by the smaller member nations of the Security Council, for lifting the blockade. By employing the veto in the Korean issue the Soviet Union thwarted the Council's efforts to put a stop to Communist Chinese military intervention.

Nonuse of the veto, however, is not a guaranty that an actual settlement will be attained even though hostilities may be inhibited. The Kashmir dispute is a case in point. In this instance, the issue was brought to the Council in 1948 and a cease-fire was obtained. The veto has not been involved but a genuine solution to the Kashmir question has not been achieved.

A number of important disputes have been transferred to the General Assembly or some other agency, largely because the Security Council has been unable to progress toward a peaceful solution. The Greek case and the Korean conflict both shifted from the Council to the Assembly. The Corfu Channel case went to the International Court. In the Iranian case and the Berlin blockade the disputants negotiated a settlement outside the United Nations. Settlements of the Korean question and the Kashmir dispute have become subjects of direct negotiation between the parties concerned. However, the United Nations may resume consideration of these questions.

Reference to the tables of disputes which follow shows that in 1946 there were 5 political disputes brought before the Security Council;

in 1947, 3; in 1948, 5. Until the very recent cases of Thailand and Guatemala, the Korean conflict was the only new dispute of outstanding importance since 1948, considered by the Security Council, and the Korean question arose when the Soviet Union had absented itself from the Council. Most of the other disputes which came before the Council in subsequent years were outgrowths of Communist propaganda relating to the hostilities in Korea.

The decline in the number of disputes considered by the Security Council represents in part at least an adjustment to the dissension among the permanent powers. Types of questions which the San Francisco drafters contemplated would be handled by the Council have been referred instead to the General Assembly, or have not been taken to the United Nations at all. Among issues recently considered by the Assembly have been those involving German unification and the Austrian peace treaty. In the Tunisian and Moroccan cases, the Security Council kept the issues off its agenda and they then went to the Assembly. Recently the problem of reaching peaceful settlements in Indochina and Korea was placed before an international conference of the countries concerned.

It is, of course, difficult to estimate the extent to which United Nations action contributes to settlement of particular disputes since there are always other factors which bear on international problems and their solution. Among the questions, however, that have been solved or in which conditions have markedly improved since the time they were first brought before the Security Council are those involving Iran, Indonesia, Syria and Lebanon, Greece, and the Berlin blockade. On the other hand, the Palestine, Kashmir, and Korean disputes remain unsettled although hostilities have been halted in these cases. With respect to Indonesia both a termination of fighting and a political settlement were achieved under the auspices of the Security Council.

In the case of disputes which have been before the General Assembly the record is also a mixed one. As previously indicated, the Greek situation has greatly improved, but the Palestine and Korean disputes are still unsettled, although hostilities have halted. No final solutions have been reached in the problems of German unification, the Austrian treaty, the Indian minority in South Africa, and the Tunisian and Moroccan controversies. The case of the Italian colonies has been disposed of, but success in this instance was practically assured by the previous agreement of the great powers to accept the Assembly's recommendations in this matter.

It is not easy to summarize the activity of the United Nations in the field of pacific settlement. In the first place, there is a question of definition as to what constitutes a "dispute" or "situation." Furthermore, certain questions have been considered by both the Security Council and the General Assembly. In the summary for the Security Council which follows are included all disputes and situations actually placed on the agenda of that body. The summary for the General Assembly contains only disputes between specific nations, including those also considered by the Council. It does not include controversies of a general nature such as those involved in disarmament.[8]

---

[8] The appendix contains a detailed narrative of each of the disputes and situations liste

A list of disputes or situations before the Security Council, 1946–54 (Sept. 1) [9]

Dispute or situation	Introduced by—	Date	Status
Iranian question	Iran	Jan. 19, 1946	Soviet forces withdrew from Iran in 1946.
Greek question	U. S. S. R. Ukrainian S. S. R. Greece	Jan. 21, 1946 Aug. 24, 1946 Dec. 3, 1946	In 1947 the Council dropped from its agenda the question of Communist-backed guerrilla activity in Greece. It was then taken up by the Assembly. (See Assembly list below.)
Indonesian question	Ukrainian S. S. R. Australia and India	Jan. 21, 1946 July 30, 1947	In 1949 with the agreement of the Dutch, an independent state of Indonesia was established.
Syrian and Lebanese question	Syria and Lebanon	Feb. 4, 1946	Britain and France withdrew their troops from Syria and Lebanon in 1946.
Spanish question	Poland	April 1946	The Soviet Union vetoed several resolutions providing that the Assembly take what it regarded as too limited action on Franco Spain. The Council then dropped the question from its agenda. (For subsequent developments see Assembly list below.)
Corfu Channel incidents	United Kingdom	Jan. 10, 1947	The Council recommended that the dispute be submitted to the International Court of Justice.
Egyptian question	Egypt	July 8, 1947	The Council did not agree on what action to take regarding British troops in Egypt.
Palestine question	Secretary General	Dec. 2, 1947	Israel and the Arab States concluded armistice agreements in 1949. (See also Assembly list below.)
India-Pakistan (Kashmir) question.	India	Jan. 1, 1948	The Council arranged a cease-fire in 1949 but thus far no political settlement of the dispute has been achieved.
Czechoslovak situation	Chile	Mar. 12, 1948	The Soviet Union vetoed a proposal to appoint a committee of investigation.
Trieste question	Italian Peace Treaty Yugoslavia	1947 July 29, 1948	The Council failed to agree on a Governor for Trieste and rejected Yugoslav charges that agreements between the Allied Command in Trieste and Italy were invalid.
Hyderabad question	Hyderabad Pakistan	Aug. 21, 1948 Oct. 6, 1948	After India occupied Hyderabad the Council discontinued discussion of the matter.
Berlin blockade	United Kingdom, United States, and France.	Sept. 29, 1948	In 1949 an agreement to lift the blockade was reached outside the United Nations by the countries concerned.
Korean question	United States	June 25, 1950	During the temporary absence of the Soviet Union the Council recommended that the members of the United Nations furnish aid to South Korea to repel the Communist attack. Later when the Soviet Union vetoed a resolution on Chinese intervention the Council removed the Korean question from its agenda. (See Assembly list below.)
Formosa question	Communist China	Aug. 24, 1950	The Council rejected Communist resolutions accusing the United States of "aggression" in Formosa.
Bombing China mainland	do	Aug. 28, 1950	The U. S. S. R. vetoed a commission to investigate Communist Chinese allegations of American air attacks on China.
Anglo-Iranian question	United Kingdom	Sept. 28, 1951	The question lapsed when the International Court ruled it had no jurisdiction over it.
Geneva Protocol on bacterial warfare.	U. S. S. R.	June 14, 1952	The Council rejected a Soviet resolution appealing for ratification of protocol on bacterial warfare.
Bacterial warfare	United States	June 20, 1952	The Soviet Union vetoed an investigation of Communist charges that United Nations forces in Korea had employed bacterial warfare.

See footnote at end of table, p. 127.

A list of disputes or situations before the Security Council, 1946–54 (Sept. 1)[9]—Con.

Dispute or situation	Introduced by—	Date	Status
Threat to Thailand from Indochina conflict.	Thailand_____	May 29, 1954__	The Soviet Union vetoed a resolution providing for dispatch of United Nations observers to Thailand.
"Aggression" against Guatemala.	Guatemala_____	June 19, 1954__	The Soviet Union vetoed referral of Guatemalan complaint to the Organization of American States. The Council then called for "immediate termination" of hostile action and requested all members of U. N. not to assist in hostilities.

[9] Based partly on L. Larry Leonard, International Organization, New York, McGraw-Hill Book Co., 1951, p. 185.

List of political controversies before the General Assembly, 1946–54 (Sept. 1)

Controversy	Introduced by—	Date	Status
Indians in South Africa_____	India_____	1946	The Assembly attempted to assist negotiations between South Africa and India and Pakistan for a settlement of the problem of the South Africa Indian minority.
Spanish question_____	Belgium, Czechoslovakia, Denmark, Norway, and Venezuela.	1946	In 1950 the Assembly withdrew its previous recommendation that diplomatic representatives be recalled from Franco Spain and that Spain be barred from certain international agencies.
Palestine question_____	United Kingdom_____	1947	The Assembly has not succeeded in achieving a final political settlement.
Greek question_____	United States_____	1947	Communist-supported guerrilla activity has now subsided.
Korean question_____	(a) Korean independence: United States.	1947	A truce has been achieved but not the unification of Korea.
	(b) Communist China's intervention. United States. United Kingdom. Cuba. Ecuador. France. Norway.	1950	Communist China was found to be an aggressor in Korea and the adoption of economic sanctions was recommended to member countries. An armistice between the United Nations Command and the Communist forces was concluded in 1953. No political settlement has been reached.
Italian colonies_____	United States, United Kingdom, France, and U. S. S. R.	1948	By prior agreement of the great powers the Assembly made political disposition of the former Italian colonies of Libya, Somaliland, and Eritrea.
Human rights in Bulgaria, Hungary, and Rumania.	Bolivia, Australia_____	1949	Despite Assembly resolutions, the 3 countries in question have not observed their treaty obligations regarding human rights.
Soviet threat to Chinese independence.	Nationalist China_____	1949	The Assembly adopted a resolution in 1952 declaring the Soviet Union had failed to carry out its treaty with China.
"Aggression" against Communist China	U. S. S. R_____	1950	The Assembly rejected Soviet charges of United States "aggression" against China.
German unification_____	United States, United Kingdom, and France.	1951	Because of Soviet noncooperation a United Nations commission was unable to complete its investigation of election conditions in Germany.
Hostile activities against Yugoslavia.	Yugoslavia_____	1951	The Assembly recommended that Communist governments in Eastern Europe settle their disputes with Yugoslavia in the spirit of the United Nations Charter.
"Aggressive acts" of the United States.	U. S. S. R_____	1951	The Assembly rejected a Soviet resolution condemning the United States Mutual Security Act.
Morocco_____	13 Arab-Asian States_____	1952	The Assembly expressed its "hope" that France and Morocco would continue negotiations for developing the "free political institutions" of the latter.

List of political controversies before the General Assembly, 1946-54—Continued

Controversy	Introduced by—	Date	Status
Tunisia	13 Arab-Asian States	1952	The Assembly expressed its confidence that France and Tunisia would continue negotiations to promote self-government in the latter country.
Austrian treaty	Brazil	1952	The Assembly appealed to the powers occupying Austria to reach agreement on a treaty with that country.
Race conflict in South Africa	13 Arab-Asian States	1952	The Assembly called on "all" member states to observe the charter provisions on human rights.
Chinese troops in Burma	Burma	1953	The Assembly urged evacuation of the Chinese forces in Burma.

IV. PACIFIC SETTLEMENT AND THE VETO

THE "CHAIN OF EVENTS" CONCEPT

A principal issue with respect to pacific settlement concerns the veto right of the five permanent members. As previously pointed out, there was considerable sentiment at San Francisco in favor of eliminating the veto in decisions in this category. This sentiment was based on the view that the Security Council should not be tied up by the unanimity rule at a stage when only recommendations for settlement of disputes were involved. Recommendations did not place any greater burden on the permanent powers than on other members as, it was conceded, would be the case in enforcement measures.

The permanent powers, however, maintained at the time that the veto was necessary in both categories of decisions, justifying their insistence by the concept of the "chain of events." By this was meant that the right of veto could be safeguarded in connection with enforcement measures only if the permanent powers also had the right of veto in the earlier stages of action on a dispute. Otherwise they maintained they might become so committed, so enmeshed, in the efforts to settle a dispute that they could not, or at least would find it difficult, to exercise freedom of choice if a decision on enforcement action eventually became necessary. Consequently, to guarantee the efficacy of the veto right in regard to enforcement action under chapter VII, the permanent members claimed the right also to veto measures relating to pacific settlement under chapter VI.

Opponents of the "chain of events" concept have argued [10] that there is no direct connection between chapters VI and VII of the charter, and that it is entirely possible to make the veto applicable in the latter category and not in the former. At one stage in the drafting of the charter a specific link between measures for pacific settlement and enforcement action was actually considered.[11] Its adoption would have established a definite bond between chapters VI and VII.[12]

---

[10] Eduardo Jimenez de Arechaga, Voting and the Handling of Disputes in the Security Council, New York, Carnegie Endowment for International Peace, 1950, pp. 40-42.

[11] The Dumbarton Oaks proposals included a paragraph at the beginning of the section on enforcement action which stated: "Should the Security Council deem that a failure to settle a dispute in accordance [with recommendations for pacific settlement] constitutes a threat to the maintenance of international peace and security, it should take any measures necessary for the maintenance of international peace and security in accordance with the purposes and principles of the Organization." This passage would have imposed a duty upon the Security Council to make a decision as to whether failure to act according to its recommendations for pacific settlement had generated a threat to the peace, and if so, to go ahead with enforcement measures. Quoted in U. S. Congress, Senate Committee on Foreign Relations, Charter of the United Nations Hearings, 1945, Washington, Government Printing Office, 1945, p. 275. This section of the hearings contains a discussion of the relationship between chs. VI and VII.

[12] Jimenez, op. cit., pp. 40-41.

At the San Francisco Conference, however, the proposal was not adopted. The link which it provided, therefore, does not now exist between chapters VI and VII of the charter.

As it is now, before the gap between the two chapters can be bridged and before enforcement action can be taken under chapter VII, opponents of the "chain of events" doctrine argue, the Council must decide either explicitly or implicitly that there is a threat to the peace, a breach of the peace, or an act of aggression. According to this view, then, even if the veto were removed on pacific settlement, any permanent member could prevent a dispute from crossing the gap and could conceivably block action under chapter VII simply by vetoing a finding that an unsettled dispute involves a threat to the peace, a breach of the peace, or an act of aggression.

THE VANDENBERG RESOLUTION

At San Francisco in 1945 the United States supported the use of the veto in decisions on pacific settlement. By 1948, however, this position had changed. On June 11 of that year the Senate passed the Vandenberg resolution [13] by a vote of 64 to 4. The first point of the resolution expressed the sense of the Senate that the United States should attempt to obtain in the United Nations:

Voluntary agreement to remove the veto from all questions involving pacific settlements of international disputes and situations, and from the admission of new members.

Senator Vandenberg contended that, if the pacific settlement provisions of the charter could be made to work, it would rarely be necessary to bring into operation those portions of the charter providing for enforcement action. The report of the Senate Foreign Relations Committee on the resolution stated that it was precisely in the areas of pacific settlement and admission of new members that the Security Council had been hampered up to that time. The committee thought that if the veto could be removed at these two points, the Security Council would be freed to a great extent from the undesirable features of its voting procedure.[14]

The United States subsequently supported recommendations, approved by the General Assembly on April 14, 1949, which advocated a curb on use of the veto in the Security Council. In effect the recommendations of the Assembly called among other things for the elimination of the veto in decisions under chapter VI of the charter. Thus far, however, Soviet opposition has prevented the adoption of these recommendations.

PARTIAL ELIMINATION OF THE VETO

Under the present practice of the Security Council, the right of veto does not extend to such matters as placing a dispute on the agenda and determining times and places of Council meetings to discuss it. These are "procedural matters" which are exempt from the veto. Beyond this point, however, the device has been invoked repeatedly. As a possible method of curbing the use of the veto

[13] S. Res. 239, 80th Cong. Senate Foreign Relations Committee Subcommittee on the United Nations Charter, Review of the United Nations Charter, Collection of Documents, U. S. Government Printing Office, 1954, pp. 140-141, hereinafter referred to as Collection of Documents.
[14] Ibid., pp. 134-135.

simply by a revised interpretation of present procedures, it has been argued that—

When the Security Council merely recommends methods of adjustment to the disputant parties, its function amounts purely to a choice of what the charter calls "procedures" and therefore, should, under the charter, be governed by a procedural vote * * * [15]

This interpretation of chapter VI would eliminate the veto in "calling upon" states to settle their disputes and in recommending procedures of settlement; it would not remove the veto, however, on recommendations of terms of settlement.[16] Presumably the revision of interpretation could be carried further, perhaps even to the point of total elimination of the veto in questions of pacific settlement, provided there was agreement to this effect among the permanent members. The fact is, however, that they have not so interpreted chapter VI and the Soviet Union particularly has shown no inclination to do so. Time and practice have tended to harden the interpretation currently in effect.

THE VETO AND INTERNATIONAL AGREEMENT

Elimination of the veto in cases of pacific settlement may not necessarily facilitate solutions of international problems. In the first place, the charter provisions in this category confer only recommendatory powers on the Security Council. Without the veto the Council could have conceivably recommended procedures or even terms of settlement in a great many more disputes than has actually been the case. While such recommendations might carry the pressure of international public opinion behind them, the fact is that one or more of the disputants could still reject them without necessarily violating the charter since there is nothing in the document compelling acceptance of such recommendations. Beyond this consideration, it is contended that the ultimate objective in pacific settlement is agreement. As long as there is fundamental disagreement between the Communist and Western Powers, according to some observers, a ban on the veto would not necessarily promote international harmony. For instance, the Soviet Union in 1947 used the veto to block a resolution in the Security Council designed to relieve international tension between Greece and Albania, Bulgaria, and Yugoslavia. Subsequently, the General Assembly, where the veto does not exist, successfully passed a resolution with similar provisions. But the latter resolution had no greater discernible effect on the latter three states: they continued their hostile campaign against Greece. Thus the veto might go, it is argued, but the problems may well remain. In other words the real obstacle in pacific settlement as well as in other matters involving the Security Council, according to this view, lies in the conflict between the Communist and Western Powers and not in the device of the veto.

---

[15] Jimenez, op. cit., p. 38.
[16] See the above categories of decisions mentioned in sec. II.

V. Proposals for Strengthening the Power of the Security Council in Pacific Settlement

The charter does not obligate any country to comply with the Security Council's recommendations under chapter VI. When the Council "calls upon" countries to settle their disputes by mediation, arbitration, or some other pacific procedure, or when it proposes a settlement, these are only recommendations and, although they possess a certain moral force, they are not binding under the charter. Even in chapter VII, which authorizes the Security Council to take enforcement action against states that threaten or break the peace, the authority extends only to maintaining or restoring peace and security. It does not include enforcement of a solution.

EFFORTS TO STRENGTHEN THE COUNCIL

A number of changes have been proposed to strengthen the voluntary procedures of pacific settlement. One such proposal was contained in a resolution which the General Assembly passed on April 28, 1949. The resolution recommended that the Security Council adopt the procedure of appointing a rapporteur or conciliator for disputes brought to the attention of the Security Council.[17] The resolution noted that in the League of Nations cases were presented to the Council of the League by a rapporteur who had the function of conciliation—

and that this practice allowed private conversations among the parties and the rapporteur and avoided the crystallization of views that tends to result from taking a stated public position.

According to the resolution, the parties to a dispute before the Security Council should be invited to meet with the President of the Council and attempt to agree upon a member of the Council to act as rapporteur or conciliator. If a rapporteur or conciliator were appointed, the resolution suggested that—

it would be desirable for the Security Council to abstain from further action on the case for a reasonable interval during which actual efforts at conciliation are in progress.

The Security Council on May 24, 1950, agreed to base itself, on appropriate occasions, on the principles of the resolution, but has not yet used the recommended procedure.[18] If it were utilized, the rapporteur in many cases might be able to progress toward solution of the dispute before positions became crystallized on the open stage of the Council. On the other hand, utilization of the procedure might lead to delays and to charges of "secret" proceedings.

ENFORCEMENT OF SOLUTIONS

The adoption of the practice of using rapporteurs would not alter the recommendatory nature of the Security Council's functions. Such is not the case, however, with the change suggested by the action of the General Assembly in the Palestine problem. The Assembly proposed that the Security Council enforce the partition

---

[17] Yearbook of the United Nations, 1948–49, pp. 412–416.
[18] However, the President of the Security Council entered into private consultations with various representatives during the course of the India-Pakistan and Berlin questions, Jimenez, op. cit., pp. 71–72.

plan. But the Council maintained that it did not have such authority under the charter. In 1948 when the Palestine question was before the Security Council, Ambassador Warren Austin of the United States argued that [19]—

The Charter of the United Nations does not empower the Security Council to enforce a political settlement whether it is pursuant to a recommendation of the General Assembly or of the Security Council itself.
  * * * The Security Council, under the charter, can take action to prevent aggression against Palestine from outside. * * * But this action must be directed solely to the maintenance of international peace. The Security Council's action, in other words, is directed to keeping the peace and not to enforcing partition.

If the Security Council possessed the power to enforce solutions of controversies,[20] it has been argued that many disputes might be prevented from ever reaching a fighting stage. To the extent that the Council would be able to compel resort to arbitration or judicial processes, the final settlements might also be more in accordance with law or justice. As it is, the voluntary procedures of pacific settlement now used are largely based on political compromise which may or may not arrive at solutions which are "just." The very existence of the power to enforce peaceful solutions, moreover, might mean that solutions could be reached more quickly.

On the other hand, compulsory procedures might not safeguard what nations regard as their rights of sovereignty. Nor, under international compulsory procedures, might an individual country assure protection of what it considers to be its national interests or honor.

The present charter provisions with respect to pacific settlement reflect the fact that the states at San Francisco were reluctant on the whole to surrender what they hold to be their vital interests, their political independence and honor to the custody of other nations or to any international agency. They reflect, further, the belief that lasting solutions of disputes between sovereign states cannot be achieved except by the free consent of the parties.

VI. The General Assembly and Pacific Settlement

The General Assembly appears to have been regarded originally by the drafters of the charter as a body which might discuss controversies but not act on them, at least not on major controversies.[21] Since its inception, however, the Assembly has come more and more to the fore in United Nations activities. This development, as previously pointed out, has been due in major part to the dissension among the permanent powers of the Security Council.

Experience has shown that unity of action on the part of these powers is in fact difficult to obtain. In those few instances, when

[19] Quoted in H. Field Haviland, Jr   The Political Role of the General Assembly, New York, Carnegie Endowment for International Peace, 1951, p. 102.
[20] This power might possibly be in a form similar to that provided by the unadopted Geneva Protocol of 1924. The protocol would have given the League of Nations Council the authority to make binding decisions in disputes or to refer them to a committee of arbitrators whose decisions would have been binding. Any state which did not abide by its obligations under the League would have been considered an "aggressor" and subject to sanctions ordered by the Council.
[21] "From a study of the evolution of the text it would appear that, while the Charter was not intended to prevent the General Assembly from dealing with disputes and situations, the thought was very definitely present that a distinction should be made between disputes and situations constituting serious threats to the peace and others of ɩ less serious character, and that in the case of the more serious disputes and situations, they should be referred to the Security Council, not alone for enforcement action, but also for such other action under chapters. VI and VII as might be appropriate." Leland M. Goodrich, Development of the General Assembly, op. cit., p. 249.

there has been at least a degree of common purpose, even of a temporary nature among them, the machinery of the Council has functioned in pacific settlement somewhat in the fashion that was originally intended. This was true, for example, in the cases of Indonesia and Kashmir. Far more often than not, however, the permanent members have clashed on the issues which have come before the Council and one or more of them have frequently been directly involved in these issues.

Experience has also shown that at the present time, the most dangerous threat to peace does not originate from the source contemplated when the charter was established. Then there was a residual concern over the possible reappearance of aggression fostered by one of the Axis Powers or from some source other than the principal victors of World War II. As it has turned out, however, the principal threat to the peace of the world has originated from one of the victors, the Soviet Union, and nations and groups within its orbit of influence.

PACIFIC SETTLEMENT IN THE GENERAL ASSEMBLY

As the developments discussed above have made it extremely difficult for the Security Council to discharge its functions of peaceful settlement, members of the United Nations have turned increasingly to the General Assembly to supply the machinery for this purpose. The Assembly has not replaced the Security Council with respect to questions of pacific settlement. But it has been able to act at times when the Council has been unable to act. It has given an opportunity to the smaller powers to participate in decisions of pacific settlement and such decisions have constituted a kind of expression of world sentiment that has undoubtedly had considerable moral significance. The Assembly moreover has also obtained an additional element of power, under the Uniting for Peace Resolution of 1950, that of recommending to members the use of sanctions to restore peace.

A characteristic of the activity of the General Assembly in connection with pacific settlement has been its flexibility and lack of formal machinery.[22] Informal mediative functions have been performed by the President of the General Assembly, by committee chairmen, and by subcommittees. Subsidiary agencies have been established, such as the Mediator in Palestine and the Special Committee on the Balkans.

The various methods employed have been designed for particular purposes in connection with specific questions.[23] The device used by the General Assembly in each case has generally been tailormade, so to speak, to fit the situation. Permanent machinery of peaceful settlement has not been devised, with one or two possible exceptions which will be discussed later.

Despite the flexibility of the present system, it does not assure compliance with the recommendations of the General Assembly. The most skillfully contrived procedure of pacific settlement can be nullified by a disputant who ignores the Assembly's recommendations. In an effort to obtain compliance, the General Assembly has employed several methods.[24] First of all, disputants are reminded of

[22] Haviland, op. cit., p. 89.
[23] A possible exception is the Peace Observation Commission mentioned below.
[24] Haviland, op. cit., pp. 96–103.

the obligations they assumed when they signed the charter. Secondly, as much moral weight as possible is mustered in the form of large voting majorities on recommendations. A third method, which has been used to a very limited extent, is that of "advance commitments" from the disputants. This device was successfully employed in connection with the disposition of the former Italian colonies, when the interested parties agreed among themselves, in advance, to accept the Assembly's decision in the matter. Still another technique is "observation" or "surveillance" of disputes, often "on the spot" by committees and mediators. For example, the United Nations Special Committee on the Balkans was set up in 1947 to assist Yugoslavia, Albania, Bulgaria, and Greece to cooperate in settling their dispute. In 1948, the General Assembly appointed a Mediator for Palestine, who supervised the carrying out of the instructions of the Assembly in that troubled area. By thus keeping continuous watch over problems, the Assembly may exert considerable influence on the parties involved.

STRENGTHENING THE ASSEMBLY WITHIN THE CHARTER

The General Assembly has taken several formal steps to enlarge or reinforce its functions in pacific settlement. Among these was the creation of the Interim Committee and the establishment of a Panel for Inquiry and Conciliation. Two other proposals for strengthening the Assembly, the creation of a Permanent Committee of Conciliation and the establishment of a Permanent Commission of Good Offices, have not been adopted.[25]

The Interim Committee was established on November 13, 1947, at a time when it was becoming increasingly apparent that the permanent powers on the Security Council were seriously divided and member nations were turning more and more to the General Assembly. This Committee which was to include the full membership of the Assembly was designed primarily to give continuity to the work of that body. It was to operate in the period between sessions of the Assembly—hence its title. The Interim Committee was empowered to take action in connection with specific disputes or situations, and it was also called upon to make a systematic study of international political cooperation, including the problem of pacific settlement.

The Interim Committee, however, has not been very active. It has been assigned certain limited functions to be carried on when the General Assembly is not in session.[26] It has also carried out study assignments.[27] "Yet in the years since its establishment the Committee has never on its own initiative considered any situation or dispute or created a commission of inquiry."[28] Since the beginning of 1951, it has met only rarely and then only for organizational and procedural purposes. The General Assembly has tended, when important questions have arisen, to remain in session to deal with them itself. From the outset, the Soviet bloc has boycotted the Committee.

Another formal step taken by the General Assembly to assist in pacific settlement was the creation of a Panel for Inquiry and Con-

---

[25] The Panel for Inquiry and Conciliation and the proposed Committee of Conciliation could also be employed by the Security Council.

[26] For example, in 1948 when the Assembly was not in session, the Interim Committee gave guidance to the United Nations Commission which had been established to assist in holding Korean elections.

[27] For example, in 1947 the Assembly authorized the Interim Committee to study methods of promoting international cooperation in the political field including the problem of pacific settlement.

[28] Haviland, op. cit., p. 155.

ciliation in 1949. The panel was intended to assist member states to seek solutions of their disputes by peaceful means. Its purpose was to make readily available qualified persons for service on commissions of inquiry or conciliation.[29] To date this panel has never been used.

The Peace Observation Commission, established by the Uniting for Peace Resolution of 1950, may be employed for observing and reporting on situations likely to endanger international peace. Although not originally intended to engage in pacific settlement, the Peace Observation Commission could conceivably play a role in that field.[30]

Two other major proposals have been made within the Assembly to help the member nations carry out their pledge to settle differences peacefully, but they have not been adopted.

The first of these was advanced by Lebanon in 1948.[31] It called for the creation of a Permanent Committee of Conciliation, composed of nine members of the United Nations, as a subsidiary organ of the General Assembly. The proposed Committee would be empowered to consider disputes submitted to it by interested parties, the General Assembly, or the Security Council. If agreement were not reached, the Committee would submit a report setting forth the reasons for the quarrel and formulating proposals for the adjustment of the conflict.

A Permanent Commission of Good Offices was proposed by Yugoslavia in 1950. This proposed Commission was also envisioned as a subsidiary organ of the General Assembly, composed of 12 United Nations members, 6 of which would be the nonpermanent members of the Security Council while the remaining 6 would be elected by the General Assembly. The Good Offices Commission in appropriate cases would advise parties to a dispute to open or resume direct negotiations, or if mediation appeared feasible, the Commission would advise the parties to accept such mediation either from itself, from third states, or from individuals.

In arguing against the Permanent Committee of Conciliation and the Permanent Commission of Good Offices, opponents expressed doubt as to the need of new formal machinery for the task of conciliation, and tended to favor small temporary bodies where necessary for the purpose. Proponents of these proposals asserted that permanent organs would afford their personnel opportunities to profit from constant association and continuous experience with the problems of conciliation which members of temporary bodies do not possess. A further contention might be that the constant availability of these permanent organs could tend to influence disputing countries to resort to them. Moreover, the General Assembly and the Security Council might, on suitable occasions, give more point to their recommendations for peaceful settlement by calling attention to the availability of these permanent commissions.

THE ASSEMBLY AND COMPULSORY PROCEDURES

The actions to reinforce the role of the Assembly which have been discussed above do not affect the voluntary character of its procedures for pacific settlement under the charter. None of them contemplates

---

[29] The resolution gave rather detailed directions whereby each state might designate persons fitted to serve on such commissions and directed the Secretary-General of the United Nations to take administrative charge of the list (or panel) of such persons.

[30] Haviland, op. cit., p. 90.

[31] United Nations, Interim Committee of the General Assembly, Lebanon: Proposal for the Creation of a Permanent Committee of Conciliation, A/AC.18/15, Jan. 28, 1948.

enforcement of any kind. Other proposals have been advanced which would involve some degree of compulsion. These proposals would result in significant changes in the present charter or would establish additional machinery for pacific settlement outside the United Nations.

One of the latter type is the so-called General Act. The General Act is a draft treaty which was originally concluded in 1928 under the auspices of the League of Nations. Signatories agree that disputes of every kind that are not resolved by diplomacy must be submitted to conciliation or in some cases to the International Court of Justice or an arbitral tribunal.

On April 28, 1949, the General Assembly adopted a resolution restoring to the General Act its "original efficacy."[32] The United Nations Secretary General was instructed to hold the act open to accession by states under the title, Revised General Act for the Pacific Settlement of International Disputes. The act is automatically in force for those nations acceding to it.

A stricter regime of pacific settlement is initiated among those countries which acede to the General Act than exists at present under the United Nations. For them, resort to conciliation, arbitration or judicial settlement in disputes is compulsory.[33]

The attitude of the powers toward the compulsory and formalized procedures of the General Act is suggested by the fact that, although in 1949 in the Assembly 45 countries voted to restore its efficacy, and only 6 against (there was 1 abstention), to date only 4 countries have acceded to the act.[34]

Another proposal involving compulsion, that put forth by Messrs. Clark and Sohn, would permit either the General Assembly or the Council to "direct" that disputes involving questions of law, such as interpretation of a treaty, be submitted to the International Court of Justice.[35] The General Assembly would also decide upon measures to compel compliance with the decision of the Court. At the present time, the compulsory jurisdiction of the Court in legal cases of this kind extends only to those States which have accepted such jurisdiction.

The same proposal also provides for a World Equity Tribunal to make recommendations for settling "nonlegal" disputes referred to it by either the Assembly or the Council.[36] Compulsion to enforce the recommendations of this tribunal is not provided for under the proposal. However, it would possess authority to render binding decisions on questions voluntarily submitted to it by member nations.

VII. Concluding Comments

Some attempts have been made within the charter to strengthen the noncompulsory procedures of both the Security Council and the General Assembly in peaceful settlement. The measures proposed have often been of relatively minor importance and those which have been adopted have not been notably successful.

---

[32] Yearbook of the United Nations, 1948–49, pp. 412–416.
[33] Since the terms provide that countries may accede only to specified parts of the treaty if they do not want to accede to the whole, the obligations of the acceding states may vary.
[34] Belgium, Denmark, Norway, and Sweden.
[35] Grenville Clark and Louis B. Sohn, Peace Through Disarmament and Charter Revision: Detailed Proposals for Revision of the United Nations Charter, preliminary print, 1953, p. 65. The proposals here described apply to disputes and situations "of so serious a character as to endanger international peace and security."
[36] That is, "the questions involved should be considered from the standpoint of what is reasonable, just and fair, rather than upon strictly legal principles," Clark and Sohn, op. cit., p. 70.

The grant of some form of compulsory authority, not merely to prevent or to stop aggression, but to enforce settlements of disputes has been suggested in some proposals as a means of strengthening the role of the Assembly and the Council in keeping the peace.

Such a grant, however, would restrict the sovereign rights of member nations. The reluctance of states to accept restrictions of this kind involves questions of national prestige and honor. It also involves the absence of a commonly accepted code of international law. States are hesitant to entrust important national interests to international courts and tribunals which now must apply a law that is often uncertain or even nonexistent. In this connection, the late Senator Robert A. Taft contended that "in the long run the only way to establish peace is to write a law, agreed to by each of the nations, to govern the relations of such nations with each other and to obtain the covenant of all such nations that they will abide by that law and by decisions made thereunder." [37] At present the International Court of Justice is available to members of the United Nations for settlement of international disputes. However, in practice only a limited number of such disputes—generally those of a "legal" nature—are considered suitable for submission to the Court.[38]

Even if a code of "world law" were developed which would cover most or all of the disputes which arise among states, that in itself would not guarantee acceptance of a compulsory system for settling differences. Many nations might still be inclined to pursue first of all their own particular interests, and would refuse to agree to what they would consider a diminution of their sovereign powers.

In these circumstances would additional emphasis placed on the role of the United Nations in encouraging the peaceful settlement of dispute be meaningful? Or is the most that should be sought an improvement in procedures both in the General Assembly and the Security Council for the peaceful settlement of disputes including that which is presently United States policy, the restriction of the veto in this sphere?

Any changes in the United Nations system of pacific settlement, if they are undertaken in connection with charter review, will not be undertaken in a vacuum. There is a close relationship in the United Nations Charter between collective enforcement of security and peaceful settlement. Article 1 mentions both types of functions as means of fulfilling a primary purpose of the charter—the maintenance of international peace and security. But it assigns no greater weight or priority to either.

In practice there may be contradiction or conflict between the two functions.[39] Concentration, whether planned or accidental, on enforcement measures may engender attitudes and habits of action that are inappropriate for effective performance of pacific settlement, or vice versa.

As confidence in the Security Council was undermined by the Soviet Union's abuse of the veto, many countries began to reexamine these

[37] A Foreign Policy for Americans, Garden City, N. Y., Doubleday & Co., 1951, p. 39.
[38] Since 1945 the United States has been party to two international disputes which have been referred to the International Court. These were the cases concerning rights of United States nationals in Morocco and concerning monetary gold removed from Rome in 1943.
[39] James N. Hyde, The United Nations and the Peaceful Adjustment of Disputes, Proceedings of the Academy of Political Science, January 1953, p. 212.

two basic functions of the United Nations. The reappraisal was much more concerned with the problem of collective security than with pacific settlement. Regional and other types of security arrangements (such as the North Atlantic Treaty Organization) began to spring up in various areas of the world to supplement such protection against aggression as the charter offered. Attempts were also made to strengthen the General Assembly as a security organ. At the same time, relatively little energy was expended in efforts to improve the peaceful settlement procedures of the United Nations.

The questions posed by proposals to change the peaceful settlement provisions of the charter are essentially three:

First, it has been argued that the United Nations or some successor organization should serve as an enforcement agency directed at the Soviet bloc as the principal threat to peace.

Second, it has been contended that the United Nations should be considered essentially as a "meeting place" where disputes can be solved peacefully by negotiation while security would be protected primarily by regional and other defense arrangements associated with the organization largely in principles.[40]

Third and finally, it has been maintained that the organization must act both as an agency of enforcement and an organization of pacific settlement on the grounds that the function of pacific settlement cannot be discharged successfully unless behind it is the power to invoke measures of collective security.[41]

In Korea, for the first time, both principal functions of the United Nations have become deeply involved. As an agency of collective security the organization, acting through a supreme command established under the United States and relying heavily on this country for the necessary military force, moved to counter Communist aggression. As an organ of pacific settlement it has sought at the same time to solve the problems arising from the political division of Korea.

There is no question that the military action prevented the conquest of all of Korea by an act of aggression. It is a question, however, whether the action has assisted the efforts of the organization to settle the Korean political problem which still remains unsolved. It is also a question whether limitations on military action in Korea, adopted in part at least out of consideration for the policies of participants in the United Nations campaign, adversely affected the pursuit of our own policy.

[40] Sir Gladwyn Jebb, The Free World and the United Nations, Foreign Affairs (New York), vol. 31, April 1953, 383–391.
[41] Byron Dexter, Locarno Again, Foreign Affairs, vol. 32, October 1953, 34–47, Hamilton Fish Armstrong, The Grand Alliance Hesitates, ibid., pp. 48–67, Benjamin V. Cohen, Collective Security Under Law, Department of State Bulletin, vol. 26, Jan. 21, 1952, 98–102.

APPENDIX

Brief Summaries of Political Controversies Before the Security Council and General Assembly, 1946–54 September 1 [1]

I. THE SECURITY COUNCIL

The Iranian question.—The Iranian Government on January 19, 1946, formally complained to the United Nations that the interference of Soviet officials and armed forces [2] in the internal affairs of Iran might lead to international friction. The Security Council discussed the question but in view of the fact that both parties affirmed their willingness to settle the matter by direct negotiation, the Council adjourned discussion to give them an opportunity to do so. In April Iran asked the Security Council to drop the issue in view of the progress of the negotiations with the Soviet Union. Although Soviet forces were subsequently withdrawn, the Council retained the question as an inactive item on its agenda.

The Greek question.—The U. S. S. R. complained on January 21, 1946, that the presence of British troops in Greece constituted interference in the internal affairs of that country. The Council, after debate, decided to consider the question closed. In August 1946 the Ukrainian delegate complained about border incidents between Greece and Albania. A United States proposal for a Commission of Investigation was vetoed by the Soviet Union.

Greece in December 1946 asked the Security Council to prevent its neighbors, Albania, Bulgaria, and Yugoslavia, from assisting insurgents against the Greek Government. The Security Council appointed a Commission of Investigation, composed of all the members of the Council, which was instructed to report the facts and propose arrangements for a settlement. While the Commission was making its investigation, the United States announced its proposed program of military and economic aid to Greece. Eight of the eleven members of the Investigating Commission reported to the Security Council in May 1947 that Yugoslavia, Bulgaria, and Albania were responsible for supporting guerrilla warfare in Greece. A United States proposal to continue the Commission was vetoed by the Soviet Union in July 1947. In August of the same year the Soviet vetoed 2 more resolutions, one proposed by Australia stating that the situation on the Greek border was a threat to the peace and calling on the 4 countries concerned to enter into negotiations for a settlement, and another proposed by the United States, designating the situation a threat to the peace, fixing responsibility on Yugoslavia, Albania, and Bulgaria, and calling on these states to stop aiding guerrillas. [3] The Council in September 1947 dropped the Greek question from its agenda, thus opening the way for the General Assembly to consider it.

The Indonesian question.—India and Australia brought the hostilities in Indonesia between the Dutch and the "Republic of Indonesia" to the attention of the Security Council in July 1947. India said the situation endangered the maintenance of international peace. Australia averred that there was a breach of the peace under article 39 of the charter. A Security Council call upon both sides to cease hostilities resulted in the issuance of cease-fire orders, but the hostilities continued. The Security Council created a three-member Committee of Good Offices (the United States, Belgium, and Australia) which arranged a truce, signed aboard the U. S. S. *Renville* on January 17, 1948. However, in December 1948 the Dutch resumed the offensive and captured some of the Indonesian leaders. The Security Council in January 1949 called for a cease-fire and release of the Indonesian leaders, and reconstituted the Committee of Good Offices as the United Nations Commission for Indonesia. The latter was to assist in negotiations for the establishment of a federal, independent, and sovereign United States of

---

[1] These are summaries of the disputes and situations listed above in sec. III of this study.
[2] Soviet troops had not withdrawn from Iran following the close of World War II.
[3] The adoption of either the Australian or American proposal, by designating the Greek situation as a threat to the peace, would have opened the way for enforcement action under ch. VII of the charter.

139

Indonesia. The Indonesians and the Dutch conferred at The Hague from August to November 1949 and agreed that the Netherlands was to transfer sovereignty to the Republic of the United States of Indonesia. A resolution congratulating the parties, welcoming the Republic of Indonesia and requesting the Commission to continue its assistance in implementing The Hague agreements was vetoed by the Soviet Union. The Commission, however, continued to function until it reported on the transfer of sovereignty to Indonesia and the withdrawal of Dutch troops.

The Syrian and Lebanese question.—Syria and Lebanon on February 4, 1946, complained to the Council that British and French troops were still in their countries although the war was over. A resolution expressing confidence that Britain and France would withdraw their troops was vetoed by the Soviet Union. The latter favored a call for immediate withdrawal. However, Britain and France informed the Council of their intention to withdraw their troops and the matter was subsequently dropped from the agenda.

The Spanish question.—Poland in April 1946 called upon the Security Council to take action on the problem of Spain on the grounds that the Franco regime endangered international peace. The Council appointed a subcommittee to investigate. The subcommittee found that the Franco government was not an actual threat to international peace (which would have been grounds for enforcement action under ch. VII) but was a potential danger to international peace. The subcommittee proposed that the General Assembly recommend that the members of the United Nations break diplomatic relations with Franco Spain. The Soviet Union vetoed three resolutions framed to allow the Spanish problem to pass to the jurisdiction of the General Assembly. The Council then merely dropped the Spanish question from its agenda. It was subsequently taken up by the General Assembly.

Corfu Channel question.—A resolution finding Albania responsible for damage to a British warship which struck a mine in the Corfu Channel was vetoed by the Soviet Union. In April 1947 the Security Council recommended that the dispute be submitted to the International Court of Justice.

The Egyptian question.—Egypt in July 1947 formally complained under articles 35 and 37 of the charter that the presence of British troops in Egypt was likely to endanger international peace. The Security Council discussed the matter, but no resolution that was proposed received sufficient votes for passage. The Council retained the question on its agenda without further discussion.

The Palestine question.—At the request of the United Kingdom, which administered Palestine as a mandate from the old League of Nations, the General Assembly began examination of conflicting Jewish and Arab claims to that country in April 1947. After receiving recommendations from an 11-member United Nations Special Committee on Palestine the Assembly, on November 29, 1947, approved a resolution recommending the termination of the mandate and the partition of Palestine into a Jewish State and an Arab State. The resolution requested that the Security Council "take the necessary measures as provided for in the plan for its implementation," and also that it "determine as a threat to the peace, breach of the peace, or act of aggression, in accordance with article 39 of the charter, any attempt to alter by force the settlement envisaged by this resolution." [4] Soon after the passage of the resolution hostilities broke out between the Jews of Palestine and the neighboring Arab States. In the Security Council the United States and other members of the Council maintained that the Council did not have the authority to enforce a settlement of the Palestine problem, but only to maintain international peace. The Council passed a resolution requesting the General Assembly "to consider further the question of the future government of Palestine." [5] The Council then concentrated on ending the hostilities. On July 15, 1948, it adopted a resolution ordering an indefinite cease-fire, and declaring that failure of any government or authority to do so "would demonstrate the existence of a breach of the peace within the meaning of article 39 of the charter requiring immediate considerations by the Security Council with a view to such further action under chapter VII of the charter as may be decided upon by the Council." [6] The order was promptly complied with.

Between February and July 1949, with the assistance of the acting mediator, Dr. Ralph Bunche, armistice agreements were concluded by Israel and the neighboring Arab States of Egypt, Jordan, Syria, and Lebanon.

4 Yearbook of the United Nations, 1947–48, p. 247.
5 Yearbook of the United Nations, 1947–48, pp. 410–411.
6 Yearbook of the United Nations, 1947–48, p. 436.

The Security Council has since considered various charges of breaches of the armistice. One recent case involved diversion of the Jordan River by Israel. A resolution introduced by the United States, the United Kingdom, and France to settle the dispute was vetoed by the Soviet Union in January 1954. Another case concerned restrictions imposed by Egypt on Israel-bound shipping passing through the Suez Canal. On March 29, 1954, the Soviet Union vetoed a resolution calling on Egypt to end such restrictions.

The Kashmir question.—India in January 1948 complained that Pakistan was aiding invaders of the state of Kashmir whose ruler had placed it provisionally under the rule of India.[7] Both Indian and Pakistani troops had entered Kashmir and were engaged in fighting. Pakistan requested the Council to call for the withdrawal of Indian troops from Kashmir.

The Security Council established a United Nations Commission for India and Pakistan, eventually composed of five members, which was to recommend measures for terminating the fighting and for creating conditions for a plebiscite to determine whether Kashmir should accede to India or Pakistan. With the assistance of the United Nations Commission a cease-fire was arranged in January 1949 but no agreement could be reached upon withdrawal of troops. In March 1950 the Council decided to appoint a United Nations representative to help in arranging a withdrawal of troops and to succeed to the responsibilities of the Commission. Neither Sir Owen Dixon, of Australia, nor his successor, Dr. Frank P. Graham, of the United States, was able to arrange either a withdrawal of forces or a plebiscite. When Dr. Graham submitted his report in March 1953 he did not request an extension of his assignment, but instead recommended that India and Pakistan negotiate directly to reach an understanding. The two countries have not yet been able to arrange either a withdrawal of forces or a plebiscite.

The Czechoslovak situation.—Chile on March 12, 1948, asked the Security Council to investigate the situation in Czechoslovakia where the Communists had taken over the Government as a consequence, it was charged, of a threat of force by the U. S. S. R. Both the new and the former representatives of Czechoslovakia at the United Nations were granted an opportunity to appear before the Council. The new representative of Czechoslovakia, however, asserted that the matter was entirely within the domestic jurisdiction of his country and refused to take part in the discussion. A Chilean resolution to appoint a subcommittee of investigation was vetoed by the Soviet Union. Although the Council terminated its discussion, it retained the question on its agenda.

The Trieste question.—The Italian Peace Treaty of 1947 provided that the Governor of the Free Territory of Trieste should be appointed by the Security Council. The Council has never been able to agree on an appointee.

Yugoslavia on July 29, 1948, asked the Security Council to declare that certain agreements made by the United States and Great Britain with Italy in regard to Trieste violated the Italian Peace Treaty. The Council discussed the matter but no proposed resolution received sufficient votes for passage. The Council is still seized of the question.

The Hyderabad question.—Under the India Independence Act of 1947 the state of Hyderabad was given the choice of joining either India or Pakistan. Hyderabad on August 21, 1948, complained to the Security Council that India was threatening its independence and subsequently that it was being invaded by India. The Council took up the dispute, but several days later Hyderabad withdrew its complaint. Some observers doubted, however, whether this gesture represented the true wishes of the Hyderabad Government. Pakistan urged the Council to deal with the question, but India reported that conditions in Hyderabad were peaceful and normal. The Council eventually discontinued discussion of the question but retained it on its agenda.

The Berlin blockade.—In September 1948, the United States, the United Kingdom and France, three of the permanent members of the Security Council, formally complained of the restrictions imposed by the Soviet Union, another permanent member of the Council, on transport and communications between the western zones of Germany and the western sectors of Berlin. The Security Council discussed the matter. The six nonpermanent members of the Council proposed a solution, but it was vetoed by the Soviet Union. Eventually, negotiations between American and Soviet representatives outside the United Nations led to an agreement to lift the Berlin blockade.[8] In May 1949, the three complaining governments informed the United Nations that an agreement had been reached.

---

[7] Kashmir under the India Independence Act of 1947 was free to join either India or Pakistan. The ruler of Kashmir was Hindu but the population was predominantly Moslem, like that of Pakistan.
[8] An important step in starting the negotiations was an informal conversation between an American representative and a Soviet representative in the United Nations delegates' lounge at Lake Success.

The Korean question.—The Korean problem was brought before the Security Council on June 25, 1950, by the United States. The Council passed a resolution designating the armed attack by North Korean forces a breach of the peace and calling for a cessation of hostilities. Two days later the Council approved a resolution recommending that members of the United Nations furnish assistance to South Korea to repel the attack. The U. S. S. R. was absent from the Council at the time these resolutions were passed and thus was not in a position to veto them.

The U. S. S. R. was present, however, when the Council in November 1950, considered a resolution calling upon the Chinese Communists, who had recently entered the conflict, to refrain from assisting the North Koreans. The U. S. S. R. vetoed this resolution. The Council then removed the Korean issue from its agenda. From this point on, the General Assembly assumed the responsibility of enforcement action and of peaceful settlement in Korea.

The Formosa question.—On August 24, 1950, Communist China complained to the Security Council that the movement of United States Armed Forces in and near Formosa constituted aggression against Chinese territory. During Council discussion of the question, two Communist resolutions condemning the American action and calling for withdrawal of its forces did not receive sufficient votes for passage. The Council discontinued its discussion but kept the item on its agenda.

Bombing China mainland.—By communications of August 28 and 30, 1950, Communist China complained that United States aircraft had attacked Chinese territory. The Council rejected a Soviet resolution condemning the United States for illegal attacks on China. The Soviet Union vetoed an American resolution for the establishment of a commission to investigate the Chinese allegations. The Council terminated its discussion but retained the question on its agenda.

Anglo-Iranian question.—The United Kingdom on September 28, 1951, complained that Iran had failed to comply with certain provisional measures indicated by the International Court of Justice pending a decision whether or not it had jurisdiction in the Anglo-Iranian Oil Co. case. The Council decided to adjourn discussion pending the International Court's ruling on its competence. The Court decided in July 1952, that it had no jurisdiction in the case. Its order for provisional measures therefore automatically lapsed.

Geneva protocol on bacterial warfare.—The U. S. S. R. on June 14, 1952, submitted a resolution asking the Security Council to appeal to all states which had not ratified the Geneva Protocol of 1925 prohibiting the use of bacterial weapons to do so. The resolution evidently was a propaganda measure against the United States which had not ratified the protocol. The Soviet resolution was defeated. The Council terminated its discussion but kept the item on its agenda.

Bacterial warfare.—The United States on June 20, 1952, submitted a resolution proposing that the International Red Cross investigate Communist charges that the United Nations forces in Korea had employed bacterial warfare. The U. S. S. R. vetoed the resolution. The United States then introduced another resolution which stated that since the Soviet Union vetoed an impartial investigation, its charges of bacterial warfare must be presumed false. After the Soviet Union vetoed this resolution, the Council ended its discussion but kept the item on its agenda.

Threat to Thailand.—Thailand on May 29, 1954, sent a letter to the Security Council calling attention to the large-scale fighting in Indochina and declaring that it represented a threat to the security of Thailand. The Thai Government requested the Council to "provide for observation under the Peace Observation Commission." The Soviet Union on June 18 vetoed a resolution introduced by Thailand providing that a Peace Observation Subcommission of 3 to 5 members be created with authority to send observers to Thailand and to make recommendations to the Security Council. The resolution further provided that, if the Subcommission thought that it could not accomplish its mission without observation "in states contiguous to Thailand," it was to report to the Peace Observation Commission or to the Security Council for the necessary instructions.

"Aggression" against Guatemala.—Guatemala on June 19, 1954, complained to the Council that an "open aggression" had been committed against it by the Governments of Honduras and Nicaragua. Guatemala asked the Council under articles 34, 35, and 39 of the United Nations Charter to prevent "disruption of peace and international security" in Central America and to stop the "aggression" against it. The Soviet Union on June 20 vetoed a resolution which would have referred the Guatemalan complaint to the Organization of American States for "urgent consideration." The Council then unanimously approved a resolution

calling for the "immediate termination of any action likely to cause bloodshed," and requesting all members of the United Nations to abstain from assisting "any such action."

II. THE GENERAL ASSEMBLY

Indians in South Africa.—India on June 22, 1946, charged that South Africa was discriminating against Indians in its territory and that this was likely to impair friendly relations between the two countries. South Africa maintained that its acts were matters of domestic jurisdiction. The controversy has been a perennial problem before the Assembly. At various times the Assembly has passed resolutions recommending that the two countries negotiate their differences and that South Africa abide by its treaties with India. In 1952 the Assembly established a Good Offices Commission to assist in negotiations between South Africa and India and Pakistan, and extended it in 1953. The controversy is still unsettled.

The Spanish question.—When the Security Council dropped the Spanish question the Assembly took it up and in December 1946 passed a resolution recommending that the members of the United Nations withdraw their principal diplomatic representatives from Madrid, that the Franco government be barred from international organizations associated with the United Nations,[9] and that the Security Council consider measures to deal with the Spanish situation if a democratic government were not established in a reasonable time. In 1950 the Assembly withdrew its recommendation that diplomatic representatives be recalled from Franco Spain and that Spain be debarred from international specialized agencies.

The Palestine problem.[10]—After the Security Council decided in 1948 that it did not have the authority to enforce the Assembly's recommended settlement of the Palestine question, the Assembly resumed its attempts to effect a pacific solution. In May 1948 the mandate was terminated, the State of Israel was proclaimed, and the Assembly appointed a mediator to try to effect a pacific settlement of the dispute. Count Folke Bernadotte of Sweden was appointed mediator but was unable to effect a settlement before his assassination in September 1948. Dr. Ralph Bunche was then appointed acting mediator. Subsequently the Assembly established a Palestine Conciliation Commission, composed of France, Turkey, and the United States, to take over the functions of peacefully adjusting the situation in Palestine and of assisting the governments and authorities concerned to achieve a final settlement of outstanding issues. To date there has been no such settlement of the dispute.

The Greek question.—After the Security Council dropped the Greek problem from its agenda in September 1947 it was promptly taken up by the Assembly. During subsequent years the Assembly approved resolutions calling for a pacific settlement of the Greek situation, admonishing other governments not to aid the guerrillas, and recommending the resumption of diplomatic relations and the regulation of the frontiers between the disputant countries. An 11-member United Nations Special Committee on the Balkans was created by the Assembly to observe compliance with the resolutions. After Yugoslavia broke with Moscow in 1948, it reestablished diplomatic relations with Greece. In succeeding years guerrilla activity in Greece subsided. The United Nations Committee was continued in order to observe the situation.

The Korean conflict.—Since the end of World War II, Korea had been divided and occupied by American forces in the south and Soviet forces in the north. The United States, after negotiations with the U. S. S. R. for the establishment of a unified Korean Government had failed, submitted the problem to the United Nations in 1947. The Assembly recommended the holding of elections for a Korean Government and appointed a commission to observe them. The U. S. S. R. did not cooperate in its zone of occupation, with the result that elections were held and a republican government was established only in South Korea. The Assembly recommended the withdrawal of occupation forces and appointed another commission to attempt to achieve the unification of Korea. American forces withdrew but the United Nations Commission was not able to verify whether Soviet troops had also departed. Because of the lack of Soviet

---

[9] The Assembly in February 1946 had passed a resolution approving a decision of the San Francisco Conference that United Nations provisions on admission of members should not apply to states whose governments had been installed with the armed assistance of ex-enemy countries. The Assembly resolution was specifically directed at Spain.

[10] For previous developments on this problem in the Assembly see the discussion under the Security Council.

cooperation the Commission was unable to achieve Korean unification before the invasion of South Korea in June 1950.

Just before the Chinese intervention in the Korean conflict in the fall of 1950, the Assembly approved a resolution for the political unification and rehabilitation of Korea. After the Chinese intervened and the Security Council removed the Korean issue from its agenda, the Assembly devoted its efforts to meeting the Communist aggression in Korea, effecting a cease-fire and achieving United Nations political objectives by peaceful means. Negotiations begun in July 1951 between the United Nations Command and the Communist forces in Korea resulted in an armistice in July 1953. The armistice agreement included a recommendation by the military commanders that within 3 months a political conference be held to negotiate the withdrawal of foreign forces and the peaceful settlement of the Korean question. In August the General Assembly approved proposals for the holding of a political conference on Korea between the nations participating on the United Nations side in Korea and the Communist governments. The proposals reaffirmed the United Nations objective of achieving a unified, independent, and democratic Korea. Preparatory negotiations at Panmunjom between the United States and Chinese and North Korean representatives for arranging the political conference were broken off in December 1953 without a successful result. In February 1954 the Foreign Ministers of the United States, United Kingdom, France, and the U. S. S. R., meeting at Berlin, agreed to convoke a conference at Geneva in April 1954 "for the purpose of reaching a peaceful settlement of the Korean question." At the Geneva Conference no settlement of the Korean problem was achieved.

The Italian colonies.—The Italian Peace Treaty provided that the United States, the United Kingdom, France, and the U. S. S. R. should determine the disposition of the former Italian colonies of Libya, Eritrea, and Somaliland within 1 year after the coming into force of the treaty on September 15, 1947. If the four powers were unable to reach agreement in that period, the treaty provided that they should refer the problem to the General Assembly with the advance understanding that they would accept the latter's recommendations.

By September 1948 the four powers had been unable to reach agreements and they referred the problem to the Assembly. The latter decided that Libya should become a sovereign state not later than January 1, 1952; that Somaliland should be placed under Italian trusteeship and should become independent in 10 years; and that Eritrea should become an autonomous unit in federation with Ethiopia under the latter's sovereignty. The Assembly's recommendations are being put into effect.

Human rights in Bulgaria, Hungary, and Rumania.—During the third and fourth sessions of the General Assembly in 1949, Bolivia and Australia called the attention of the General Assembly to violations of human rights and fundamental freedoms in Bulgaria, Hungary, and Rumania. The Assembly passed a resolution expressing the hope that measures would be taken, in accordance with the peace treaties, to insure respect for human rights. The Western countries then took steps to carry out procedures provided for in the treaties for the handling of disputes among the signatories, but the three Balkan States refused to cooperate. In 1950 the Assembly passed a resolution condemning the three Balkan governments for refusing to cooperate with the treaty procedures.

Soviet threat to Chinese independence.—In September 1949 the National Government of China complained to the General Assembly that Soviet violations of the Sino-Soviet Treaty of 1945 and of the United Nations Charter threatened the political independence and territorial integrity of China and the peace of the Far East. In December 1949 the Assembly called on all states to respect the political independence of China, to observe treaties relating to China, and to refrain from seeking special rights in China. In February 1952 the Assembly adopted a resolution declaring that the Soviet Union had failed to carry out its treaty with China.

"Aggression" against Communist China.—The U. S. S. R. on September 20, 1950, complained that the United States was committing aggression against China. The U. S. S. R. declared that the "blockade" and "invasion" of Formosa by American forces and air attacks against Chinese territory constituted an act of aggression and a serious threat to international peace. The Assembly rejected a resolution proposed by the U. S. S. R. requesting the Security Council to take steps to insure an immediate end to United States "aggression" against China.

German unification.—The United States, United Kingdom, and France, at the request of the Chancellor of the West German Federal Republic, asked the General Assembly on November 5, 1951, to consider the appointment of a United

Nations Commission to investigate the possibility of holding free elections through-out Germany. The Assembly approved a resolution on December 20, 1951, appointing a Commission to investigate conditions for holding free elections and requesting authorities in the West German Federal Republic and in the Soviet Zone to permit free access to the investigators. In August 1952 the Commission, after the Soviet authorities in Germany had refused to cooperate with it, reported that it was unable to perform its task and would adjourn its activities, but would remain at the disposal of the United Nations.

Hostile activities against Yugoslavia.—Yugoslavia on November 9, 1951, complained that for more than 3 years the U. S. S. R. and other Communist governments in Eastern Europe had been applying "aggressive pressure" against it. The Assembly approved a resolution proposed by Yugoslvaia recommending that the governments concerned settle their disputes in the spirit of the United Nations Charter, conform in their diplomatic intercourse with customary international rules, and settle their frontier disputes.

"Aggressive acts" of the United States.—The U. S. S. R. on November 22, 1951, complained to the General Assembly of "aggressive acts" of the United States as evidenced in its appropriation of money to organize armed groups inside and outside the Soviet Union and other East European countries. The Soviet Union proposed a resolution condemning the United States Mutual Security Act, but the Assembly rejected it.

Morocco.—Egypt on October 4, 1951, requested that the Assembly consider the conflict between France and Morocco, arising from "the national claims of the Moroccan Government and people." The Assembly postponed discussion of the question in 1951 but in December 1952 passed a resolution expressing the hope that France and Morocco would continue negotiations for developing the free political institutions of the latter.

Tunisia.—After having failed in the spring of 1952 to induce the Security Council to admit the Tunisian question to its agenda, a group of 13 Arab and Asian States asked the General Assembly on July 30, 1952, to consider the continuing tension between France and Tunisia and to help achieve a peaceful settlement. On December 17, 1952, the Assembly passed a resolution expressing confidence that France and Tunisia would continued negotiations to promote self-government in the latter country.

Austrian treaty.—In March 1952 the Austrian Government circulated a memorandum to members of the United Nations indicating its intention, if the United States, Great Britain, France, and the U. S. S. R. remained deadlocked in their efforts to agree on a treaty restoring Austrian independence, to appeal to the United Nations to induce the occupying powers to evacuate the country and restore its freedom. During the next several months the Soviet Union continued to block negotiations, and on August 29, 1952, Brazil requested that the Austrian question be considered by the General Assembly. The latter approved a resolution on December 20, 1952, appealing to the occupying powers to make a renewed effort to reach agreement on an Austrian treaty.

Race conflict in South Africa.—A group of 13 Arab and Asian countries requested the General Assembly on September 12, 1952, to consider the question of racial conflict in South Africa resulting from the policies of the Government of that country. The complainants asserted that the situation was a threat to international peace. South Africa challenged the Assembly's competence, maintaining that the matter was strictly within its domestic jurisdiction. However, the Assembly proceeded to discuss the question and approved two resolutions on December 5, 1952, establishing a Commission to study the racial situation in South Africa and calling upon all member states to bring their policies into conformity with their obligations under the charter to promote human rights and fundamental freedoms.

Chinese troops in Burma.—On March 26, 1953, Burma complained to the Assembly that the actions of Nationalist Chinese troops on Burmese territory constituted an act of aggression. The Assembly on April 23 approved a resolution recommending that negotiations be pursued either to intern or evacuate the Chinese forces. The United States, Burma, Thailand, and Nationalist China concluded arrangements to evacuate those troops that chose to leave. Nationalist China disavowed the remainder. On December 8, 1953, the Assembly noted that limited evacuation of the Chinese troops had begun, and urged continued efforts either to evacuate or intern them.

BUDGETARY AND FINANCIAL PROBLEMS OF
THE UNITED NATIONS

STAFF STUDY NO. 6
DECEMBER 1954

PREFACE

By Alexander Wiley, *Chairman*

It has been remarked that if the nations of the world were to spend one-tenth of the sums which they spend on armaments for the purpose of promoting peace much more progress could be made in that direction. The United States Government denotes less than one-tenth of 1 percent of its annual budget as its contribution to the budget of the United Nations.

This staff study of the financial and budgetary problems of the United Nations is of particular interest to me because, as a member of the United States delegation to the Seventh General Assembly, I debated the issue involved with delegations from many countries. The study is designed to set forth the main problems in financing the organization. The subject is complicated. It is complicated in part because some 60 nations with 60 different systems of currencies and 60 different budgetary procedures must work together to construct a budget acceptable not only to the government representatives at the United Nations but in most instances to their legislatures at home.

In the case of the United States every year Members of Congress appropriate about $15 million as our share of the regular costs of the United Nations. This represents $33\frac{1}{3}$ percent of the regular United Nations budget—a disproportionately large share when one remembers that the United States has only 1 out of 60 votes. The share is not so great, however, when one considers the wealth of the United States in contrast with the wealth of the rest of the world.

It is not the purpose of this study to examine the question of whether the money is well spent. Rather, it explores the ways in which the United Nations goes about forming its budget, the various types of contributions made not only to the United Nations but to the specialized agencies and certain U. N. voluntary programs, and the proposals which have been made to change the United Nations system of handling its financial and budgetary problems.

I should like to invite particular attention to that section of the attached report concerning the costs of the U. N. enforcement action in Korea. It has been estimated that this action cost the United States in the vicinity of $5 billion each year. It also cost us heavily in casualties. The study points out that in the event of a similar action in the future the President has indicated that he would recommend that the United States give logistic support to help other nations carry their fair share of the manpower burden. It must also be noted that the United Nations itself through the Collective Measures Committee is taking steps to make certain that in the event of another enforcement action there would be maximum contributions from the members of the United Nations.

In addition to our payments to the regular U. N. budget the United States makes contributions to so-called voluntary programs such as the Korean reconstruction program and the international children's fund. Our contributions in these cases have ranged as high as 70 percent of the total budgets. Even with these heavy payments from the United States, other nations have lagged in their contributions. The study notes that there is "a disturbing tendency among states * * * to discuss" such programs to vote for them and not to contribute. I, myself, think it vitally important that all United Nations members share in the financing of these programs which they have acknowledged to be an international responsibility by setting them up in the first place.

This study should be of particular interest to my colleagues in the Senate and the House of Representatives, since they are called upon every year to appropriate the funds for our contributions to the United Nations, the specialized agencies, and the voluntary programs.

The study was written by Francis O. Wilcox, chief of staff of the Senate Foreign Relations Committee, who has long been associated with the United States delegations to the General Assembly of the United Nations. The views presented therein do not necessarily represent those of the subcommittee or any of its members.

DECEMBER 1954.

CONTENTS

BUDGETARY AND FINANCIAL PROBLEMS OF THE UNITED NATIONS

INTRODUCTORY COMMENTS

Financing the United Nations is somewhat like the job of providing for an unusually large and disparate family on a very modest income. Some worthy projects may have to be sidetracked; a portion of the funds available may be wasted; it is difficult to get each member of the family to accept his share of responsibility; and there will be a constant concern over whether both ends will meet.

It is often said that the veto is the greatest single problem facing the United Nations. But money is the lifeblood of any organization. And the financial problems the U. N. has encountered—although less spectacular—have proven almost as difficult and, in some ways, even more complex than the veto.

In spite of its importance, the financial side of the U. N. has received relatively little attention from the American public or from authors and critics. For the most part, the criticisms that have emerged are general in character. Some people complain that the U. N. is spending too much; others insist that it is not spending enough. In Congress, where these matters are discussed every year, there is some fear that the organization may be taking on too many activities—particularly in the relief and refugee fields· where large and continuing expenditures may be involved. There are also recurring criticisms that the United States is still contributing too large a proportion of the total U. N. budget and that some of the other members are slow to assume their fair share of expenses. Finally, there are some complaints that there is a certain amount of waste, mainly through overlapping and duplication of effort within the U. N. system.

How have the financial provisions of the charter worked out in practice? Where have U. N. funds come from and how have they been spent? What are the main problems that have arisen in financing the various activites of the U. N.? What suggestions have been made for changing the present arrangements? It is the purpose of this study to review these questions, with particular emphasis upon the proposals which have been made for change.

Such questions should be of considerable interest to the people and the Government of the United States. From the very beginning the United States has been by far the largest contributor to the U. N. Moreover, as the leader of the free world and as the host country to the U. N., we have a unique stake in its successful functioning. Financially and politically, we are one of its principal stockholders.

I. Provisions of the Charter

The main provisions of the charter dealing with financial matters are found in articles 17, 18, and 19.[1] Article 17 reads as follows:

1. The General Assembly shall consider and approve the budget of the Organization.
2. The expenses of the Organization shall be borne by the Members as apportioned by the General Assembly.
3. The General Assembly shall consider and approve any financial and budgetary arrangements with specialized agencies referred to in Article 57 and shall examine the administrative budgets of such specialized agencies with a view to making recommendations to the agencies concerned.

Several important points should be noted in connection with article 17. In the first place, the purse strings of the United Nations are placed squarely in the hands of the General Assembly. The power to approve the budget gives the Assembly a very strategic position, for it carries with it the power of coordinating and controlling the various activities of the United Nations. This follows the precedent established by the League of Nations and is based upon the principle that all members of the organization should have a voice in the allocation and expenditure of funds.

In the second place, article 17 bestows upon the General Assembly far-reaching authority to apportion the expenses of the U. N. among the members. At the same time, it places upon the members an international legal obligation to meet these expenses in the manner agreed upon by the Assembly. No rule of thumb is provided for the apportionment of expenses. The only limitation is that found in article 18 which provides that budgetary decisions must be approved by a two-thirds vote of the Assembly.

Flexibility is thus the keynote. As the Report to the President on the Results of the San Francisco Conference points out:

At the Conference there was some discussion of the desirability of specifying in detail the budgetary procedures and methods of apportioning expenses, but all such suggestions were in the end rejected on the ground that the charter should be held as much as possible to the description of fundamental powers and functions, and that the General Assembly could safely be left to take care of details through its own subsequent regulations.[2]

In the third place, article 17 underlines the autonomous character of the various specialized agencies—such as the Food and Agriculture Organization (FAO), World Health Organization (WHO), and United Nations Educational, Scientific, and Cultural Organization (UNESCO)—within the U. N. system. In the League of Nations days the budgets of such technical organizations were included in the League budget and subject to the control of the Assembly. In the United Nations, the situation has developed in quite a different way. From the beginning, representatives of the specialized agencies have insisted that while article 17 gives the General Assembly the right to examine their administrative budgets and make recommendations about them, the Assembly does not have the authority to exercise any

---

[1] On this subject generally see Goodrich and Hambro, Charter of the United Nations: Commentary and Documents, 1949, pp. 183–191 and 324–350 ; Vandenbosch and Hogan, The United Nations, Background, Organization, Functions, Activities, 1952, chs. 8, 10 ; E. P. Chase, The United Nations in Action, 1950, chs. 7, 13 ; Report of the Committee on Expenditures in the Executive Branch, U. S. Senate, Rept. No. 90, 82d Cong., 1st sess. ; and Carnegie Endowment for International Peace, The Budget of the United Nations, New York, 1947.

[2] Report to the President on the Results of the San Francisco Conference, 1945, p. 57.

control over their expenditures. Instead of a single, coordinated budget, a policy of financial diffusion has prevailed. Ten autonomous agencies have developed with 10 separate and independent budgets. Under the language of article 17, the General Assembly has its foot in the door of the specialized agencies, but that is about all.

One other provision of the charter should be mentioned. Article 19 imposes a penalty upon members which fall seriously behind in their financial contributions to the organization. Any member whose arrears equals the amount of the contributions due from it for the 2 preceding years loses its vote in the General Assembly. The Assembly may, however, lift the penalty if it is satisfied that the failure to pay stems from conditions beyond the control of the member. While the specific conditions are not stipulated in the charter, presumably they would include severe economic depressions or extreme natural disasters like earthquakes and floods.

II. How the U. N. Budget Works in Practice

It is often pointed out by supporters of the U. N. that the cost of maintaining the organization is quite small. We are reminded that the annual contribution of the United States to the administrative budget of the U. N. is only about 8 to 10 cents per capita or, to put it in still another way, less than the cost of cleaning the streets of New York City. We are told that the amount we contribute to the U. N. is less than the amount we spend on a single destroyer.

It is true that our normal contribution to the U. N. represents only a very small fraction of our total national budget. It should be kept in mind, however, that there are various budgets and funds within the U. N. system and it is not always easy to distinguish between them. Table I, which follows, gives U. N. expenditures in the three major categories discussed below.

TABLE I.—*United Nations and the specialized agencies and special programs, expenditures, 1946–53*

Organization	1946	1947	1948	1949	1950	1951	1952	1953	Total
A. The United Nations	$19,330,287	$27,290,241	$38,387,531	$42,575,368	$43,746,264	$48,628,383	$50,270,153	$49,292,552	$319,520,779
B. The specialized agencies:									
ILO	2,711,212	3,720,661	4,147,704	5,034,154	5,266,854	5,834,589	6,389,539	6,509,775	39,614,488
FAO	376,535	5,172,987	4,174,000	4,654,519	4,504,652	4,581,456	4,830,334	5,064,399	33,358,882
UNESCO	1,052,374	6,212,825	6,696,799	7,780,000	7,162,794	7,989,102	8,726,107	7,972,937	53,592,938
ICAO	719,254	1,690,044	2,284,865	2,344,880	2,946,080	3,020,779	3,191,748	3,150,032	19,347,682
UPU	132,095	168,608	866,510	297,388	301,837	354,100	416,978	435,413	2,972,929
WHO	116,333	1,718,860	4,442,874	4,776,608	6,108,299	6,259,247	7,938,850	8,112,605	39,473,676
ITU	(¹)	(¹)	897,289	2,994,252	1,639,639	1,382,194	1,591,875	1,455,733	9,960,982
WMO						185,755	179,259	271,911	636,925
Subtotal	5,107,803	18,683,985	23,510,041	27,881,801	27,930,155	29,607,222	33,264,690	32,972,805	198,958,502
C. Special programs financed by voluntary contributions:									
UNTA						6,642,376	22,305,988	22,662,016	51,610,380
UNRWA [2]				39,115,975	19,220,237	42,130,595	26,778,934	29,192,012	156,437,753
UNICEF		815,240	31,463,980	46,664,735	35,932,593	22,571,234	13,526,630	12,506,630	163,471,042
UNKRA					496,835	4,132,705	52,964,159	28,695,324	86,289,023
UNREF								847,908	847,908
IRO		75,675,840	132,167,476	119,401,897	85,446,702				412,691,915
ICAO, joint support				³2,017,942	906,356	1,376,391	1,515,136	1,603,731	7,419,556
Subtotal		76,491,080	163,621,456	207,200,549	142,002,723	76,853,301	117,090,847	95,507,621	878,767,577
Total	24,438,090	122,465,306	225,519,028	277,657,718	213,679,142	155,088,906	200,625,690	177,772,978	1,397,246,858

¹ Prior to 1948, the International Telecommunication Union was made up of separate bureaus with varying membership. ITU was established in its present form by the Atlantic City convention of 1947.

² Includes expenses of predecessor agency, United Nations Relief for Palestine Refugees in 1949 and 1950.

³ Covers 1947–49 on some projects.

NOTE.—The abbreviations used above stand for the following: ILO—International Labor Organization; FAO—Food and Agriculture Organization; UNESCO—United Nations Educational, Scientific and Cultural Organization; ICAO—International Civil Aviation Organization; UPU—Universal Postal Union; WHO—World Health Organization; ITU—International Telecommunication Union; WMO—World Meteorological Organization; UNTA—United Nations Expanded Program of Technical Assistance; UNRWA—United Nations Relief and Works Agency for Palestine Refugees in the Near East; UNICEF—United Nations International Children's Fund; UNKRA—United Nations Korean Reconstruction Agency; UNREF—United Nations High Commissioner for Refugees Emergency Fund; IRO—International Refugee Organization.

In the first place there is the regular U. N. budget—or the administrative budget—which covers expenditures for headquarters space, field missions, salaries, travel and transportation, equipment and supplies, printing, and other overhead expenses. The regular budget is financed by the 60 members of the U. N. who make contributions on a scale determined by the General Assembly under article 17. The budget for 1954 was approximately $48 million of which $41,300,000,000 was assessed against the members. Of this amount the United States contributed 33.33 percent, or roughly $13.7 million.

Quite apart from the regular budget are the budgets of the various specialized agencies such as the WHO, the FAO and the International Labor Organization (ILO). At present there are 10 of these specialized agencies each with a budget and a financial system of its own. In fiscal 1953 the United States contributed varying amounts to 8 of the agencies aggregating in the neighborhood of $10 million. The International Bank for Reconstruction and Development, and the International Monetary Fund finance their own operations from earnings and do not receive annual contributions from their members.

Even more important from a dollar standpoint is a third category— the so-called voluntary programs—which are financed by voluntary contributions of member states. Since these programs are of an operational nature and involve the expenditure of unusually large sums for nonadministrative purposes, they are not included in the regular budget. The United States has consistently contributed from 50 to 70 percent of the funds available to 4 of the voluntary programs—the Technical Assistance Program, the Children's Fund, the Korean Reconstruction Agency and the Palestine Refugee Program. In fiscal 1953 these contributions totaled roughly $71,500,000.

Finally, a word should be said about the kind of extraordinary expenditures incurred in the Korean conflict. While estimates vary considerably, it is probable that more than $5 billion were spent by the United States each year carrying out this enforcement action. The contributions of states—whether in the form of manpower, equipment, clothing, transportation, food, or troop maintenance generally— were not budgeted through the United Nations.

Table II below shows United States contributions in the three major categories discussed above.

TABLE II.—*United States contributions to the United Nations, fiscal years 1949–53*

Organization	1949 United States contribution	1949 United States percentage of total assessment	1950 United States contribution	1950 United States percentage of total assessment	1951 United States contribution	1951 United States percentage of total assessment	1952 United States contribution	1952 United States percentage of total assessment	1953 United States contribution	1953 United States percentage of total assessment
A. The United Nations	$13,841,032	39.89	$16,601,021	39.89	$13,576,243	39.79	$16,394,244	38.92	$15,440,860	36.90
B. The specialized agencies:[1]										
ILO	[2]1,091,739	19.13	848,058	18.35	1,269,868	22.00	1,466,412	25.00	1,538,991	25.00
FAO	1,250,000	25.00	1,250,000	27.10	1,420,800	27.10	1,355,000	30.00	1,673,750	30.00
UNESCO	[2]3,601,424	41.88	2,887,173	38.47	2,814,381	37.82	2,785,400	35.00	2,855,609	33.33
ICAO	498,004	18.69	463,979	18.47	453,319	24.98	698,610	24.97	807,273	27.00
UPU	8,781	4.43	12,056	4.34	12,341	4.38	13,867	4.31	18,520	4.63
WHO	1,860,884	38.77	1,918,220	38.54	[2]3,070,931	36.00	2,481,159	35.00	2,886,667	33.33
ITU	58,393	7.76	146,311	8.04	457,376	12.00	[2]109,264	7.83	113,150	7.98
WMO							[2]24,855	12.67	36,253	12.67
Subtotal	8,369,225		7,525,797		9,499,016		8,934,567		9,910,213	
C. Special programs financed by voluntary contributions:										
UNTA	8,000,000		10,000,000		12,007,500		11,400,000		8,171,333	
UNRWA[3]	25,491,692		15,356,361		25,450,000		50,000,000		16,000,000	
UNICEF					7,106,114				6,666,667	
UNKRA									40,750,000	
UNREF[4]										
IRO	70,643,728		70,447,729		25,000,000		10,000,000			
ICAO, joint support	1,103,366		547,939		650,000		676,312		653,814	
Subtotal	105,238,786		96,352,029		70,213,614		72,076,312		72,241,814	
Total	127,449,043		120,478,847		93,288,813		97,405,123		97,592,887	

[1] This list does not include the International Bank for Reconstruction and Development or the International Monetary Fund, which are financed by capital subscriptions from member governments and income from operations rather than by annual contributions.
[2] Amounts include advances to the working capital fund, which stand to the credit of the United States.
[3] Includes expenses of predecessor agency in 1949 and 1950.
[4] No contributions made from appropriated funds prior to fiscal year 1954.

NOTE.—The abbreviations used above stand for the following: ILO—International Labor Organization; FAO—Food and Agriculture Organization; UNESCO—United Nations Educational, Scientific, and Cultural Organization; ICAO—International Civil Aviation Organization; UPU—Universal Postal Union; WHO—World Health Organization; ITU—International Telecommunication Union; WMO—World Meteorological Organization; UNTA—United Nations Expanded Program of Technical Assistance; UNRWA—United Nations Relief and Works Agency for Palestine Refugees in the Near East; UNICEF—United Nations International Children's Fund; UNKRA—United Nations Korean Reconstruction Agency; UNREF—United Nations High Commissioner for Refugees Emergency Fund; IRO—International Refugee Organization.

THE REGULAR BUDGET: APPORTIONMENT OF EXPENSES

In accordance with a resolution of the General Assembly approved in 1946, the expenses of the U. N. are "apportioned broadly according to capacity to pay." In calculating the relative capacity of members to contribute the Committee on Contributions [3] is under instructions from the General Assembly to take into account available estimates of national incomes together with the following principal factors:

(1) The temporary dislocation of national economies arising out of the war;
(2) Comparative income per head of population; and
(3) The ability of members to obtain foreign currency.

There is one other important limiting factor approved by the General Assembly; that is, that no member should be required to contribute more than one-third of the regular budget. In 1946 the Committee on Contributions recommended that the United States, based on its ability to pay, should contribute 49.89 percent of the total. The United States delegation vigorously protested this apportionment on the ground that the U. N. is an organization of sovereign equals and that it would be unwise for any one member to bear a preponderance of the administrative costs. "Such a situation," argued Senator Arthur Vandenberg, "makes the organization too dependent upon a single member and invites the member in question to attempt to exert an undue influence in the management of the organization."

As a result, the United States finally agreed to a temporary assessment of 39.89 percent. This figure was reduced to 39.79 percent in 1949, and a year later cut still further to 38.92 percent. Subsequent to that time additional annual reductions took place until 1954 when the one-third ceiling finally went into effect.

While the United States has insisted upon the principle of the ceiling with respect to the regular budget, our Government has indicated a willingness in special cases to pay more than one-third of the expenses of major operational programs. This is not, as it might first appear, a distinction without a difference, since it is clear that if heavy contributions had not been made by the United States it would have been difficult if not impossible for the U. N. to launch such voluntary programs as those referred to above.

---

[3] The Committee on Contributions is a special committee of 10 members elected by the General Assembly and serving as individuals. The committee is charged, among other things, with the responsibility of determining the capacity of states to pay and of recommending to the General Assembly the apportionment of expenses among the members.

The 1954 scale of assessment for United Nations members is as follows:

TABLE III.—*United Nations: Regular Budget—Scale of assessment for 1954*[1]

Member State	Percent	Member State	Percent
Afghanistan	0. 08	Lebanon	0. 05
Argentina	1. 40	Liberia	. 04
Australia	1. 75	Luxembourg	. 06
Belgium	1. 38	Mexico	. 75
Bolivia	. 06	Netherlands	1. 25
Brazil	1. 40	New Zealand	' 48
Burma	. 13	Nicaragua	. 04
Byelorussian Soviet Socialist Republic	. 50	Norway	. 50
Canada	3. 30	Pakistan	. 75
Chile	. 33	Panama	. 05
China	5. 62	Paraguay	. 04
Colombia	. 41	Peru	. 18
Costa Rica	. 04	Philippines	. 45
Cuba	. 34	Poland	1. 73
Czechoslovakia	1. 05	Saudi Arabia	. 07
Denmark	. 78	Sweden	1. 65
Dominican Republic	. 05	Syria	. 08
Ecuador	. 04	Thailand	. 18
Egypt	. 47	Turkey	. 65
El Salvador	. 06	Ukrainian Soviet Socialist Republic	1. 88
Ethiopia	. 10	Union of South Africa	. 78
France	5. 75	Union of Soviet Socialist Republics	14. 15
Greece	. 21		
Guatemala	. 07	United Kingdom of Great Britain and Northern Ireland	9. 80
Haiti	. 04		
Honduras	. 04	United States of America	33. 33
Iceland	. 04	Uruguay	. 18
India	3. 40	Venezuela	. 39
Indonesia	. 60	Yemen	. 04
Iran	. 28	Yugoslavia	. 44
Iraq	. 12		
Israel	. 17	Total	100. 00

[1] From United Nations Document A/2461.

LIMITATIONS ON CAPACITY TO PAY

The principal headache of the Committee on Contributions in determining the capacity of members to pay has resulted from the unavailability of adequate statistics. Complete and accurate data on production, national incomes, and related matters often do not exist, and when they do exist they are subject to different interpretations. The Communist states particularly have been inclined either to withhold their economic statistics or to twist them to suit their own purposes. Senator Alexander Wiley reports that on one day in 1952, for example, he listened to a member of the Ukrainian delegation in one committee of the General Assembly speak with great pride of the remarkable economic progress his country had made since the war. The Senator then went to another committee where he heard a second member of the Ukrainian delegation explain with equal fervor why his Government was unable to increase its contribution to the U. N. budget.

Still another complicating factor has been the serious dollar shortage suffered by many members since the war. Inasmuch as the headquarters is located in New York, most U. N. expenditures must be made in dollars. This imposes a hardship on some members over and above their actual financial capacity to pay.   In order to alleviate this situation, the Secretary General has been authorized to accept as large a proportion of member payments as possible in currencies other than dollars.   During 1953 some 28.55 percent of the contributions to the regular budget was made in other currencies—mainly in Swiss francs. This practice can be encouraged to the extent that the U. N. continues to spend additional funds in countries outside the United States.

Finally, a word should be said about capacity to pay and per capita income.   In 1946 the General Assembly resolved that in normal times the per capita contribution of members should not exceed the per capita contribution of the member bearing the highest assessment.   In effect, this meant that countries like Canada and Sweden, with relatively small populations and high incomes, should not contribute more per capita than the United States.

This principle has not proved entirely practicable, especially since the United States contribution has been reduced to 33.33 percent.   A comparable reduction for other high-income countries could only mean that a greater financial burden would fall on the poorer nations.   Our per capita contribution to the 1954 regular budget was 8.6 cents; Canada's contribution amounted to 9.2 cents; New Zealand's, 9.7 cents; and Sweden's, 9.5 cents.   Iceland topped the list with 11 cents per capita.

THE BUDGET PROCESS

The U. N. budget probably is given as careful a scrutiny as any budget of a similar size anywhere in the world.   Representatives from member states in the General Assembly often spend days debating relatively modest sums which would be considered by some national legislative bodies in a matter of hours or even minutes.   Rarely have so many important people taken so much time to spend so little in the way of public funds.

In general, U. N. budget procedure is comparable to that used by the Federal Government of the United States.   When budget estimates for a particular fiscal year have been carefully worked out in the Secretariat, they are submitted to the Secretary General for his approval.   They are then sent to the General Assembly's Advisory Committee on Administrative and Budgetary Questions, where they are studied in minute detail.   This committee normally spends 4 or 5 months reviewing the various programs, hearing witnesses, and preparing its recommendations for the use of the General Assembly.

The final hurdle comes when the General Assembly convenes in September.   At that time the Assembly's Fifth Committee puts the budget under a microscope, normally devoting most of its 10 or 11 weeks session going over the estimates and debating financial and administrative matters generally.   Both the Secretary General, or his representative, and the chairman of the advisory committee, participate actively in the meetings of the Fifth Committee.   The final result, which is usually a bundle of compromises somewhere between the recommendations of the advisory committee and the Secretary General, is submitted to the General Assembly for its approval.

This is not the place to examine the budget procedures of the 10 specialized agencies.   In general, they follow a procedure somewhat comparable to that described above.

SOME BUDGET FACTS

A study of the regular budget figures since 1946 reveals some interesting facts. While the United States contribution has been reduced to 33.33 percent, the Soviet assessment has been increased by about the same amount, from 7.73 percent in 1946 to 14.15 percent in 1954. The five great powers take care of more than two-thirds of the budget with the United States contributing about almost as much as the U. S. S. R., the United Kingdom, France, and China combined. During the current year (1954) some 44 states contributed less than 1 percent and 15 states contributed less than $25,000 each. Table A in the Appendix illustrates these facts.

The striking disparity between member contributions and voting strength is even more noteworthy. The six Arab States, for example, pay less than 1 percent of the budget, yet they cast 10 percent of the votes in the General Assembly. Similarly, the 20 Latin American countries, while controlling one-third of the General Assembly votes, contribute somewhat less than 6 percent of the budget. On the other hand the 12 North Atlantic Treaty Countries, in voting power at least, receive far less than they pay for. Thus the United States contributes one-third of the budget but has only one-sixtieth of the vote.

THE COLLECTION OF CONTRIBUTIONS

While the United Nations has encountered the usual amount of difficulty in collecting dues from member states, up to the present time the situation has not become serious. A number of offenders lag behind in their payments but always manage to complete their contributions before the 2-year period provided by the charter has expired. For example, some 27 members were in arrears at the end of 1952. Yet 2 years later all the contributions for 1952 had been collected and no state was sufficiently in arrears to justify the penalty set forth in article 19.

China, of course, faces the toughest problem. At present her resources are limited to the island of Formosa with a population of something less than 10 million. Yet she continues to pay the fifth largest assessment in the United Nations calculated upon the productive capacity of continental China with its huge population of more than 450 million. At the end of 1952 China was in arrears $4,823,-680—which was more than half the total amount still owed the United Nations by all the members combined.

Since some members customarily do not make their contributions until late in the fiscal year, the United Nations draws heavily upon its working capital fund to meet current obligations. It is also available to meet emergency expenses. This revolving fund, which was established in 1946 for the purpose of financing the first year of the organization, is now maintained at a level slightly in excess of $21 million.

U. N. EXPENDITURES

It is not the purpose of this study to present in any detail the expenditures of the United Nations. Moreover, although the regular budget figures are broken down in several ways, no bird's-eye view of expenditures for the total U. N. system is available. It may be worth while, however, to call attention to several rather significant trends which the table on p. 4 illustrates.

If figures for the regular U. N. budget and the budgets of the specialized agencies are any indication, it would appear that the period of rapid expansion is over. The regular budget began at $19.3 million in 1946, rose rapidly to a high of $50.3 million in 1952, dropping to $47.8 million in 1954. The budget approved for 1955 is $46.5 million. The figures are somewhat comparable for the specialized agencies although the termination of the International Refugee Organization (IRO) in 1952 marked a very considerable reduction for the group as a whole. For the rest of the agencies the trend continued slightly upward in 1954 and 1955.

This leveling-off period is probably due to two main factors. The first is the persistent efforts put forth on behalf of economy by the Advisory Committee and the Fifth Committee of the General Assembly. The second is the legislative ceilings which Congress has placed upon the contribution of the United States to several of the specialized agencies. The fact that our contribution to FAO, ILO, and WHO is now limited by law to a fixed sum each year should have a deterring effect upon expansionist tendencies in these agencies.

It may be possible to look forward to a rather substantial reduction, within the next few years, in the size of the voluntary programs. Most of these programs are of a relief character arising out of the war or stemming from U. N. activities in Korea and Palestine. The Children's Fund, which was launched in 1948, and Technical Assistance, which began its activities in 1950, are long-range programs and probably will be a charge on the U. N. budget for a good many years. In both cases, however, the sums involved are relatively modest. On the other hand, the Palestine Relief and Works Agency and the Korean Reconstruction Agency, which will both require large annual outlays during the next few years, are agencies with temporary mandates. They can be terminated, as in the case of the IRO, when their tasks are completed. Unless, therefore, some other large-scale U. N. activity is launched, such as an economic development program, total expenditures under the U. N. conceivably could be reduced considerably within a relatively short time.

III. Proposals for Change in U. N. Methods of Financing

It is not possible, in a limited study of this kind, to examine in any detail the budgetary and administrative practices of the United Nations. Instead, in the pages that follow, seven specific questions are raised. It is believed that a consideration of these questions will cover the main problems facing the U. N. in the financial field and the principal suggestions that have been made for change.

1. THE AUTHORITY OF THE GENERAL ASSEMBLY

Should the charter be amended so as to take away from the General Assembly the authority to determine the budget of the United Nations and to apportion its expenses among the members?

From time to time, since the ratification of the charter, Members of the Senate and House have expressed surprise that the charter bestows upon the General Assembly the power to apportion the expenses of the U. N. among its members. "Do you mean to say," some have inquired, "that our Government is obligated to pay into the U. N. treasury whatever amount the Assembly determines to be our share of the expenses? Suppose it should decide to authorize large sums for the economic development of the underdeveloped areas? Does article 17 mean that the United States would be bound to contribute 50 or 60 percent of such amounts if the Assembly voted that much as our fair share?"

From the point of view of our international legal obligations, the answer to these questions is "Yes." Under article 17 the General Assembly apportions the regular budgetary expenses of the organization by a two-thirds vote, and the resulting assessments constitute binding obligations upon the members. Practically, however, it is very doubtful that the Assembly would resort to this authority and impose upon our Government huge financial responsibilities which it is unwilling to assume.

In any event, such questions reflect a very legitimate desire to protect the national interests of the United States by keeping the U. N. what it was designed to be in the first instance—an organization of sovereign states. They reflect a determination not to leave the United States, by far the wealthiest member of the U. N., vulnerable to unreasonable financial demands from poor and underdeveloped countries.

At San Francisco there was relatively little debate on this point. It is significant, however, that Committee II of the Conference approved a revision of the Dumbarton Oaks proposals relating to expenditures which had the effect of imposing a direct obligation upon the members to bear the expenses as apportioned by the Assembly. "In approving the text," say the rapporteur's report, "the committee took into account the view of the Advisory Committee of Jurists that this obligation should be clearly stated in the charter."[4]

In practice there has been little indication of discrimination by the General Assembly against the United States. To the contrary, the success of United States efforts in obtaining a steady reduction in our assessment over the years would seem to reflect a fairly general desire on the part of U. N. members to be equitable in their approach to such matters.

This is not to say that the system has worked perfectly. Every year when the Contributions Committee makes its recommendations there is a certain amount of grumbling from states whose contributions have been raised; and by no means the least of these is the Soviet Union whose assessment has been increased from 7.73 percent in 1946 to 15.08 percent in 1955. But by and large the members have accepted the apportionment of the General Assembly with good grace. Since the regular budget is now fairly well stabilized there should be no serious trouble on this score in the immediate future.

Those who object to the present procedure would probably be hard pressed to come up with anything better. Obviously if each member, mindful of national budget pressures and domestic politics, were allowed to determine the amount it could conveniently contribute every year, the U. N. would be plunged into fiscal anarchy. Confronted thus with no sure source of funds, it would be subject to the financial whims of 60 different states each convinced of the justice

4 UNCIO Doc. 1092, II/1/39, June 19, 1945.

of its cause in seeking to reduce its own contribution to the lowest possible level.

Suppose, however, the General Assembly attempts to step beyond the proper bounds of its competence under article 17? This is not likely to happen inasmuch as U. N. members are restrained from approving large programs because of their own budget limitations. But, if it should, and if we should find ourselves unable to secure the support of the 20 states necessary to block action, then at least two courses would be open to the United States. In the first place, the Congress could withhold the funds. The effect of that action would be that the United States would lose its vote in the General Assembly after 2 years. In the second place, as a last resort, we might even withdraw from the organization.

Actually, of course, there is an automatic, though unprecise, limit on Assembly assessments against the United States through increases in the overall budget. This limit operates through the fact that, if the U. N. budget were doubled, it would be more difficult for some of the small states to meet even a portion of the increase than for the United States to double its contribution.

The general consensus, in U. N. circles at least, seems to be that article 17 has worked fairly well. There appears to be little sentiment for Charter change, either in stripping the General Assembly of its authority to apportion expenses, or in modifying the two-thirds vote.

2. U. N. BUDGET CEILING

Should a ceiling be placed upon the budget of the United Nations so that annual expenditures can be kept within reasonable limits agreed upon in advance?

It is desirable that the annual expenditures of the United Nations and the specialized agencies be stabilized at a level which will permit the organization to perform its proper functions in an effective manner. Equally important, of course, is the corollary that the budget should never be allowed to reach a point which might compel members to withdraw from the U. N. because of their inability to pay their fair share of expenses. As Senator Vandenberg often put it:

The United Nations must never become a rich man's club; the dues must be kept low enough so that the smallest and poorest states can afford to belong.

During the first 5 or 6 years of the U. N., members were confronted with the grim specter of ever-increasing expenditures at a time when many of them could ill afford to pay. Expenditures under the regular budget grew from a modest $19.3 million in 1946, to $38.4 million in 1948, to a high of $50.3 million in 1952. At the same time, the birth of UNESCO, IRO, FAO, WHO, and the other specialized agencies, together with heavy outlays for certain voluntary activities like the Children's Fund and the Palestine refugee program, began to take their toll. These growing contributions, coupled with the added expenses involved in establishing permanent missions at U. N. headquarters and attending meetings all over the world, began to give many governments serious concern. The problem was complicated by the fact that a large proportion of their new obligations was payable

in hard currency. In 1950, the report of the General Assembly's Fifth
Committee warned that—

if costs continued to increase, there would be a grave danger that essential activities might be seriously limited by lagging contributions.[5]

These factors have given rise to repeated suggestions that a ceiling
be imposed upon the regular U. N. budget and that expenditures
for the year be kept within the stipulated amount. This could be
done either by the passage of a simple General Assembly resolution
or by the approval of a formal charter amendment. In the former
case, the stipulated amount—$35 million is the figure most often sug-
gested—could be revised upward or downward in accordance with the
will of the Assembly; in the latter case, the ceiling figure could not
be changed without going through the difficult process of amending
the charter.

There are sound arguments in favor of stabilizing the level of
regular U. N. expenditures at or near the present level. As the Australian delegate pointed out in 1950, it would be helpful for planning
purposes if the member governments could know for some years in
advance approximately what their commitments would be with respect
to United Nations activities.[6] Even more important is the legitimate
fear shared by many people that if the organization moves too far
and too fast in the direction of taking on new activities and new
responsibilities, it would subject the U. N. to undue stresses and strains
and jeopardize the entire program. If a reasonable limit is not imposed upon expansion, the argument runs, worthwhile programs might
suffer and serious damage be done to an already overburdened staff.

A good many delegations, however, have vigorously opposed the
budget ceiling as being neither practicable nor desirable. While they
favor economy in U. N. expenditures, they insist that the organization
should have the financial means at its disposal at all times so that
it can discharge effectively its essential functions. Some are particularly anxious not to hamper U. N. activity in the field of social and
economic advancement. Still others point out that the special responsibilities of the U. N. in the political field, and the uncertainties of
the future, constitute a sufficient justification for not limiting requests
which might come from the General Assembly in this respect.

The most persuasive argument, however, is the fact that through
economy measures inaugurated during the past few years, the regular
budget has stopped its upward climb. Following a high of $50.3
million in 1952, expenditures dropped to $48.3 million in 1953 and
$47.8 million in 1954. The budget approved for 1955 is an even lower
$46.5 million. As a result, by October 1954—with the exception of
the Communist states whose representatives favor the elimination
from the budget of certain activities which they deem to be "incompatible with the principles and provisions of the charter"—the pressure to establish a budget ceiling was gradually subsiding.

One final point should be made in this connection. It should be
kept in mind that the regular U. N. budget comprises a relatively
small portion—in 1952 it was less than 20 percent—of the funds spent
in the United Nations system. The real danger, therefore, does not
come from that source. If the U. N. should encounter financial dis-

---

[5] United Nations document A/1734, December 14, 1950.
[6] United Nations document A. C. 5/L. 96.

tress, it will not be because of the regular budget; it will be because of the heavy burdens imposed upon the members by the voluntary programs.

3. THE PROBLEM OF THE VOLUNTARY PROGRAMS

Should the present distinction between the regular U. N. budget and the voluntary programs be broken down and one overall budget established for United Nations activities?

By far the most important aspect of the U. N. budget is that concerned with voluntary contributions to various operational programs like the United Nations Expanded Program for Technical Assistance (UNTA), and the programs of the United Nations Korean Reconstruction Agency (UNKRA), the United Nations Relief and Works Agency for Palestine Refugees in the Near East (UNRWA), and the United Nations International Children's Fund (UNICEF). As one would expect, this type of financing has given rise to various criticisms. In the first place, the distinction between the regular budget and the voluntary programs is not a logical one; it developed primarily because voluntary contributions offered the only practical basis on which the U. N. could get certain programs financed and agreed to. Moreover, a certain amount of criticism has been leveled at both the extent and the use of these various funds. No doubt there has been some duplication and overlapping of effort as well as excessive expenditures for administrative purposes.

The main criticism, however, which has been raised in the United States, stems from the fact that a number of U. N. members are reluctant to contribute their share of the expenses. Indeed, one of the current crises facing the U. N. is the possibility that some of the voluntary programs, such as UNKRA and UNRWA, are in danger of collapsing because of a shortage of funds.

A few statistics may serve to highlight this point. As of September 15, 1954, only 14 of the 60 member states had pledged contributions to each of the four voluntary programs for the current year.[7] Although 58 members pledged assistance to the Technical Assistance program, only 21 were listed as supporting UNRWA, and 30 as promising aid to UNKRA. Some 33 members pledged assistance to UNICEF.

The response to UNKRA has been especially disappointing. In spite of an authorized target figure of $266 million, which the General Assembly in 1953 approved by an overwhelming majority, payments from governments had totaled only $112 million by September 15, 1954. Because of lack of support, UNKRA was forced to cut back its authorized 1953–54 program from $130 million to $85 million, and even then less than half the funds required for the reduced program had been collected by September 15, 1954. Moreover, 95 percent of the assistance received by the agency has come from four governments.

These results were recorded in the face of the persistent efforts of the General Assembly's Negotiating Committee for Extra-Budgetary Funds to stimulate contributions. In 1953 the Committee invited all the delegations to a special meeting at which the Secretary General and other top officials discussed the financial requirements of the voluntary programs and encouraged pledges to them. Throughout the

---

[7] See United Nations Document A/2730, September 20, 1954.

year the Committee continued its efforts in a variety of ways including meetings with delegations, letters addressed to member states, and diplomatic approaches to various governments.

The reasons for this lack of enthusiasm for certain U. N. programs are not difficult to find. In some cases it may be due to the chronic shortage of dollars which has plagued the organization since its inception. In other cases it may be due to the unfamiliarity of people in various parts of the world about the work of the United Nations. When important gaps in popular understanding often exist even in the United States, where the headquarters is located, it is easy to understand how such gaps might be multiplied in faraway countries like Liberia, Peru, Burma, and Yemen.

It should also be kept in mind that UNICEF and Technical Assistance are programs with a well-nigh universal appeal carrying with them tangible and immediate benefits for a great many countries. On the other hand, both UNKRA and UNRWA have only a local or regional impact and, as such, reflect tangible returns for relatively few states.

Moreover, the U. N., like most human institutions, has to face up to political realities. Many of the underdeveloped countries, for understandable reasons, take a pretty dim view of the idea of making contributions to large-scale programs of a relief character in some distant part of the world when they need to exert every effort to raise the standard of living within their own borders. A man who is hard pressed to feed his own family is not likely to make sizable contributions to the Community Chest.

Even so, there is a disturbing tendency among many states, some of which are in fairly sound financial condition, to discuss, to vote and not to contribute. One of the compelling needs of the U. N. today is the development among the members of a deeper sense of individual and collective responsibility for the successful completion of multilateral programs launched by the organization.

One possible answer to the present dilemma would be to take Technical Assistance, UNICEF, UNRWA, and UNKRA off the present voluntary basis, provide for them in the regular U. N. budget, and assess the members for their fair share of the programs. If this could be done, it would not only guarantee participation in important U. N. activities by the total membership; it would do away with inherent weaknesses which have beset the voluntary programs from the beginning.

Take the technical assistance program as an example. As things stand now, funds are pledged on a year-to-year basis with pledges subject to parliamentary approval in many different states. With financial resources so uncertain, it is extremely difficult for the agencies concerned to plan their programs with any degree of efficiency. Moreover, it becomes almost impossible to launch long-term projects or to enter into long-run commitments with staff members or consultants. These are formidable handicaps for any enterprise of this kind to overcome.

If the program were incorporated into the regular U. N. budget it would put technical assistance funds on a more stable plane and would enable the agencies concerned to carry out their projects on a continuing basis instead of in the disjointed, haphazard manner they are sometimes forced to operate.

On the other side of the picture, there are three significant advantages to the present voluntary arrangement:

1. Each member may contribute what it wishes each year in accordance with its interest in the various programs and its ability to pay.

2. It does not increase the regular U. N. budget to a level where it is beyond the capacity of the members to support over a period of years.

3. So far as the United States is concerned, Congress has indicated its willingness to contribute more than one-third of the budgets of some of the voluntary programs if they are not on a continuing obligatory basis.

Budget figures are inescapably harsh. If all U. N. expenses—excluding the specialized agencies—were incorporated into a single overall budget the result would be a total annual budget of something less than $200 million for 1955. This would mean a figure of approximately four times the present regular U. N. budget. It is obvious that if individual contributions were increased by that amount it would put a serious strain on the financial position of a number of states. Some members no doubt would be compelled to withdraw from the organization.

From a practical point of view, therefore, it is doubtful that the objective referred to above could be achieved unless one of two things were to happen: (1) either it would be necessary to reduce drastically the amounts spent for the voluntary programs; or (2) the United States would have to raise its contribution to the regular budget far in excess of its present 33⅓ percent level.

If it is not yet possible to do away with voluntary financing, consideration could still be given to the possibility of moving in that general direction. Would it not be possible, for example, to increase the regular budget to $100 million and then make sizable contributions from that budget to each of the voluntary programs? This would mean that every member, through doubling its contribution to the regular budget, would be assuming at least a limited share of the financial responsibility for each U. N. program. States with more ample means would still be called upon to make relatively large amounts available on a voluntary basis. As the voluntary programs are reduced in scope, a larger proportion of their total costs could be charged against the regular budget.

In fact, the technical assistance program has already reached a point where, with relatively minor adjustments, it could be absorbed into the regular budget, although the participation of non-U. N. members would present a problem. At present, only two U. N. members do not contribute. Moreover, with three major exceptions, the members contribute to Technical Assistance in about the same ratio as they are assessed for the regular budget. The United States contributes some 55 percent as contrasted with our regular contribution of 33.33; China contributes 0.06 percent as against her regular budget assessment of 5.62 percent; and the U. S. S. R., which is assessed 14.15 percent for 1954, agreed to contribute 3.95 percent of the technical assistance fund. It appears, therefore, that the bulk of the deficiency the United States is making up by contributing in excess of 33.33 percent can be attributed to the U. S. S. R. and China.

One additional point should be kept in mind. If our Government should decide to urge the consolidation of the voluntary programs with the regular budget, we should consider carefully the effect of such a move on the control of the programs in question. So long as they are kept on a voluntary basis the United States, as the largest contributor, is in a position to exercise greater influence than would be the case if the voluntary programs were covered into the regular budget.

4. PRIVATE SOURCES OF INCOME FOR THE U. N.

Could private or nongovernmental sources of income be tapped in such a way as to relieve member states of a substantial portion of their U. N. financial burdens?

From time to time, the suggestion has been made that the United Nations should put forth greater efforts to secure funds from private sources. In 1951, for example, the Senate Committee on Expenditures in the Executive Departments had this to say:

> Independent sources of income must be found for the United Nations and the specialized agencies in order to relieve member governments of their present heavy financial burdens. These sources might be developed by the performance of services for private business and educational concerns, or by obtaining private grants in support of some portions of their work.[8]

Thus far, the United Nations has derived only an insignificant fraction of its annual budget from nongovernmental sources. An unusual exception occurred in 1947–48 when the Children's Fund collected some $12 million in a special worldwide appeal for voluntary contributions. The success of this drive hinged upon the unique humanitarian appeal which this particular program had at the end of the war when people in many countries were suffering because of the severe shortage of food and medical supplies. While UNICEF has encouraged various campaigns for funds in individual countries since that time, it is significant that it has not been found possible to repeat the successful 1947–48 experiment. From 1947 to 1953, the Fund received from private sources (including organized campaigns) a total of $13,655,000—with only $144,000 collected in 1952, and $828,000 in 1953. This represents about 7 percent of its total income during these years.

In U. N. circles, the UNICEF experience has demonstrated quite conclusively that this doorbell approach, while helpful in isolated instances, is certainly no solution to the difficult problem of financing international agencies over the long pull. Moreover, as a general principle, it would seem unwise for the U. N. to seek funds through regular governmental channels and then proceed to supplement those funds by going, hat in hand, to solicit private contributions within the member states. Certainly, if very many such appeals were made, U. N. prestige could eventually suffer serious setbacks.

Nor can the private foundations and other nongovernmental agencies be expected to assume a sizable proportion of the burden. They carry on a number of helpful activities in many countries which tie in closely with U. N. programs—especially in the fields of health and agriculture—but the funds expended are not a part of the U. N. budget. They have extended the U. N. a few small grants, the most notable of which is the $3,100,000 given the U. N. High Commissioner for Refugees by the Ford Foundation in 1952. This was for the pur-

---

[8] 82d Cong., 1st sess., Rept. No. 90, pp. 69–70.

pose of undertaking a pilot project working toward a permanent solution to the so-called hard-core refugee problem.

The private foundations have been inclined to shy away from grants to the U. N. for several reasons. In the first place, they do not want to make it possible, through their grants, for U. N. agencies to launch projects which the member states themselves have not actively approved or supported. Perhaps even more important, they do not want to get bogged down contributing to large-scale programs of a relief character which could easily drain off their resources for years to come. As a result of these factors, together with the desire not to move into areas which are more properly the responsibility of the international community, the few grants they have made have been relatively small and for very special purposes.

So far as the regular U. N. budget is concerned, efforts to augment the income derived from member contributions have certainly not been crowned with success. The two most promising sources are the guided tours of the U. N. headquarters, which will return an estimated $400,-000 gross for 1954, and the sale of U. N. postage stamps which will net about the same figure. Somewhat less is derived from rentals and the sale of U. N. publications. Unless new fund-raising activities are launched, however, such sources probably cannot be counted upon to return more than 2 or 3 percent of the annual budget figure.

Meanwhile, a number of proposals—generally without supporting analysis—have been advanced with the thought of uncovering some yet untapped source of revenue for the U. N. There is, for example, the suggestion that member governments might agree to impose a small fee on certain types of international commerce or upon tourists going from one country to another, for the benefit of the U. N. There is also the suggestion that nongovernmental agencies which have a particular interest in certain aspects of U. N. activity might be willing to supplement the contributions of the members. Finally, one writer has suggested that profits accruing from the International Bank, international development corporations, international canals and airways, and other internationally controlled monopolies administered for the benefit of the international community, might also be used in this way.[9]

Some of these schemes would probably call for a formal charter amendment. Others could be brought to fruition by agreement among the member states. In any event, it can be assumed that any proposal which would have the effect of throwing the United Nations into competition with private-business concerns, or of granting to the United Nations even a very limited taxing power, would raise a storm of protest and would meet with bitter opposition.

5. U. N. AUTHORITY TO LAY TAXES

Should the U. N. be granted the authority to lay and collect a limited amount of taxes within the member states for the support of the organization?

A good many proponents of world government believe that the only satisfactory way to cure the U. N. of its financial ills is to give it the power to levy and collect taxes within the member states. A vari-

---

[9] C. W. Jenks, Some Legal Aspects of Financing International Institutions, Grotius Society Transactions, vol. 28, p. 93.

ety of proposals supporting this view have been set forth by individuals and organizations. The most detailed of these will be found in the Clark-Sohn proposals wherein it is suggested that the General Assembly should have power—

to lay and collect an income and other taxes which, taken together, shall in no event exceed in any year 2 percent of the estimated world gross product for that year.[10]

The proponents believe this amount would be necessary for the U. N. to carry out the greatly expanded program of activities which they recommend in the economic and collective security fields. U. N. revenues would come from income taxes collected from taxpayers in the upper brackets, from excise taxes on such items as motor vehicles, gasoline, liquor, and tobacco, or from export and import duties. A United Nations Revenue Officer would be stationed in each member state to receive directly the taxes of those individuals called upon to pay.

Most of the other proposals are more general in character and somewhat less ambitious in scope. The United World Federalists, for example, suggest that the kind of world organization they have in mind "should have authority to raise dependable revenue under a carefully defined and limited but direct taxing power independent of national taxation." Two other world federalist groups, the World Movement for World Federal Government, and the World Association of Parliamentarians for World Government, have expressed much the same view. In a joint meeting held in Copenhagen, in 1953, they recommended that the world assembly should be given the power to raise revenue for United Nations purposes. "The maximum percentage of estimated world income to be collected for United Nations purposes," declared the conference, "must be defined in the charter, and should be levied proportionately to the national income of each member state."[11] The Committee to Frame a World Constitution, as well as the Federal Union and Atlantic Union groups would also bestow upon a central world or regional legislative body the right to levy taxes.

The proponents of world government argue their case vigorously. Their main contentions, however, can be boiled down to one essential point: reliability of revenue. "How can the U. N. or any other world organization do its job effectively," they argue, "if it does not have a reliable source of income from year to year?"

This argument would seem more valid if the U. N. were to expand its functions in a manner contemplated by the Clark-Sohn proposals. Certainly it is doubtful if the organization could meet an annual budget of the magnitude contemplated in these proposals if it did not resort to extraordinary means to secure funds.

The world government point of view was summed up at the Copenhagen Conference in these words:

A new tax collector can hardly expect to be greeted with loud and prolonged cheers; but unless the U. N. has its own taxing power, it cannot act independently of national governments, and can therefore have no real authority. The United Nations at present relies on contributions from the nations, which are liable to withhold the money if they dislike what U. N. is doing; in fact, certain countries have already withdrawn their help from the specialized agencies.

---

[10] Clark and Sohn, Peace Through Disarmament and Charter Revision, 1953, p. 25 ff.
[11] John Pinder, U. N. Reform, Proposals for Charter Amendment, Federal Union, London, September 1953, p. 23.

Taxation of individuals is just a special example of the enforcement of law on individuals described above; it is likewise necessary, because people who fail to pay taxes can be brought to book, while nations cannot.[12]

This question of the independence of the U. N. goes to the heart of the issue. Supporters of the concept of state sovereignty insist that sovereign nations cannot afford to supply the U. N. with an independent source of income precisely because they want to be in a position to hold back contributions in the event they disapprove what the organization is doing. To lose control of U. N. purse strings would be tantamount to losing control, to a considerable degree, of its programs.

There is also vigorous opposition to the idea of U. N. taxation on the ground that it would invade, in a dangerous way, an area which has been traditionally reserved within the exclusive jurisdiction of the member states. Even groups like the Parliamentarians for World Government are restrained by that fact. At their London Conference in 1952 the group pointed out that they were "attracted" by the idea that the U. N. should be allowed to levy taxes on individual citizens. "We finally decided to recommend against it," they added. "The incidence of taxation is peculiarly a matter of domestic consideration." [13]

Apart from the fact that such far-reaching proposals would require amendments to both the charter and the United States Constitution, many difficult questions remain to be answered. For example: (1) Would not a direct tax on individuals cause resentment among the people and lose public support for the U. N.? (2) Would the American people, already objecting to extensive foreign-aid programs, agree to substantial increases in U. N. expenditures? (3) Could agreement be reached on the kind of taxes that would be fair and equitable in view of the various conditions that exist in different states? (4) Who would be responsible for the collection of such taxes? (5) What machinery would be set up for the enforcement of tax laws against individual citizens?

These may not be insuperable problems. But given the present state of world affairs they are tough enough to make unlikely the adoption of any U. N. tax system in the near future.

6. COORDINATION OF SPECIALIZED AGENCIES

Should the General Assembly be given more authority to coordinate the activities of the specialized agencies particularly through approval of their budgets and programs?

It has already been pointed out that the United Nations system is made up of a dozen relatively autonomous entities. Each of the specialized agencies has its own constitution, its own headquarters, its own constituent organs, its own program, and its own budget. As a result, it has been extremely difficult to develop effective coordination between the United Nations and the various specialized agencies and among the specialized agencies themselves.

This lack of coordination has taken various forms. In some cases it has given rise to overlapping and duplication of effort on the part of the specialized agencies. This is not surprising, for it is only

[12] Ibid., p. 12.
[13] Report of the Second London Parliamentary Conference on World Government, Sept. 20–26, 1952, p. 115.

natural that agencies with such intimately related programs as health and food and agriculture would tend to elbow their way into each other's fields.   In other cases it has resulted in embarrassing conflicts of policy within the United Nations system.   This, too, is understandable, for with so many agencies in the field it has not always been possible for the right hand in FAO to know just what the left hand in WHO, UNESCO, or ILO is up to.   Finally, and more importantly, it has encouraged a running competition among the specialized agencies for larger portions of United Nations funds with various special-interest groups exerting pressure on behalf of their particular agencies.

It is true that a considerable amount of coordinating machinery already exists.   The specialized agencies have been "brought into relationship" with the United Nations by means of agreements negotiated by the Economic and Social Council and approved by the General Assembly.   These agreements cover such matters as reciprocal representation at meetings, provision for consultation, and the transmission of reports to the United Nations by the specialized agencies.   Each year their budgets are "examined" by the Advisory Committee on Administrative and Budgetary Questions, which makes various recommendations.   Relatively little attention, however, has been given these recommendations by the General Assembly.   Moreover, the Secretary General presides over an Administrative Committee on Coordination, which consists of the Directors of the specialized agencies.

It is in the administrative and financial fields particularly that real progress has been achieved.   The United Nations and the specialized agencies have agreed upon uniform fiscal and accounting procedures, personnel regulations, pension benefits, salary scales and allowances, and where practicable, the coordination of administrative services.

The point remains, however, that the present sprawling system of independent agencies is extremely complex and creates a great deal of confusion in the public mind.   Its greatest weakness lies in the fact that it does not permit any central planning through which the members may determine in a balanced and logical way the most effective use of the United Nations total resources.

On this point the Senate Committee on Expenditures in the Executive Branch stated in 1951 that—

effective coordination can be achieved only if some measure of real control over the budgets and programs of the specialized agencies is given to the General Assembly.   This, in turn, can be accomplished only by amendment of the constitutions of the specialized agencies, designed either to afford to the General Assembly effective control over programs and projects of the agencies, or to provide for the inclusion of the budgets of the agencies within a consolidated budget of the United Nations, to be approved by the General Assembly.[14]

If this procedure were followed, each of the specialized agencies would approve its own budget and submit it to the United Nations for consideration.   The various budgets would then be consolidated with the regular United Nations budget and would be subject to the same overall scrutiny and review as the regular budget.   As an alternative the budgets of the specialized agencies could be reviewed separately by the United Nations, instead of in a single package form.   In either event the results would be approximately the same.   Member states would have an opportunity to look at the total United Nations program and thus be in a much better position to give overall guidance and

_____
[14] Rept. No. 90, 82d Cong., 1st sess., p. 57.

direction to United Nations activities.   Effective control over programs and projects could be established, duplication and overlapping avoided, and substantial savings brought about.

These may sound like good and sufficient reasons for a consolidated budget.   Why, then, has consolidation not taken place?   The most obvious answer lies in the solid opposition of the specialized agencies which are anxious to retain their position of autonomy within the U. N. system.   In the United States they have won the support of various farm, labor, health, and educational groups whose influence is felt in the Nation's Capital.   As a result, there are conflicting pressures on Congress: On the one hand there is desire to consolidate and coordinate; on the other hand, there is a desire to permit the specialized agencies to develop their own programs in their own independent way.

The tradition of autonomy is deeply ingrained in the U. N. system. At San Francisco the framers of the charter considered the possibility of establishing a centralized, unitary system but finally rejected it.   They chose instead to support the creation of a galaxy of semi-autonomous agencies which were to be brought into relationship with the United Nations proper by means of special agreements concluded under articles 17, 57, and 63.

In 1948 the Administrative Committee on Coordination pointed out that at least four steps were necessary before a consolidated budget could be put into effect.   These were: (1) the constitutions of the various specialized agencies would have to be amended in order to transfer to the General Assembly sufficient power to handle the new combined budget; (2) state delegations to the General Assembly would have to be changed so as to include specialists equipped to discuss the budgets and programs of the specialized agencies; (3) General Assembly sessions would have to be lengthened to enable it to handle the heavy workload involved in examining carefully a greatly enlarged budget; and finally, (4) some way would have to be found to get around the fact that some United Nations members do not belong to the specialized agencies.   Moreover, most of the agencies have a fairly large number of members who are not represented in the General Assembly because they do not belong to the United Nations.

Because of these complications, the Committee agreed that, however desirable a consolidated budget might be as a long-range goal, it did not offer a practicable solution for the problem in the immediate future.   As an alternative, the Committee recommended that every effort be made to put the existing machinery for coordination to a fair test.[15]

The problem of overlapping membership is especially important. Some of the specialized agencies have been able to make significant progress precisely because the Communist countries have remained aloof.   Under the circumstances, it would not be appropriate to permit the U. S. S. R. and its satellites in the General Assembly to take part in the debate on the budgets of some of the agencies to which they do not belong.

There are still other potent political factors which make the specialized agencies shy away from any further consolidation of the U. N. system.   Rightly or wrongly, they strongly believe that they can make more persuasive gains in such technical fields as health, labor, and

[15] U. N. Document E/614, January 29, 1948, annex V.

agriculture, if they are allowed to keep a safe distance from the political turmoil of the General Assembly. Likewise, in the event the United Nations should collapse, they would be in a better position to carry on their work as independent agencies if they are not too closely identified with the parent organization.

Meanwhile, there is another step that has been suggested which would bring in its wake many of the advantages of a centralized budget. The Economic and Social Council and the General Assembly could review the activities of the United Nations and the specialized agencies and then on the basis of that review, recommend overall budget figures for each of the specialized agencies. These target figures would be in the nature of recommendations only; the competent organs of the specialized agencies would still possess the authority to give final approval to their particular agency's program and budget. Since the General Assembly already has ample power to make such recommendations, no formal charter amendment would be necessary to bring about this change.

Even though the General Assembly would still be unable to compel the specialized agencies to do its bidding, such a procedure could have a very salutary impact upon the U. N. system. As in the case of the centralized budget, it would make possible a comparative analysis of various U. N. programs and enable the members, for the first time, to apportion the total resources of the U. N. in a logical way. It would also compel each government to hammer out a coherent, unified policy with respect to the specialized agencies so it could speak with the same voice in the General Assembly as it would in each of the agencies to which it belongs.

It is doubtful, for reasons already outlined above, that the specialized agencies would accept willingly even such half-way measures. As the director-general of one of the agencies commented in October 1954:

> We are making good progress with the coordinating machinery we already have. The new Secretary-General is doing a splendid job in giving us the leadership we need to pull the U. N. system together. I believe if we are permitted to give the existing machinery a good trial we can satisfy the demands of those people who are insisting upon more effective coordination.

Actually, since the General Assembly and the specialized agencies have a large overlapping membership, the problem could be resolved any time the members agree on a solution—and it does not really matter whether they agree as members of the General Assembly or as members of the specialized agencies. Much of the difficulty arises from internal schizophrenia of governments; and if the governments of sovereign states insist on following conflicting policies in the U. N. and in the specialized agencies, reorganization of the U. N. will not cure them.

7. U. N. CONTRIBUTIONS AND WEIGHTED VOTING

Should some form of weighted voting be instituted so that the voting strength of member states could be brought more into line with their contributions to the United Nations?

The suggestion has been made that some method should be devised so that member states might receive more tangible benefits from their contributions to the United Nations. As things stand, the United

States, even though it has only one vote, receives a considerable amount of prestige and influence because it contributes the lion's share of the budget. No similar benefits accrue to the rank and file of members who stand further down the contributions scale. If proper incentives could be arranged, the argument runs, certain states might be willing to increase their annual outlay.

One possible incentive is additional voting strength. In 1950, the New Zealand delegate in the First Committee of the General Assembly suggested that it might be a good idea to grant voting power to each member——

roughly equal to the proportions which its financial contribution to the funds of the U. N. bears to the total contribution. * * * [16]

This principle has been applied successfully in a few specialized international organizations. In the International Bank for Reconstruction and Development and in the International Monetary Fund, for example, the voting power of the member states reflects the share of capital which the members have subscribed. It should be pointed out, however, that the idea has never been transplanted from agencies of a technical character to a general international organization like the United Nations.

There can be no doubt but what the principle of sovereign equality— which gave birth to the prevailing practice of giving to each state but one vote—has resulted in bestowing upon the smaller countries a voting strength in international affairs far out of proportion to their position in the world. In 1953, for example, 9 members of the U. N. contributed less than $20,000 each to the regular budget. In contrast, the United States, likewise with 1 vote in the General Assembly, contributed $13,765,290. The 5 great powers, with only one-twelfth of the votes, contributed roughly 70 percent of the total budget.

Yet clearly any formula which would award states votes in rough proportion to their financial contributions would result in a disequilibrium of power that would be unacceptable to the small nations. Can anyone imagine the small states approving a General Assembly in which 3 or 4 of the permanent members would possess a majority of the votes? Or one in which the United States would be given one-third of the total voting strength?

On the other hand, it might be possible to work out a weighted voting formula combining contributions, population, and perhaps certain other factors, with a relatively modest voting bonus given to states whose contributions are in the upper brackets. Such a tentative proposal was put forth for discussion in Staff Study No. 4. In that proposal it was suggested that states contributing less than $20,000 to the regular U. N. budget might receive 1 vote; $20,000 to $100,000, 2 votes; $100,000 to $500,000, 3 votes; $500,000 to $2 million, 4 votes; and all over $2 million, 5 votes. Additional votes would also be accorded to countries with large populations.[17]

If some such system were adopted, national pride might impel a certain number of states to strain their budgets a bit more in order to be placed in a higher voting category. On the other hand, on the thesis that states have only so much to contribute to the U. N. system,

---

[16] Statement made October 11, 1950, during the Fifth General Assembly.
[17] U. S. Senate Committee on Foreign Relations, Subcommittee on the U. N. Charter, Staff Study No. 4: Representation and Voting in the United Nations General Assembly, pp. 19–23.

increased contributions to the regular budget might well be offset in some cases by decreased contributions to the various voluntary programs. If states were inclined to offset their contributions in this way, there would be little or no net gain for the U. N.

As logical as the concept of weighted voting might appear on the surface, there are telling arguments against it. In the first place, it would draw an undesirable distinction between rich and poor countries, and tend to place too much emphasis on the purely financial aspects of the United Nations. In the second place, it runs counter to the long-established principle of the sovereign equality of states; for this reason it would probably meet with the firm opposition of the smaller countries. Finally, any reasonable system of weighted voting based on such factors as population and financial contribution to the U. N. would adversely affect the position of the United States in the General Assembly since it would take voting strength away from the little states, many of whom have been staunch supporters of the free world position. Of the 9 states contributing less than $20,000 per year, for example, 6 are Latin American countries.

If it is not feasible to develop a system of weighted voting that would take into account the contributions of member states to the regular U. N. budget, it might still be possible to award additional votes to states making large contributions to the U. N.'s voluntary programs. A special voting formula could be devised for the Executive Board of the Children's Fund, for example, which has general supervision of that particular program. In this way those governments that volunteer heavy contributions to special U. N. activities would be given some additional control over the expenditure of the funds.

In U. N. circles a good many people are inclined to discount the importance of extra votes. Weighted voting, they argue, would make little or no real difference in the existing distribution of power in the General Assembly. The influence of a country would continue to be reflected more in the size of its contribution to the U. N. budget (and in other factors) than in the size of its vote. The United States may have only one vote but it has a great deal of influence inasmuch as its contribution is essential before vital programs can be carried out. For that reason, most countries which are on the receiving end of U. N. programs, normally exercise considerable restraint in pressing to a vote matters which are unacceptable to our Government.

Up to this point the problem of weighted voting has ordinarily been approached in terms of giving to states voting power more commensurate with their responsibility in the organization. Perhaps it should also be approached in terms of encouraging members to make further contributions to the U. N. budget.

IV. Contribution of U. N. Members To Enforcement Action

United Nations action to stem aggression in Korea put the contributions problem in a somewhat different perspective. The total amount spent on various U. N. activities prior to June 25, 1950, appeared insignificant indeed when compared to the vast resources in both manpower and materiel, that were poured into the Korean conflict. Since the greatest share of the burden fell upon the United States, this raised in a very pointed way the question as to what can be done under the charter to encourage each of the U. N. members to assume its fair share of the responsibility in any future enforcement action.

During the 3 years of hostilities in Korea only 15 nations, besides the Republic of Korea and the United States, contributed armed forces. As against the 45,000 men furnished by our 15 allies, the United States contributed over 450,000 and actually rotated more than a million men through Korea. We also furnished a considerable portion of the equipment and supplies required for the total U. N. effort.

There are reasons advanced—including the limited number of ground forces available and the total defense requirements of the free world—why our allies did not respond more effectively to the call for action in Korea. Some nations had already committed certain of their forces to areas which were considered of vital importance to them as well as to us. Still others were ready to send troops to Korea if the U. N. were willing to guarantee their territorial integrity while their armed forces were fighting elsewhere. Even so some 46 U. N. members gave the U. N. their economic support, 43 governments contributed to the Korean relief program, and some 40 countries pledged cooperation in the United Nations embargo against the shipment of strategic materials to Communist China. A few countries contributed naval vessels or dry-cargo ships. Others sent field hospital units and medical supplies. Some contributed fighter squadrons and air-transport facilities while others made available sea and air bases.

Nevertheless, as Senator Knowland, of California, has pointed out—

both in the Congress and in the country there is a very real concern that the burdens ought to be more evenly spread, in the event of future necessity for collective security action. If nations are to benefit by the system of collective security, they should be prepared to assume their full obligations.[18]

In view of the duration of hostilities in Korea and the large number of casualties involved, it is unlikely that many members of the U. N. will be inclined to regard any similar venture in the future with any real enthusiasm. Nevertheless, two recent developments indicate that, if another enforcement action should become necessary, it may be possible for the U. N. to approach with somewhat greater success a larger number of states for contributions in armed forces and in other types of military assistance.

In the first place, the President has outlined a new policy which may have some appeal to states that are willing to make troops available but are unable to furnish them with the necessary logistic support. On March 3, 1954, Ambassador Lodge testified before the Senate Foreign Relations Committee that if our Government, during the Korean crisis—

had not required states having valuable manpower to reimburse us in dollars for the supplies which we provided them, we might well have had perhaps as much as three divisions more.[19]

Some nations, he pointed out, were unable to participate in the Korean enterprise because they did not have the mechanized equipment, the transportation facilities, or the dollars necessary to put their troops on the battlefront so far away from home. These factors tended to re-

---

[18] Senate Committee on Foreign Relations, hearings on the U. N. Charter, 1954, pt. I, p. 14.
[19] Hearings, op. cit., p. 40.

duce considerably the manpower contribution of various U. N. members.

Presumably, our Government does not intend to let this happen again for want of logistic support. "The President's policy," said Ambassador Lodge, "is that, while in principle each nation involved in a United Nations effort to repel an aggression should equip and supply its own troops to the extent that it is able, the overriding consideration should be the maximum contribution of effective manpower. When any such nation is willing to contribute effective manpower but not able to provide for logistic support, the Department of Defense should furnish to such nation military equipment, supplies, and services; without requirement of payment to the extent that the Department of State, in consultation with the Departments of Treasury and Defense, may determine such nation cannot reasonably be expected to pay."

In the second place, the Collective Measures Committee of the United Nations has undertaken a comprehensive study of the techniques for organizing and coordinating the contributions of armed forces and other types of assistance which members might make to any future collective action against an aggressor. In the event the United Nations is called upon to take enforcement action the Committee points out that "a primary objective shall be to secure the maximum contribution of effective military forces." [20] At the same time, it emphasizes the fact that the contributions of states "may be military, political, economic or financial; direct or ancillary." The Committee then analyzes in some detail the various types of assistance that can be given and, in accordance with the terms of the Uniting for Peace Resolution, calls upon U. N. members to earmark certain units of their armed forces for possible U. N. use.

Obviously, no catalog of collective measures, no matter how detailed, will guarantee an effective response when an aggressor puts in his appearance. But in Korea the U. N. started from scratch. Now, at least, with the analysis of the Collective Measures Committee available, member states should have an increasing awareness of their responsibilities toward collective security and a much better notion of the types of assistance they can render.

One further point should be made in this connection. As originally drafted, the charter envisaged a system in which member nations, in accordance with special agreements provided for in article 43, would be obligated to make armed forces, assistance, and facilities available to the Security Council for enforcement purposes. Since article 43 remains a dead letter, any such contributions must now be made on a purely voluntary basis. This inevitably means that, if the U. N. should be faced with another Korea, some governments would find other more urgent uses for their armed forces.

Theoretically, there are several ways in which this problem could be met. Article 43 might be reactivated and further attempts made to conclude the agreements which that article contemplates between the member states and the Security Council. The fruitless efforts of the Military Staff Committee during the past 9 years, however, would indicate that there is not much hope in that direction. Similarly, any attempt formally to amend the charter so as to bestow upon the General Assembly compulsory powers comparable to those outlined in

[20] United Nations document, A/2713: S/3283, August 30, 1954.

the charter for the Security Council would be foredoomed to failure.

Still a third possibility was put forth in 1950 by the late Senator Thomas, of Utah, and Senator Douglas, of Illinois, in the form of a general collective defense pact under article 51. The signatories to such a convention would pledge themselves to support enforcement measures against any nation voted an aggressor by a two-thirds vote of the General Assembly including three of the permanent members of the Security Council. Moreover, they would agree in advance to make available to the Security Council or to the General Assembly upon call certain designated military, naval, and air components for enforcement purposes.

This proposal would have the merit of letting the U. N. know precisely what it could count on in the way of military assistance from its members to keep the peace. From the point of view of the United States, however, it would have a serious drawback. It would mean that our Government would agree to abandon the veto in decisions involving the use of our Armed Forces.

So long as the manpower and other contributions to U. N. enforcement action remain on a voluntary basis, this will constitute one of the burning issues of the U. N. Regardless of how the issue is resolved, one thing is certain. The people of the United States might be expected to be more willing to contribute generously to the regular U. N. budget and its various special programs if the other members of the U. N. could be counted upon to contribute their fair share of manpower, money, and materiel when the chips are down.

V. Concluding Summary

From the day of its creation, the United Nations has been riding the horns of a fiscal dilemma. It was recognized, on the one hand, that a relatively small budget might prove inadequate to meet the many demands placed upon the organization. On the other hand, the U. N. is made up of sovereign states. A very large budget would tend to make it impossible for many members to meet their financial obligations and participate in the work of the organization on a basis of sovereign equality.

The problem may be put in still another way. The expenditures of the United Nations must remain within such reasonable limits that the cost of membership is financially tolerable for the poorest as well as the wealthiest member on the roll. This means that the U. N. must not be overburdened with functions and projects it is not prepared to carry out. At the same time, if important tasks need to be performed and the organization should assume the responsibility for them, then proper ways and means must be found to make effective action possible.

In spite of the principle of sovereign equality, the devastation brought by the war, the shortage of dollars, and the wide variation in the national incomes of its 60 member states, the United Nations has met its financial problems reasonably well. The regular U. N. budget has been stabilized. No urgent and important task legitimately within the scope of action of the U. N. has been left undone because of a lack of funds. And no member has been forced to withdraw because it could not pay its dues.

Apart from the heavy cost involved in U. N. enforcement action, the most critical problem now is the financial plight of the so-called voluntary programs. If more satisfactory methods are not devised soon for the financing of such important activities as the relief and reconstruction programs in Palestine and Korea, they may suffer serious setbacks because of dwindling contributions.

As a result of the experience of the past 9 years, a number of suggestions have emerged relating to the financing of the U. N. These proposals range all the way from the idea that the General Assembly should be shorn of its power to apportion the expenses of the organization among its members, to the suggestion that the U. N. be given limited authority to levy and collect taxes in order to supplement its income. Other proposals include the following:

1. That a ceiling be placed upon the U. N. budget so as to limit annual expenditures to a fixed sum.

2. That the voluntary programs be incorporated into the regular U. N. budget and all members required to contribute to them.

3. That greater efforts be made to tap nongovernmental or private sources of income for U. N. purposes.

4. That the General Assembly coordinate the activities of the specialized agencies by exercising budgetary control over them.

5. That voting power in the General Assembly be given to member states in accordance with their financial contribution to the U. N.

6. That steps be taken to insure more effective participation by the members in any future U. N. enforcement action, particularly with respect to the use of armed forces.

In some cases—such as those relating to U. N. taxation and weighted voting—these proposals would necessitate formal charter amendments. In most instances, however, the objectives contemplated could be achieved by informal agreement among the member states.

Some of these proposals, if adopted, might help the United Nations to function more smoothly. But what is needed more than anything else in the financial realm is a recognition on the part of all members of their responsibility in the job to be done. No agreements, formal or informal, can take the place of a determination on the part of individual states to carry their full share of the burden.

This spirit of cooperation cannot be engendered overnight. It involves, among other things, a long educational process by which the people and the governments of many countries become better acquainted with the work of the United Nations.

There is one potential source of income that should not be ignored. At the present time, some 20 applications for membership—including such countries as Italy, Japan, Austria, Portugal, Ireland, and Finland—are pending before the U. N. If the 14 countries judged by the General Assembly to be qualified for membership were admitted, together with Western Germany, contributions to the regular U. N. budget could be increased by nearly 15 percent without any corresponding increase in expenditures.

It would seem, therefore, that every effort should be made to break the current logjam on membership. In the opinion of many people the admission of these states would add greatly to the effectiveness of the U. N. in dealing with the world's political problems. Their contributions to the budget would be just as helpful in strengthening the financial posture of the organization.

Meanwhile, there is one thing U. N. members can do which would contribute to the effectiveness of the voluntary programs, and that is to make their contributions sufficiently in advance so that adequate planning can be done.   Ordinarily contributions must be approved by the legislative bodies of the member states.   This sometimes involves considerable delay in part because the fiscal year of the U. N., which corresponds to the calendar year, does not coincide with the fiscal year of some of the members.

The technical assistance program is a case in point.   As of December 1954, those administering the program did not know whether approximately half their budget for the coming year would materialize.   As a result, their plans for 1955 had to be tentative and uncertain.   This is an extremely difficult situation for any administrator who must allocate funds, hire personnel, and coordinate the various aspects of a complex program.

If the members of the United Nations should decide to make no contribution to the voluntary programs, that is within their sovereign right.   But if they are going to contribute, it undoubtedly would be helpful if they would make known their intentions far enough in advance so the funds could be spent with the maximum degree of effectiveness.

One final conclusion seems inescapable.   The regular and voluntary financial burdens which the United Nations imposes are small when compared with the cost of war; they represent only a minor fraction of the national budgets of the member states.   That this is the case is indicated by the cost of the Korean enforcement which has been many times the total of all other expenditures for the U. N. since its inception.   When measured against the probable cost of fighting an atomic war, the normal financial burdens of the United Nations are infinitesimal.

The U. N. is one of the insurance policies we hold against the outbreak of another world war.   In every insurance policy there is a certain risk involved.   But if the U. N. can make a vital contribution to the maintenance of peace, if it can be instrumental in preventing a third great war, the premium payments would be very well spent.

APPENDIX

TABLE A.—*Member assessments for the United Nations, 1946–54* [1]

Country	1946 Per-cent	1946 Assessment	1947 Per-cent	1947 Assessment	1948 Per-cent	1948 Assessment	1949 Per-cent	1949 Assessment	1950 Per-cent	1950 Assessment	1951 Per-cent	1951 Assessment	1952 Per-cent	1952 Assessment	1953 Per-cent	1953 Assessment	1954 Per-cent	1954 Assessment
Afghanistan		$3,192	0.05	$13,725	0.05	$17,349	0.05	$20,808	0.05	$17,085	0.06	$25,542	0.08	$34,352	0.08	$35,360	0.08	$33,040
Argentina	1.94	373,062	1.85	507,825	1.85	641,913	1.85	769,915	1.85	632,145	1.85	787,545	1.62	695,628	1.45	640,900	1.40	578,200
Australia	2.00	384,600	1.97	540,765	1.97	683,551	1.97	819,855	1.97	673,149	1.92	817,344	1.77	760,038	1.75	773,500	1.75	722,750
Belgium	1.42	273,066	1.35	370,575	1.35	468,423	1.35	561,830	1.35	461,295	1.35	574,595	1.35	579,690	1.37	605,540	1.38	569,940
Bolivia	.08	15,384	.08	21,960	.08	27,758	.08	33,294	.08	27,336	.08	34,056	.06	25,764	.06	26,520	.06	24,780
Brazil	1.94	373,062	1.85	507,825	1.85	641,913	1.85	769,915	1.85	632,145	1.85	787,545	1.62	695,628	1.45	640,900	1.40	578,200
Burma						34,063	.15	62,425	.15	51,255	.15	63,855	.15	64,410	.13	57,460	.13	53,690
Byelorussian S. S. R.	.23	44,229	.22	60,390	.22	76,336	.22	91,557	.22	75,174	.24	102,168	.34	145,996	.43	190,060	.50	206,500
Canada	3.35	644,205	3.20	878,400	3.20	1,110,336	3.20	1,331,744	3.20	1,093,440	3.30	1,404,810	3.35	1,438,490	3.30	1,458,600	3.30	1,362,900
Chile	.47	90,381	.45	123,525	.45	156,141	.45	187,277	.45	153,765	.41	174,537	.35	150,290	.33	145,860	.33	136,290
China	6.30	1,211,490	6.00	1,647,000	6.00	2,081,880	6.00	2,497,020	6.00	2,050,200	6.00	2,554,200	5.75	2,469,050	5.62	2,484,700	5.62	2,321,060
Colombia	.39	74,997	.37	101,565	.37	128,383	.37	153,983	.37	126,429	.37	157,509	.37	158,878	.35	154,700	.41	169,330
Costa Rica	.04	7,692	.04	10,980	.04	13,879	.04	16,647	.04	13,668	.04	17,028	.04	17,176	.04	17,680	.04	16,520
Cuba	.30	57,690	.29	79,605	.29	100,624	.29	120,689	.29	99,093	.31	131,967	.33	141,702	.34	150,280	.34	140,420
Czechoslovakia	.95	182,685	.90	247,050	.90	312,282	.90	374,553	.90	307,530	.99	421,443	1.05	450,870	1.05	464,100	1.05	433,650
Denmark	.81	155,763	.79	216,855	.79	274,114	.79	328,774	.79	269,943	.79	336,303	.79	339,226	.78	344,760	.78	322,140
Dominican Republic	.05	9,615	.05	13,725	.05	17,349	.05	20,808	.05	17,085	.05	21,285	.05	21,470	.05	22,100	.05	20,650
Ecuador	.05	9,615	.05	13,725	.05	17,349	.05	20,808	.05	17,085	.05	21,285	.05	21,470	.04	17,680	.04	16,520
Egypt	.81	155,763	.79	216,855	.79	274,114	.79	328,774	.79	269,943	.71	302,247	.60	257,640	.50	221,000	.47	194,110
El Salvador	.05	9,615	.05	13,725	.05	17,349	.05	20,808	.05	17,085	.05	21,285	.05	21,470	.05	22,100	.06	24,780
Ethiopia	.08	15,384	.08	21,960	.08	27,758	.08	33,294	.08	27,336	.08	34,056	.10	42,940	.10	44,200	.10	41,300
France	6.30	1,211,490	6.00	1,647,000	6.00	2,081,880	6.00	2,497,020	6.00	2,050,200	6.00	2,554,200	5.75	2,469,050	5.75	2,541,500	5.75	2,374,750
Greece	.17	32,691	.17	46,665	.17	58,987	.17	70,749	.17	58,089	.18	76,626	.18	77,292	.19	83,980	.21	86,730
Guatemala	.05	9,615	.05	13,725	.05	17,349	.05	20,808	.05	17,085	.06	25,542	.06	25,764	.06	26,520	.07	28,910
Haiti	.04	7,692	.04	10,980	.04	13,879	.04	16,647	.04	13,668	.04	17,028	.04	17,176	.04	17,680	.04	16,520
Honduras	.04	7,692	.04	10,980	.04	13,879	.04	16,647	.04	13,668	.04	17,028	.04	17,176	.04	17,680	.04	16,520
Iceland		2,558	.04	10,980	.04	13,879	.04	16,647	.04	13,668	.04	17,028	.04	17,176	.04	17,680	.04	16,520
India	4.09	786,507	3.95	1,084,275	2 3.95	1,370,571	3.25	1,352,553	3.25	1,110,525	3.41	1,451,637	3.53	1,515,782	3.45	1,524,900	3.40	1,404,200
Indonesia															.60	265,200	.60	247,800
Iran	.47	90,381	.45	123,525	.45	166,141	.45	187,277	.45	153,765	.45	191,565	.40	171,760	.33	145,860	.28	115,640
Iraq	.17	32,691	.17	46,665	.17	58,987	.17	70,749	.17	58,089	.17	72,369	.14	60,116	.12	53,040	.12	49,560
Israel								27,085	.12	41,004	.12	51,084	.17	72,998	.17	75,140	.17	70,210

	%	Amount	%	Amount	%	Amount	%	Amount	%	Amount	%	Amount	%	Amount	%	Amount	%	Amount
Lebanon	.06	11,538	.06	16,470	.06	20,819	.06	24,970	.06	20,502	.06	25,542	.06	25,764	.05	22,100	.05	20,650
Liberia	.04	7,692	.04	10,980	.04	13,879	.04	16,647	.04	13,668	.04	17,028	.04	17,176	.04	17,680	.04	16,520
Luxembourg	.05	9,615	.05	13,725	.05	17,349	.05	20,808	.05	17,085	.05	21,285	.05	21,470	.06	22,100	.06	24,780
Mexico	.66	126,918	.63	172,935	.63	218,598	.63	262,187	.63	215,271	.63	268,191	.65	279,110	.75	309,400	.75	309,750
Netherlands	1.47	282,681	1.40	384,300	1.40	485,772	1.40	582,638	1.40	478,380	1.35	574,695	1.27	545,338	1.25	552,500	1.25	516,250
New Zealand	.52	99,996	.50	137,250	.50	173,490	.50	208,085	.50	170,850	.50	212,850	.50	214,700	.48	212,160	.48	198,240
Nicaragua	.04	7,692	.04	10,980	.04	13,879	.04	16,647	.04	13,668	.04	17,028	.04	17,176	.04	17,680	.04	16,520
Norway	.52	99,996	.50	137,250	.50	173,490	.50	208,085	.50	170,850	.50	212,850	.50	214,700	.50	221,000	.50	206,500
Pakistan					(²)	(²)	.70	291,319	.70	239,190	.74	315,018	.79	339,226	.75	349,180	.75	309,750
Panama	.05	9,615	.05	13,725	.05	17,349	.05	20,808	.05	17,085	.05	21,285	.05	21,470	.05	22,100	.05	20,650
Paraguay	.04	7,692	.04	10,980	.04	13,879	.04	16,647	.04	13,668	.04	17,028	.04	17,176	.04	17,680	.04	16,520
Peru	.21	40,383	.20	54,900	.20	69,396	.20	83,234	.20	68,340	.20	85,140	.20	85,880	.18	79,560	.18	74,340
Philippines	.30	57,690	.29	79,605	.29	100,624	.29	120,689	.29	99,093	.29	99,093	.29	124,526	.39	172,380	.45	185,850
Poland	1.00	192,300	.95	260,775	.95	329,631	.95	395,361	.95	324,615	1.05	446,985	1.36	583,984	1.58	698,360	1.73	714,490
Saudi Arabia	.08	15,384	.08	21,960	.08	27,758	.08	33,294	.08	27,336	.08	34,056	.08	34,352	.07	30,940	.07	28,910
Sweden	.78	150,628	2.35	645,075	2.04	707,839	2.00	832,340	1.98	676,566	1.85	787,545	1.73	742,862	1.65	729,300	1.65	681,450
Syria	.12	23,076	.12	32,940	.12	41,638	.12	49,940	.12	41,004	.11	46,827	.09	38,646	.08	35,360	.08	33,040
Thailand					.27	93,685	.27	112,366	.27	92,259	.24	102,168	.21	90,174	.18	79,560	.18	74,340
Turkey	.93	178,839	.91	249,795	.91	315,752	.91	378,715	.91	310,947	.91	387,387	.75	322,050	.65	287,300	.65	268,450
Ukrainian S. S. R.	.88	169,224	.84	230,580	.84	291,463	.84	349,583	.84	287,028	.92	391,644	1.30	558,220	1.63	720,460	1.88	776,440
Union of South Africa	1.15	221,145	1.12	307,440	1.12	388,618	1.12	466,110	1.12	382,704	1.04	442,728	.90	386,460	.83	366,860	.78	322,140
U. S. S. R.	6.62	1,273,026	6.34	1,740,330	6.34	2,199,853	6.34	2,638,518	6.34	2,166,378	6.98	2,971,386	9.85	4,229,590	12.28	5,427,760	14.15	5,843,950
United Kingdom	11.98	2,303,754	11.48	3,151,260	11.37	3,983,331	11.37	4,731,853	11.37	3,885,129	11.37	4,840,209	10.56	4,534,464	10.30	4,552,760	9.80	4,047,400
United States	39.89	7,670,847	39.89	10,949,805	39.89	13,841,032	39.89	16,601,021	39.79	13,596,243	38.92	16,568,244	36.90	³15,844,860	35.12	15,523,040	33.33	13,765,290
Uruguay	.18	34,614	.18	49,410	.18	62,456	.18	74,911	.18	61,506	.18	76,626	.18	77,292	.18	79,560	.18	74,340
Venezuela	.28	53,844	.27	74,115	.27	93,685	.27	112,366	.27	92,259	.30	127,710	.32	137,408	.35	154,700	.39	161,070
Yemen			.04	3,660	.04	13,879	.04	16,647	.04	13,668	.04	17,028	.04	17,176	.04	17,680	.04	16,520
Yugoslavia	.34	65,382	.33	90,585	.33	114,503	.33	137,336	.33	112,761	.36	153,252	.43	184,642	.44	194,480	.44	181,720
Total	100.00	19,386,378	100.00	27,527,775	100.00	34,732,063	100.00	41,644,085	100.00	34,243,100	100.00	42,570,000	100.00	42,940,000	100.00	14,200,000	100.00	41,300,000

1 Tables prepared by Department of State. The assessments for new members are shown in the columns for the year of assessment, not the year when they were paid.

2 The Government of India undertook to pay the total assessment for India and Pakistan for 1948 subject to an intergovernmental adjustment between the 2 states.

3 Gross assessment. Due to credit of $404,000 as result of adjustment of advances to working capital fund on basis of 1952 scale of assessments, United States net assessment is $15,440,860.

ENFORCEMENT ACTION UNDER THE
UNITED NATIONS
STAFF STUDY NO. 7
JANUARY 1955

PREFACE

By Alexander Wiley, *Chairman*

The most pressing question facing the people of this Nation today is the preservation of our freedoms in a world at peace. If there is one overriding reason for our membership in the United Nations, it is to be found in the hope and expectation that the organization can make a significant contribution to this end.

The United Nations does not offer an ironclad guaranty of peace; nor do we expect that it should. No manmade institution of itself will ever be able to do that. What the United Nations can do, what the charter intends that it shall do, what indeed, it must do, is to provide effective facilities for preventing and curbing international conflicts. The successful employment of these facilities depends ultimately on the nations of the world, especially the great powers, and their leaders.

The United Nations Charter provides two principal lines of defense against war. One is generally termed peaceful settlement. In this connection, the organization serves as an international forum, a "crossroads of the world" where nations meet and seek to talk out their quarrels with the aid of other nations and in the full light of world opinion. This defense against war was discussed in detail in a previous staff study.[1]

The present study deals with the second line of defense, so to speak, against war, enforcement action to prevent or curb breaches of the peace. This is the "teeth" of the United Nations. The power to prevent breaches of the peace can take many forms, including diplomatic and economic sanctions and, as we have seen in Korea, military action.

The evolution of this function during the past decade has not moved in the direction that many expected when the organization was established. If international communism had not embarked on a program of expansion in a war-weakened world, we might now have a world in which peace would be maintained largely by the cooperative efforts of the great powers acting together in the Security Council. That has not been the case. Nevertheless, the urge of nations toward peace has been so strong that we have seen developed within the United Nations system other means to prevent war. Regional security arrangements like the North Atlantic Treaty Organization and the Organization of the American States have evolved to provide new means of keeping the peace in vast and important areas of the globe. When the Security Council faltered under the repeated use of the veto, the General Assembly was brought more strongly into play by the nations of the world to bolster sagging defenses against aggression. We have seen still other proposals advanced to preserve the peace. Some of them are far reaching in their implications, such as those for

[1] See U. S. Senate Committee on Foreign Relations. Subcommittee on the United Nations Charter. Staff Study No. 5: Pacific Settlement of Disputes in the United Nations.

an international army or a worldwide security arrangement aimed at Communist aggression.

All of these developments and ideas, as this study so ably points out, have their advantages and disadvantages. The problem of the subcommittee is to study and weigh these ideas in the context of past experience and with one primary consideration in mind, the safety and continued progress of our country and its institutions.

In a world of atomic and hydrogen bombs, our future and the future of all peoples on the face of the globe are inextricably related to the prevention of the holocaust of world conflict. This was made remarkably clear by the President, who a short time ago stated that—

The soldier can no longer regain a peace that is usable to the world. I believe the best he could do would be to retain some semblance of a tattered nation in a world that was very greatly in ashes and the relics of destruction.

In the years since the end of World War II, the nations have several times skirted the edge of disaster. They have so far managed to avoid it. We must continue to explore every means which offers any prospects of further reducing the possibility of war. The nations of the earth cannot claim to have met their responsibilities to their peoples so long as the ingenuity of man has not exhausted every possibility of assuring a world at peace in which individual freedom can grow.

This study, Enforcement Action Under the United Nations, is the seventh in a series of analyses for the background use of the Subcommittee on the United Nations Charter. It was prepared by Mrs. Ellen Collier of the Legislative Reference Service of the Library of Congress under the direction of the staff of the subcommittee. The views expressed do not necessarily represent those of any member of the subcommittee.

JANUARY 1955.

CONTENTS

ENFORCEMENT ACTION UNDER THE UNITED NATIONS

A. INTRODUCTION

The League of Nations, whatever its achievements, was considered a failure by some because it was unable to prevent the Second World War. Similarly, the success of the United Nations may well be measured in terms of its contribution to keeping the peace of the world. Some would challenge the validity of this criterion, citing the importance of the United Nations activities in the economic, social, cultural, and humanitarian fields and in developing international law. They would say it is too much to expect that the organization will be able to reverse in a moment the traditional pattern of alternating war and peace which has characterized the history of mankind. Nevertheless, the fundamental test of the United Nations in the view of many people may well be the manner in which it fulfills the basic promise of the charter; that is, preservation of durable peace in the world.

The charter adopted at the San Francisco Conference establishes two principal types of machinery for maintaining international peace and security through the United Nations. One method is to encourage the settlement of international disputes by peaceful means before such disputes lead to attempts by the parties involved to gain their purposes by force.[1]

In the event this first line of defense against war is unsuccessful the charter provides for a second line. This line is enforcement action, the use of collective measures, including military force if necessary, to prevent and remove threats of war and to suppress acts of aggression or other breaches of the peace.

There is a point of view which holds that it was a mistake to charge the United Nations with responsibility for peace enforcement. The contention is that the force of the United Nations is a pretense; that nations are not yet ready to utilize their national power to support the principle of collective security in a world organization, and will not do so unless it coincides with their national interest.

Shortly after the United Nations was established the suggestion was made that the charter be amended so that—

* * * [the United Nations] be deprived of its warmaking threat and function and become an assembly for the consideration of mutual problems, notably in the economic sphere, and become the agency for recommending and, if possible without force, effecting peaceful change by a two-thirds vote in the Assembly and in the Security Council.
* * * the profession to direct force be eliminated, since the promise of force merely begets counterforce and defeats any hope of the limitation of armaments.[2]

The view that the peace-enforcement function of the United Nations should be allowed to lapse informally if not eliminated by amendment has become more widespread in the face of the split between the Soviet and the free nations. Some hold that the United

---
[1] See U. S. Senate Committee on Foreign Relations. Subcommittee on the United Nations charter. Staff Study No. 5: Pacific Settlement of Disputes in the United Nations.
[2] Edwin Borchard. The Impracticability of "Enforcing" Peace. Yale Law Journal (New Haven), vol. 55, August 1946, pp. 971-972.

Nations cannot successfully carry out enforcement action when the main danger of aggression stems from the Soviet Union, a principal member state. Collective resistance to Communist aggression, the argument runs, should be organized outside the United Nations. The United Nations would then serve, if at all, as one of the sole remaining ties between the two camps, a bridge on which the opponents could at least meet and make an attempt to discuss and settle specific issues.[3]

The fact is, however, that the charter establishes the United Nations not merely as a device for peaceful settlement of this kind but also as an agency of enforcement. It is with the latter function that this study is concerned.

B. THE CHARTER PROVISIONS ON ENFORCEMENT ACTION

The enforcement provisions of the charter were designed to give the United Nations the "teeth" the League of Nations had seemed to lack, as for example, when it unsuccessfully attempted to cope with the invasion of Manchuria in 1931 and the aggression against Ethiopia in 1935. For this purpose, the primary responsibility for maintaining peace and security was vested in a Security Council, which in theory was to be more powerful and effective than the Council of the old League.

The 11-member Security Council was organized to function continuously so that it would be able to act promptly. Provision was made for all decisions to be taken by a seven-vote majority rather than on the basis of unanimity as had been the case in the League Council.[4] However, each of the five principal victors of World War II, the United States, the U. S. S. R., the United Kingdom, China, and France, was given the right to veto these decisions except in the case of procedural matters and all were seated in the Council on a permanent basis.

The effect of this arrangement is that enforcement of peace by the Security Council under the charter, for practical purposes, is limited to those instances in which the 5 permanent members of the Security Council and a minimum of 2 nonpermanent member-states agree.[5] If this prerequisite exists then the charter provides that decisions of the Security Council are binding on all other members of the United Nations.[6] Reliance upon the Security Council to maintain and enforce peace and security in these circumstances means reliance primarily upon joint action of the five permanent members. If they are in agreement, any decision which might be taken to enforce the peace would have preponderant power behind it.

On the other hand, any one of the permanent powers can employ the veto to block an enforcement action directed against itself or

[3] The peaceful settlement functions of the United Nations have been discussed fully in Staff Study No. 5, previously cited.
[4] Originally the League Council had eight members, including Great Britain, France, Italy, and Japan as permanent members. Later, Germany and the Soviet Union were added as permanent members and the number of nonpermanent members was increased to 11. The total membership varied, however, because of withdrawals and the expulsion of the Soviet Union.
[5] That the Council acted in the Korean situation despite the disagreement of the Soviet Union was due to the circumstance of the latter having absented itself from the proceedings at the time the issue arose. Subsequently, the Soviet veto did prevent further action and forced the Korean issue out of the Security Council into the General Assembly.
[6] It should be noted, however, that decisions of the Security Council bind other member-states only in regard to the prevention or suppression of a conflict. In other matters, including the actual settlement of the conflict, the Council can only make recommendations. Cross reference to Staff Study No. 5, previously cited.

against any nation or area which it considers of special interest. Under the present charter, moreover, there is no assurance that action will be taken automatically in every conflict that threatens or breaks out in some part of the world.   In each instance, the Security Council must determine that a "threat to the peace, breach of the peace or act of aggression" does exist.   Enforcement action other than of a provisional nature must await such a determination.   Attempts were made in the preparatory stages to write into the charter a definition of aggression in order to insure automatic action by the Council but the sponsoring governments of the San Francisco Conference, particularly the United States, were opposed on the grounds that it would be impossible to cover all possible forms of aggression.   Accordingly the Security Council has wide discretion in determining what contitutes a threat to or breach of the peace or act of aggression.

Chapter VII of the charter outlines the measures which the Security Council may take in the way of enforcement action and the obligations and rights of the members with respect to such decisions.   In this connection the Council may call upon member-states to impose economic and diplomatic sanctions.   It may also call upon some or all of the members to apply military sanctions.   Before this latter provision can come into operation, the charter requires that member-states conclude special military agreements with the Security Council. Once this has been done, national military forces presumably would be immediately available under the agreements for possible call by the Council in the event of an act of aggression.[7]   No agreements have been concluded to date.

Provision is also made in the charter for a Military Staff Committee composed of personnel of the permanent members of the Security Council.   The staff is to assist the Council in military matters relating to the maintenance of peace, the command of forces, and the regulation of armaments.   In addition, this committee would have responsibility, under the Council, for the strategic direction of armed forces should any ever be made available for use by the United Nations under the agreements previously mentioned.

The Security Council is given authority under the charter to determine what specific members of the United Nations are to be charged with a given enforcement action.[8]   Under article 49, however, all members obligate themselves to join in affording mutual assistance in carrying out the measures decided upon by the Security Council.

While primary responsibility for maintaining international peace and security rests with the Security Council, the charter left the way open for the General Assembly to participate in this function.   Article 11 specifically confers on the Assembly the authority to discuss questions relating to the maintenance of international peace and security. In this connection, it may make recommendations to the states concerned or the Security Council, and it may call to the attention of the Security Council situations likely to endanger peace and security. Such questions on which action is necessary are to be referred to the

---

[7] As envisioned in the charter, the agreements were to govern the numbers and kinds of forces, their general location and degree of readiness, and the nature of the facilities and assistance to be provided.

[8] A member not represented on the Council was to be permitted participation in Council decisions concerning the employment of its contingents.

Security Council. However, article 10 confers upon the Assembly the additional right to discuss and make recommendations on any matter within the scope of the charter.[9]

Both article 10 and article 11 are limited by article 12 which prohibits the Assembly from making recommendations on any matter while the Security Council is functioning with respect to it, unless the Council so requests. Even this limitation does not preclude the Assembly from discussing the matter.

Regional arrangements in enforcement

The charter encourages regional organizations of nations to participate in the maintenance of peace. Chapter VIII requires, however, that any action for the enforcement of peace which may be taken by such organizations have the authorization of the Security Council and that the Council be kept fully informed of developments.[10]

At San Francisco a further provision was added largely to meet the fear of the American Republics that action by them under inter-American regional arrangements might be blocked by the veto in the Security Council. This was article 51 (ch. VII) which stated that—

Nothing in the present charter shall impair the inherent right of individual or collective self-defense if an armed attack occurs against a member of the United Nations, until the Security Council has taken the measures necessary to maintain international peace and security. Measures taken by members in the exercise of this right of self-defense shall be immediately reported to the Security Council and shall not in any way affect the authority and responsibility of the Security Council under the present charter to take at any time such action as it deems necessary in order to maintain or restore international peace and security.

Transitional security arrangements

The charter recognized in article 106 that special security arrangements would be necessary until the military agreements previously referred to were signed and the Security Council had the means with which to enforce the peace. In the interim period the five permanent members were to have responsibility for taking military enforcement action, if such were necessary. They were to consult with each other and with other members of the United Nations as occasion demanded with a view to joint action on behalf of the United Nations. This article presupposed continued cooperation and agreement of the permanent members, and the same dissension among the permanent members of the Council which has prevented the military agreements from being completed has also precluded joint action under this transitional arrangement.

Unlike the League of Nations, the United Nations was to have no connection with the peace settlements following World War II. Article 107 of the charter makes clear that this responsibility lies with the governments that had defeated the enemy states in that conflict.

---

[9] This broad authority grew out of several amendments to the Dumbarton Oaks proposals submitted at the San Francisco Conference. The Soviet Union strongly objected to expanding the role of the Assembly, but finally agreed to article 10 after the United States expressed a willingness to support it even if the Soviet Union withdrew from the Conference.

[10] Except that directed against the renewal of aggression by an enemy state of World War II. The enemy states included any state which during World War II had been an enemy of any signatory of the charter. This exception was to last until the United Nations was "on request of the governments concerned * * * charged with the responsibility for preventing further aggression" by enemy states.

C. THE PEACE ENFORCEMENT MACHINERY IN PRACTICE

The enforcement machinery of the Security Council was one of the first parts of the charter to be affected by the collapse of relationships among the permanent members after World War II. This machinery, as has been noted, was tightly bound to the principle of unanimity. Without the common consent of the five permanent members, the Council could make neither recommendations nor binding decisions and hence could not begin to fulfill its principal functions. Thus, a major segment of the charter, that of peace enforcement, began to become inoperative shortly after the United Nations was established.

The military agreements

The machinery, for example, by which the Security Council was to have the power to enforce decisions depended on the provision of armed forces by the member states. Early in 1946, the Council established the Military Staff Committee and directed it to make recommendations on this question. On April 30, 1947, the Committee presented a report [11] which included 25 recommendations agreed upon unanimously on the "general principles governing the organization of the armed forces made available to the Security Council by Member Nations of the United Nations." The report also contained 16 proposals on which agreement was not reached in the Committee nor when they were later discussed in the Security Council. On most of the disputed issues the United States, the United Kingdom, China, and France took one position and the Soviet Union another.

Before armed forces could be subject to United Nations direction, agreement had to be reached by the permanent members not only on these basic principles, but on the strength of the forces to be contributed by each member state, and on the text of the agreements. In addition, the agreements would have had to be ratified by the member states according to their constitutional processes. Progress has been halted since 1948 at the first step, the agreement on general principles.[12]

From time to time recommendations have been made calling for a renewed attempt to end the stalemate. One such recommendation was contained in the Vandenberg resolution, passed by the Senate on June 11, 1948. It called for "maximum efforts to complete the enforcement machinery of the United Nations." However, there has been little actual effort along this line since 1948.[13]

D. THE SECURITY COUNCIL AND PEACE ENFORCEMENT

The absence of the military agreements has not entirely blocked the Security Council from fulfilling the enforcement role assigned to it by the charter. For example, measures of a provisional nature, at least,

[11] For text, see Senate Foreign Relations Committee Subcommittee on the United Nations Charter, Review of the United Nations Charter, Collection of Documents, U. S. Government Printing Office, 1954, pp. 581–592, hereinafter referred to as Collection of Documents.
[12] On August 6, 1948, the Chairman of the Military Staff Committee informed the Security Council an impasse had been reached. Collection of Documents, p. 592. The Military Staff Committee has continued meeting every 2 weeks, but its meetings generally last only a few minutes and apparently are merely a formality.
[13] At the time of the passage of the Uniting for Peace resolution in 1950, the General Assembly also adopted a resolution sponsored by the Soviet Union to recommend to the Security Council:
"That it should devise measures for the earliest application of articles 43, 45, 46, and 47 of the Charter of the United Nations regarding the placing of armed forces at the disposal of the Security Council by the states members of the United Nations and the effective functioning of the Military Staff Committee" (Collection of Documents, p. 561.)

were taken in regard to the Palestine question. Large-scale hostilities there were ended after one Council resolution specifically threatened enforcement action if the resolution were violated. Moreover, in Indonesia, the cease-fire resolutions passed by the Security Council played an important role in ending hostilities.[14]

The action in Korea, however, was the first instance in which the United Nations took enforcement action in the full sense of the term. It is the only occasion on which the United Nations has declared an act of aggression to have been committed and subsequently acted to repel the aggressor.

The Korean aggression, however, occurred in circumstances which made impossible its handling in accordance with the procedure envisaged in the charter. In the first place, the invasion of South Korea by the North Korean Communist regime had the support of one of the permanent members of the Council, the Soviet Union. In the second place, the military agreements which were to provide power for the Security Council had not come into existence.

On the other hand, there were also certain circumstances which made enforcement action in Korea more likely than would otherwise have been the case. Foremost was the self-decreed absence of the Soviet Union from the Security Council at the time the aggression occurred.[15] Consequently, at the outset the Security Council operated unhampered by the veto.[16]

The presence of a United Nations Commission in South Korea at the time was another factor which greatly aided action. This Commission could report on the situation and make recommendations. It eliminated the need for the time-consuming process of forming and sending out an investigating group. Thus, the experience of the League of Nations with the Lytton Commission, which had taken many months to investigate and make a report on the invasion of Manchuria in 1931, was avoided.

Still another unusual circumstance made possible prompt action, in this case the close proximity to the scene of aggression of active and equipped forces of a principal member state such as the United States had in Japan, and the willingness of the country controlling the forces to use them on behalf of the United Nations. The President of the United States ordered naval and air forces to give assistance to the Republic of Korea on the basis of the June 25 resolution and within a few days also dispatched ground troops.[17]

[14] There is disagreement whether United Nations action in Indonesia fell within ch. VII, that is, the enforcement provisions of the charter. The United States representative took the position that the cease-fire resolutions were provisional measures under art. 40, ch. VII, and hence binding, even though art. 40 was not mentioned. The Belgian representative, however, contended that ch. VII had not been applied because it had not been specifically invoked. Eduardo de Arechaga Jimenez, Voting and the Handling of Disputes in the Security Council. United Nations Studies, No. 5. New York, Carnegie Endowment for International Peace, 1950. Pp. 153–154.

[15] The Soviet Union had absented itself from the Security Council meetings over the Council's refusal to unseat the representative of the Nationalist Chinese Government. Much of the material in this section is taken from Leland Goodrich. Korea, Collective Measures Against Aggression. International Conciliation(New York), October 1953.

[16] On the same day of the invasion of South Korea, June 25, 1950, the Council was able to label the action a breach of the peace. At the same time, it called for an immediate cessation of hostilities and the withdrawal of North Korean forces and urged all member states "to render every assistance to the United Nations in the execution of this resolution and to refrain from giving assistance to the North Korean authorities" (Collection of Documents, p. 593).

[17] On June 27, 1950, the Security Council adopted a second resolution which noted that the North Koreans had not ceased hostilities nor withdrawn their forces to the 38th parallel, and recommended: "that the members of the United Nations furnish such assistance to the Republic of Korea as may be necessary to repel the armed attack and to restore international peace and security in the area." On July 7 the Security Council recommended that all member states provide military forces and other assistance and make them available to a unified commander designated by the United States. Collection of Documents, pp. 593–594.

On August 1, 1950, when the Soviet Union's turn to assume the chairmanship of the Security Council came by rotation, the Soviet representative returned to the Council meetings. By that time, the basis for action in Korea had already been laid. After two Soviet vetoes, the Security Council dropped the question from its agenda on January 31, 1951, and it was pursued thereafter by the General Assembly.

E. LIMITATIONS OF THE SECURITY COUNCIL IN ENFORCEMENT

Until Korea, the Security Council had brought into play only its prestige and implied or overt warnings of the use of force in an attempt to bring an end to hostilities. Actions of this kind in the first instance were frequently not heeded and were even violated by the disputants.[18] In the Korean question the Security Council went further and invoked the use of force to repel an aggression. Even in this case, the Council confined itself to recommendations that members take such action. The powers of the charter fully utilized presumably could have resulted in an order to use force, provided of course that the military agreements previously referred to had come into force. Although 53 members indicated a willingness to support the principle of voluntary action called for by the Security Council in the Korean situation (only the Soviet bloc specifically objected), the responses actually varied considerably. One group of nations, primarily Asian and African, approved the concept of collective security but maintained a degree of detachment from the actual enforcement measures. Another group, including most of the Latin American states, expressed complete approval of the principle but felt able to make only token contributions. Armed forces, in most cases small in size, actually were sent to Korea by 16 members of the United Nations.[19]

The basic factor underlying the Security Council's limitations in enforcing peace in the manner intended by the charter has been the attitude of the Soviet Union. Enforcement action in the Korean situation under the auspices of the Council was possible only so long as that country absented itself from Council meetings.

In two cases, Indonesia and Palestine, the Council played a significant role in restoring the peace, largely because the five permanent members were at least in partial agreement on a course of action. Even in these questions the veto was invoked but not in a manner as to forestall action entirely.

In a far greater number of disputes, the Security Council has been completely stalemated. The veto has prevented issues from being classified as threats to the peace within the meaning of chapter VII, and hence subject to enforcement action, and has blocked measures attempting to deal with such situations. For example, in September 1948, France, the United Kingdom, and the United States drew attention to the Berlin blockade as a threat to the peace within

---

[18] Among the resolutions not heeded in the Palestine case, for example, were an appeal of March 5, 1948, to all governments and peoples to prevent disorders, a resolution of April 16, 1948, calling on the parties to cease acts of violence immediately, and a resolution of May 22, 1948, calling upon all parties, without prejudice to their rights or position, to issue a cease-fire order. Jimenez, op. cit., ch. V.

[19] Australia, Belgium, Canada, Colombia, Ethiopia, France, Greece, Luxembourg, the Netherlands, New Zealand, the Philippines, Thailand, Turkey, the Union of South Africa, the United Kingdom, and the United States.

The unified command took the position that contributions from any country should be at least of the strength of a reinforced battalion (1,200 men) with supporting artillery, and that other units should be of such size and organization as to be able to function as a unit. Several offers of assistance were refused, therefore, because they fell short of these standards. Goodrich, op. cit., p. 159.

the meaning of chapter VII. At the same time, a resolution was introduced in the Security Council by the six nonpermanent members calling upon the disputants in the situation to take steps to end the controversy. This resolution was vetoed by the Soviet Union. In the Greek question, the Soviet delegate vetoed resolutions determining that the situation constituted a threat to the peace within the meaning of chapter VII.

In May 1954, Thailand called attention to "large-scale fighting * * * in the immediate vicinity of Thai territory * * * [in Indochina]," as "a threat to the security of Thailand, the continuance of which is likely to endanger the maintenance of international peace and security." The Thai delegate suggested that the Security Council provide for objective observation of the situation. Use of the Peace Observation Commission for this purpose was vetoed by the Soviet Union, and the hostilities in Indochina continued to remain entirely outside the purview of the United Nations. A short time later, a proposal that Guatemala's complaint of aggression be taken to the Organization of American States before being considered by the Security Council received 10 favorable votes. Nevertheless, it was vetoed by the Soviet Union.

The number of vetoes does not portray fully the effect of the disunity in the Security Council. Tension among the permanent powers has not only reduced the capacity of the Council to operate; it has also undermined faith within the United Nations and elsewhere in the ability of that body to discharge primary responsibility for maintaining international peace and security.

F. THE GENERAL ASSEMBLY AND PEACE ENFORCEMENT

The Security Council's difficulties have led to the devising of new machinery within the United Nations for organizing collective security.[20] Prior to Korea, the General Assembly had already taken over consideration of several controversies because of the Council's inability to act. However, there was little available machinery through which enforcement-type action could be pursued by the Assembly.

After the Korean aggression, the United States, Canada, France, the Philippines, Turkey, the United Kingdom, and Uruguay sponsored the Uniting for Peace Resolution. On November 3, 1950, this resolution passed by a vote of 52 to 5 (Soviet bloc) and 2 abstentions (India and Argentina). It provided a new framework for voluntary collective enforcement action by member states.

The resolution acknowledged the primary responsibility of the Security Council for the enforcement of peace but contended in effect that the deadlock in that body did not relieve other members of the right or duty to act in this connection. It provided that if the veto prevented the Council from exercising its responsibility for maintaining peace, the General Assembly:

* * * shall consider the matter immediately with a view to making appropriate recommendations to members for collective measures, including in the case of a

---

[20] As early as 1947, a major attempt was made by member states to reorganize the structure of the General Assembly. At that time an interim committee, popularly called the Little Assembly, was established. This change was aimed at eliminating a major limitation on the activity of the General Assembly, the fact that it did not remain in continuous session. The revision was proposed by the United States at almost the same time that the Greek case had reached a stalemate in the Security Council and the General Assembly was beginning to discuss the question. In recent years the interim committee has fallen into disuse, the General Assembly choosing instead to extend its sessions when necessary. This permits the first, or political, committee to remain active even though the Assembly may be in recess.

breach of the peace or act of aggression the use of armed force when necessary, to maintain or restore international peace and security * * * [21]

Established by the resolution was a Peace Observation Commission to observe and report on situations of tension which might endanger peace. With the consent of the state into whose territory the Commission would go, the Peace Observation Commission could be used by the General Assembly by a two-thirds vote, or by the Security Council.[22]

Another part of the resolution recommended that each member state maintain—

* * * within its national armed forces elements so trained, organized and equipped that they could promptly be made available, in accordance with its constitutional processes, for service as a United Nations unit or units, upon recommendation by the Security Council or General Assembly.[23]

John Foster Dulles, speaking for the United States at the time of the adoption of the resolution said:

* * * The action which is contemplated is indeed momentous. It may determine, perhaps decisively and finally for our generation, whether or not the nations of the world really want an effective, as against a paper, system of collective resistance to aggression * * *.[24]

The point has been made that the resolution substantially changed the enforcement role of the General Assembly from that envisioned at the San Francisco Conference. As one observer writes:

Although one can * * * argue that the Uniting for Peace Resolution is constitutionally valid, it is at the same time clear that such an innovation is a significant modification of the spirit, if not the letter, of the charter, which obviously intended that the Security Council should direct the use of collective force under the United Nations.[25]

One of the sequences to the Uniting for Peace Resolution was an invitation to member states to submit information on measures taken to maintain within their armed forces units readily available for use by the United Nations. They were asked to report these measures to the Collective Measures Committee, established by the Uniting for Peace Resolution.[26] Of the 38 members who replied, most supported the principle, although some considered their military or economic resources insufficient to set aside troops for United Nations use.

---

[21] In the event of an emergency a special session of the Assembly could be called at the request of the Security Council on the vote of any 7 members or at the request of a majority of members of the United Nations.

[22] Originally the 14-member Peace Observation Commission, provided for under the Uniting for Peace Resolution, was intended to exclude the great powers in the interests of objectivity. However, when the Soviet Union indicated that it would participate, other delegations accepted the proposal to include all the permanent members. The only time the Peace Observation Commission has been utilized has been in connection with Greece. In 1951 the General Assembly wished to end the Special Committee on the Balkans and, as a tide-over measure, requested the Peace Observation Commission to dispatch observers to the area and make reports. In 1954 Thailand requested the Security Council to send the Commission to its territory to observe hostilities in the area but the request was vetoed by the Soviet Union.

[23] The resolution requested the Secretary General to appoint, with the approval of the Collective Measures Committee, a panel of military experts who could give technical advice to members who requested it.

[24] Collection of documents, p. 555.

[25] H. Field Haviland, Jr. The Political Role of the General Assembly. United Nations Studies No. 7. New York, Carnegie Endowment for International Peace, 1951, p. 159.

[26] This committee has submitted three reports analyzing enforcement action possible under the present charter with or without unanimity of the permanent members. These measures include political, economic and financial, and military sanctions. The committee has also formulated an arms embargo list and a list of strategic items for use in the event a United Nations-sponsored embargo should be invoked. For the text of the reports, see Collection of Documents, p. 606. U. N. Document A/2215, 1952, and Department of State Bulletin, Sept. 20, 1954, p. 420. For summary of replies, see First Report of the Collective Measures Committee, Annex II. United Nations General Assembly, Official Records, Sixth Session, Supplement No. 13 (A/1891).

The United States pointed out that it already had contingents and facilities serving the United Nations in Korea, and that the forces in Europe in support of the North Atlantic Treaty could in appropriate circumstances, in accordance with constitutional processes, serve the United Nations in collective measures.

Upon the recommendation of the Collective Measures Committee, in January 1952, the General Assembly urged the members to—

take further steps to maintain elements in their armed forces so trained, organized and equipped that they could promptly be made available in accordance with their constitutional processes, for service as United Nations units.

Moreover, it recommended that states should survey their resources and examine their legislation in order to take the necessary legal and administrative measures to place them in a position to carry out both economic and military enforcement measures expeditiously and effectively.

In response to a request of the General Assembly for a report on this matter, the United States advised that—

* * * the legislative and administrative arrangements of the United States are such that by appropriate governmental action in accordance with its constitutional processes this Government can promptly make available assistance and facilities in appropriate circumstances.[27]

Other replies indicated, however, that little concrete progress had been made in obtaining, in advance, pledges of troops even among those countries which supported the principle of the Uniting for Peace Resolution.

The Collective Measures Committee has emphasized that the most important aspect of this problem is securing the largest possible participation in enforcement action from the maximum number of states. In addition, the committee has adopted a United States proposal that contributing countries should give logistical support to other nations which are willing to supply troops in the event of collective action but which are unable to equip, train and supply their own forces.

G. LIMITATIONS OF THE GENERAL ASSEMBLY IN PEACE ENFORCEMENT

Despite developments which have enlarged the capacity of the General Assembly for enforcement, there are inherent limitations on what that organ can do in this field. The Assembly is too large and cumbersome to be expected to act quickly. Moreover, its system of voting in no way reflects a linking of power and responsibility. A two-thirds majority of the Assembly, for example, could recommend action for enforcement. If this majority, however, did not contain at least some of the more powerful states and they chose to ignore the recommendation, the resolution might lack the force necessary to support it.[28] Moreover, the Assembly must depend on recommendations which might not necessarily be carried out by the members or which might be carried out inequitably. On the other hand, the distinction between recommendatory action of the General Assembly and imperative action of the Security Council may be more theoretical than real. In the first place, the veto power insures

---

[27] Collection of Documents, p. 674–675.
[28] See U. S. Senate Committee on Foreign Relations. Subcommittee on the United Nations Charter. Staff study No. 4. Representation and Voting in the United Nations General Assembly.

that a permanent member cannot be bound to any enforcement action of the Security Council to which it is opposed. Moreover, the extent of the real obligation of all other members to carry out imperative enforcement decisions of the Council is not clear since it has never been adequately tested. In the Korean instance, the Council recommended; it did not order enforcement. As at least one writer has pointed out, the obligations of members under article 25, to accept and carry out the decisions of the Security Council are—

* * * imperfect obligations in that no action is stipulated that may be taken against members refusing to abide by the Council's decisions.[29]

The Korean case indicated, nevertheless, that enforcement action could be taken on the basis of recommendations. An embargo on strategic items recommended against North Korea and China by the General Assembly, for example, was accepted by most of the member nations,[30] although opinions differ as to the effectiveness of its application. On the other hand, Korea revealed a major defect in recommendatory enforcement action. In the first place, the burden of the sacrifices was not evenly distributed among member states. The United States and to a lesser extent a few other nations bore a disproportionate share of the sacrifices entailed in enforcement.[31] This condition tended to detract from the United Nations character of the operation and led to some tension between other members of the United Nations and the United States.
One observer contends:

* * * that the major weakness of United Nations collective action in Korea, from the point of view of organization and procedure, has been the failure to develop adequate organs and procedures for giving political guidance to the military measures taken to coerce the North Korean authorities and later the Chinese Communists.[32]

On the other hand, some observers in this country have expressed the view that undue interference by the United Nations in the Korean question hampered the military operations of the United States acting as the command for the organization against the aggressor. For instance, Gen. James A. Van Fleet, former commander in Korea, stated:

* * * in battle, as in any business, you must have a single head to make decisions. You must have fixed responsibility and unity of command. And where it is American effort, we should have American decision and freedom of action and not have to account for it to the United Nations.

    *   *   *   *   *   *   *

The very fact is that we did weaken our command structure to do as [our U. N. allies] would have us do * * *[33]

H. DEVELOPMENT OF REGIONAL ARRANGEMENTS AND AGREEMENTS

At the time of the San Francisco Conference, the inter-American system and the League of Arab States were the principal formal regional arrangements for security purposes. The attitude and actions of the Soviet Union have since served to stimulate the formation of numerous other bilateral and multilateral defensive arrangements.

---

[29] Stefan T. Possony. Peace Enforcement, Yale Law Journal (New Haven), vol. 55, August 1946, p. 939.
[30] Third report to Congress on the Battle Act. Department of State Bulletin, October 27, 1953, p. 57.
[31] However, South Korea, the victim of the aggression, which was not a member of the United Nations, sustained the greatest burden of casualties in its own defense.
[32] Goodrich, op. cit., p. 164.
[33] Senate Internal Security Subcommittee Hearings on Interlocking Subversion in Government Departments. Pt. 24, September 29, 1954, pp. 2044–2045.

This development has been in large measure a response to the evident limitations of the United Nations in providing adequate defense against aggression, particularly when a principal member nation is the major threat to peace. Special collective security agreements to which the United States is now, or has indicated an intention to become, a party are [34] (see map facing this page)

1. The Inter-American Treaty of Reciprocal Assistance, signed at Rio de Janeiro on September 2, 1947; [35]

2. The North Atlantic Treaty, signed April 4, 1949; [36]

3. Security treaty between Australia, New Zealand, and the United States, signed September 1, 1951; [37]

4. Southeast Asian Collective Defense Treaty, signed September 8, 1954; [38]

Other important regional agreements of recent formation to which the United States is not directly a party are the Western European Union, the Arab League, and the Balkan Pact. The British Commonwealth of Nations is sometimes regarded as a "regional" arrangement for defense although formal undertakings to that end do not exist.

The Communist states do not have a formal open multilateral treaty which binds all to act in the event of conflict in which one becomes involved.[39] There is, however, a network of bilateral treaties between the Soviet Union and the other Communist states and among the latter themselves.[40] The text of these treaties pledge the signatories to give military aid and any other assistance possible to each other in the event of attack.

The original intent of chapter VIII was to make a place within the United Nations system for regional arrangements already in existence at the time the charter was adopted and to permit the development of others within this framework. Article 51 of chapter VII was added to insure that such arrangements could function within certain limits without the danger of being frustrated by a veto in the Security Council.[41]

Some observers feel that regional arrangements, as they have developed in the last few years, may impair the capacity of the United Nations to enforce peace. The Commission To Study the Organization of Peace, for instance, reported in 1953:

Since World War II the Soviet system, including the Soviet Union, its European satellites and China, has developed as an aggressive agency of Russian imperialism and Communist expansion. To defend the free world, the United States, Canada, the United Kingdom, and Western Europe have created the North Atlantic Treaty Organization now joined by Greece and Turkey. These two gigantic

---

[34] This listing includes only multilateral treaties. In addition the United States has bilateral defense treaties with the Philippines. Japan. and the Republic of Korea. Another has been negotiated with the Republic of China but has not yet been ratified.

[35] The signatories are Argentina, Bolivia, Brazil, Chile, Colombia, Costa Rica, Cuba, Dominican Republic, Ecuador, El Salvador, Guatemala, Haiti, Honduras, Mexico, Nicaragua, Panama, Paraguay, Peru, the United States, Uruguay, and Venezuela. Guatemala has not yet ratified. For text, see Collection of Documents, p. 682.

[36] The signatories are Belgium, Canada. Denmark, France, Iceland, Italy, Luxembourg, the Netherlands, Norway, Portugal, the United Kingdom, and the United States, and it was later adhered to by Greece and Turkey. For text, see ibid., p. 700. An additional protocol has been signed which would bring the Federal Republic of Germany into the arrangement. For text, see Department of State Publication 5659. London and Paris Agreements, p. 30.

[37] Collection of Documents, p. 704.

[38] The signatories are Australia, Britain, France, New Zealand, Pakistan, Philippines, Thailand, and the United States. This treaty will come into force between the states which ratify as soon as the ratifications of a majority of the signatories have been deposited. For text, see New York Times, September 9, 1954. p. 4.

[39] That they may be on the verge of forming such a treaty, however, was indicated by a recent conference of these states in Moscow.

[40] In the Soviet system of alliances the treaties usually contain some statement to the effect that they will be carried out in the spirit of the United Nations Charter. Collection of Documents, p. 692.

[41] See L. M. Goodrich and E. Hambro, Charter of the United Nations, Commentary and Documents, Boston, World Peace Foundation, 1949, pp. 297–298.

systems have functioned relatively independently of the United Nations.   The result of their rivalry and mutual fears has been an arms race tending to draw states to one side or the other, to weaken the United Nations as an agency of collective security, and to threaten a new world war.[42]

The regional arrangements entered into by the United States were not intended to weaken the United Nations.   On the contrary, the Vandenberg resolution, passed by the Senate on June 11, 1948, endorsed a policy of—

* * * progressive development of regional and other collective arrangements for individual and collective self-defense in accordance with the purposes, principles, and provisions of the charter * * * [43]

At the same time it recommended strengthening the United Nations directly by maximum efforts to obtain the military agreements envisioned in the charter and by removing the veto from questions of membership and pacific settlement.   The Vandenberg resolution constituted recognition that at the time the United Nations, without supplemental machinery, was unable to assure international peace and security.   The report of the Senate Foreign Relations Committee on this resolution stated:

* * * a constructive program for the strengthening of the United Nations is essential for world peace * * *   World peace—the paramount objective of the United States, can and should be bulwarked by the development of regional and other collective arrangements among free nations for their self-defense consistent with the charter.[44]

Similarly, other nations signing the North Atlantic Treaty regarded it as a supplement to the United Nations necessary for their security. In signing the treaty Halvard M. Lange, Minister of Foreign Affairs of Norway, for example, stated:

We believe today as firmly as ever in the rightness of the words and spirit of that great [United Nations] Charter and in the fundamental soundness and necessity of the universal idea of the United Nations.
We cannot close our eyes, however, to the fact that—for reasons which we all know— the United Nations cannot today give us or any other nation the security to which we had confidently looked forward.[45]

The texts of the regional agreements which the United States has entered into all refer to the identity of their purpose with that of the United Nations.   In more recent years, however, the language of these treaties has tended to be less specific in its reference to the machinery of the United Nations.   The Rio Treaty, the first of these agreements, was the one most closely geared to the machinery of the United Nations.   Although this agreement is based primarily on article 51 in chapter VII, which emphasizes that nothing in the United Nations Charter impairs "the inherent right of individual or collective self-defense," it also adheres specifically to article 54, chapter VIII, which requires that the Security Council be kept informed of activities undertaken or planned by regional organizations with respect to the maintenance of peace.   Thus chapter VIII of the charter, which subordinates enforcement action by regional agencies to the United Nations, is recognized.

The North Atlantic Treaty, signed a year and a half later, however, mentions only article 51, and requires only that measures taken against an armed attack be reported to the Security Council.   Such

[42] Commission To Study the Organization of Peace.   Regional Arrangements for Security and the United Nations.   8th report, New York, June 1953, p. 9.
[43] Collection of Documents, p. 140.
[44] Collection of Documents, p. 139.
[45] The Signing of the North Atlantic Treaty, Washington, D. C., April 4, 1949, Department of State Publication 3497, p. 25.

measures, the treaty provides, should be terminated when the Security Council has taken the necessary steps to restore peace and security. The Southeast Asian treaty, signed 5 years later, continues the principle that regional collective security arrangements do not alter the rights or obligations of the parties under the United Nations Charter, and still requires that action taken against a common danger be reported to the Security Council. However, it does not refer to any specific article of the United Nations Charter. Nor does it call for the termination of regional defensive action in the event the Security Council acts to restore peace.

Thus, in phraseology at least, the regional agreements seem to place less emphasis than in the past on specific coordination with the United Nations. It would be a mistake, of course, to put too much emphasis on the language of the treaties. Nevertheless, concern with this trend was indicated in the eighth annual report of the Secretary-General on the work of the United Nations. Secretary-General Dag Hammarskjold noted that while the use of regional arrangements, when appropriate, was encouraged in the charter, "where resort to such arrangements is chosen in the first instance, that choice should not be permitted to cast any doubt on the ultimate responsibility of the United Nations."

There also appears to be a changing emphasis in purpose in the more recent regional arrangements. The principle of universal collective security embodied in the United Nations Charter calls for aid to the victim of aggression, no matter what the source of aggression and whether or not a country's own immediate interests are involved. In contrast, the aim of recent regional arrangements has been to provide more specifically for collective security against Communist aggression.

For example, the Organization of American States, the only regional security arrangement to which the United States belongs which has roots deeper than the postwar resistance to Communist expansion, originally followed the general principle of opposition to aggression from any source. In the recent Declaration of Caracas,[46] however, the specific danger of Communist aggression was highlighted.

The North Atlantic Treaty Organization was formed largely as a result of the Communist threat, but was nevertheless couched in terms of general opposition to aggression. When the Soviet Union expressed its "readiness to join with the interested governments in examining the matter of having the Soviet Union participate in the North Atlantic Treaty," the United States replied:

It is unnecessary to emphasize the completely unreal character of such a suggestion. It is contrary to the very principles on which the defense system and the security of the Western Nations depend.[47]

In the most recent regional agreement entered into by the United States, the Southeast Asia Collective Defense Treaty, the United States had specifically incorporated into the text the understanding that for its part, it would consider only Communist aggression as

---

[46] The Declaration of Caracas, adopted by the Tenth Inter-American Conference in March 1954, declared:
   "That the domination or control of the political institutions of any American state by the international Communist movement, extending to this Hemisphere the political system of an extracontinental power, would constitute a threat to the sovereignty and political independence of the American states, endangering the peace of America, and would call for a meeting of consultation to consider the adoption of measures in accordance with existing treaties."
[47] Department of State Bulletin, May 17, 1954, v. 30, pp. 756-757.

an aggression which would automatically require it to act to meet the common danger in accordance with its constitutional processes.[48]

Thus, on the part of the United States at least, regional arrangements apparently are increasingly being regarded primarily and specifically as a part of our defense against Communist aggression. From this country's point of view, therefore, regional agreements would seem to supplement the United Nations system particularly to the extent that the threat is from a Communist source.

In general planning against aggression the United Nations may still remain the focus of enforcement action. That the organization should be a center for organizing collective security against aggression in general, while regional arrangements assume primary responsibility for preparing for aggression from a specific source, has already been suggested by Sir Gladwyn Jebb.

* * * [Regional arrangements] are all perfectly consonant with the Charter of the United Nations, but they are not the United Nations itself. Nevertheless they exist and it is on them and on the actual military strength which they represent that the defense of the free world will have to be based if world war III ever breaks out. After all, it stands to reason that the United Nations itself cannot be used to prepare military plans against specified possible aggressions (and this is the only realistic form of military planning to meet aggression) because such plans would have to be directed against one or more members * * *.
* * * [It] is not possible in the United Nations to go beyond general planning for defense against aggression from any quarter and with no definite aggressor named. * * * [Strategic] planning against specific aggressions can be done only by regional or collective self-defense organizations.[49]

The only trial to date of the working relationship between regional arrangements and the United Nations has been the Guatemala case. On June 19, 1954, Guatemala complained to the Security Council and the Organization of American States of aggression on the part of Honduras and Nicaragua. In this case a majority of the Security Council approved the handling of the complaint in the first instance by the Organization of American States. However, a resolution referring the matter to that organization was vetoed by the Soviet Union which took the position that the issue should be dealt with at once by the Security Council. The Security Council then passed a resolution calling for the "immediate termination of any action likely to cause bloodshed." Subsequently the Organization of American States sought to bring about a settlement.

Upon complaint by Guatemala that the Security Council's resolution was not being observed, the Council refused to take further action on the grounds the matter was being handled by the Organization of American States. The United States among others insisted that the inter-American organization was the proper place for handling the matter. Moreover, Ambassador Lodge contended that Guatemala had an obligation under the charters of both organizations to move first through the regional organization.

The United States and the other members of the Security Council, except the Soviet Union, based their position to a considerable extent on the contention that a dispute rather than an act of aggression was involved. The Guatemalan representative, supported by the Soviet Union, contended there had been acts of aggression against Guatemala, and argued for immediate intervention of the Security Council

[48] Department of State Bulletin, September 20, 1954, p. 395.
[49] Sir Gladwyn Jebb. The Free World and the United Nations. Foreign Affairs (New York), April 1953, pp. 385–386.

largely on this basis.   Thus, as at the San Francisco Conference, the question of what constitutes aggression again raised its head.[50]   As one observer pointed out, the issue in the Guatemalan case was essentially—

Does the United Nations have the right to insist on prior attempts at peaceful negotiations through regional organizations or does it have the obligation to look immediately into any complaint of aggression, right or wrong?   Put another way, do members of the United Nations have the sovereign right to insist on United Nations investigation of their charges, or can they be referred by the United Nations to another organization?[51]

I. PROPOSED CHANGES IN THE CHARTER

Elimination of the veto in the Security Council

One of the most frequently proposed amendments to the charter affecting enforcement action is the curbing of the veto.   Some suggest that the veto be eliminated from defined matters of aggression even though they do not propose that it be abolished entirely.[52]   This proposal involves a fundamental change in the United Nations as it was conceived at San Francisco.   As previously pointed out, the charter was based on the premise that the five permanent members of the Security Council would bear most of the responsibility for any enforcement action of the United Nations.   The desire to couple power with responsibility was a main reason for establishing the veto.   Involved in the premise was the belief that it would be preferable that the United Nations not attempt enforcement action rather than act with too little power to be successful.   Also involved was the view that if enforcement action were indicated against one of the permanent members, a world war would probably be inevitable.

Many people have never agreed with this view primarily because of its exemption of the big powers themselves from the enforcement system.   For instance, one writer has stated:

Only by checking major aggression can the intentions of the general pact be fulfilled, that is, world peace be preserved.   Checks against the strongest potential aggressor must be the keystone of any peace system.[53]

If the veto were entirely removed on questions relating to enforcement, any 7 of the 11 members of the Security Council would be able to order diplomatic, economic, and other nonmilitary sanctions against an aggressor.   In the event the military agreements previously discussed were concluded, the Council presumably would be able to direct the troops of any nation into action against the aggressor, regardless of the wishes of one or more of the great powers.   Such a change could be a long step away from the original concept that enforcement action would only be undertaken in cases in which the Big Five make their preponderant power jointly available.   On the other hand, it could imply that the United States, as well as other members, would be obligated to support with force an action which it might not approve.

An alternative to complete abolition of the veto would be to require that decisions on enforcement gain the concurrence of 2, 3, or 4 but not all 5 permanent members.   In this way, action could not be

---

[50] A possible definition of aggression had again been studied by a special committee established by the General Assembly in 1952, which reported in 1953.   Opinion still varied on the matter.   See report of the Special Committee on the Question of Defining Aggression.   Supplement No. 11 (A/2683) 1954.
[51] A. M. Rosenthal. New York Times, June 23, 1954, p. 3.
[52] ABC proposal, S. Res. 133, 81st Cong., 1st sess.   Collection of Documents, p. 868.
[53] Stefan T. Possony.   Op. cit., p. 947.

blocked by any single nation and decisions would nevertheless be assured of varying degrees of supporting power. From a national point of view, however, any such arrangement would still hold the possibility that, if the United States were in the minority, it could be bound without its consent. The same situation would exist, of course, for any of the other permanent powers.

A proposal which tends in the opposite direction is that the Security Council be divested of the power to order enforcement. The argument is based on the view that if the big powers were not bound by action of the Council they could afford to give up their veto.[54] The Security Council then would act, much as the General Assembly has acted in the Korean case, exclusively by recommendations on enforcement. The principal difference would be that such recommendations could be conceived and administered by a smaller body, the Security Council, rather than the General Assembly. This arrangement presumably would make for more prompt and efficient action. At the same time, a majority decision in the Council might be more likely to be representative of the actual distribution of power in the world. Under this proposal the Council could recommend action which a permanent power like the United States did not approve, but we would not be bound to support such action. A byproduct of this proposal would be to free the smaller nations from whatever compulsion they may be under at present to carry out "orders" approved by the requisite majority of the Council.

Strengthening the role of the General Assembly

Although the General Assembly has no clearly defined responsibilities for enforcement under the charter, in practice it has established procedures for exercising such responsibilities in the event that the Security Council fails to act because of the veto. There is a point of view which holds that the General Assembly could be more effective in enforcement if its role in this connection were formalized or strengthened through charter revision.

One change suggested has been that the General Assembly be given coequal responsibility with the Security Council in enforcement.[55] The Assembly, as well as the Council, would have power to determine the existence of a threat to or breach of the peace, to decide what measures of enforcement, including the use of a United Nations armed force, should be taken. It is further suggested under this proposal that only the General Assembly be permitted to call national armed services into use on behalf of the United Nations.

Such a change would permit the General Assembly to take stronger, more binding measures than are now possible. Unless simultaneous changes were made in the structure and voting procedures of the General Assembly, however, the grant of power to the Assembly would not solve two of the basic problems which confront that body in taking enforcement action, namely, unwieldy size and the one-state-one-vote formula which in no way links power with responsibility. Consequently, proposals which call for a strengthening of the role of the General Assembly in enforcement measures are often tied into a

---

[54] Clement Davies, MP, Revised Charter To Safeguard Peace. New Commonwealth (London), vol. 25, March 16, 1953, p. 264, and Dr. Gilbert Murray, Buttressing an Agency for Building World Peace, New Commonwealth (London), vol. 25, March 30, 1953, pp. 320–321.

[55] This, along with other changes, is suggested in the Clark-Sohn proposals for charter revision. See Grenville Clark and Louis B. Sohn, Peace Through Disarmament and Charter Revision, Detailed Proposals for Revision of the United Nations Charter, July 1953.

system of weighted voting in the General Assembly so that decisions will have power as well as votes behind them. Such proposals also frequently include an executive council of some kind as the instrument of action to meet the problem of unwieldiness. In effect, this would mean a modification or replacement of the present Security Council.

If the Assembly were to be capable of maintaining the strengthened role indicated in the above proposal, two differences from the present concept of the Security Council would appear essential. It would have to be subordinate and responsible to the General Assembly rather than the equal or superior body that the Security Council is under the present charter. Moreover, a veto by any single member of the Council would be out of the question.

Proposals respecting regional arrangements

Some observers feel that the enforcement of peace can be bulwarked by tying regional arrangements more closely to the United Nations organization. The general objective of proposals in this connection is to promote a simultaneous strengthening of the United Nations and the regional groupings and to prevent the two from working at cross purposes. The Collective Measures Committee has already considered the use of regional forces by the United Nations under the present charter. To this end, it has proposed that the member states of regional organizations seek to obtain regional support for collective measures of the United Nations. The Committee also recommended that the United Nations in turn take all appropriate steps to support regional enforcement action when it is consistent with the charter.

Another group of proposals has been advanced which would move closer to subordination of the regional or other collective defense arrangements to the United Nations.[56] The aim would be to strengthen the United Nations and reduce the fear that forces committed under regional agreements would be used for purposes other than defense. Subordination to the United Nations under these proposals would be achieved by requiring regional groupings (1) to discontinue any defensive action when so directed by the General Assembly, (2) to modify any provision of their organic treaties if any seven members of the Security Council or two-thirds of the General Assembly find them to be inconsistent with the purposes of the United Nations, (3) to respect recommendations for use of regional forces made by a similar vote in either body, and (4) to keep the General Assembly as well as the Security Council informed of any action contemplated or taken by the regional agencies.

The principal effect of these proposals would be to bring the General Assembly into the machinery for coordinating United Nations and regional action. At the present time, both the United Nations Charter and the principal regional agreements provide for coordination through the Security Council. Linkage of the regional groups with the General Assembly as well as the Security Council might reduce the apprehension that specific ties with United Nations action would hamper effective regional action. Some of the changes to bring this about could be made by the regional groupings themselves and would not necessarily require revision of the charter. On the other hand, revision of the charter might be conducive to the establishment of more uniform relationships among the United Nations and all regional groupings.

---

[56] Commission To Study the Organization of Peace, Eighth Report, op. cit., pp. 9–11.

The above group of suggested revisions also calls for ending the special status of any enforcement arrangements or action directed against ex-enemy states. At the present time, under article 53, any such activity is exempt from controls which the Security Council otherwise exercises over regional arrangements formed under chapter VIII.   It is primarily the bilateral treaties of the Communist countries which would be affected by this proposal, since they are largely characterized by specific reference to ex-enemy states.

Another proposal for achieving closer coordination is that regional organizations as such be represented in the Security Council.[57]   The nonpermanent members of the Security Council are already chosen so that major geographic areas are represented on that body, but they do not sit specifically as representatives of regions or regional organizations.

If this proposal were followed, the Council's primary function would probably become that of a coordinator among regional groupings with most of the military power of the world represented in the Security Council. Some members of the United Nations, however, do not belong to regional groupings and consequently would not have representation under this plan. Others, such as the United Kingdom and the United States, belong to several, and in effect would be overrepresented. Moreover, this approach tends to divide the world more or less permanently into superpower blocks which would probably become increasingly exclusive in time. Such a development has already occurred in the Soviet sphere whose votes in the United Nations, invariably the same, reflect the monolithic structure of the block.

An alternative along these lines might be to have authoritative spokesmen for the regional groups available whenever a major issue relating to enforcement were before the Council or the Assembly. Such an arrangement should at least facilitate coordination of actions of the regional organization and the United Nations. It might even have the effect of encouraging regional agencies to formulate their positions on the issue and could lead to prompt commitments of support for United Nations collective measures.

There are possible drawbacks in any attempts to link the United Nations too closely with regional arrangements. A tight relationship could impair the ability of the regional organizations to act quickly and efficiently, as presumably they can at present. It might also have the effect of making the United Nations dependent on 1 or 2 powerful regional groupings. In any situation where these groupings would not be willing to act, the United Nations might find itself unprepared to draw on alternative sources of support.

A proposal which is distinct from present regional defense concepts, but nevertheless shares in some degree their purposes, is the idea of a supplementary treaty under article 51 (ch. VII), which would be open for signature to all members of the United Nations. Signatories would agree to maintain specified forces for use by the United Nations against an aggressor as determined by a majority vote of either the Security Council or General Assembly, provided that this vote in-

[57] Robert D. Hayton, at Meeting of American Society of International Law, April 23, 1949. See Proceedings of the American Society of International Law, 1954, p. 64.   In 1943, Winston Churchill favored a plan which called for postwar peace enforcement to be carried out by 3 regional councils under the direction of a Supreme World Council. Another proposal for organizing the world community on a regional basis is discussed by R. W. G. Mackay in the Annals of the American Academy of Political and Social Science, November 1954, pp. 101–102.

cluded at least three permanent members.[58]   This proposal would have the effect of extending the collective defense concept involved in many regional pacts to a worldwide basis and circumventing the single-power veto.   Yet, all action would still be under the general auspices of the United Nations.

Under this proposal, there need not be any change in the present scope or membership of the United Nations.   At the same time a broader base of defense would be provided against the Soviet threat, broader than any existing regional organization.   Nor would the adoption of the proposal require the consent of the Soviet Union as would an amendment to the charter.

However, the same argument applies here as it does in all suggestions which would eliminate the veto, namely, that there is no stopping a third world war if one of the permanent members is intent upon precipitating it.   If that is the case, whether regional organizations are small or large in size may have technical significance in dealing with the aggressor, but they would not prevent war which is a fundamental purpose of the United Nations.

A more powerful United Nations

Some who favor an extensive enlargement of the powers of the United Nations advocate establishing a world police force or an international army of some type which would be directly under the command of the United Nations for peace enforcement.   Until such a police force is established, it is held, the United Nations cannot be certain of having sufficient forces to quell breaches of the peace.   Any instance of enforcement action, the argument runs, depends on the willingness of member states to make national troops available. Meanwhile, national governments are forced to maintain a high level of armaments to be prepared for aggression.

Proposals for an international police force or army vary as to organization, composition, size, relationship to armies of national governments, and other particulars.[59]   However, they generally have in common the concept that peace can be effectively enforced by the United Nations only if the international organization has under direct command an armed force which is large enough to repel aggression by any national state.   To achieve a satisfactory ratio in this respect, a corollary of the proposals is usually some degree of disarmament on the part of national states.

The proposals generally recognize, however, that acceptance of a plan calling for a large international police force which would be stronger than the forces of any single power, the United States, for example, and the use of which could not be vetoed, would involve the loss of important national prerogatives.   It would be a substantial step toward converting the United Nations from a league of sovereign states into a supranational government even though its powers may be rigidly circumscribed.

In 1950 the Senate Foreign Relations Committee held hearings on proposals to revise the United Nations Charter.   Several of the ideas advanced were aimed in the direction of developing the peace-enforcement machinery of the United Nations into a world police force or international army.   Some suggested the formation of a new

---

[58] This was the proposition in the Thomas-Douglas resolution (S. Con. Res. 52, 81st Cong., 1st sess.)

[59] For examples, see Clark-Sohn, op. cit., pp. 28–32, and p. 144; John Pinder, U. N. Reform, Proposals for Charter Amendment. London, Federal Union, 1953; The ABC proposal, Collection of Documents, p. 868.

international organization without the Soviet Union if the Soviet Union refused to agree to the establishment of such a force under the United Nations.

The committee, in its report, stated:

> For the most part the proposals before the committee involved serious constitutional questions. It would not be proper for the committee to take a position on propositions as fundamental as proposals for world federation which would involve extensive amendments of the United States Constitution until the issues have been debated, discussed, and understood the length and the breadth of this land.[60]

Attention was given to the idea of an international police force by the Collective Measures Committee in studying a proposal made by Secretary General Trygve Lie to create a small United Nations military legion capable of putting down local breaches of the peace. The committee felt that the term "legion" was a misnomer and that United Nations Volunteer Reserve would be a more accurate title. Both the Secretary General and the Committee expressed the view that creation of even a small supranational self-contained standing force, internationally recruited and subject to the control of a self-contained United Nations command, was administratively, financially, and militarily impractical for the present.[61]   Later the former Secretary General made it clear he did not even wish to proceed with the establishment of a United Nations Volunteer Reserve at this time.[62]

Proposed changes along a different line but still leading to a much stronger organization call for broadening the entire base of enforcement action.   Enforcement measures would be applied not merely to keep or restore the peace but to enforce the decisions of the organization concerning the settlement of disputes.   Some would go even further; as one writer has put it:

> * * * the centralization of the legitimate use of force is a problematical achievement if not accompanied by the establishment of compulsory adjudication of all conflicts by decisions of a central organ, and the guaranty of prompt enforcement of these decisions through a centralized machinery [63]

Others share this view in the belief that merely "enforcing peace" and "repelling aggression" actually mean "to maintain the status quo." [64]   Unless there is some way to effect peaceful change, enforce settlements or bring an end to situations likely to continue to cause international tension, it is held, there is little gain in the long run in enforcing "peace."   Was the Korean action worthwhile, such advocates would ask, when, after the fighting ended, the basic problem remained unsettled, still a threat to the peace of the world?   On the other hand, it may be asked, if it is difficult for the United Nations to organize collective measures to maintain peace, how much more difficult might it be for the organization to enforce international "legislation"?   What nations, moreover, will endorse the extensive limitations on their sovereignty which are inherent in this approach?

[60] Collection of Documents, p. 866.
[61] Second Report of the Collective Measures Committee, op. cit.
    This was not the same as a United Nations guard force proposed earlier by the Secretary General, designed primarily to police and protect United Nations headquarters or missions abroad.   These were authorized by the General Assembly, in the form of a United Nations Field Service, on November 22, 1949.   For full study of this see "United Nations Guards and Technical Field Service," Commission To Study the Organization of Peace, September 1949.
[62] Third Report of Collective Measures Committee, op. cit.
[63] Hans Kelsen.   Collective Security Under the Charter of the United Nations, American Journal of International Law (Washington) vol. 42, October 1948, p. 790.
[64] Edwin Borchard, op. cit., p. 970.

J. CONCLUDING COMMENTS

The machinery of peace enforcement within the United Nations system has evolved in considerably different fashion from what was envisioned at San Francisco a decade ago.   At that time, the Security Council, designed as the principal organ of enforcement, was charged with potentialities in this field which were far reaching in scope. Under article 43 it would have been possible to establish, in effect, an international army under control which was supranational over member states except the five permanent members of the Security Council. The latter would have been largely responsible for deciding when this international army should move against aggression or threat of aggression and, each of them, through the instrumentality of the veto, when it would not.

These potentialities of the Council, however, have not developed. On the contrary, the Security Council has fallen largely into disuse insofar as enforcement is concerned, primarily because of the attitudes and policies of the Soviet Union.

Instead, the nations have sought elsewhere for means to bulwark their individual security in common defense against aggression.   They have developed substitutes or supplements for the peace enforcement machinery of the Security Council.   This development has taken two principal directions.   The role of the General Assembly in enforcement has been enlarged and regional defense organizations have multiplied. In both cases, the influence of the United States has been extensive. This country led in encouraging the General Assembly to adopt the Uniting for Peace resolution, largely as a response to the Korean aggression.   The United States has also been a principal sponsor and supporter of regional defense arrangements.

Recently, Secretary of State Dulles named security as one of the major questions which might be brought before the Charter Review Conference, and raised the following questions concerning charter amendment in this field:

By the charter, article 24, the Security Council is supposed to exercise "primary responsibility for the maintenance of international peace and security."   Can charter changes better enable it to discharge that responsibility?   Or must that primary responsibility be left to security organizations the formation of which is authorized by article 51?   Or should greater responsibility be given to the General Assembly, where there is no veto? [65]

Because security is at the heart of the conflict between Communist and free countries, it is the field in which charter changes would seem the least likely to be accepted as long as the Organization contains both camps and the unanimity of the permanent powers is required for adoption of amendments.   Apart from this problem, however, this country needs to be clear as to whether any changes in the charter in this vital field are desirable from our national point of view.   Some of the proposals which have been advanced are far reaching in their effect.   Elimination of the veto is a case in point.   Unquestionably, the use of the veto by the Soviet Union in recent years has seriously circumscribed the capacity of the Security Council to discharge its function of enforcement.   Proposals to curb the device suggest remedies for this situation but they also raise other questions which must not be overlooked.   Would the United States be willing, for

[65] Senate Subcommittee on the United Nations Charter.   Hearings on review of the United Nations Charter (pt. 1, p. 6).

example, to supply armed forces for a United Nations enforcement action of which we did not approve? That could be a consequence of at least some of the proposals for the elimination of the veto. Furthermore, would the United States be willing to assign enforcement functions beyond those of a voluntary nature to a General Assembly in which it has only 1 out of 60 votes?

The rapid development of regional organizations and the trend away from close links between them and the United Nations raise additional questions. In size and composition, these groupings appear to possess advantages in organizing common defense against aggression, particularly Communist aggression. On the other hand, will the cumulative effect of the regional arrangements in time lead to the division of the world into superpower blocs existing largely, if not wholly, apart from the United Nations system? In these circumstances the importance of the United Nations might be reduced considerably at least insofar as its principal objective, that is, maintenance of peace, is concerned. Can regional arrangements be so tied into the system as to prevent this development, if indeed it is desirable to prevent it?

Questions such as these are implicit in the present trends relative to the enforcement functions of the United Nations system. They need to be examined, not only in connection with the policies we are presently pursuing in the United Nations, but also in connection with proposed changes in the charter and in U. N. procedure involving these functions.

THE INTERNATIONAL COURT OF JUSTICE

STAFF STUDY NO. 8
MAY 1955

PREFACE

By Walter F. George, *Chairman*

The development of rules of law to regulate the conduct of nations in their relations with each other in such a way that war may be avoided is perhaps the most important single task man can perform in his eternal quest for peace. This great goal may not be realized in our lifetime. But it is one we should all help to achieve.

Some of the greatest men of history have devoted their lives to this problem, and, by and large, most people have supported the efforts to establish moral and legal principles to guide the conduct of nations. Unfortunately, there have been recurrent instances in which the governments of some countries have relied upon force instead of law to seek fulfillment of their objectives.

It is incontrovertible that today Communist ideologists view international law simply as a device to bring free men under Communist control and to further Communist concepts. Even in the mid-Twentieth century the shortsightedness of men has prevented the development of an adequate international law applicable to nations in their critical relationships with each other. The International Court of Justice, the subject of this staff study, is the principal judicial organ of the international community as it exists today. As such, the Court can hardly rise higher than the community of which it is a part. The United Nations is an international organization based on the concept of the sovereign equality of states. As this study shows, the International Court obtains jurisdiction in cases only with the consent of sovereign states and can only declare what it finds the law to be.

Nevertheless, the Court is an instrumentality available for the use of states to settle their legal disputes. Able, conscientious men versed in the law of nations stand ready to help states settle disputes by peaceful means based on principles of international law and equity. The Court has not been used as much as many have wished. The fault is not with the instrument, but with the attitude of states which all too often still seem to prefer political settlements to those based on law and reason.

It is my belief that more use should be made of the International Court of Justice. Our common law was developed over the centuries. Men gradually found it to their mutual advantage to settle disputes by appeal to law and courts rather than to the sword. International law and the International Court are in their infancy as compared to the laws and codes that guide men in their relationships one with the other within nations. If men are to live at peace, international law must grow and the Court must be used.

The United States can be proud of the historic role it has played in the development of international jurisprudence. From participation in the creation of the first arbitral tribunals to the acceptance of the compulsory jurisdiction provision of the statute of the International Court, our Nation has been in the forefront. Leaders of the American bar have helped, officially and unofficially, to promote the concept that if nations are to live at peace their relationships should develop in a framework of accepted international legal principles.

The study was prepared by Mrs. Ellen Collier of the Legislative Reference Service of the Library of Congress, and Carl Marcy of the staff of the subcommittee. It is a record of the workings of the Court during the past 9 years and a discussion of some of the proposals which have been advanced respecting the functions of the Court. The study is for the background use of the subcommittee and does not necessarily represent the views of any of its members.

MAY 1955.

CONTENTS

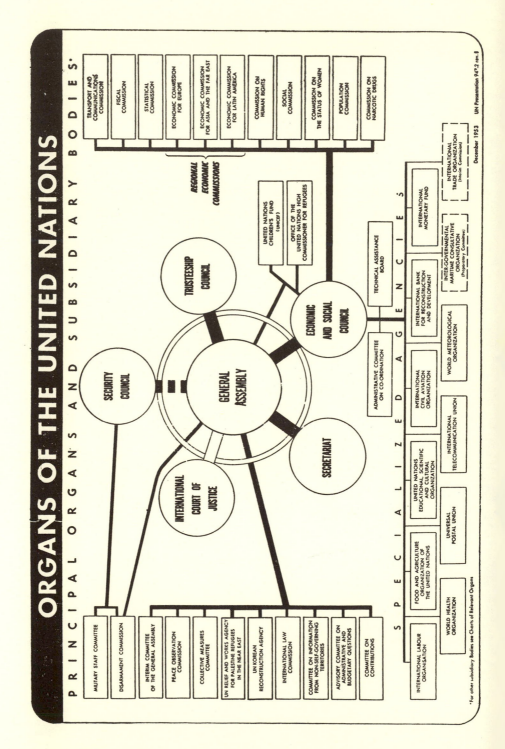

ORGANS OF THE UNITED NATIONS

PRINCIPAL ORGANS AND SUBSIDIARY BODIES*

TRANSPORT AND COMMUNICATIONS COMMISSION

FISCAL COMMISSION

STATISTICAL COMMISSION

ECONOMIC COMMISSION FOR EUROPE

ECONOMIC COMMISSION FOR ASIA AND THE FAR EAST

ECONOMIC COMMISSION FOR LATIN AMERICA

COMMISSION ON HUMAN RIGHTS

SOCIAL COMMISSION

COMMISSION ON THE STATUS OF WOMEN

POPULATION COMMISSION

COMMISSION ON NARCOTIC DRUGS

REGIONAL ECONOMIC COMMISSIONS

UNITED NATIONS CHILDREN'S FUND (UNICEF)

OFFICE OF THE UNITED NATIONS HIGH COMMISSIONER FOR REFUGEES

TRUSTEESHIP COUNCIL

SECURITY COUNCIL

GENERAL ASSEMBLY

INTERNATIONAL COURT OF JUSTICE

ECONOMIC AND SOCIAL COUNCIL

SECRETARIAT

TECHNICAL ASSISTANCE BOARD

ADMINISTRATIVE COMMITTEE ON CO-ORDINATION

MILITARY STAFF COMMITTEE

DISARMAMENT COMMISSION

INTERIM COMMITTEE OF THE GENERAL ASSEMBLY

PEACE OBSERVATION COMMISSION

COLLECTIVE MEASURES COMMITTEE

UN RELIEF AND WORKS AGENCY FOR PALESTINE REFUGEES IN THE NEAR EAST

UN KOREAN RECONSTRUCTION AGENCY

INTERNATIONAL LAW COMMISSION

COMMITTEE ON INFORMATION FROM NON-SELF-GOVERNING TERRITORIES

ADVISORY COMMITTEE ON ADMINISTRATIVE AND BUDGETARY QUESTIONS

COMMITTEE ON CONTRIBUTIONS

SPECIALIZED AGENCIES

INTERNATIONAL LABOUR ORGANISATION

WORLD HEALTH ORGANIZATION

FOOD AND AGRICULTURE ORGANIZATION OF THE UNITED NATIONS

UNIVERSAL POSTAL UNION

UNITED NATIONS EDUCATIONAL, SCIENTIFIC AND CULTURAL ORGANIZATION

INTERNATIONAL TELECOMMUNICATION UNION

INTERNATIONAL CIVIL AVIATION ORGANIZATION

WORLD METEOROLOGICAL ORGANIZATION

INTERNATIONAL BANK FOR RECONSTRUCTION AND DEVELOPMENT

INTERNATIONAL MONETARY FUND

INTER-GOVERNMENTAL MARITIME CONSULTATIVE ORGANIZATION (Preparatory Committee)

INTERNATIONAL TRADE ORGANIZATION (Interim Commission)

*For other subsidiary Bodies see Charts of Relevant Organs

December 1953   UN Presentation 947-2 rev.6

THE INTERNATIONAL COURT OF JUSTICE

I. Introduction

The International Court of Justice has probably had virtually a uniformly favorable acceptance among the member states of the United Nations. Perhaps the two most important factors in this acceptance are these: (1) The Court has continued to maintain the high standards of jurisprudence which characterized predecessor tribunals; and (2) it has handled a limited number of cases which have not generally involved the more controversial political issues of the day.

The fact that the Court has been used only infrequently is not a critical reflection on the Court. Its primary function, as in the case of any court, is to interpret and apply the principles of the legal system of the society which it serves so that the society may conduct its affairs in a peaceful and orderly manner. Seen from this point of view, the Court reflects the realities of the international system. It is not, as in the case of domestic courts, a part of a society which, for example, has a legislative body to enact laws, an executive to administer laws, and a police force to enforce the law and the decisions of the court. Given the present state of world society, some would go so far as to say that the Court's intrinsic value at this time is to be measured not so much by its contribution to pacific settlement of disputes as by its contribution to the development of international law.

Bearing these qualifications in mind, this staff study examines briefly the background of the International Court of Justice; its position within the United Nations; its organization, procedures, and jurisdiction; the volume and nature of its work; and certain proposals to change the nature of the Court or to broaden its jurisdiction.

II. Origins of the Court

INTERNATIONAL ARBITRATION

The International Court of Justice evolved out of the Permanent Court of International Justice, established in 1921 in accordance with the Covenant of the League of Nations. The origins of both courts, however, are to be found in the modern development of efforts to settle international disputes on the basis of law, the first steps in this direction being the establishment of arbitration procedures. Throughout this development the United States has played a leading role.

The first notable instance of international arbitration in modern times, for example, was the provision in the American-British Treaty of 1794 (the Jay Treaty). Significant advances with respect to international arbitration were made at The Hague Conferences in 1899 and 1907. The United States played a prominent part in both Conferences. At the latter Conference, the first serious effort was made to establish a true international "court." Again it was the United States that took the lead. The nations represented at the Conference proceeded to draw up plans for an International Court of Arbitral Justice. The project failed because the large nations and the small nations could not agree on a method for selecting the judges.[1]

THE PERMANENT COURT OF INTERNATIONAL JUSTICE

The first World Court was established through and in close connection with the League of Nations. Though never a party to the statute of the Court, the United States had an important part in its establishment. This country signed the protocol of signature of 1920 to which the statute of the new Court was attached, and in 1923 President Harding asked the Senate for its advice and consent to ratification. Following action by the Senate in 1926 setting forth reservations and conditions under which the United States might ratify, negotiations were carried on over a period of years with the parties to the statute and with members of the League of Nations. The statute was revised in an effort to meet the Senate's views, but in 1935 the Senate, by a vote of 52 for and 36 against, failed to provide the necessary two-thirds majority for approval.[2]

The Permanent Court of International Justice sat from 1922 until 1940. During this period it rendered 32 judgments and 27 advisory opinions.[3] The Court is generally regarded as having performed its duties fairly and competently and there was no instance of its decisions being disregarded. During the negotiations concerning post-World War II arrangements, it was fully agreed that the record of the old Court was such that it should be reinstituted or a new one established along the same general lines.

THE INTERNATIONAL COURT OF JUSTICE [4]

The Dumbarton Oaks proposals, drawn up in 1944, provided that there should be an international court as the principal judicial organ of the proposed new international organization, and that the statute of the Court should be a part of the charter. At San Francisco, it was decided—because of the practical difficulties involved in reconstituting the Permanent Court—to establish a new court to be called the International Court of Justice. The change was largely formal, for the new statute approved at San Francisco was very similar to the old.[5]

[1] The 1907 Hague Conference did provide conditionally for the establishment of an International Prize Court, but this never came into being. Through the influence of The Hague Conferences, the five Central American States established the Central American Court of Justice, which actually functioned from 1908 to 1918.

[2] Four citizens of the United States—John Basset Moore, Charles E. Hughes, Frank P. Kellogg, and Manley O. Hudson—served at one time or another as judges of the Court.

[3] Lissitzyn, Oliver J. The International Court of Justice. New York, Carnegie Endowment for International Peace, Martin Press, 1951, pp. 23–24.

[4] For annual reports on the work of the Court see articles by Manley O. Hudson in January issues of the American Journal of International Law.

[5] As for the two issues on which the Committee of Jurists had not been able to agree—the method of nominating the judges and compulsory jurisdiction—the Conference decided in both matters to retain, with minor modifications, the provisions of the 1920 statute.

III. The Organization, Jurisdiction, and Procedure of the Court

RELATIONSHIP OF THE COURT TO THE UNITED NATIONS

The new Court is one of the principal organs of the United Nations, whereas the old Court, though it had close connections with the League of Nations was not an integral part of it. This is in fact the major point of difference between the two courts.

The position of the new Court in the United Nations is defined in chapter XIV (arts. 92–96) of the charter. The Court—

is the principal judicial organ of the United Nations, and the Statute of the Court is an integral part of the present Charter. All Members of the United Nations are automatically parties to the Statute, and other states may become parties to the Statute on conditions determined by the General Assembly upon the recommendation of the Security Council.

Each member of the United Nations undertakes to comply with the decision of the International Court of Justice in any case to which it is a party. If any party fails to perform the obligations incumbent upon it under a judgment of the Court, the other party may have recourse to the Security Council. That body may make recommendations or decide upon measures to be taken to carry out the judgment.

In addition to its function of adjudication, the General Assembly and the Security Council may request the Court to give advisory opinions on any legal question. Other organs of the United Nations and specialized agencies may also be authorized by the General Assembly to request such opinions on legal questions within the scope of their activities.

Article 36 of the charter, dealing with the authority of the Security Council in peaceful settlement, states:

In making recommendations under this Article, the Security Council should also take into consideration that legal disputes should as a general rule be referred by the parties to the International Court of Justice in accordance with the provisions of the Statute of the Court.

No attempt is made, however, to preclude resort to tribunals other than the International Court. Article 95 of the charter provides that—

Nothing in the present Charter shall prevent Members of the United Nations from entrusting the solution of their differences to other tribunals by virtue of agreements already in existence or which may be concluded in the future.

THE JUDGES

Under its statute, the Court is composed of 15 judges, no 2 of whom may be nationals of the same state. The judges are to be—

elected regardless of their nationality from among persons of high moral character, who possess the qualifications required in their respective countries for appointment to the highest judicial offices, or are juris-consults of recognized competence in international law.

In their selection, however, it is expected not only that the justices should possess the qualifications required, but also that in the Court as a whole the representation of the main forms of civilization and of the principal legal systems of the world should be assured.

The term of office is 9 years, as was the case under the previous statute, but in order to assure greater continuity, provision is made in the new statute for election of one-third of the members every 3 years. Members are eligible for reelection. No justice may engage in any political or administrative function, or other occupation of a professional nature during his tenure.

Inability to agree on a method of selecting the judges defeated the attempt to establish an international court of justice at The Hague in 1907, and the same issue was the subject of sharp differences of opinion in the drafting of the 1920 statute. The issue was resolved in 1920 by an elaborate procedure of nomination and election which is retained in the present statute. Panels of jurists in each state may nominate not more than 4 persons, of whom not more than 2 shall be of that nationality. From the persons so nominated, the General Assembly and the Security Council proceed independently of one another to elect the members of the Court. An absolute majority in each body is required for election. Detailed procedures are outlined to be followed in the case of a disagreement.

PROCEDURES AND JURISDICTION

The seat of the Court is at The Hague, but the Court may sit and exercise its functions elsewhere if it considers it desirable. The Court is permanently in session. It is authorized to establish its own rules of procedure, and did in fact adopt those of its predecessor.

The expenses of the Court are provided for in the United Nations budget. The salaries of the judges are fixed by the General Assembly, and "may not be decreased during the term of office."

The Court has two different types of jurisdiction. One is jurisdiction with respect to contending parties—the so-called contentious cases; the other is its role with regard to the rendering of advisory opinions.

In contentious cases, only states (not individuals or international organizations) may be parties before the Court.[6] It is open to states which accept the jurisdiction of the Court and which adhere to the statute, and to other states on conditions laid down by the Security Council.[7]

The jurisdiction of the Court is defined in article 38 of the statute, which reads as follows:

1. The jurisdiction of the Court comprises all cases which the parties refer to it and all matters specially provided for in the Charter of the United Nations or in treaties and conventions in force.

2. The states parties to the present Statute may at any time declare that they recognize as compulsory *ipso facto* and without special agreement, in relation to any other state accepting the same obligation, the jurisdiction of the Court in all legal disputes concerning:

    a. the interpretation of a treaty;

    b. any question of international law;

    c. the existence of any fact which, if established, would constitute a breach of an international obligation;

---

[6] The statute provides, however (art. 34), that the Court "may request of public international organizations information relevant to cases before it, and shall receive such information presented by such organizations on their own initiative."

[7] It is specifically provided that such conditions shall not place the parties in a position of inequality before the Court. Conditions established by the Security Council October 15, 1946, provide that the Court is to be open to states which are not parties to the statute on condition that they deposit with the Registrar of the Court a declaration accepting the Court's jurisdiction in accordance with the U. N. Charter and the statute and rules of the Court, undertaking to comply in good faith with the Court's decisions, and accepting the obligations of a member of the U. N. under art. 94 of the charter. See International Court of Justice Yearbook, 1953, pp. 35–36.

d. the nature or extent of the reparation to be made for the breach of an international obligation.

*   *   *   *   *   *   *

3. In the event of a dispute as to whether the Court has jurisdiction, the matter shall be settled by the decision of the Court.

In dealing with disputes submitted to it, the Court is directed to apply international conventions; international custom; "the general principles of law recognized by civilized nations"; and with certain limitations, "judicial decisions and the teachings of the most highly qualified publicists of the various nations." The Court is also authorized to decide cases ex aequo et bono [in justice and good dealing] if the parties agree.

Cases may be brought before the Court by agreement of the parties, or on application of one of the parties. If one party does not appear, or fails to defend its case, the other party may call on the Court to decide in favor of its claim, but—

the Court must, before doing so, satisfy itself, not only that it has jurisdiction * * * but also that the claim is well founded in fact and law.

All questions are decided by a majority of the judges present (assuming a quorum). The judgment must state the reasons on which it is based, and must contain the names of the judges who took part in the decision. Any judge may deliver a separate opinion.

The statute specifically provides that a decision of the Court "has no binding force except between the parties and in respect of that particular case." The judgment, however, is final and without appeal although applications may be made under specified conditions for revision of a judgment.[8]

Article 65 of the statute provides that—

the Court may give an advisory opinion on any legal question at the request of whatever body may be authorized by or in accordance with the Charter of the United Nations to make such a request.[9]

COMPULSORY JURISDICTION

It has been noted above that under article 36, provision is made for the automatic or compulsory jurisdiction of the Court as between States under certain conditions. As applied to international disputes, the origin of compulsory jurisdiction is to be found in the history of efforts made to provide for obligatory arbitration. Some sort of special agreement between the disputants was nearly always necessary in order to bring arbitration machinery into operation, so that in the last analysis each party to a dispute was in a position to decide for itself whether the agreement to arbitrate was applicable.

In drafting a statute for the predecessor of the present Court, an Advisory Committee of Jurists proposed that the jurisdiction of the Permanent Court of International Justice be compulsory for all states for certain broad types of disputes. There was substituted for this provision the so-called optional clause, under which each state could, at its option, confer on the Court compulsory jurisdiction in

[8] Any state which considers that it has an interest of a legal nature which may be affected by the decision in a case may request the Court to be permitted to participate (art. 62).
[9] The request must contain "an exact statement of the question upon which an opinion is required," and must be accompanied by "all documents likely to throw light upon the question" (art. 65). Notice is given to all States entitled to appear before the Court, and they are entitled, as are any international organizations "likely to be able to furnish information on the question," to present written or oral statements to the Court (art. 66).

the designated categories of disputes; i. e., disputes concerning the interpretation of a treaty; any question of international law; the existence of any fact which, if established, would constitute a breach of an international obligation; and the nature or extent of the reparation to be made for the breach of an international obligation.

Another provision gave the previous Court jurisdiction over "all matters * * * in treaties and conventions in force." Under this provision whenever the parties to a treaty or convention agreed to refer to the Court disputes arising thereunder, any such dispute could be brought before the Court by one of the parties, even over the objections of another.

The effect of the above provisions was strengthened by empowering the Court, in the event of a dispute as to whether it had jurisdiction, to decide the matter itself.

By the above provisions, a foundation was laid for the exercise of compulsory jurisdiction by the previous Court. The actual extent of such jurisdiction, however, remained dependent on the willingness of States to commit themselves in advance to accept the Court's jurisdiction in provisions of treaties and conventions, and to file declarations under the optional clause. In point of fact, 45 States at one time or another filed declarations under the optional clause, while provision for reference of disputes to the Court was made in approximately 400 treaties and conventions.

The Committee of Jurists which met in 1945 to prepare the draft of a statute for the present Court could not agree on the issue of compulsory jurisdiction. A majority favored elimination of the optional clause and provision for compulsory jurisdiction in the statute itself. Others wanted the optional clause retained. The debate was continued at the San Francisco Conference where there was considerable support for immediate recognition of the compulsory jurisdiction of the Court. Both the United States and the U. S. S. R. were opposed, however, and it was finally decided to retain the optional clause. Declarations of acceptance of compulsory jurisdiction under the previous statute were made applicable to the new one and it was likewise provided that agreements in existing treaties and conventions for reference of disputes to the old Court should be applicable to the new one.

AMENDMENTS

The 1920 statute contained no provision for amendment. This has been changed by providing that amendments to the new statute may be made by the same procedure employed in amending the U. N. Charter.[10] The Court itself may also propose amendments.

IV. The Work of the Court

As in the case of its predecessor, the new Court was resorted to infrequently at the beginning. By the end of 1947 it had been presented with 1 dispute (the Corfu Channel dispute, which eventually gave rise to 3 judgments) and 1 request for an advisory opinion.

---

[10] "Subject, however, to any provisions which the General Assembly upon recommendation of the Security Council may adopt concerning the participation of states which are parties to the present Statute but are not Members of the United Nations" (art. 69).

At its second session, on November 14, 1947, the General Assembly adopted a resolution,[11] which the United States supported, to encourage resort to the Court. The resolution stated that "it is * * * of paramount importance that the Court should be utilized to the greatest practicable extent in the progressive development of international law * * *." It went on to recommend that organs of the United Nations and the specialized agencies should, from time to time, review the difficult and important points of law which arose in the course of their activities, and refer such questions to the Court for advisory opinions. It also called to the attention of the member states of the United Nations the advantage of inserting in conventions and treaties clauses providing "for the submission of disputes which may arise from * * * [their] interpretation or application * * * preferably and as far as possible to the International Court of Justice." It was further recommended that states should as a general rule submit their legal disputes to the Court, and it was pointed out that it would be desirable if "the greatest possible number of States" accepted the Court's jurisdiction "with as few reservations as possible."

While it can hardly be said that the Court has been "utilized to the greatest practicable extent," much greater use was made of it after 1948 than had been the case up to that time.

Altogether, there have been 18 contentious proceedings and 7 requests for advisory opinions. Six of the contentious cases developed out of two disputes—the Corfu Channel dispute and the Colombian-Peruvian Asylum dispute—so that a total of 14 separate disputes have been referred to the Court.

Year	Cases submitted [1]	Judgments	Advisory opinions requested	Advisory opinions rendered
1946	0	0	0	0
1947	2	0	1	0
1948	0	1	1	1
1949	[2] 4	2	3	1
1950	3	2	1	[3] 4
1951	4	2	0	1
1952	0	[4] 3	0	0
1953	2	[5] 3	1	0
1954	[6] 3	[6] 3	0	1

[1] Counting 3 separate proceedings in the Corfu Channel dispute and 3 separate proceedings in the Colombian-Peruvian Asylum dispute.
[2] 1 case withdrawn in 1950.
[3] Interpretation of peace treaties with Bulgaria, Hungary, and Rumania—2 opinions: Mar. 30 (pt. I), July 18 (pt. II).
[4] Including judgment of July 1952 (preliminary objection) in the Ambatielos case.
[5] Including judgment of May 19, 1953 (merits) in the Ambatielos case.
[6] Includes proceedings instituted by the United States against the U. S. S. R. and Hungary, respectively, for damages on account of seizure and detention of an U. S. Air Force C-47 aircraft. Applications removed from calendar of Court because U. S. S. R. and Hungary refused to submit to jurisdiction.

The size of the Court's docket, of course, is an inadequate index of the role it has played in the pacific settlement of international disputes. The mere existence of the Court may encourage states to settle their disputes "out of court."

[11] Resolution 171 (II). For full text, see Senate Foreign Relations Committee Subcommittee on the United Nations Charter, Review of the United Nations Charter, Collection of Documents, U. S. Government Printing Office, 1954, pp. 482–483.

ADVISORY OPINIONS

The General Assembly and the Security Council are authorized directly by the United Nations Charter to request advisory opinions on any legal questions. In accordance with the charter, the General Assembly in turn has authorized 11 organs and specialized agencies to request advisory opinions from the Court on legal matters.[12]

Up to the present time, only the General Assembly has made use of this authority. It has requested advisory opinions on seven occasions.

Two of the requests made dealt with the interpretation of the membership provisions of the U. N. Charter (art. 4); one with the capacity of the United Nations to bring an international claim against a state for reparation for injuries suffered by U. N. employees; one with the interpretation of the peace treaties with Bulgaria, Hungary, and Rumania; one with the status of former German South-West Africa (involving the interpretation of the trusteeship provisions of the U. N. Charter); one with the subject of reservations to the Genocide Convention; and one with the right of the General Assembly to refuse to give effect to awards of compensation to staff members dismissed by the Secretary General. (See appendix, table I, for brief summaries of the requests and opinions.)

In some instances the competence of the Court to render advisory opinions has been challenged and its opinions have been disregarded by states affected (though not by the General Assembly as a whole). In 1947, for example, the General Assembly requested an opinion on whether a member of the United Nations could make its consent to the admission of a new state subject to conditions other than those set forth in the Charter, and, more specifically, on the condition that other states be admitted. The request was made because the Soviet Union had consistently used the veto to prevent the membership of a number of states, and had indicated that it would admit the states in question only on the condition that certain other states be admitted. The Court's competence was challenged by the Soviet bloc chiefly on the grounds that the question of admitting new members was a political question. The Court held that the question as asked, in abstract form, was a purely legal one and within the Court's competence. The Court went on to say that no conditions on admission of members could be imposed beyond those specified in the Charter. The Court did say, however: "Article 4 [the membership provision of the charter] does not forbid the taking into account of any factor which it is possible reasonably and in good faith to connect with the conditions laid down in that Article * * *" (ICJ Reports, 1947–48, p. 63). The Court was divided 9 to 6, with 2 judges writing concurring opinions. The dissenting judges took the position that the admission of new members involved political as well as juridical considerations, and that the General Assembly and the Security Council could consider conditions other than those mentioned in the charter.

[12] Economic and Social Council; Trusteeship Council; Interim Committee of the General Assembly; International Labour Organization; Food and Agriculture Organization of the United Nations; United Nations Educational, Scientific, and Cultural Organization; International Civil Aviation Organization; World Health Organization; International Bank for Reconstruction and Development; International Monetary Fund; International Telecommunications Union. United Nations Secretariat, Department of Public Information, Research Section; The International Court of Justice. Background Paper No. 66. 31 pp.

The General Assembly recommended that the members of the Security Council and the General Assembly act in accordance with the Court's opinion in voting on the admission of states. The Soviet Union, however, took the position that the "opinion of the Court" was actually a minority view, supported by only 7 votes, whereas 8 judges (6 dissenting, 2 concurring) were opposed to this view.[13] The Soviet Union continued to veto the admission of a number of applicant states. A later opinion of the Court expressed the view that the General Assembly could not proceed to vote on the admission of new members without a recommendation from the Security Council.[14]

The request for an advisory opinion relating to the peace treaties with Bulgaria, Hungary, and Rumania arose out of the contention that human rights guaranteed in the peace treaties had been violated in these countries. The three countries at no time recognized the competence of either the General Assembly or the Court, on the grounds that human rights questions were matters of domestic jurisdiction and therefore outside the purview of the charter. The Court said that the question before it was solely one of interpretation of the treaties, and that the question of domestic jurisdiction was not presented. Nevertheless, the three countries did not observe the Court's opinion.

In the South-West Africa case, the General Assembly asked for the advisory opinion of the Court with respect to the status of South-West Africa—a former League of Nations mandate under the administration of the Union of South Africa. The Court held that South Africa was not obligated to put South-West Africa under the U. N. trusteeship system and stated that—

the competence to determine and modify the international status of the Territory rests with the Union of South Africa acting with the consent of the United Nations.

According to the President's Report on United States Participation in the United Nations, 1951:

South Africa indicated that, while it would not accept the Court's opinion, it would accept international responsibility in regard to South-West Africa in conformity with the spirit of the League of Nations mandate, but not to the greater extent set forth under the United Nations trusteeship system.[15]

This case suggests that while advisory opinions do not bind states, or the United Nations organs requesting such opinions, in some instances they may serve the purpose of inducing states to move in the direction suggested by the Court.

CONTENTIOUS CASES

One of the twelve disputes brought before the Court in contested cases is still in the process of litigation. [See appendix, table II, for brief summaries of these cases.] In two others, the controversy arising out of the nationalization by Iran of the Anglo-Iranian Oil Co, and the case involving four U. S. airmen forced down in Hungary—the Court found that it lacked jurisdiction. One case was withdrawn.

Up to the present time, the Court has issued judgments relating to eight different disputes. Two of these disputes resulted in nonobserv-

[13] See Sloan, F. Blaine, Advisory Jurisdiction of the International Court of Justice. California Law Review, vol. 38, December 1950, p. 856.
[14] See appendix, below, p. 246.
[15] President's Report, 1951, pp. 237-238.

ance of the Court's judgments. In the Corfu Channel dispute between Great Britain and Albania, the Court's third and final judgment was an award of damages to Great Britain. Albania has never paid the damages assessed. While the Court is technically not to be concerned with political matters such as relieving tensions between disputants, its earlier judgment on the points of law involved in the Corfu Channel case may have helped to relieve the tension which the dispute had created.

In the Colombian-Peruvian asylum dispute, a considerable period of time elapsed before effect was given to the judgment of the Court. The Court held in November 1950 that the asylum accorded by the Colombian Embassy to the Peruvian, Haya de la Torre, should be terminated. Colombia refused to surrender the fugitive, and could not come to agreement with Peru on any other method of terminating the asylum. A later judgment of the Court in June 1951 held that Colombia should have terminated the asylum, in accordance with the Court's judgment, but that Colombia did not have to terminate it by surrendering Haya de la Torre to the Peruvian authorities. Senor de la Torre was finally able to leave Peru in March 1954—a satisfactory, though tardy, compliance with the Court's decision.

The United States has been party to one of the contentious cases in which a judgment has been rendered—that between France and the United States concerning treaty rights of United States nationals in Morocco. The case arose out of legislation promulgated in 1948 for the French zone of Morocco under which the importation of goods into Morocco by United States nationals was subjected to a system of licensing control. The French contended that this legislation did not contravene economic rights reserved to the United States by the United States-Moroccan treaty of September 16, 1836, and by a provision of the Act of Algeciras of April 7, 1906, which pledged France and Morocco to "the principle of economic liberty without any inequality." The Court ruled unanimously that the 1948 legislation did contravene United States rights by discriminating between imports from the United States and imports from France.[16]

On March 3, 1954, the United States Government filed with the Court applications instituting proceedings against the Soviet and Hungarian Governments on account of their conduct in connection with four United States airmen who were forced down on Hungarian soil in a United States military aircraft, November 19, 1951. Because of Soviet and Hungarian objections to the jurisdiction of the Court, it was necessary to dismiss the proceedings.

V. Extension of Jurisdiction of the Court

As previously pointed out, the Court has compulsory jurisdiction when members accept it in advance by filing declarations under the optional clause (art. 36), and then only in the four types of legal disputes specified therein. The present Court started out with 17 states bound to accept compulsory jurisdiction in such disputes by

[16] A number of issues were also raised concerning the extraterritorial rights of the United States based on the 1836 treaty, the Court ruling for the United States in 2 of these, and against it in 2. Additional rulings were made on questions of taxation and customs evaluation (International Court of Justice Yearbook, 1952-53. The Hague, 1953, pp. 69-74).

virtue of declarations made under the optional clause of the statute of its predecessor. Since then 20 more states have filed declarations under the new statute.[17] A majority of member states of the United Nations along with several nonmembers have now accepted the optional clause. Twenty-six members, however, including the Soviet Union, have not.

Even among the states which have made declarations binding themselves to accept the Court's compulsory jurisdiction in the four types of legal disputes, some have attached conditions or reservations of an extensive nature. The United Kingdom's acceptance, for example, provides that the statute shall be applicable: [18]

For all disputes arising after February 5, 1930, with regard to situations or facts subsequent to that date, other than:
> disputes in regard to which the Parties to the dispute have agreed or shall agree to have recourse to some other method of peaceful settlement;
> disputes with the government of any other Member of the League which is a Member of the British Commonwealth of Nations, all of which disputes shall be settled in such manner as the Parties have agreed or shall agree;
> disputes with regard to questions which by international law fall exclusively within the jurisdiction of the United Kingdom;
> disputes arising out of events occurring at a time when His Majesty's Government in the United Kingdom were involved in hostilities.
The right is reserved to suspend judicial proceedings under certain conditions in the case of disputes under consideration by the Council.

The declarations of Australia, Canada, India, New Zealand, and the Union of South Africa contain reservations almost identical with those in the United Kingdom declaration. A considerable number of declarations by other states have a provision similar to the first one quoted above.

The United States filed a declaration of acceptance of the Court's compulsory jurisdiction in 1946, on a reciprocity basis and subject to termination after 5 years, on 6 months' notice. The United States declaration further stipulates:

That the declaration does not apply to:
> (a) disputes the solution of which the Parties shall entrust to other tribunals by virtue of agreements already in existence or which may be concluded in the future; or
> (b) disputes with regard to matters which are essentially within the domestic jurisdiction of the United States of America as determined by the United States of America; or
> (c) disputes arising under a multilateral treaty, unless (1) all Parties to the treaty affected by the decision are also Parties to the case before the Court, or (2) the United States of America specially agrees to jurisdiction.

Reservations similar to those in the United States declaration have been made by Pakistan and, with respect to the matter of domestic jurisdiction, by France, Liberia, and Mexico as well.

The legality of the reservation stipulating that the state itself is to determine whether a dispute concerns matters essentially within its domestic jurisdiction has been questioned. It is contended that this reservation may be irreconcilable with the provision of the Court's statute which specifies that in the event of a dispute over jurisdiction, the Court itself shall decide the matter.[19]

In addition to voluntary acceptance of the optional clause, the Court's compulsory jurisdiction has been extended by approximately

---

[17] One of these, Iran, withdrew its declaration in 1951. Four declarations had expired by July 15, 1954.
[18] All declarations made under art. 36 of the statute can be found in the International Court of Justice Yearbooks.
[19] See Lawson, the Problems of the Compulsory Jurisdiction of the World Court, op. cit., p. 238. Views on each side are cited in footnote 85 (same page).

100 treaties and conventions made since 1945, which provide for reference of disputes growing out of the treaties to the Court.[20]   In the view of some advocates of the Court, such provisions, coupled with the acceptance of the optional clause by a majority of the members of the United Nations, represent a—

start * * * in the right direction although * * * further progress must of necessity be slow.[21]

It has been contended by others, however, that the compulsory jurisdiction of the Court in legal disputes is not extensive enough. Disappointment has been expressed because so many states have not filed declarations under the optional clause (art. 36).   Even the acceptances of compulsory jurisdiction which have been forthcoming have been questioned on the grounds that their value has been "diminished in many cases by crippling reservations." [22]

Some of those who share this view seek an extension of the Court's compulsory jurisdiction in legal disputes to a greater number of states.   Such an extension, of course, could be achieved at any time by additional voluntary acceptances of the optional clause as provided for in the present statute.   As pointed out earlier, this course was advocated by the General Assembly in 1947.   At that time, the Assembly urged that more states adopt the optional clause, with as few reservations as possible, that states include in treaties provision for submission to the Court of disputes concerning the treaty, and that as a general rule states submit their legal disputes to the Court.

It is difficult to determine what further might be done to encourage acceptance of the optional clause by some states which have so far not done so, notably the Soviet Union.   For some time that country has taken the position that it will not allow itself to be bound by decisions which cannot be vetoed as long as a majority of states, or a majority of judges in the case of a court, represent a different political philosophy.[23]

It has also been suggested that to help strengthen the Court, states which have attached extensive reservations to their acceptance of the optional clause should abandon them.   In 1950, a resolution referred to the Senate Foreign Relations Committee for consideration included the proposition that the United States cooperate with other governments by—

* * * elimination of the reservations made by the United States to its acceptance of the optional clause of the Statute of the International Court of Justice; and acceptance by all states of the optional clause without reservations, so as to give the Court compulsory jurisdiction in legal disputes as defined in article 36 of the statute; * * * [24]

Another proposal to broaden the Court's jurisdiction in legal matters which would not require charter revision calls for the General Assembly and Security Council to refuse to consider legal disputes and instead refer them to the Court.[25]   While states would not have to accept the jurisdiction of the Court, the recommendation of the Council or Assembly that they do so might carry enough prestige in

[20] International Court of Justice Yearbooks.
[21] Lissitzyn, op. cit., p. 101.
[22] Louis B. Sohn.   The Development of International Law: The Jurisdiction of the International Court of Justice, 35 American Bar Association Journal 924, November 1949.
[23] Lissitzyn, op. cit., p. 63–64.
[24] S. Con. Res. 72, 81st Cong., 2d sess.   Collection of Documents, p. 872.
[25] Clyde Eagleton.   Proposals for Strengthening the United Nations.   Foreign Policy Reports, September 15, 1949, p. 110.

some cases to influence them to have recourse to the Court. Such a procedure would serve to emphasize that under the United Nations system, the Court is the proper place for consideration of international legal disputes, and hence the prestige of the Court might be enhanced.

To expand the jurisdiction of the Court in legal disputes, except by encouraging acceptance of compulsory jurisdiction and greater recourse to the Court, would probably require revision of the charter or the Court's statute. At the San Francisco Conference a majority of states sought to have the compulsory jurisdiction of the Court in the four categories of legal disputes previously referred to, written into the statute, without option. At that time it was largely the opposition of the United States and the Soviet Union which prevented this course from being followed. Since the consent of all permanent members of the Security Council would be required, an amendment to this effect would certainly be difficult to obtain. In the case of the Soviet Union, as pointed out earlier, it has not even accepted the optional clause, while France, the United Kingdom, and the United States have attached extensive reservations to their acceptances.[26]

The Clark-Sohn proposals for charter revision [27] would make the Court's jurisdiction compulsory in legal disputes between states if the General Assembly or Executive [Security] Council so directed, thus leaving it up to the two principal organs of the United Nations to set the Court's jurisdiction. This would abrogate the principle of national consent of individual states on which the Court's jurisdiction is now based.

Suggestions for broadening the Court's jurisdiction along a different line concentrate on its potentialities in political, as distinguished from legal, disputes. It has been proposed, for example, that an International Equity Tribunal be established, to which would be referred all disputes coming before the Security Council or General Assembly which other methods of peaceful settlement had failed to resolve. The decisions of this Tribunal would be binding on the parties.[28] A similar proposal calls for the establishment of a World Equity Tribunal which would be a section of the International Court. In this proposal, the Tribunal would have jurisdiction to hear and report on all non-legal disputes, but the decisions would only be advisory unless states consented in advance to being bound.[29]

The assumption underlying proposals which would take political disputes to the International Court is that any conflict can be settled in a way more conducive to an orderly international society if only they are handled by an impartial body according to standards of justice, rather than by a political group acting primarily from political motives.

One international lawyer, for instance, has written:

A positive legal order can always be applied to any conflict whatever. * * * Political as well as legal conflicts are justiciable in the true sense of the term * * *.[30]

---

[26] Actually, because of the amending process of the charter, any amendment along these lines would signify voluntary acceptance of the Court's jurisdiction by two-thirds of the members of the United Nations, including the five powers with the right of veto in the Security Council. Only the dissenters would, in effect, be bound involuntarily.

[27] Grenville Clark and Louis B. Sohn. Peace Through Disarmament and Charter Revision. Detailed proposals for revision of the United Nations Charter. July 1953, p. 147.

[28] An Equity Tribunal in the Context of Present Policy. The New Commonwealth for Justice and Security, vol. 9, September 1949, p. 213.

[29] Report of the Third World Parliamentary Conference on World Government, Copenhagen, 1953. World Association of Parliamentarians for World Government, 1954, p. 131.

[30] Hans Kelsen, quoted in F. B. Schick, Toward a Living Constitution of the United Nations. International Law Quarterly, spring 1948 (reprint, p. 11). See also J. L. Brierly, loc. cit.

On the other hand, some feel that it would be disastrous for the Court to accept jurisdiction in disputes which are primarily political. Edwin Borchard, for example, in discussing the suggestion that the determination of an aggressor be left to the International Court, wrote:

> It is blandly assumed that the Court would assume jurisdiction of such a case. Acceptance of such jurisdiction would be likely to terminate the Court's existence, since the Court depends for its existence upon the cooperation of the constituent members. * * * [31]

Moreover, a judicial determination of a dispute composed primarily of political facets may not contribute to a solution of the underlying problem.   This leads to the contention that it is much more realistic to allow political considerations full sway.

Even if the Court should attain broader jurisdiction, unless the enforcement procedures of the United Nations were simultaneously widened and strengthened, the question of making its decisions effective would remain.   In present circumstances, increasing the number of cases coming to the Court without the consent of the parties concerned also would increase the likelihood that a greater number of its decisions would not be observed, and that its prestige would fall rather than rise as a result.

To provide additional enforcement power for the Court's decisions would involve changes in the United Nations which concern more directly parts of the charter other than those dealing with the Court. Under article 94 of the charter each member already undertakes to comply with the Court's decisions in cases to which it is a party.   In the event a party fails to comply, the other party is authorized to have recourse to the Security Council—

> * * * which may, if it deems necessary, make recommendations or decide upon measures to be taken to give effect to the judgment.

This provision appears to provide ample authority to the Security Council to see that the Court's decisions are carried out.   In practice, however, the Security Council's ability to take action of this kind has been undermined by the dissension in that body and the differences among the great powers.

A proposal to break this deadlock is suggested in the Clark-Sohn proposals which call for recourse to the General Assembly in the event a decision of the Court is ignored.   Further, these proposals would make it mandatory rather than discretionary that the Assembly take steps to see that the judgment is carried out.[32]   This suggestion is made in the context of a much more powerful United Nations than exists at present.   All proposals of this type, moreover, as well as those which would confer jurisdiction on the Court without the con-sent of the parties concerned, imply a willingness of states to abandon significant traditional concepts of national sovereignty which, hereto-fore, for the most part, they have been unwilling to do.

VI. The Court and Interpretation of the Charter

Another direction in which suggestions have been made which would increase the authority of the International Court involves making the International Court the official organ for interpretation

---

[31] Edwin Borchard. The Impracticability of "Enforcing" Peace. Yale Law Journal, (New Haven) vol. 55, August 1946, pp, 969–970.
[32] Clark-Sohn, op. cit., pp. 123. 124.

of the United Nations Charter. At the present time the charter contains no specific provisions for its interpretation, and some consider this a serious defect. In the words of one commentator:

> The charter's glaring deficiency in neglecting to provide for a single authoritative organ of interpretation has made each United Nations organ almost a law unto itself, with no obligation to submit to an external body, questions concerning its own competence or procedure. This structural deficiency is matched by an equally serious substantive limitation. The charter specifies no criteria to be followed by the United Nations organs in determining questions of legality.[33]

Member states often make the point in debates in the United Nations that some suggested course of action is contrary to the charter, or that the United Nations lacks competence to act, usually on the grounds that the matter lies within a member's domestic jurisdiction. Frequently such a point is made merely as part of the general oratory or to delay an action. Often, however, serious questions of interpretation of the charter are raised.

Sometimes the majority passes the challenged resolution over the objection of the minority; sometimes a compromise resolution is effected; and sometimes the minority objections prevent the adoption of the resolution. On occasion, the majority has offered to take the matter to the Court for an advisory opinion, and the minority has objected. On the other hand, the majority has also at times exhibited a reluctance to bring the Court into the decision. The members as a whole have preferred to make the decision concerning competence within the organ involved, while ignoring charges of lack of competence. A special committee of the American Society of International Law, which reported on this matter in 1950, stated:

> * * * one may be surprised at the general tendency to brush aside all challenges to the competence of the United Nations * * * due in large measure to the multitude of such challenges and to the desultory manner in which they are raised * * *.[34]

A Belgian proposal at the San Francisco Conference in 1945 would have given the Court the power of judicial review over actions of the Security Council. This proposal was rejected, with the understanding that each organ could itself interpret those portions of the charter applicable to itself, although it might ask the Court for an advisory opinion, or the states concerned could submit their dispute over interpretation to the Court for a decision.

One authority has pointed out that the present freedom of each organ to interpret the charter for itself could lead to the abuse of rights of individual members or the minority, or a distortion of the purposes of the United Nations:

> At present, the weakness of the organization largely protects its members from abuse of power. If the organization is to gain strength, the authority to give binding interpretations of the charter, at least in matters directly affecting the rights and duties of states, must be lodged somewhere, preferably in a judicial organ. The long-range purposes and policies laid down in the charter must be given some protection against the possible short-range aberrations of the political organs.[35]

Only the General Assembly has referred questions involving interpretation of the charter to the Court for an advisory opinion. In its

[33] Philip E. Jacob. The Legality of United Nations Action, University of Pittsburgh Law Review, vol. 9, fall 1951, p. 38.
[34] Report of special committee on reference to the International Court of Justice of questions of United Nations competence. Proceedings of the American Society of International Law at its 44th annual meeting held at Washington, D. C., April 27–29, 1950. Washington, 1950, p. 258.
[35] Lissitzyn, op. cit., p. 96, 97.

first advisory opinion concerning membership, the Court held that it was within the jurisdiction of the Court to determine the meaning of treaty provisions when so requested.

Several suggestions have been made that the Court, without formal charter amendments, could increasingly be used as the official organ for interpreting the charter. More questions could be referred to it, and the organs or states could agree to consider as binding the Court's advisory opinion on matters of charter interpretation.

It has also been suggested that individual states as well as United Nations organs be permitted to seek advisory opinions of the Court. A change of this kind would appear to require charter revision since article 96 explicitly limits the right to request advisory opinions to the General Assembly, the Security Council, and other organs of the United Nations or specialized agencies authorized by the Assembly.

If adopted, it would give a state an opportunity to secure a judicial opinion if it thought its rights were being abused by a United Nations organ. At the present time it does not have this recourse unless another state is involved in such a way that the matter can be submitted as a legal dispute or unless one of the authorized bodies of the United Nations agrees to take the question to the Court for an advisory opinion. In the past there has been an obvious reluctance on their part to do so.

The disadvantages in this change have been concisely summarized as follows:

It might make the states less willing to accept the jurisdiction of the Court with binding effect. Should advisory opinions be given at the request of states and disregarded by them, the Court's authority would be impaired. Should the states agree in advance or develop a uniform policy to give effect to the opinions, they would amount to judgments in a different form. The advisory opinions of the Court are often useful in the work of international organs, but there is danger of diluting the tribunal's authority by an undue extension of its advisory functions.[36]

The special committee of the American Society of International Law recommended that organs of the United Nations make a practice of referring to the Court matters involving interpretation of the charter where the competence of the organ was questioned, and where a legal decision would contribute to the solution of the problem. Moreover, in such cases, the committee suggested that the organ might make the referral to the Court conditional on the advance agreement of the state or states contesting the competence to abide by the Court's opinion.[37]

Several general charter revision plans call for states and United Nations organs to be allowed to refer to the Court for decision (not advisory opinion) any question relating to interpretation of the charter. The Clark-Sohn proposals, for example, would include in article 96 of the charter an additional paragraph stating:

Any question or dispute relating to the interpretation or application of this charter including its annexes, or the constitutionality, interpretation or application of any law enacted thereunder, may be submitted for decision to the International Court of Justice by any member nation, either on its own behalf or on behalf of any of its citizens.[38]

---

[36] Lissitzyn, op. cit., p. 96. Such a proposal was rejected at the San Francisco Conference.
[37] Report of special committee on reference to the International Court of Justice of questions of United Nations competence, op. cit., p. 268.
[38] Peace Through Disarmament and Charter Revision, by Grenville Clark and Louis B. Sohn, p. 125.

The World Federal Government Conference held in Copenhagen in 1953 called for a provision—

to entrust the interpretation of the charter to (the World Court) and to provide that any member * * * may refer for the decision of the Court any provision of the charter the meaning of which is disputed or doubtful.[39]

The far-reaching implications of this proposal are suggested in its description as one of a series of proposed charter amendments which would be—

possible first steps to secure the strengthening of the present United Nations Charter in the direction of world federal government.

Acceptance of the Court's role as official interpreter of the meaning and obligations of the charter would signify a readiness to accept judicial, as against political, determinations of many questions which might be as important to sovereign states as whether a given matter lies within its domestic jurisdiction.

The Soviet Union has denied that the Court has competence to interpret the charter, even when the Court was being asked for an opinion that was advisory rather than binding. Existing evidence indicates that many other states are also generally unwilling to have such questions referred to the Court. Adoption of proposals which would go even further and give the Court the power to interpret the charter with binding effect would involve greater inroads on the prerogatives of member states. It might offer states a judicial method for protecting their rights against abuse by organs of the United Nations but it would also constitute recognition that they could be bound by decisions of these organs in the first place. Except in the actions by a seven-vote majority of the Security Council which is not vetoed by any of the permanent members that is not now the case.

VII. EXTENSION OF THE COURT'S JURISDICTION TO INDIVIDUALS

Under the present charter and statute, individuals are excluded from access to the Court. Proposals have been advanced which would alter this arrangement. They are generally based on the theory that individuals have rights and duties under international law and therefore should also have the capacity to take legal action under it. The doctrine that only states are subjects of international law, it is held, is out of date.

At the present time the only way the complaint of an individual can be brought before the International Court is for his state to espouse his cause. That this course of action be employed more often has been suggested as one way of increasing the accessibility of the Court to individuals without the necessity of charter revision. However, if a person were stateless, or if his state did not wish to take up his cause, for political or other reasons, an individual would still be without recourse to the international tribunal.

One proposal which would allow individuals to appear before the Court calls for the Court's jurisdiction to be extended to disputes between states and private and public bodies or private individuals in cases in which states agree and arrange in advance to appear as defendants before the Court.[40]

[39] World Frontiers (Northfield, Minn.), summer 1954, p. 19.
[40] H. Lauterpacht. The Subjects of the Law of Nations. The Law Quarterly Review. vol. 63, October 1947, pp. 458–459.

By maintaining the right of the state involved to refuse to accept the Court's jurisdiction in a particular case, it is felt, this proposal would not introduce a principle of obligatory judicial settlement. Nevertheless, it would allow an individual some recourse if he had a claim against a foreign state and his own state refused to espouse it.

Suggestions which would bring the individual into international judicial jurisdiction, although not necessarily that of the International Court itself, call for the establishment of various types of subsidiary, associate, or other international courts. For instance, it has been proposed that there be subsidiary courts to deal with disputes of individuals of different nationality, an International Criminal Court, and an International Court of Human Rights.

While it is not always clear in such suggestions that these other courts would have a direct connection with the present International Court or the United Nations, the proposals are usually advanced in the context of the United Nations system. One group which has spelled out the relationship of the proposed courts to the International Court has recommended that—

The charter shall provide for the creation of lower courts of the United Nations, empowered to decide on violations by individuals of the charter and laws enacted thereunder. The International Court shall have appellate jurisdiction with respect to judgments of such lower courts.[41]

The proposal that individuals be given access to international courts for disputes against individuals of other nationalities is suggested as an alternative to the present system under which a claimant must rely on the courts of a given nation. The laws, procedures, and enforcement methods of states are so varied, it is held, that the end results are often unsatisfactory.

However, problems inherent in this proposal have been pointed out as follows:

There is * * * much force in the proposal that international judicial authorities or courts should be established and given jurisdiction to deal with disputes between individuals of different nationalities, but there are many difficulties which would face the individual litigants; the expense of such proceedings, and the necessity that sovereign states should agree to enforce the judgments under their own municipal law, being among them.[42]

Moreover, if claims of an individual were not screened by the national's own state, as states presumably now do, the proposed international courts could well be swamped with claims not having sufficient merit for their attention.

Among the proposals which would bring individuals under the jurisdiction of an international court are those which call for the establishment of an international criminal court. Heretofore, violations of international law by individuals, such as piracy, have been handled in national courts. However, the international tribunals established to try war criminals at Nuremberg and Tokyo are instances in which individuals were tried and held responsible before the international community. The willingness of the victorious powers to try nationals of a defeated state as war criminals in an international tribunal, however, should not be taken as evidence of a similar willingness to allow their own nationals, or criminals who have committed felonies within their jurisdiction, to be so tried in normal times.

41 Report of the Third World Parliamentary Conference on World Government, Copenhagen, 1953, World Association of Parliamentarians for World Government, 1954, p. 130.
42 E. A. S. Brooks. Subsidiary Judicial Authorities of the United Nations To Hear and Decide Claims by Individuals and Corporations Against States. The International Law Quarterly, vol. 3, October 1950, pp. 525–526.

The Committee on International Criminal Jurisdiction, created by a General Assembly resolution in December 1952, which studied the implications of and methods for establishing an international criminal court, concluded that—

* * * there was no evidence that states wished to establish a court, or that, even if it were established, states would be willing to give it the measure of consent and cooperation which was vital to its functioning.[43]

Moreover, there was considerable feeling that the substance of the law which could be applied by such a court was not sufficiently developed.

Other proposals involving extending international jurisdiction to individuals revolve around the concept of protecting human rights. It has been suggested that an International Court of Human Rights be established to protect individuals from infringement of their rights. It is held that if human rights are to be guaranteed in any way by the United Nations, there must be some sort of tribunal to protect such rights. One proposal would give a human rights court the authority to issue an equivalent of the writ of habeas corpus.[44]

This suggestion makes most apparent that all proposals tending to subject the individual directly to international law have profound implications on the present relationship of an individual and the state of which he is a national, and on the rights of a sovereign state. It would offer an individual a clear-cut right of appeal to an authority outside his state if his intrinsic human rights as set down in an international bill of rights, were violated by his state. In so doing, it would extend the international judicial system into a field which until now has been a most jealously guarded area of the domestic jurisdiction of states. It would suggest, in short, the existence of an organization with some limited attributes of supranational government.

If the international court were to have a well-developed law to apply and adequate means to enforce its decisions concerning individuals, changes in the present organization of the international community beyond those affecting the judicial system would be involved. These changes would involve establishment of supranational bodies in the field of legislation and enforcement as well as the judiciary.

Without this far-reaching change the Court would have to depend for enforcement on the voluntary cooperation of the states themselves, which cannot always be considered reliable, especially if an individual were appealing to the international body precisely because he had not been able to receive satisfactory relief in his own state. The prestige of an international court's decision might influence a state to enforce the decision. On the other hand, if many decisions were not heeded, the Court's authority and prestige would rapidly decline.

Like proposals which would extend compulsory jurisdiction of the Court beyond its present limits, proposals which would bring individuals within the jurisdiction of the Court have far-reaching implications for the sovereign state system.

VIII. The Future of the Court

A comparison of the Covenant of the League of Nations with the Charter of the United Nations reveals many substantial differences

---

[43] Report of the 1953 Committee on International Criminal Jurisdiction, August 24, 1953, U. N. Document A/AC.65/L.13, p. 61.
[44] Luis Kutner. A Proposal for a United Nations Writ of Habeas Corpus and An International Court of Human Rights, vol. 28, Tulane Law Review, June 1954, pp. 417-441.

between the United Nations and the League. That is not true with respect to the statutes of the old Permanent Court and the postwar International Court of Justice. As noted, the Committee of Jurists which prepared the draft statute for consideration at San Francisco proposed only minor changes in the statute of the old Court.

The fact that the statute of the Permanent Court of International Justice drafted in 1919 was accepted with only minor changes as the basis of the statute of the International Court in 1945 indicates that the status of the Court in the international system of the 20th century has become reasonably well fixed.[45]

Despite the fact that the statutes of the two Courts have stood virtually unchanged for 35 years, there have been several important criticisms relating to the jurisdiction and operation of the International Court since World War I—criticisms which do not run to the Court itself, its conduct, or the conduct of the judges, but, rather, criticisms which arise from the general attitudes of states toward the Court, attitudes which in turn are traceable in part to the East-West tensions in the postwar world.

The General Assembly has expressed its concern that not enough use is being made of the Court. It emphasized the importance of utilizing the Court "to the greatest practicable extent." Literature on the work of the International Court contains many comments on the frustration of the Court's potentialities.[46]

There has also been extensive criticism of the tendency of organs of the United Nations to interpret for themselves charter provisions relative to their jurisdiction, rather than ask the Court for advisory opinions as to the scope of the charter authority under which they operate. This criticism has focused attention on the fact that there is no agency, other than the organs themselves, that has authority to interpret charter provisions, thus defining their metes and bounds.

A third criticism which has been made of the place of the Court in the international structure is that though the majority of the United Nations have made declarations accepting the compulsory jurisdiction of the Court, the acceptance of this jurisdiction has been limited by extensive reservations. It is recognized, of course, that many treaties provide for compulsory jurisdiction, but the fact remains that a number of people who had hoped for widespread acceptance of compulsory jurisdiction have been disappointed to find acceptance of this provision limited by reservations. The significance of these reservations cannot be estimated in the absence of a substantial body of applicable precedents—which are not being rapidly accumulated if the current Court docket is any indication.

These three—(1) the lack of business, (2) the inability of the Court to interpret the charter, and (3) reservations to compulsory jurisdiction—are the main criticisms that have been leveled at the judicial system of the United Nations. There have been numerous proposals

[45] See Brierly, J. L., International Law: Some Conditions of Its Progress, International Affairs, vol. 22, No. 3, 1946, July, pp. 353 ff., in which he notes that there is little difference, except in name, between the Permanent Court and the new International Court. He suggests: "We do not urgently need either more or better international courts, or more or better rules of law. But we do need a comprehensive organization in which law will cease to be a detached limb and become an integrated member of an international body politic" (p. 360).

[46] See, for example, Wehle, Louis B., The United Nations Bypasses the International Court as the Council's Adviser. A Study in Contrived Frustration, 98 University of Pennsylvania Law Review, February, 1950, pp. 285–319

to expand the scope of the Court's jurisdiction. They have ranged in magnitude from those proposing an enforceable world law (which may imply some elements of a world legislature, a world citizenship, and a world police force to enforce court judgments) to more limited types of proposals that would authorize individuals to become complainants before the Court in certain types of claims cases.

The late Senator Robert A. Taft wrote in 1951 that the fundamental difficulty with the United Nations Charter "is that it is not based primarily upon an underlying law and an administration of justice under that law." He then observed that the veto power in the charter "completely dispels the idea that any system of universal law is being established * * *." There was "an opportunity * * * in the case of the Atlantic Pact," he noted, for those nations to agree "to a new form of international organization based on law and justice without veto." Such an organization could "operate between themselves and settle all disputes among them." [47]

These comments touch on the underlying problem. Law cannot exist outside of the society of which it is a part. To the extent that there exists a world community that in general accepts the same basic premises of right and wrong, of freedom and slavery, there may be a possibility of formulating an international law in some respects like that which exists in the domestic sphere. But even granted the possibility that a body of law might receive general acceptance in a cohesive international community (which does not exist today), there still remains the job of interpreting such law (a job primarily for the courts) and the job of enforcing the interpretation of the law—a matter which under some circumstances might involve the creation of an international police force.

In effect, therefore, any proposal to bring about substantial changes in the realm of international law and its enforcement quickly raises questions going to the fundamental nature of the United Nations.

Changes which would permit individuals to appear before the Court would tend to derogate from the proposition that the United Nations is an organization of "states." Such changes would tend to encourage development of the concept that individuals have a "United Nations citizenship," with legal rights and duties deriving from some source other than the national state. A state's treatment of its citizens which might be construed as a violation of fundamental human rights, for example, might no longer be viewed as a matter of domestic jurisdiction.

Similarly, it can be argued that changes that would give the Court authority to render binding judgments without the consent of the states parties to a dispute would tend to negate the concept that the United Nations is an organization "based on the principle of the sovereign equality of all its Members." In short, substantial changes in the statute of the International Court of Justice cannot take place outside the political realities of the day. This means that the future of the Court is closely linked not only to the United Nations, with its strengths and its weaknesses, but also to international developments generally.

<hr>

[47] Taft, Robert A., A Foreign Policy for Americans, pp. 37–46.

APPENDIX

TABLE I—ADVISORY OPINIONS

1. CONDITIONS OF ADMISSION OF A STATE TO MEMBERSHIP IN THE UNITED NATIONS

Requested by the General Assembly on November 17, 1947. The request arose out of the failure of the Security Council to recommend certain states applying for admission.

Question

Is a Member of the United Nations which is called upon, in virtue of Article 4 of this Charter, to pronounce itself by its vote, either in the Security Council or in the General Assembly, on the admission of a State to membership in the United Nations, juridically entitled to make its consent to the admission dependent on conditions not expressly provided by paragraph 1 of the said Article?

In particular, can such a Member while it recognizes the conditions set forth in that provision to be fulfilled by the State concerned, subject its affirmative vote to the additional condition that other States be admitted to membership in the United Nations together with that State?

Opinion

Noting that the question related not to the vote itself, but to "the statements made by a Member concerning the vote it proposes to give," the Court answered both questions in the negative, by a vote of 9 to 6. The Court said that the conditions established by article 4 of the charter "are not merely necessary, they suffice," and that "considerations other than those prescribed by the terms and spirit of article 4 could not prevent the admission of an applicant."

2. REPARATION FOR INJURIES SUFFERED IN THE SERVICE OF THE UNITED NATIONS

Requested by the General Assembly on December 3, 1948. The request resulted from the assassination in September 1948 of Count Folke Bernadotte, United Nations Mediator on Palestine and member of the observing staff, and from injuries to other United Nations employees.

Question

I. In the event of an agent of the United Nations in the performance of his duties suffering injury in circumstances involving the responsibility of a State, has the United Nations, as an Organization, the capacity to bring an international claim against the responsible de jure or de facto Government with a view to obtaining reparation due in respect of the damage caused (a) to the United Nations, (b) to the victim or to persons entitled through him?

II. In the event of an affirmative reply on point I (b), how is action by the United Nations to be reconciled with such rights as may be possessed by the State of which the victim is a national?

Opinion

The Court gave affirmative answers to questions I (a) and I (b), in the former case by a unanimous decision, in the latter by an 11 to 4 vote. The opinion with regard to question II, on a 10 to 5 vote, was as follows:

When the United Nations as an Organization is bringing a claim for reparation of damage caused to its agent, it can only do so by basing its claim upon a breach of obligations due to itself; respect for this rule will usually prevent a conflict between the action of the United Nations and such rights as the agent's national State may possess, and thus bring about a reconciliation between their claims; moreover, this reconciliation must depend upon considerations applicable to each particular case, and upon agreements to be made between the Organizations and individual States, either generally or in each case.

On the basis of this opinion, the General Assembly authorized the Secretary General to seek reparation for damages caused to the United Nations and to the agents involved (or those entitled through them).

3. INTERPRETATION OF THE HUNGARIAN, BULGARIAN, AND RUMANIAN PEACE TREATIES

Requested by the General Assembly on October 22, 1949. The request arose out of accusations that Hungary, Bulgaria, and Rumania had violated provisions in the treaties with respect to human rights and fundamental freedoms.

Question

I. Do the diplomatic exchanges between Bulgaria, Hungary and Rumania, on the one hand, and certain Allied and Associated Powers signatories to the Treaties of Peace on the other, concerning the implementation of Article 2 of the Treaties with Bulgaria and Hungary and Article 3 of the Treaty with Romania, disclose disputes subject to the provisions for the settlement of disputes contained in Article 36 of the Treaty of Peace with Bulgaria, Article 40 of the Treaty of Peace with Hungary, and Article 38 of the Treaty of Peace with Romania?

In the event of an affirmative reply to Question I:

II. Are the Governments of Bulgaria, Hungary and Romania obligated to carry out the provisions of the Articles referred to in Question I, including the provisions for the appointment of their representatives to the Treaty Commissions?

In the event of an affirmative reply to Question II and if within thirty days from the date when the Court delivers its opinion, the Governments concerned have not notified the Secretary-General that they have appointed their representatives to the Treaty Commissions, and the Secretary-General has so advised the International Court of Justice:

III. If one party fails to appoint a representative to a Treaty Commission under the Treaties of Peace with Bulgaria, Hungary and Romania where that party is obligated to appoint a representative to the Treaty Commission, is the Secretary-General of the United Nations authorized to appoint the third member of the Commission upon the request of the other party to a dispute according to the provisions of the respective Treaties?

In the event of an affirmative reply to Question III:

IV. Would a Treaty Commission composed of a representative of one party and a third member appointed by the Secretary-General of the United Nations constitute a Commission, within the meaning of the relevant Treaty articles competent to make a definitive and binding decision in settlement of a dispute?

Opinion

The Court's opinion (11 to 3) was that there did exist disputes subject to the provisions for settlement of disputes in the peace treaties, and that the Governments of Bulgaria, Hungary, and Rumania were obligated to carry out these provisions (First Phase, opinion rendered March 30, 1950). In reply to question III, the

Court gave the opinion that the Secretary General could not proceed to name a third member of the Commission until each party had appointed its representative (Second Phase, opinion rendered July 18, 1950).

4. COMPETENCE OF THE GENERAL ASSEMBLY FOR THE ADMISSION OF A STATE TO THE UNITED NATIONS

Requested by the General Assembly in a resolution of November 22, 1949. The request arose out of the fact that 14 applications for admission were pending from previous years on which the Security Council had made no recommendation. Nine of these had failed to receive a recommendation because of the Soviet Union's veto, and five had not received as many as seven affirmative votes.

Question

Can the admission of a State to membership in the United Nations, pursuant to Article 4, paragraph 2, of the Charter, be effected by a decision of the General Assembly when the Security Council has made no recommendation for admission by reason of the candidate failing to obtain the requisite majority or of the negative vote of a permanent Member upon a resolution so to recommend?

Opinion

The answer, by a vote of 12 to 2, was in the negative. If the General Assembly acted without the recommendation of the Security Council it "would almost nullify the role of the Security Council in the exercise of one of the essential functions of the Organization," and "both these acts are indispensable to form the judgment of the Organization."

5. THE INTERNATIONAL STATUS OF SOUTH-WEST AFRICA

Requested by the General Assembly in a resolution of December 6, 1949. The request resulted from the refusal of the Union of South Africa, which by the Covenant of the League of Nations was entrusted with the mandate over the former German South-West Africa, to consent in 1946 to transform the mandated territory into a trust territory under the Charter of the United Nations.

Question

What is the international status of the Territory of South-West Africa and what are the international obligations of the Union of South Africa arising therefrom, in particular:

(a) Does the Union of South Africa continue to have international obligations under the Mandate for South-West Africa and, if so what are these obligations?

(b) Are the provisions of Chapter XII of the Charter applicable and, if so, in what manner, to the Territory of South-West Africa?

(c) Has the Union of South Africa the competence to modify the international status of the Territory of South-West Africa, or, in the event of a negative reply, where does competence rest to determine and modify the international status of the Territory?

Opinion

The Court rendered the opinion that "the Union of South Africa continues to have the international obligations stated" in the covenant and the mandate agreement, "the supervisory functions to be exercised by the United Nations, to which the annual reports and the petitions are to be submitted   *   *   *" (by a vote of 12 to 2); that the U. N. Charter provisions are applicable to the Territory "in the sense that they provide a means by which the Territory may be brought under the Trusteeship System" (unanimously); but that they "do not impose on the Union of South Africa a legal obligation to place the Territory under the Trusteeship System" (by a vote of 8 to 6); and (unanimously)—

that the Union of South Africa acting alone has not the competence to modify the international status of the Territory of South-West Africa, and that the competence to determine and modify the international status of the Territory rests with the Union of South Africa acting with the consent of the United Nations.

6. RESERVATIONS TO THE CONVENTION OF THE PREVENTION AND PUNISHMENT OF THE CRIME OF GENOCIDE

Requested by the General Assembly in a resolution of November 16, 1950.

Question

I. Can the reserving State be regarded as being a party to the Convention while still maintaining its reservation if the reservation is objected to by one or more of the parties to the Convention but not by the others?

II. If the answer to Question I is in the affirmative what is the effect of the reservation as between the reserving State and:

(a) the Parties which object to the reservation?

(b) those which accept it?

III. What would be the legal effect as regards the answer to Question I if an objection to a reservation is made:

(a) by a signatory which has not yet ratified?

(b) by a State entitled to sign or accede but which has not yet done so?

Opinion (by a 7 to 5 vote)

On question I:

A state which has made and maintained a reservation which has been objected to by one or more of the parties to the Convention but not by the others, can be regarded as being a party to the Convention if the reservation is compatible with object and purpose of the Convention; otherwise, that state cannot be regarded as being a party to the Convention.

On question II:

(a) If a party to the Convention objects to a reservation which it considers to be incompatible with the object and purpose of the Convention, it can in fact consider that the reserving state is not a party to the Convention;

(b) If, on the other hand, a party accepts the reservation as being compatible with the object and purpose of the Convention, it can in fact consider that the reserving state is a party to the Convention.

On question III:

(a) An objection to a reservation made by a signatory state which has not yet ratified the Convention can have the legal effect indicated in the reply to question I only upon ratification. Until that moment it merely serves as a notice to the other State of the eventual attitude of the signatory state;

(b) An objection to a reservation made by a state which is entitled to sign or accede but which has not yet done so, is without legal effect.

7. EFFECT OF AWARDS OF COMPENSATION MADE BY THE UNITED NATIONS ADMINISTRATIVE TRIBUNAL

Question:

Following an inconclusive debate in the fall of 1953 the General Assembly adopted a resolution, 785A (VIII) of December 9, in which it asked for an advisory opinion from the International Court of Justice in answer to the following two questions:

(1) Having regard to the Statute of the United Nations Administrative Tribunal and to any other relevant instruments and to the relevant records, has the General Assembly the right on any grounds to refuse to give effect to an award of compensation made by that Tribunal in favour of a staff member of the United Nations whose contract of service has been terminated without his assent?

(2) If the answer given by the Court to question (1) is in the affirmative, what are the principal grounds upon which the General Assembly could lawfully exercise such a right?

The questions grow out of awards made by the Administrative Tribunal of the United Nations during 1953 to certain staff members of the United Nations who had been dismissed by the Secretary General after they had refused to answer questions concerning Communist Party membership or activity, and espionage.

Opinion (by a vote of 9 to 3)

On question I:

In answer to the first question the Court replied that "the General Assembly has not the right on any grounds to refuse to give effect to an award of compensation of the Administrative Tribunal of the United Nations in favor of a staff member whose contract of service has been terminated without his assent."

On question II:

Since the answer to the first question was in the negative, it is unnecessary to answer the second question.

TABLE II.—*Contentious cases*

Proceeding	Parties	Method of submission	Dispute	Issue	Judgment	Vote
1. Corfu Channel case	United Kingdom and Albania.	Application by United Kingdom (registered May 22, 1947).	Destruction of 2 British destroyers by a mine explosion in the Corfu Channel, Oct. 22, 1946, and subsequent mine-sweeping operation by the United Kingdom in the Corfu Channel under the protection of a covering force.	(1) Is Albania responsible for the damages and does it have a duty to pay compensation?	Yes [1]	11-5
				(2) Did the United Kingdom's actions violate Albanian sovereignty?	Passage of British warships through channel did not; subsequent mine-sweeping operation did (Apr. 9, 1949).	14-2
Corfu Channel case (preliminary objection).	do	Preliminary objection filed by Albania (Dec. 1, 1947).		Admissibility of United Kingdom's application.	Albania held to have accepted Court's jurisdiction voluntarily (Mar. 25, 1948).	16-0 / 15-1
Corfu Channel case (damages).	do	Court's judgment of Apr. 9, 1949.		Amount of compensation to be paid by Albania.	Amount fixed at £843,957 ($2,363,051) (Dec. 15, 1949).	12-2
2. Fisheries case	United Kingdom and Norway.	Application by United Kingdom under art. 36 (2) of statute (registered Sept. 28, 1949).	Seizure of British fishing boats by Norway.	Legality of Norwegian decree of 1935 delimiting fisheries zone.	Decree found not to be contrary to international law (Dec. 18, 1951).	[2] 10-2
3. Protection of French nationals and protected persons in Egypt.	France and Egypt	Application by France under the Convention of 1937 (Oct. 13, 1949).	Detention of French nationals and seizure of their property, May 1948.	Did action of Egypt violate Convention of May 8, 1937, regarding the abrogation of capitulations in Egypt?	Case withdrawn at the request of France (Mar. 29, 1950).	8-4
4. Asylum case	Colombia and Peru	Application by Colombia on basis of Act of Lima, Aug. 31, 1949. (Oct. 15, 1949).	Peruvian citizen given asylum in Colombian Embassy at Lima, Peru refused to grant safe conduct.	(1) Was Colombia competent to qualify the offense for the purpose of asylum under Habana Convention on Asylum, Feb. 20, 1928?	No	14-1
				(2) Was Peru bound to grant safe conduct?	No	15-1
				(3) Did grant of asylum by Colombia violate the Habana Convention?	In part (Nov. 29, 1950). [3]	10-6
Interpretation of the judgment in the Asylum case.	do	Request by Colombia (Nov. 20, 1950).		Request of interpretation of judgment.	Request declared inadmissible (Nov. 27, 1950).	12-1

[1] The Court further held, by a vote of 10 to 6, that it had jurisdiction to assess the amount of compensation to be paid.

[2] The 10 to 2 vote was on the method employed by the decree for delimiting the zones; the 8 to 4 vote was on the baselines fixed.

[3] The Court held, by 15 votes to 1, that there was no violation of the Convention's provision prohibiting asylum in respect to "common crimes," but that there was a violation of the provisions as to urgency and limit of time.

TABLE II.—*Contentious cases*—Continued

Proceeding	Parties	Method of submission	Dispute	Issue	Judgment	Vote
4. Haya de la Torre case.	Colombia and Peru.	Application by Colombia under treaty of 1934 (Nov. 28, 1950).	Request by Peru for immediate delivery of Haya de la Torre by Colombia.	Did Court's judgment of Nov. 20, 1950, require Colombia to deliver Haya de la Torre to Peru?	Asylum should have terminated; Colombia need not deliver refugee, since delivery not only possible way of terminating asylum (June 13, 1951).	Unanimous 13–1
5. Rights of nationals of the United States in Morocco.	France and the United States.	Application by France (Oct. 28, 1950).	Application to United States nationals of Moroccan decree establishing licensing control for importation of goods into Morocco.	(1) Are treaty rights of the United States violated by the application of the decree to United States nationals? (2) United States consular law jurisdiction.	Yes.	Unanimous
6. Ambatielos case.	Greece and United Kingdom.	Application by Greece (Apr. 9, 1951).	Nondelivery of steamships by British Government to Greek citizen under contract.	Was United Kingdom obligated to submit dispute to arbitration under treaty of 1886?	(4) Yes (May 19, 1953).	10–1
7. Anglo-Iranian Oil case.	United Kingdom and Iran.	Application by United Kingdom under art. 36 (2) of statute, and treaties (May 26, 1951).	Nationalization of Anglo-Iranian Oil Co. alleged by United Kingdom to violate 1933 concession agreement.	(1) Does Court have jurisdiction? (2) Did nationalization violate 1833 agreement?	No (July 22, 1952). do.	9–5
8. Minquiers and Ecrehos case.	United Kingdom and France.	Special agreement (Dec. 6, 1951).	Sovereignty over Minquiers and Ecrehos group of islets.	Does the United Kingdom or France have sovereignty over these islets and rocks?	The United Kingdom (Nov. 17, 1953).	Unanimous.
9. Nottebohm case.	Liechtenstein and Guatemala.	Application by Liechtenstein (Dec. 17, 1951).	Action on person and property of Nottebohm, citizen of Liechtenstein.		Pending.	
10. Case of the monetary gold removed from Rome in 1943.	Italy, France, United States, and United Kingdom.	Application by Italy (May 19, 1953).	Gold removed from Italy by Germany in 1943, property of Albanian National Bank.	Can Albania or Italy legally claim the gold?	Court could not take jurisdiction without consent of Albania (June 15, 1954).	(6)
11. Société Electricité de Beyrouth case.	France and Lebanon.	Application by France (Aug. 15, 1953).	Dispute over certain concessions held in Lebanon by the Société Electricité de Beyrouth, a French limited company.		Removed from list after notice from French Government (July 26, 1954) that it was not continuing proceedings.	

| 12. United States planes in Hungary. | United States and Hungary. | Application by United States (Mar. 3, 1954). | Action by Hungary and U.S.S.R. with respect to 4 United States airmen who landed (Nov. 19, 1951) on Hungarian soil in a United States military aircraft. | | Court could not accept jurisdiction over Hungarian and Soviet objections. |

[4] The Court ruled (Aug. 27, 1952) for the United States position on 2 issues, and against it on 2. The Court also passed on various questions relating to taxation and customs evaluation.

[5] In a judgment on a preliminary objection entered by the United Kingdom, the Court ruled that it had jurisdiction.

[6] Unanimous and 13-1.

THE UNITED NATIONS AND DEPENDENT TERRITORIES

TERRITORIES

STAFF STUDY NO. 9
JUNE 27, 1955

PREFACE

By Walter F. George, *Chairman*

During the first 10 years of the United Nations, great progress has been made in bringing freedom and independence to the colonial peoples of the world. No less than 13 countries with a total population of over half a billion people have won their independence.

The United Nations is not, of course, solely responsible for this development. Some of it, probably a large part of it, might have taken place even if the United Nations had not existed. The fact remains that the work of the United Nations in connection with dependent territories is highly important and deserves our careful study.

It is my belief that too often the policies of the United States in the field covered by this study have seemed to put the United States on the side of colonialism. Our Nation was once a colony. It wrested its freedom from England only some 170 years ago. This fact gives us much in common with peoples seeking national freedom and independence. We must never lose sight of the deep desire, indeed, the right, of people to self-government. This aspiration must be satisfied as soon as peoples are able to protect their own freedom and govern themselves. It is incumbent upon governing powers to make a great and continuous effort to develop these capacities among dependent peoples. Despite the fact that throughout many of the dependent areas of the world there is a tendency to associate the United States with the policies of colonial powers, the action of this Nation in giving independence to the Republic of the Philippines is good evidence of the sincerity of our desire to advance the cause of human freedom everywhere.

I must underline one other factor to keep in mind as people move from a colonial or dependent status to independence. Independence means freedom of choice and international communism seeks constantly to take advantage of the inexperience and weakness of newly independent states to bring them under Communist control. In encouraging the development of self-government we must ever be wary of this danger.

Secretary of State Dulles has voiced the concern of the United States over United Nations actions in the field of dependent overseas territories as well as recognition of the importance of this work in these words:

"The United Nations has helped to transform colonialism into self-government. The role played by the United Nations in this matter has been controversial and it is in some respects subject to legitimate criticism. Undoubtedly, however, it has exerted a useful influence in promoting peaceful rather than violent developments."

Similar concern was expressed by a number of nations at the 1953 General Assembly session during discussions on preparatory measures for a charter review conference. The issue of colonialism, as raised by the chapters of the charter on trusteeship and non-self-governing territories, is likely, therefore, to be a matter of controversy in the event of a charter review conference.

The question, broadly phrased, is "Should the powers of the United Nations over dependent areas be expanded, contracted, or left alone?" Our Nation's direct interest in this issue stems from four factors:

(1) Our possession of dependent Territories—American Samoa, the Virgin Islands, Guam, Alaska, and Hawaii.

(2) Our responsibility for the Trust Territory of the Pacific Islands, formerly under Japanese mandate from the League of Nations.

(3) Our interest in broad problems of equal economic opportunity for and in dependent areas.

(4) Our tradition of sympathetic interest in the aspirations of dependent peoples for self-government and independence.

The conflicts and problems in this area of United Nations activity are the subject of this staff study, The United Nations and Dependent Territories. The study depicts the areas of disagreement between some nations which have important dependent overseas territories and others which do not. The latter in general seek a broad extension of United Nations influence over the administration of these territories in the belief that this will hasten the elimination of the vestiges of colonialism. The administering countries, while recognizing certain international obligations to the dependent people, believe the charter permits them a greater use of their own judgment on such basic questions as these peoples' readiness for self-government or independence. This conflict runs through most aspects of United Nations activities with respect to dependent territories. Efforts to resolve it are complicated by the fact that the issue of trusteeship is interwoven with other international problems, such as those concerning relations among allies and the creation of effective opposition to Communist expansion.

This study was prepared under the direction of the subcommittee staff by Charles R. Gellner of the Legislative Reference Service of the Library of Congress. It is for the background use of the subcommittee and does not necessarily represent the views of any of its members.

June 27, 1955.

CONTENTS

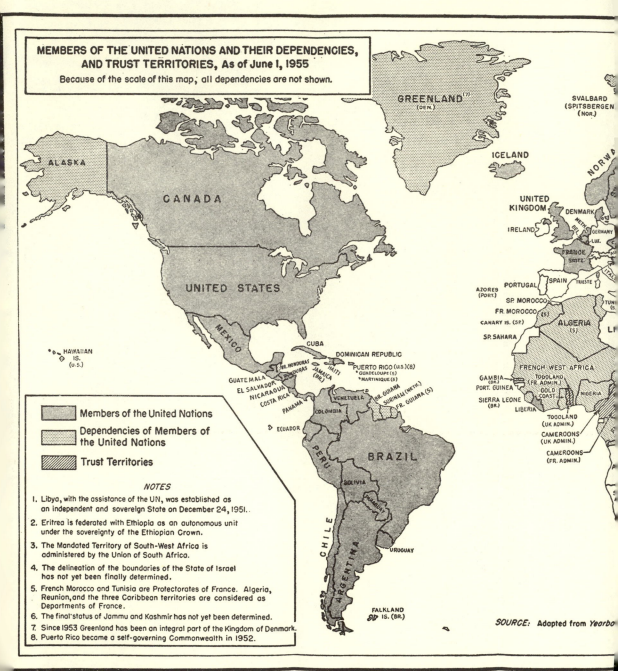

MEMBERS OF THE UNITED NATIONS AND THEIR DEPENDENCIES, AND TRUST TERRITORIES, As of June 1, 1955

Because of the scale of this map, all dependencies are not shown.

GREENLAND (7)
(DEN.)

SVALBARD
(SPITSBERGEN)
(NOR.)

ICELAND

NORWAY

ALASKA

CANADA

UNITED KINGDOM

DENMARK

IRELAND

NETH.
BEL.

GERMANY
LUX.

FRANCE
SWITZ.

ITALY

UNITED STATES

PORTUGAL

SPAIN

TRIESTE

AZORES
(PORT.)

SP. MOROCCO

FR. MOROCCO (5)

TUNISIA
(5.)

MEXICO

CANARY IS. (SP.)

ALGERIA
(5)

LI

SP. SAHARA

HAWAIIAN
IS.
(U.S.)

CUBA

DOMINICAN REPUBLIC

PUERTO RICO (U.S.)(8)

GUADELOUPE (5)

MARTINIQUE (5)

FRENCH WEST AFRICA

GAMBIA
(BR.)

PORT. GUINEA

TOGOLAND
(FR. ADMIN.)

GOLD
COAST

NIGERIA

GUATEMALA

EL SALVADOR

HONDURAS

BR. HONDURAS

JAMAICA
(BR.)

HAITI

SIERRA LEONE
(BR.)

LIBERIA

TOGOLAND
(UK ADMIN.)

NICARAGUA

COSTA RICA

PANAMA

VENEZUELA

BR. GUIANA

SURINAM (NETH.)

FR. GUIANA (5)

CAMEROONS
(UK ADMIN.)

COLOMBIA

ECUADOR

CAMEROONS
(FR. ADMIN.)

PERU

BRAZIL

BOLIVIA

PARAGUAY

CHILE

URUGUAY

ARGENTINA

FALKLAND
IS. (BR.)

SOURCE: Adapted from *Yearbo*

Legend

- Members of the United Nations
- Dependencies of Members of the United Nations
- Trust Territories

NOTES

1. Libya, with the assistance of the UN, was established as an independent and sovereign State on December 24, 1951.

2. Eritrea is federated with Ethiopia as an autonomous unit under the sovereignty of the Ethiopian Crown.

3. The Mandated Territory of South-West Africa is administered by the Union of South Africa.

4. The delineation of the boundaries of the State of Israel has not yet been finally determined.

5. French Morocco and Tunisia are Protectorates of France. Algeria, Reunion, and the three Caribbean territories are considered as Departments of France.

6. The final status of Jammu and Kashmir has not yet been determined.

7. Since 1953 Greenland has been an integral part of the Kingdom of Denmark.

8. Puerto Rico became a self-governing Commonwealth in 1952.

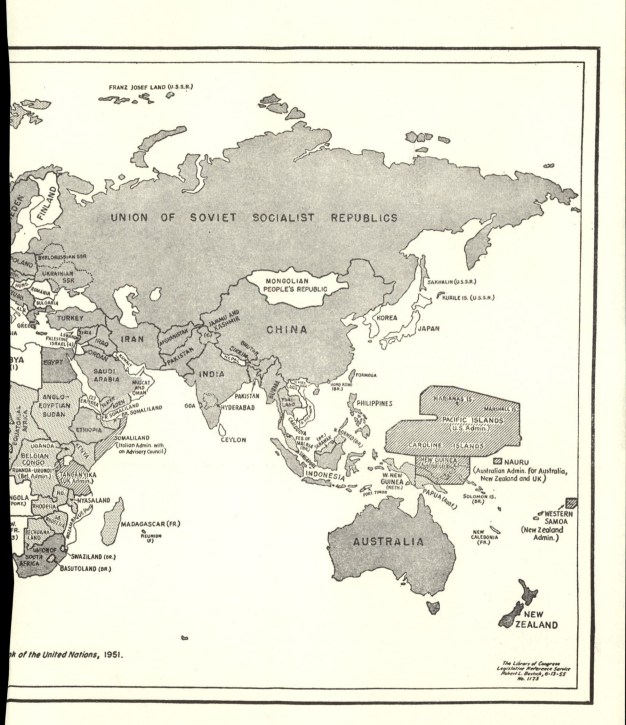

FRANZ JOSEF LAND (U.S.S.R.)

UNION OF SOVIET SOCIALIST REPUBLICS

FINLAND

SWEDEN

BYELORUSSIAN SSR

UKRAINIAN SSR

POLAND

CZECH.

HUNG.

YUGO.

ROMANIA

ALB.

BULGARIA

GREECE

TURKEY

SYRIA

LEBANON

PALESTINE
ISRAEL (4)

IRAQ

JORDAN

IRAN

KUWAIT

SAUDI
ARABIA

MUSCAT
AND
OMAN

AFGHANISTAN

PAKISTAN

JAMMU AND
KASHMIR

(6)

SIKKIM

BHUTAN

NEPAL

MONGOLIAN
PEOPLE'S REPUBLIC

SAKHALIN (U.S.S.R.)

KURILE IS. (U.S.S.R.)

KOREA

JAPAN

CHINA

INDIA

PAKISTAN

HYDERABAD

GOA

CEYLON

BURMA

THAI-
LAND

LAOS

N. VIET
NAM

S. VIET
NAM

CAMBODIA

FORMOSA

HONG KONG
(BR.)

PHILIPPINES

FED. OF
MALAYA
(BR.)

SARAWAK
(BR.)

N. BORNEO (BR.)

SINGAPORE

INDONESIA

MARIANAS IS.

MARSHALL IS.

PACIFIC ISLANDS
(U.S. Admin.)

CAROLINE ISLANDS

NEW GUINEA
(Australian Admin.)

NAURU
(Australian Admin. for Australia,
New Zealand and UK)

W. NEW
GUINEA
(NETH.)

PORT. TIMOR

PAPUA (Aust.)

SOLOMON IS.
(BR.)

WESTERN
SAMOA
(New Zealand
Admin.)

NEW
CALEDONIA
(FR.)

LYBA
(1)

EGYPT

ANGLO-
EGYPTIAN
SUDAN

FR.
EQUATORIAL
AFRICA

ERITREA

FR. SOM.

ADEN

(2)

BR. SOMALILAND

ETHIOPIA

SOMALILAND
(Italian Admin. with
an Advisory Council)

UGANDA

KENYA

BELGIAN
CONGO

RUANDA-URUNDI
(Bel. Admin.)

TANGANYIKA
(UK Admin.)

NO.

SO.

RHODESIA

ANGOLA
(PORT.)

MOZAMBIQUE (Port.)

NYASALAND

MADAGASCAR (FR.)

REUNION
(F.)

W.
FR.
(3)

BECHUANA-
LAND

UNION OF
SOUTH
AFRICA

SWAZILAND (BR.)

BASUTOLAND (BR.)

AUSTRALIA

NEW
ZEALAND

ok of the United Nations, 1951.

The Library of Congress
Legislative Reference Service
Robert L. Bostick, 6-13-55
No. 1173

THE UNITED NATIONS AND DEPENDENT TERRITORIES

A. INTRODUCTORY COMMENT

Since the end of World War II about one-quarter of the population of the world has achieved self-government. This surge toward independence has resulted in the creation of many new sovereign states, such as India, Pakistan, Indonesia, the Republic of the Philippines, Israel, and Burma. Other countries, such as Puerto Rico and the Gold Coast, although not fully independent, have received either complete, or a large measure of, self-government.

Despite the many political transformations that have occurred since the end of the war, however, there are still many millions of people in a dependent status, concentrated primarily in Africa, southeast Asia, the Caribbean, and Pacific areas. The Communist "satellite" or "captive" countries, although they are in a state of political subjection, are generally excluded from discussions of the "colonial" question. The areas with which this study is concerned, therefore, are territories that are in some state of dependency to the non-Communist nations, for it is to these territories that the provisions of the Charter on trusteeship and non-self-government have been applied.

Except for the United States, Australia, and New Zealand, the principal powers retaining dependent territories are located in Western Europe. They include France, Great Britain, Belgium, Portugal, Spain, and The Netherlands. These so-called European colonial powers acquired most of their dependencies during the 18th and 19th centuries.

The breakup of the German and Turkish empires during the First World War heralded a trend toward contraction of the colonial system. It was a trend that greatly accelerated after the Second World War, deriving in many instances from the unsettling conditions of the war with its relaxation of overseas governmental controls. It was also due to other causes. Many dependent peoples, for example, had grown in political maturity to a point where they believed themselves capable of self-government. Large numbers had taken to heart the war aims of "freedom" and "democracy" proclaimed by the Allied countries. Many of them also thought they deserved recognition in the form of independence for the contributions they had made to the victory over the Axis. Finally, the dependent peoples were becoming increasingly eager to improve their economic condition, and this they believed could better be accomplished if they controlled their own political destiny.

The "colonial question" and international tension

Such transitions from dependence to independence or self-government as have occurred since the end of the war for the most part have not been free of bloodshed. Hostilities occurred, for example, in the cases of Israel, Indonesia, India, and Pakistan. Only in Indonesia. however, were hostilities primarily between the dependent territory and the administering country—in this instance The Netherlands. In the case of Israel, there was a military clash between the Jews and the neighboring Arabs. In the shift to independence in India and Pakistan, religious rioting on a massive scale occurred and subsequently the two countries became temporarily engaged in armed conflict over the status of Kashmir.

Although, during the postwar period, open warfare between dependent and administering countries has not often occurred, relations have frequently been characterized by tension, recrimination, and sporadic outbreaks of disorder. Such tension has often persisted even after a dependent people has achieved independence or self-government. In some instances these tendencies appear to be abating. Nevertheless, attitudes of suspicion have carried over and are frequently manifested in the policies of certain former colonies.

The Communists in their propaganda sharply attack what they call imperialism and seek to win the allegiance of dependent peoples. Communist leaders proclaim that one of their aims is to ally themselves with the "oppressed" peoples in a common revolutionary front. In other words, the Communists seek to employ national liberation movements as a means of vaulting themselves to power.

The problem for the United States

For the American people this situation poses a dilemma between historic sympathies on the one hand and strategic logic on the other. By tradition this country is "anticolonial." The United States, nevertheless, has sometimes appeared restrained in its practical measures for promoting the political advancement of dependent peoples, especially those under the dominion of the leading nations of Western Europe with which we have close defense relationships. Secretary of State John Foster Dulles, however, gave the following assurance regarding dependent areas: [1]

* * * The United States is pushing for self-government. We do so more than is publicly known, for in these matters open pressures are rarely conducive to the best results.

* * * The United States will never fight for colonialism.

The Secretary also asserted that when the United States exercises restraint in colonial matters—

It is because of a reasoned conviction that quick action would not, in fact, produce true independence.

In some cases hasty action in favor of independence for peoples not fully prepared for it has had unfortunate results. However, experience has shown that unfortunate results also arise from delaying or thwarting the political advancement of peoples who desire to govern themselves. The problem for the United States has been to achieve a balance in its policies toward the administering and the dependent countries—to reconcile its historical traditions with present realities. In the United Nations this has resulted in the pursuit of a "middle course" by this country. The policy is often expressed in a refusal to adopt a partisan attitude in controversies between administering and nonadministering countries. As commonly happens to neutrals, the effort to avoid alinement with either side has satisfied neither.

[1] Speech at Seattle, Wash., June 10, 1954. Department of State Bulletin, June 21, 1954, p. 937.

Although the United States follows a moderate course in regard to specific colonial controversies, nevertheless it pursues a general policy favoring the political advancement of dependent peoples.   For instance, when President Eisenhower and Prime Minister Churchill met in Washington in the summer of 1954, they jointly declared, in what is sometimes called the "Potomac Charter," that they upheld the "principle of self-government" and would "earnestly strive by every peaceful means to secure the independence of all countries whose peoples desire and are capable of sustaining an independent existence." [2]

On September 8 the United States joined seven other western and Asian countries at Manila in sponsoring the "Pacific Charter." [3]   In it they pledged themselves to—

strive by every peaceful means to promote self-government and to secure the independence of all countries whose peoples desire it and are able to undertake its responsibilities.

Scope of the study

The great stresses produced by the colonial issue are beneath the surface of many of the political questions which come before the United Nations.   As they relate directly to charter review, however, they have manifested themselves in two types of problems.   First are those which arise in connection with the provisions of the charter dealing with the advancement of dependent territories.   Second are those like the Indonesian question, that spring from a dispute or situation between former colonial areas and metropolitan powers which endangers the peace.   The latter come more directly under those chapters of the charter concerned with pacific settlement of disputes and enforcement action and are treated in detail in Staff Studies 5 and 7.   This study is primarily concerned with the chapters that deal with "trusteeship" and "non-self-governing" areas—how these articles originated, how they are being carried out, the problems that have arisen since they first went into operation, and proposals for dealing with those problems.

B. BACKGROUND

At the end of the First World War considerable sentiment in the United States and elsewhere supported the idea that nations holding colonies had a responsibility to advance the welfare of dependent peoples and to extend to all nations the principle of equal economic opportunity in colonial areas.   This attitude found expression in the mandates system which was incorporated into the League of Nations.   Under the mandates system the 14 territories taken from Germany and Turkey were not transferred outright to the victors.   Instead, their control was entrusted to certain of the Allied Powers of World War I, such as Great Britain, France and Japan.   The League of Nations was given responsibility for supervising the way in which these nations carried out the mandates.   To assist the League in this task a Permanent Mandates Commission was set up, composed of independent specialists on colonial affairs.

---

[2] New York Times, June 30, 1954, p. 3.
[3] The Pacific Charter was proclaimed by delegates to the Manila conference from the United States, Great Britain, France, Australia, New Zealand, the Philippines, Thailand, and Pakistan on the same day they signed the Southeast Asia Collective Defense Treaty.

During the Second World War the question of the mandates system came under consideration in connection with preparations for the formation of the United Nations. At Yalta in early 1945 the United States, Great Britain, and the Soviet Union decided that, prior to the forthcoming San Francisco Conference on the United Nations Charter, they would consult each other on creating machinery for dealing with what they called "territorial trusteeship."

The intent at that time was that the proposed trusteeship system, at least in the beginning, should be primarily a means of handling the mandates held under the old League of Nations and such territories as would be detached from enemy states as a result of the Second World War.[4] Provision for a third type—territories voluntarily placed under trusteeship—was made in the hope that in time the success of the system would induce countries with dependencies to take this step.[5]

At the San Francisco Conference it soon became clear that the agreement reached at Yalta provided too narrow a foundation on which to build the kind of international structure for dependencies desired by many of the participating nations. Some delegations proposed that the charter should provide not just for the territories that might be brought under trusteeship by one of the methods mentioned above but for all dependencies.

It was finally agreed at San Francisco to devote separate chapters of the charter to trusteeships and to non-self-governing territories. Chapters XII and XIII of the charter create a system of international supervision for a particular category of non-self-governing territories, the trust territories. Chapter XI contains a "Declaration" of principles for all other non-self-governing territories, but specifically provides for little or no international supervision.[6]

In working out the final wording of these chapters, controversy arose over whether "independence" should be stipulated as a goal for all dependent peoples. It was finally decided to mention only "self-government" as the objective for non-self-governing territories under chapter XI. For the trust territories, however, the objective was set forth as—

progressive development towards self-government or independence as may be appropriate to the particular circumstances of each territory * * *.[7]

The trusteeship system as finally set forth in the Charter is a modernization and heir of the former mandates system of the League of Nations. The purposes of the trusteeship system are stated in more positive terms than those of the old mandates regime. Under the United Nations system, for example, "progressive development toward self-government or independence" is established as a goal for all trust territories. Under the League, however, independence was specifically recognized as an objective for only some of the mandated

---

[4] In practice, only these 2 types of territories have actually been placed under trusteeship.
[5] This interpretation of the agreement at Yalta is given in the United Nations and Non-Self-Governing Territories. International Conciliation (New York) No. 435. November 1947: 703.
[6] See sec. F below for a description of the controversy over supervision of the non-self-governing territories.
[7] It appears to be a matter of dispute whether or not the objective of "self-government" under chapter XI includes the goal of "independence." See, for example, L. Larry Leonard, International Organization, New York, McGraw-Hill Book Co., 1951, p. 491; and Josef L. Kunz, Chapter XI of the United Nations Charter in Action, American Journal of International Law (Washington), vol. 48, January 1954: 105.
At the San Francisco Conference those who opposed the use of the term "independence" in connection with non-self-governing territories gave various arguments, among which was the contention "that the use of 'self-government' alone did not exclude the possibility of independence. * * * In the discussion the delegate of the United Kingdom stated that his Government had never ruled out independence as a possible goal for dependent territories in appropriate cases but objected to putting it forward as a universal coequal alternative goal for all territories." Leland M. Goodrich and Edvard Hambro, Charter of the United Nations: Commentary and Documents. Boston, World Peace Foundation, 1949, p. 410.

territories. Other stated purposes of the trusteeship system, more-over, include encouragement of respect for human rights and freedoms in the dependent areas and equal treatment in social, economic, and commercial matters for members of the United Nations and their nationals. Specific objectives of this scope were not embodied in the League mandate system.

C. THE TRUSTEESHIP SYSTEM

Under the United Nations Charter an agreement must be negotiated for each area brought into the trusteeship system. Its terms must be agreed upon "by the states directly concerned," and approved by the General Assembly. Special provision is made for a state to designate all or part of a trust territory as "strategic" and in this case the agreement must be approved by the Security Council. Under this provision the United States in 1945 was designated to administer as a strategic trusteeship the Central Pacific Islands captured from Japan during World War II.[8]

At the present time the following territories are under trusteeship. All of them, except Somaliland, were previously League-mandated territories.[9]

Territory	Area (square miles)	Population (thousands)	Administering state
Cameroons	34, 081	991	United Kingdom.
Do	166, 797	2, 703	France.
New Guinea	93, 000	1, 006	Australia.
Nauru	82	3	Australia (on behalf of the United Kingdom, New Zealand, and Australia).
Pacific Islands [1]	687	60	United States.
Ruanda-Urundi	20, 916	3, 719	Belgium.
Somaliland	194, 000	915	Italy.
Tanganyika	362, 688	7, 080	United Kingdom.
Togoland	13, 040	382	Do.
Do	21, 236	944	France.
Western Samoa	1, 133	73	New Zealand.
Total	907, 660	17, 876	

[1] This is the only strategic trust territory.

Responsibility for governing these territories in accordance with the trusteeship agreements rests with the administering states. The General Assembly and the Trusteeship Council supervise the operation of the agreements.

The Trusteeship Council is composed of all states holding trust territories and those permanent members of the Security Council which do not have them, that is, the Soviet Union and China. In addition, it includes as many elected states as are necessary to insure that the membership is evenly divided between administering and nonadministering countries.[10]

[8] The text of the trusteeship agreement for the strategic territory of the Pacific Islands is given in U. S. Senate Foreign Relations Committee, Review of the United Nations Charter: Collection of Documents, Washington, Government Printing Office, 1954, pp. 722-725. (Hereafter referred to as Collection of Documents).

[9] The Union of South Africa has refused to place the mandated territory of Southwest Africa under trusteeship.

[10] Chosen by the General Assembly for 3-year terms. The present members of the Trusteeship Council are: Administering countries—Australia, Belgium, France, New Zealand, United Kingdom, United States; nonadministering countries—El Salvador, China, Haiti, India, Syria, U. S. S. R. In addition, Italy which has responsibility for the trusteeship of Somaliland, but which is not a member of the United Nations, participates without vote in the work of the Council.

Administering states are required by the charter to make annual reports to the United Nations. The reports pertain to the political, economic, social, and educational advancement of the inhabitants of the trust territories. Under the charter, petitions may be and are submitted to the United Nations by the inhabitants of the trust territories or by anyone else. Finally, the Trusteeship Council may and does send out visiting missions to gather firsthand data on developments in the trust territories.

The administrative structure of the United Nations trusteeship system differs from the mandates system of the League of Nations in certain respects. The League Council, rather than the Assembly, for example, had responsibility for supervision of the mandates, and states administering mandates were strongly represented in that body. In the case of the United Nations, however, the General Assembly has ultimate authority for supervising the trusteeships. The administering states are greatly outnumbered in the Assembly by the nonadministering countries and many of the latter are out of sympathy with what they regard as colonialism.

Another significant difference lies in the fact that representatives on the United Nations Trusteeship Council, although they are expected to be "specially qualified," are delegates of governments rather than independent technical experts as was the case in the League Mandates Commission. This has tended to accentuate the political character of the Trusteeship Council.

D. THE NON-SELF-GOVERNING TERRITORIES

In addition to the 11 trust territories which come within the purview of chapters XII and XIII of the Charter, some 60 other dependencies are at present considered as non-self-governing under chapter XI of the Charter. These territories contain about 120 million inhabitants and cover an area of more than 6½ million square miles.[11] It is to them that the Declaration Regarding Non-Self-Governing Territories applies.

According to the declaration, the administering states "accept as a sacred trust" the obligation not only to develop free political institutions and self-government in their dependencies, but also to insure the economic, social, and educational advancement of the peoples of these areas. The administering states promise "to transmit regularly to the Secretary-General for information purposes" statistical and other technical data relating to the economic, social, and educational conditions in the dependencies. Transmission of political information on these territories, however, is not specifically mentioned, as in the case of trusteeships.

The declaration, which is contained in chapter XI, has been described as—

the first general international instrument in history in which all States administering Non-Self-Governing Territories have agreed to be bound by a set of principles applying to all such territories.[12]

---

[11] For a recent listing see Collection of Documents, p. 726. The total area of the United States, including all its outlying territories, is about 3,600,000 square miles.

[12] International Responsibility for Colonial Peoples: The United Nations and Chapter XI of the Charter. International Conciliation (New York) No. 458, February 1950: 52. "This is the first time in any international agreement that the interests of dependent peoples have been placed ahead of any other consideration." United Nations. What the United Nations is Doing: Non-Self-Governing Territories. New York. Lake Success, 1949, p. 3.

STRUCTURE OF THE
UNITED NATIONS
TRUSTEESHIP
SYSTEM

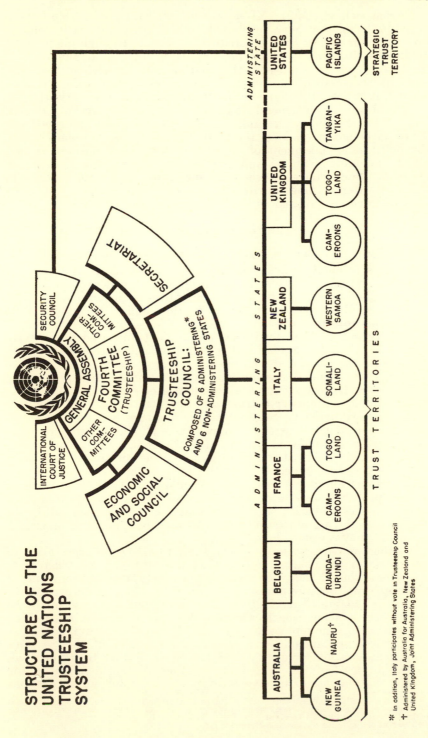

INTERNATIONAL COURT OF JUSTICE

SECURITY COUNCIL

GENERAL ASSEMBLY

OTHER COMMITTEES

FOURTH COMMITTEE (TRUSTEESHIP)

OTHER COMMITTEES

SECRETARIAT

ECONOMIC AND SOCIAL COUNCIL

TRUSTEESHIP COUNCIL:* COMPOSED OF 6 ADMINISTERING AND 6 NON-ADMINISTERING STATES

ADMINISTERING STATES

AUSTRALIA

NEW GUINEA

NAURU†

BELGIUM

RUANDA-URUNDI

FRANCE

CAM-EROONS

TOGO-LAND

ITALY

SOMALI-LAND

NEW ZEALAND

WESTERN SAMOA

UNITED KINGDOM

CAM-EROONS

TOGO-LAND

TANGAN-YIKA

ADMINISTERING STATE

UNITED STATES

PACIFIC ISLANDS

STRATEGIC TRUST TERRITORY

TRUST TERRITORIES

* In addition, Italy participates without vote in Trusteeship Council

† Administered by Australia for Australia, New Zealand and United Kingdom, Joint Administering States

Four aspects of chapter XI, as will be seen later, have been factors in the problems that have developed in the United Nations in connection with non-self-governing territories. First, although chapter XI applies to "territories whose peoples have not yet attained a full measure of self-government," the charter does not define "self-government" nor does it specify which territories are non-self-governing. Second, it is provided that reports on conditions in the territories are to be sent not to the General Assembly or to the Trusteeship Council, but to the Secretary-General, for the purpose of "information." Third, although members of the United Nations pledge themselves to the political advancement of dependent territories, nothing is said about including political information in these reports. Fourth, although the charter expresses the concern of the United Nations in the non-self-governing territories, machinery for channeling this concern is not elaborated as in the case of trust territories.

E. THE TRUST TERRITORIES: PROBLEMS AND PROPOSALS

The conflict between administering and non-administering countries

Rising sentiment against colonialism in many areas of the world since the end of World War II has resulted in a clash of opinion between "colonial" and "anti-colonial" countries in the United Nations. The Soviet Union has contributed to the conflict by injecting its propaganda into the issue.

With regard to trust territories the conflict appeared at an early stage. In 1946 five administering countries submitted draft agreements for eight mandated territories.[13]

During the General Assembly's consideration of the agreements, the U. S. S. R. pressed for the acceptance of the principle that no nation should administer a trust territory "as an integral part" of other territory under its control. Some countries also proposed that the duration of the trusteeship agreements should be limited to 10 years, subject to review at the end of that period. An Indian resolution suggested that trust territories should be administered "solely for the benefit of" their peoples and the latter's right to independence upon termination of the trusteeships should be recognized. All three of these proposals were accepted by the Assembly's Fourth Committee which is concerned with trusteeship matters, but they imposed conditions that the administering countries did not think wise or practicable and they rejected them.[14]

Another controversy arose at the same time over interpretation of the clause in the charter stating that the terms of the trusteeship agreements should be agreed upon by the "states directly concerned." This somewhat obscure phrase was subject to varying interpretations.

The United States maintained that the disputed phrase might be interpreted to mean, in each case, only the state or states administering the territory. The representative of the Soviet Union contended that the term should include the permanent members of the Security Council. As a matter of practical procedure, it was finally decided, on the proposal of the United States, that all the members of the United Nations were to have an opportunity to make suggestions

---

[13] Australia submitted a draft agreement for New Guinea; Belgium for Ruanda-Urundi; France for French Cameroons and French Togoland; New Zealand for Western Samoa; and United Kingdom for Tanganyika, British Cameroons, and British Togoland.

[14] Yearbook of the United Nations, 1946–47, pp. 186–187.

for changes.   The states that submitted the draft agreements would then have the right to accept or reject such suggestions.   On December 13, 1946, the Assembly finally approved the trusteeship agreements with the understanding that no state had waived its right to be considered a "state directly concerned;" and that the procedure to be followed in the future was still to be determined.   In short, the Assembly put off the fundamental issue in order to set the trusteeship system in motion.

During the years that the trusteeship system has been in operation the clash between the administering and nonadministering countries has been evident in almost every important issue affecting the trust territories.   It has appeared in practically every organ of the United Nations, particularly in the Trusteeship Council, in the General Assembly, and in the Assembly's Fourth Committee.   Nonadministering countries, in general, have favored measures which they believe would hasten the development of trust territories and encourage their political advancement.   They have sought by a very free interpretation of the Charter to win political concessions for the trust peoples and have opposed measures that they view as prejudicing or delaying the ultimate independence or self-government of these people.   The administering states also have argued for the economic and political development of the trust territories, but have opposed what they regard as intrusions upon their authority in those territories and have resisted many demands which they consider hasty or unrealistic. The United States has followed a moderate policy, avoiding the extreme positions taken by the two groups.   These different attitudes are revealed in the controversies which have occurred over the questions of administrative unions, association of the trust peoples in supervision of trust territories, and target dates for the achievement of self-government or independence.

Administrative unions

Some of the trusteeships are adjacent to other dependent territories governed by the same administering power.   In these cases, many of the trusteeship agreements authorize the formation of customs, fiscal or administrative unions, and the establishment of common services.[15] The administering states maintain that such unions have advantages in increased efficiency and lower costs.   They also contend that in those instances where a trust territory is joined to a more highly developed colony, the union may accelerate the political advancement of the former.   Nonadministering states, however, have expressed the fear that these unions may jeopardize the development of the trust territories as distinct political entities and may lead to their annexation by the administering country.   Resolutions have been passed by the General Assembly pointing out that annexation of the trust territories is not authorized by the charter and warning that administrative unions must not hamper free evolution toward self-government or independence.   The Assembly has also expressed the hope that the "freely expressed wishes of the inhabitants" will be taken into account and that the Trusteeship Council will be consulted before such unions are established.[16]

[15] Thus, the trust territory of British Togoland in West Africa is joined administratively with the neighboring British area of the Gold Coast.

[16] See, for instance, the text of the resolution passed by the General Assembly on December 20, 1952, in Yearbook of the United Nations, 1952, p. 742.

Association of trust peoples in the United Nations supervision of trust territories

In the latter part of 1952 a group of nonadministering countries proposed that a native representative from each trusteeship be selected and allowed to speak independently but not to vote in certain discussions before the Trusteeship Council. While ostensibly designed to increase indigenous participation in the operation of the trusteeship system, there was also in this proposal an implication that the interests of the indigenous peoples were not being fully represented by the trusteeship powers. It contained, in short, a suggestion of going over the heads of the administering powers.

Most of the latter, including the United States, opposed the resolution. They maintained that the form of representation of the trust territory on the Council was their sole responsibility and that visiting United Nations missions authorized in the charter furnished the trust inhabitants with adequate opportunities to make known their views. On the proposal of the United States, the Assembly adopted a compromise. It approved a resolution expressing the hope that the administering authorities would associate suitably qualified trust inhabitants with the work of the Trusteeship Council as part of their delegations or in any other manner they deemed advisable.[17]

Target dates for independence

Under the charter, an obligation exists to promote the development of the trust peoples toward self-government or independence. The manner and pace at which this development is to take place is apparently left to the discretion of the administering authorities, under the surveillance, however, of the Trusteeship Council and the General Assembly. Arguing that it would give encouragement to the people of the trust territories, a group of nonadministering states proposed a resolution, in January 1952, inviting annual reports on measures which were intended to lead the trust territory to self-government or independence, and the period of time regarded as necessary to reach this goal. Administering states opposed the proposal on the ground that it was impossible to foretell the date. Nevertheless, a resolution to this effect was passed by the General Assembly. The administering states did not respond to its recommendations. In December 1953 the Assembly reaffirmed the earlier measure and requested the Trusteeship Council to report on the steps taken to carry out both resolutions.[18] The United States did not vote on either resolution.

In only one trusteeship—Somaliland—is there an established target date for independence. This date (1960) was set by the Assembly, which was authorized by the Peace Treaty with Italy to dispose of the former colonies of that country. The Somaliland trusteeship will probably be considered a test case for the effectiveness of assigning target dates. Moreover, the impact of the Somaliland example upon more advanced dependent peoples who have not been assigned a date for independence or self-government will probably be closely observed.

[17] Yearbook of the United Nations, 1952, pp. 731–732. A similar question also arose in connection with the work of the Committee on Information from Non-Self-Governing Territories (see sec. F below). In 1952 the General Assembly approved a resolution inviting the administering countries to associate representatives in the work of the Committee on Information. See Yearbook of the United Nations, 1952, pp. 576–579.
[18] The texts of the resolutions are given in Collection of Documents, pp. 728–729 and 748–749.

Proposed changes in the relationship of the General Assembly and the Trusteeship Council

The typical controversies discussed above indicate that the administering and nonadministering states in general differ as to the means of reaching the goals of the trusteeship system and possibly as to the goals themselves. As a result, the machinery of trusteeship as envisioned in the charter tends to be impeded.

In the Trusteeship Council there is, as previously pointed out, an even division of the membership between administering and nonadministering countries, and hence an even division of votes. Under present circumstances, this division has had the effect at times of hampering or deadlocking operations.

As one commentator points out:

* * * In its fourth session, the Trusteeship Council actually could not come to conclusions about certain operations because the six Administering Authorities insisted on one point of view and the six nonadministering powers insisted on another. In a case involving the examination of conditions in one Trust Territory, the split vote was maintained throughout that session, and the Trusteeship Council could not fulfill its obligations under the Charter.[19]

The difficulties have diminished of late but have not disappeared. Since the elective membership of the Council and other factors affecting its operations are subject to change, the conflict may revert on some future occasion to its earlier and more acute form.

The basic controversy is also evident in the attempts of the General Assembly to assert supremacy over the Trusteeship Council. In the Assembly, the nonadministering states outnumber and, therefore, can outvote the administering powers. Under the charter, the Trusteeship Council operates "under the authority of the General Assembly," and assists the latter in carrying out its functions. On the other hand, it is clear from the terms of the charter that the Council, rather than the Assembly, was intended to exercise direct supervision over the trusteeship system.[20] It has been pointed out that:

* * * A constitutional dilemma arises * * * from the fact that while the General Assembly can pass a resolution and say what it wishes with regard to all of the operations of the Trusteeship System, it cannot force the Trusteeship Council to agree. The Trusteeship Council is composed of sovereign Members of the United Nations who cannot be influenced in their individual vote by any Assembly action.[21]

Thus the stage is always set for a tug-of-war between the General Assembly and the Trusteeship Council. Nor is the situation likely to clarify itself unless there is a major shift in the international political scene or a change in the relationship established between the two bodies by the charter. To end the dilemma, this change would have to take the form either of removing or loosening the authority which the Assembly has over the Council or conversely of subjecting the

---

[19] H. A. Wieschoff. Trusteeship and Non-Self-Governing Territories, in Clyde Eagleton and Richard N. Swift. Annual Review of United Nations Affairs, 1952. New York, New York University Press, 1953, p. 117. Mr. Wieschoff is an official of the United Nations secretariat.
    The deadlocked vote occurred when the U. S. S. R. placed critical remarks in the annual report on French Togoland and France attempted to enter a reply. In a series of tie votes approval of the report was blocked.
[20] "Acting under the authority of the General Assembly * * *, the Trusteeship Council is the directly responsible organ of the United Nations for the operation of the Trusteeship System. * * * The Council has the responsibility and general power of supervising the administration of the Trust Territories, in achieving the objectives defined in the Charter and in accordance with its functions and powers." United Nations. Department of Public Information. What the United Nations Is Doing for Trust Territories. New York, 1952, p. 3.
[21] Wieschoff. Op. cit., p. 121. The word "influenced" in the last sentence of the above quotation requires clarification. Assembly action may have a persuasive effect upon the sovereign members of the Trusteeship Council, but it cannot have a coercive effect.

Council to even closer control.   The first alternative would probably entail shifting the main responsibility for trusteeship from the General Assembly to the Trusteeship Council.   If the change were made, the Trusteeship Council might well become the principal scene of conflict between administering and nonadministering powers.   As such its operations could remain deadlocked, or near-deadlocked, unless some alteration were also made in its present evenly divided membership.   The nonadministering countries are not likely to look with favor on a shift of principal responsibility from the General Assembly since it would deny them the influence in trusteeship matters they now have by virtue of their majority in that body. Almost certainly they would oppose shifting it to a Trusteeship Council in which they had less than or at best equal influence with the administering countries.

If, on the other hand, the Trusteeship Council were to be placed under closer Assembly control, one reform might be to make the Trusteeship Council a body of experts, much like the former Mandates Commission, rather than official representatives of member states. This new expert Council might then be made clearly subordinate to the General Assembly which it would serve in only an advisory capacity.

The possibility of this change is suggested by observations such as the following:

In some respects machinery for international supervision of trust territories is weaker than the comparable machinery in the mandates system * * * the Trusteeship Council is an organ through which the member states voice their respective policies on matters before it.   These policies are * * * determined by the complex of factors * * * that enter into the formulation of any foreign policy position.   The Permanent Mandates Commission * * * was, on the contrary, composed of individuals, experts in colonial affairs, public finance, and the like, who were free to voice personal opinions on matters before them without regard to the foreign policies of their respective governments.   Add to this the fact that much of their work was done in private, and it becomes evident that there could and, in fact, did exist an objectivity about their activities that in its nature cannot be true of the Trusteeship Council.[22]

Those who favor a greater measure of United Nations influence over the trust territories generally think in terms of increasing the General Assembly's control over the Trusteeship Council.   One proposal along these lines would give the Assembly the right of electing all the members of the Trusteeship Council; the nonadministering would outnumber the administering members of the Council and the entire membership of that body would be subject to removal by an Assembly vote.[23]   Needless to say, proposals along this line are likely to be vigorously opposed by most, if not all, administering countries.   They have already made clear that in their view the United Nations is even now interfering excessively in the management of the trusteeships.

Another approach designed to increase the influence of the United Nations over trust territories is contained in proposals that the organization itself act as the administering authority.   Although this is already authorized by the charter (article 81), thus far only states have been so designated.[24]

[22] Ruth C. Lawson.   Trusteeship, 1945–50.   Current History, vol. 19, November 1950: 261.
[23] Grenville Clark and Louis B. Sohn.   Peace Through Disarmament and Charter Revision: Detailed Proposals for Revision of the United Nations Charter.   Preliminary print, 1953, p. 116 ff.
[24] Specific proposals for designating the United Nations as an administering authority have been made from time to time.   In 1948, for instance, the United States proposed that the United Nations administer a trusteeship over Palestine, but this was not adopted.

Insofar as it might provide them with a greater opportunity to participate in the control of trust territories, the anticolonial countries would probably welcome a more active role for the United Nations as administering authority. However, the grant of such a role to the international organization involves difficulties. One commentator has remarked that the charter provisions on trusteeship were apparently written primarily to fit situations in which states would be charged with trusteeship administration. He maintains, consequently, that many of these provisions would not be applicable if the United Nations itself were the administrator. He argues, for instance, that if the United Nations were both administrator and supervisor, no supervision in the true sense of the term would be possible.[25] If this view is correct, then the assignment of a more extensive role to the United Nations as a direct administrator of trusteeships might necessitate clarification of those clauses of the charter (for instance, articles 87 and 88) giving supervisory functions to the Assembly and the Trusteeship Council.

At the San Francisco Conference some delegates argued that the organization would not be effective in the role of administering authority. A grant to the United Nations of administrative authority over a trust territory also raises questions pertinent to the fundamental nature of the organization. As it is now, the United Nations is regarded as an "international" body, that is, as not possessing sovereign powers. But what would happen to its status if it were clothed with governmental powers similar to those exercised by sovereign states?

F. NON-SELF-GOVERNING TERRITORIES: PROBLEMS AND PROPOSALS

Supervision of non-self-governing territories

A comparison of the charter provisions on non-self-governing [26] and those on trust territories shows a number of differences.[27] Perhaps the most obvious is that the provisions affecting the former provide explicitly only for a very limited United Nations administrative concern. The administering countries are merely called on to report annually to the Secretary General on the economic, educational, and social conditions in their dependent territories (art. 73).

Administering and nonadministering states have repeatedly clashed over the interpretation of this obligation.[28] On the basis of this provision, as one commentator has expressed it, the General Assembly has—

assumed greater powers with regard to non-self-governing territories than a strict interpretation of article 73 of the charter warrants.[29]

He cites in point: the creation of a special committee of the Assembly similar in some respects to the Trusteeship Council to examine the information reported by the administering powers; the formulation of a standard form of reporting on dependent territories, similar to the

[25] Hans Kelsen. The Law of the United Nations: A Critical Analysis of Its Fundamental Problems. London, Stevens & Sons, 1950, p. 651. The author maintains, for instance, it would be meaningless to impose upon the United Nations the obligation of making reports to itself, which would be the case if the organization were an administering authority.
[26] The term "non-self-governing territories" refers to those dependent territories, excluding territories under trusteeship, on which reports are made under chapter XI of the charter.
[27] See the discussion on charter provisions in sections B and C above.
[28] Seven member states transmit information on non-self-governing territories. They are Australia, Belgium, France, the Netherlands, New Zealand, the United Kingdom, and the United States.
[29] S. Engel. The Changing Charter of the United Nations. Year Book of World Affairs, 1953. London, Stevens and Sons, Ltd., 1953, pp. 80–81.

Trusteeship Council's questionnaire; the encouragement of transmission of information relating to political developments in the dependent areas; and the tendency on the part of the Assembly to assert its authority to determine whether or not territories are self-governing. In other words, the Assembly has been gradually building a structure of supervision over 'non-self-governing territories which resembles that specifically provided in the Charter for the trust territories. This tendency has been opposed by the administering countries.

The Committee on Information

Much of the controversy with respect to the above development has centered on what is now called the Committee on Information from Non-Self-Governing Territories. This Committee had its genesis in 1946 when the Assembly established a procedure for dealing with the information which the administering countries were beginning to transmit on these territories. The Assembly decided that such information, after being summarized and analyzed by the Secretary-General, should be examined by a special committee before being presented to it for consideration.

The Committee on Information from Non-Self-Governing Territories was continued on an annual basis until 1949 when it was voted a 3-year term (subsequently renewed in 1952). It is composed of the member states transmitting information on non-self-governing territories and an equal number of nonadministering members. The Committee makes procedural recommendations to the General Assembly "relating to functional fields generally but not with respect to individual Territories." [30]

In 1952, when the Assembly was debating extension of the Committee, three principal points of view were advanced by the member countries. The United Kingdom, Belgium, and France, all principal holders of non-self-governing territories, opposed the renewal of the Committee. They argued that there was no basis in the charter for the establishment of the Committee and that the responsibility of the United Nations ended when the Secretary-General received the information transmitted by the administering countries. They also contended that the charter made no provision for a system of supervision of the non-self-governing territories such as it authorized for the trust territories. They asserted that if the Committee on Information were continued on a permanent basis, the existence of an obligation on the part of administering powers to be subject to United Nations supervision would be implied. Moreover, they announced that if the Committee were made permanent, they would not participate in its work.

Pakistan, Egypt, Ecuador, the U. S. S. R., and others spoke in favor of continuing the Committee on a permanent basis. They maintained that as long as non-self-governing territories existed, then the General Assembly needed some kind of machinery to assist it in fulfilling its responsibilities in regard to these territories; and that the Committee could not be terminated without adverse psychological repercussions in the dependent areas.

The United States, supported by Denmark, Australia, and the Netherlands, favored continuation of the Committee for another 3-year term. The American delegate expressed the opinion that the

---

[30] The texts of the General Assembly resolutions on the Committee in 1949 and 1952 are given in Collection of Documents, pp. 727–728 and 730.

Committee had done useful work. In view of the differences of opinion on whether the Committee should be continued at all, however, he advocated only that it be extended for another period of 3 years.

The General Assembly finally passed a resolution providing for a 3-year extension, with the added proviso that in 1955 the General Assembly consider whether the Committee should be "renewed for a further period." [31]

Transmission of political information

Another aspect in the conflict has centered on the "standard form"—a questionnaire similar to that specifically authorized by the charter for the Trusteeship Council—for reporting on conditions in the nontrust territories. The form provides, among other things, for the transmission of political information, although such transmission is classified as "optional." [32]

Some countries have maintained that the transmission of political information should be made obligatory. The question was debated in the United Nations as early as 1947. A group of states, including the U. S. S. R., Egypt, India, and Pakistan, asserted that chapter XI constituted a treaty and not merely a unilateral declaration. They claimed the administering countries had assumed the obligation of promoting the political development of the non-self-governing peoples. The United Nations had the right to know, they contended, whether the administering countries were fulfilling their obligations. Consequently, they concluded, the administering states were under the obligation of transmitting information on the political progress of the territories under their control.[33]

Other members, including the United States, the United Kingdom, France, the Netherlands, and Belgium, argued that chapter XI of the charter was merely a unilateral declaration of policy on the part of the administering countries by which they incurred no specific obligation except to transmit economic, social, and educational information, the only categories mentioned in article 73. At the San Francisco Conference, they asserted, a deliberate decision had been made to exclude political information from the article.

Thus far the General Assembly has not formally held that an obligation exists to transmit political information. However, it has repeatedly encouraged the member countries to submit such information voluntarily.[34]

Some nations, including the United States, on their initiative have consistently transmitted to the Secretary General information on political developments. Others, such as the United Kingdom and Belgium, have consistently refrained from doing so.

It is evident from the developments discussed above that there is a definite movement in the General Assembly to exercise supervisory

[31] Collection of Documents, p. 730. Belgium in August 1953, charging that the Assembly was extending the powers of the Committee on Information beyond what was authorized by the charter, announced that it would no longer participate in the Committee's work.

[32] This form was originally adopted in 1947 on the basis of a draft submitted by the United States.

[33] Yearbook of the United Nations, 1947–48, p. 152.

[34] Resolutions have been passed by the Assembly declaring that the voluntary transmission of political information is in conformity with the spirit of art. 73 and expressing the hope that those members who have not transmitted such information would voluntarily do so in the future. (See for instance the resolution of Dec. 2, 1949, in Yearbook of the United Nations 1948–49, p. 734.) In 1952 the Assembly passed resolutions recognizing the right of self-determination for non-self-governing and trust peoples and recommending that states administering non-self-governing territories voluntarily report "the extent to which the right of peoples and nations to self-determination is exercised by the peoples" of such territories. (Texts of the resolutions are given in Collection of Documents, p. 730–731).

powers in regard to non-self-governing territories, resembling those which it clearly has over trusteeship areas. It has established a Committee on Information on Non-Self-Governing Territories of a composition similar to that of the Trusteeship Council. It has also adopted a questionnaire and has encouraged the reporting of political information. This movement to assimilate non-self-governing territories into a sort of trusteeship regime is being resisted by administering states on the grounds that such action is not specifically authorized by the charter and that it represents intervention in matters of domestic jurisdiction.

A method of resolving the conflicts in interpretation of chapter XI would be to specify more clearly the obligations it imposes. The administering states would probably approve changes strictly limiting their obligations to those at present expressly mentioned in the chapter. An alternative procedure, which would probably accord with the desires of many nonadministering states, would be specifically to authorize the Assembly to employ those supervisory devices, such as the Committee on Information, that it has at present adopted without clear authorization. Or, as has been suggested by some observers,[35] the United Nations might even be granted authority over all dependent areas equaling or at least approaching that which it now has over trusteeship territories.

Definition of "non-self-governing territory"

Although the charter uses the terms "non-self-governing territories" and "territories whose peoples have not yet attained a full measure of self-government," it nowhere defines these terms nor does it specify who is to have the authority to make such a determination.

A definition of these terms was discussed in the early sessions of the General Assembly without conclusive result. As a practical procedure, administering states merely informed the United Nations of the territories on which they would transmit information. In turn, the General Assembly listed these 74 territories, in a resolution adopted in December 1946.

However, in 1948, information was received on only 63 territories. This immediately raised a series of questions. Under what conditions should the obligations of chapter XI cease to apply? Was the administering authority obliged to explain why it was no longer transmitting information? What was the responsibility of the United Nations in the matter?

In November 1948 the Assembly passed a resolution stating that—

it is essential that the United Nations be informed of any change in the constitutional position and status—

of any territory on which information was no longer transmitted. It requested the countries concerned to transmit appropriate information—

including the constitution, legislative act or executive order providing for the government of the territory and the constitutional relationship of the territory to the Government of the metropolitan country.[36]

[35] A proposal to apply the trusteeship system to all colonies was considered at the San Francisco Conference. See Documents of the United Nations Conference on International Organization, San Francisco, 1945. New York, United Nations Information Organizations, 1945, v. 10, p. 429 and 440. See also Ernst B. Haas. The Attempt to Terminate Colonialism: Acceptance of the United Nations Trusteeship System. International Organization, v. 7, February 1953: 10–12.

[36] The text of the resolution is given in Collection of Documents, p. 727.

Although some administering countries protested the resolution, they submitted the explanations.

But the fundamental questions of how to determine when a non-self-governing territory became self-governing, and who was to make this determination, remained unanswered. In 1949, when the matter was discussed in the Assembly, administering states denied that the United Nations had a right to intervene in these questions. They asserted that only the country concerned was in a position to determine its constitutional relationship with the territories it controlled.

Many of the nonadministering states, on the other hand, maintained that once a territory had been placed on the list as non-self-governing the administering state no longer had the sole responsibility. It could not discontinue transmitting information, they asserted, until self-government had been attained and the United Nations had a responsibility in deciding when that stage was reached.

The viewpoint of the nonadministering states prevailed and the Assembly passed a resolution in December 1949 in which it claimed the right—

to express its opinion on the principles which have guided or which may in future guide—

the members in listing non-self-governing territories under chapter XI.[37]

In 1953 the Assembly made reference to its "competence" in deciding whether a non-self-governing territory had attained a full measure of self-government.[38]

It approved a list of factors to be considered in determining the status of non-self-governing territories. These factors were grouped into three categories: Those indicative of the attainment of independence; those indicative of the attainment of other forms of self-government; and those indicative of the free association of a territory on an equal basis with the metropolitan or other country as an internal part of that country. It was emphasized in the resolution that the factors should be used by both the General Assembly and the administering members only as a "guide" in determining whether a territory was within the scope of chapter XI.[39]

Thus the issue is posed. The General Assembly has claimed competence in determining whether or not territories are or are not self-governing. The administering states, on the other hand, maintain that they alone are the judges. When the question was discussed in the United Nations in 1953, the representative of the United States held that the General Assembly could recommend to the administering powers the consideration of a definition of "non-self-governing territories," and that this country had no objection to Assembly discussion of the information transmitted by the administering powers in explanation of their decision to cease reporting on territories which had become self-governing. However, the American representative pointed out that under the United States Constitution only the United States Congress had the sovereign power to decide

[37] Yearbook of the United Nations, 1948–49, p. 732.
[38] See Collection of Documents, pp. 740–745.
[39] The resolution emphasized that the factors "should in no way be interpreted as a hindrance to the attainment of a full measure of self-government" by a nontrust territory, and declared that the manner in which such territories "can become fully self-governing is primarily through the attainment of independence." It did not exclude the possibility, however, that self-government could also be achieved by association with another state "if this is done freely and on the basis of absolute equality."

upon constitutional changes in the status of American Territories, and that only the United States could determine when one of its Territories had become self-governing within the terms of the charter.[40]

The problem could be resolved either by assigning to the Assembly alone the specific authority to determine whether or not territories are self-governing, or by stipulating that such authority belongs solely to the administering states. Another possibility would be for the Assembly and the administering states to share this authority according to some specific formula.

G. CONCLUDING COMMENTS

Because numerous factors are involved, it is frequently difficult to assess the influence of the United Nations on a dependency's attainment of independence or self-government. Of the dozen or so countries that have become independent since the end of the war only two have had any direct relationship with the charter provisions dealing with non-self-governing territories. The Netherlands Indies (Indonesia) and Indochina (Laos, Cambodia, and Vietnam) had been designated as non-self-governing territories under chapter XI. Israel and Jordan, it should be noted, had been mandates under the League of Nations.

The more conspicuous role of the United Nations in furthering independence or self-government has been related to those provisions of the charter dealing with peaceful settlement of disputes and enforcement action. Even here, however, the extent and effectiveness of UN influence is difficult to measure. In Indonesia, for example, the Security Council brought about a truce between Indonesian and Dutch forces; it recommended the establishment of an independent and sovereign Republic of Indonesia; and it set up a special commission to assist the parties in arriving at a settlement. In 1949 Indonesia became an independent sovereign state. In Palestine, however, the General Assembly attempted to settle the rival claims of Jews and Arabs by recommending the creation of an Arab state and a Jewish state. This recommendation was not accepted. The Jews proclaimed the independence of the new State of Israel, and part of Palestine was annexed by Jordan.

In the case of the Italian colonies, the great powers agreed that if they were unable to decide on the disposition of the colonies within 1 year after the Italian Peace Treaty came into effect, they would abide by the decision of the General Assembly. The General Assembly decided that Libya should become independent, that Eritrea should become autonomous in a federation with Ethiopia, and that Somaliland should become independent after a 10-year period under Italian trusteeship.

After the surrender of Japan, the United States and the U. S. S. R. agreed that Korea should temporarily be under four-nation trusteeship but that it should eventually be independent. When the two could not agree on the establishment of a provisional Korean Government, the United States placed the case before the United Nations. It was under the auspices of the United Nations that an independent Republic of Korea was established in 1948.

---

[40] United Nations Bulletin, New York, vol. 15, Oct. 15, 1953: 343. The United States voted against the Assembly resolution approving the list of "factors."

From time to time suggestions have been made that the island of Formosa might be placed under United Nations trusteeship.[41] Usually such proposals do not specify who would actually administer the trusteeship.   However, both the United States [42] and the Chinese National Government [43] have been mentioned for this role.   It has also been suggested in some quarters that the United Nations itself might be designated as the administering authority.   Such proposals are usually advanced in connection with the political questions surrounding the Formosan Straits tension.   It has been argued, however, that a U. N. trusteeship would be "a form of multiple colonialism for such a trusteeship would undermine if not destroy the sovereignty of the Republic of China." [44]

As regards those territories still in a state of dependency, there is little disagreement that an objective of the charter is to further a change of this status to that of self-government at least.   Nevertheless, there is sharp conflict between the administering and nonadministering countries over the pace and method by which this goal shall be achieved.   The conflict has grown out of a movement against "colonialism," initiated and sustained largely by countries of Asia, Africa, and Latin America, some of them recently dependent territories themselves.   The Communist states also, for their own reasons, have added support to the campaign.

The administering powers, relatively few in number, have frequently been outvoted by the nonadministering countries in the United Nations General Assembly.   An anomalous situation, moreover, is created by the fact that under the terms of the charter "questions relating to the operation of the trusteeship system," in which the charter clearly assigns the United Nations an extensive interest, require a two-thirds vote for passage by the Assembly, whereas some matters relating to other non-self-governing dependencies may be approved by only a simple majority vote.[45]   The relatively large group of nonadministering countries, therefore, can more easily enact resolutions in regard to territories clearly under the control of administering states than they can in regard to areas under the international supervision of the trusteeship system.

Nonadministering states probably registered their furthest advance to date in what they consider their campaign on behalf of the trust territories when the Assembly recommended in 1952 that "target dates" be established for the attainment of self-government or independence in the trust territories.

In regard to the nontrust territories, a structure of supervision resembling that over the trust territories has been erected by the General Assembly, without specific authorization of the charter and in spite of the protests of practically all of the administering countries.   The latter are in the embarrassing position of having either to accept the gradual encroachment of United Nations supervision into a sphere that they regard as preponderantly internal or of ignoring

[41] See, for example, Friends Committee on National Legislation, Supplement to Washington Newsletter 133, October 1954. See also statements by Clement R. Attlee and Winston Churchill in the New York Times, July 15, 1954.
[42] Dorothy Thompson. Formosa Problem Isn't Simple. Washington Star, February 21, 1955, p. A31.
[43] What's Ahead for Formosa. Editorial. Christian Science Monitor, February 7, 1955, p. 14.
[44] Address of Senator William F. Knowland before the Indiana Republican Editorial Association, Indianapolis, April 16, 1955. Printed in Congressional Record, April 18, 1955, pp. A2518–A2520.
[45] Under art. 18 the Assembly may decide what categories of questions, in addition to those specified in the charter, require a two-thirds rather than a simple majority vote.

world opinion as expressed in the resolutions of the General Assembly. The structure of supervision has been extended to the point at which the Assembly now asserts its competence to decide whether or not territories are self-governing. It may be that the Assembly has gone almost as far as it can go within the present framework of the charter. Matters may now be approaching a critical point where at least advisory opinions of the World Court, or perhaps amendments to the charter, would be essential if the General Assembly is to obtain appreciably greater supervisory power over the non-self-governing territories or conversely if it is to be prevented from seeking such power.

THE UNITED NATIONS AND THE SPECIALIZED AGENCIES

STAFF STUDY NO. 10
JULY 25, 1955

PREFACE

By Walter F. George, *Chairman*

This staff study examines the relationship of the United Nations to the specialized agencies and the problems occasioned by this interconnection. The concern of the United States about this relationship has been voiced by both the Secretary of State, Mr. John Foster Dulles, and our permanent representative at the United Nations, Ambassador Henry Cabot Lodge, Jr.

Secretary Dulles told the subcommittee that there was a "curious" and in his opinion "inadequate" control over these bodies. "I believe," he said, "that the whole galaxy of satellites which revolves around the United Nations deserves some consideration, although those bodies are not themselves technically organs of the United Nations."

Ambassador Lodge, in his testimony before the subcommittee, supplemented this statement with more detailed comments of his own. He stated that "for practical purposes the specialized agencies are independent," despite some formal coordination. This status "has been the source of many troubles." He raised with the subcommittee, therefore, "the question as to whether the present provisions of the United Nations Charter are adequate for the sort of coordination we want, and, if not, whether the system of coordination should be improved, and if so, by what changes in the charter."

From time to time I have noted a disturbing tendency on the part of the specialized agencies to go their own separate ways. In some cases they are supported in this tendency by special interest groups within member states which seek funds and status for the particular agency in which they are interested.

I can readily understand why the specialized agencies would resist any integration process that would place them under the immediate authority and control of the General Assembly. For the Assembly is primarily a political body and the specialized agencies fear their technical work would be jeopardized if it were subjected to the political pressures that are released every year in New York.

Both the United Nations proper and the specialized agencies have as one of their main objectives the kind of cooperative action that will strengthen the fabric of peace in the world. Whether the work of the various agencies and instrumentalities in the total U. N. system might be more effectively coordinated is certainly one of the questions our subcommittee must examine.

During the past several years, a number of important steps have been taken to coordinate the activities of the specialized agencies and thus to avoid duplication and overlapping of effort. Much can still be done without recourse to formal charter amendments or without getting these agencies enmeshed in the cold war. Our best hope, it seems to me, lies with the Secretary-General of the United Nations. I believe that his vigorous and enlightened leadership can do much to accomplish the objectives we all have in mind.

This staff study was prepared to help the subcommittee consider the question. It summarizes the existing relationship between the United Nations and its specialized agencies, and discusses some of the major problems created by the system and some of the suggestions which have been advanced by way of a solution.

This study was prepared for the subcommittee by Dr. Hugh L. Elsbree, senior specialist in government and public administration with the assistance of Mary Shepard, Foreign Affairs Division, Legislative Reference Service, Library of Congress, under the direction of the subcommittee staff. It does not necessarily reflect the views of the Subcommittee on the United Nations Charter.

JULY 25, 1955.

CONTENTS

283

Coordination Between the United Nations And the Specialized Agencies

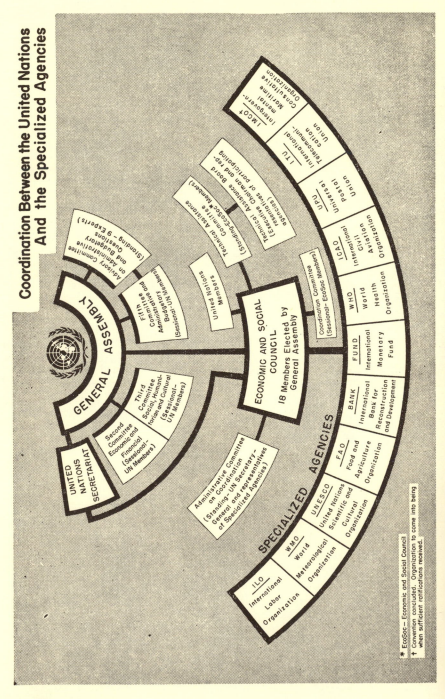

GENERAL ASSEMBLY

UNITED NATIONS SECRETARIAT

Advisory Committee on Administrative and Budgetary Questions (Standing - 9 Experts)

Fifth Committee Administrative and Budgetary (Sessional-UN Members)

Third Committee Social, Humanitarian and Cultural (Sessional- UN Members)

Second Committee Economic and Financial (Sessional- UN Members)

United Nations Members

Technical Assistance Committee (Sessional-EcoSoc Members)

Technical Assistance Board (Executive Chairman and rep- resentatives of participating agencies)

ECONOMIC AND SOCIAL COUNCIL 18 Members Elected by General Assembly

Coordination Committee (Sessional- EcoSoc Members)

Administrative Committee on Coordination (Standing- UN Secretary - General and representatives of Specialized Agencies)

SPECIALIZED AGENCIES

ILO International Labor Organization

WMO World Meteorological Organization

UNESCO United Nations Scientific and Cultural Organization

FAO Food and Agriculture Organization

BANK International Bank for Reconstruction and Development

FUND International Monetary Fund

WHO World Health Organization

ICAO International Civil Aviation Organization

UPU Universal Postal Union

ITU International Telecommuni- cation Union

IMCO† Intergovern- mental Maritime Consultative Organization

* EcoSoc — Economic and Social Council

† Convention concluded. Organization to come into being when sufficient ratifications received.

THE UNITED NATIONS AND THE SPECIALIZED AGENCIES

A. Introduction

In the drafting of the United Nations Charter great importance was attached to international economic, social, and cultural cooperation. Considerable difference of opinion developed, however, as to the most effective method of promoting this objective. Some favored a centralized system, in which the social, cultural, and economic objectives expressed in the charter would be the direct responsibility of the United Nations organization. Others felt that it would be desirable to keep these functions largely separate from political and security matters, and to handle them through more or less autonomous international agencies, existing or to be established.

In the end the principle of decentralization was the one relied on chiefly, although not exclusively. The provisions of the charter on this point are somewhat unprecise.

This study discusses a number of problems and proposals concerning the relationship of the specialized agencies to the U. N. It seeks to identify and analyze briefly only those more general problems in existing relationships involving either possible amendment of the United Nations Charter, or relatively far-reaching changes falling short of charter amendment. The study does not deal with the internal organization and programs of the specialized agencies as such. Moreover, the study makes no effort to identify and discuss all of the significant problems and issues of coordination that have arisen. For example, discussion of difficulties in the actual execution of programs, as well as in the provision of administrative services, is almost entirely omitted. This is not because these problems are in any sense lacking in importance, but rather because they involve a host of highly detailed cooperative administrative arrangements.

B. Provisions of the Charter

The social, economic, and cultural objectives of the United Nations are stated in broad terms in the charter.[1] The organization is to promote solutions of international economic, social, health, and related problems; international cultural and educational cooperation;

---

[1] See preamble and arts. 1 (3), 13 (1b), and 55.

higher standards of living and full employment; the observance of human rights and fundamental freedoms for all without regard to race, sex, language, or religion.

The charter recognizes a division of responsibility between the United Nations and what are called the specialized agencies in the carrying out of these objectives. The U. N. is assigned a direct function under article 62 to initiate and undertake studies and to make recommendations respecting international economic, social, and cultural objectives. The charter recognizes, however, that similar functions reside in the specialized agencies.

These agencies are to be brought into relationship with the United Nations, through the General Assembly and the Economic and Social Council. The United Nations may make recommendations for coordinating the policies and activities of existing agencies and, where appropriate, for creating additional agencies.

Thus the responsibility of the United Nations with regard to the social, economic, and cultural objectives of the charter is twofold: (1) it has a direct responsibility for promoting these objectives; and (2) it has responsibilities with respect to coordinating the work of the specialized agencies, which are engaged in the pursuit of similar objectives.

The latter responsibilities are described in some detail in articles 17, 63, 64, and 70. These articles deal with the financial and budgetary arrangements between the United Nations and the specialized agencies, coordination of the activities of the agencies, reporting of their activities, and the interchange of representatives. The language of the articles is such, however, as to leave unclear the specific extent of control of the United Nations over the agencies. This is undoubtedly due in part to the fact that some of the agencies predated the United Nations and it was uncertain in 1945 how the new organization would affect them. Nor was it clear at that time to what extent the membership of the agencies and the United Nations would parallel each other. In any event, the assumption appears to have been that the proper division of responsibilities would be achieved through the exercise of the United Nations' power to make recommendations on coordination.[2]

C. Relationships of the Specialized Agencies With the United Nations

Ten operating specialized agencies now have agreements in effect with the United Nations in accordance with article 63.[3] Four of the agencies involved—the International Labor Organization (ILO), the International Telecommunications Union (ITU), the Universal Postal Union (UPU), and the World Meteorological Organization— formerly the International Meteorological Organization—(WMO)—

---

[2] For a detailed discussion of the United Nations Charter and the specialized agencies, see L. M. Goodrich and Edvard Hambro, Charter of the United Nations (Boston, 1949) chaps. 9 and 10. Also, Gustav Pollaczek, The United Nations and the Specialized Agencies, American Journal of International Law, vol. 40, pp. 592-619 (July 1946).

[3] Twelve agreements have been approved by the General Assembly. An agreement was approved with the International Refugee Organization (IRO), which was established as the result of U. N. initiative in 1948. The IRO was abolished at the end of 1951. In 1948 the General Assembly approved an agreement with the Inter-Governmental Maritime Consultative Organization (IMCO), also initiated by the U. N. The IMCO Convention has not yet been ratified by the number of states required to bring it into existence.

The facts of the agreements are all published in Agreements Between the United Nations and the Specialized Agencies, U. N. Doc. ST/SG/1.

were in existence prior to the Second World War. The other six agencies—the Food and Agricultural Organization (FAO), the International Bank for Reconstruction and Development (IBRD), the International Monetary Fund (IMF), the International Civil Aviation Organization (ICAO), the United Nations Educational, Scientific and Cultural Organization (UNESCO), and the World Health Organization (WHO)—were founded during the closing years of the Second World War or shortly thereafter. One of them—the World Health Organization—was established through the initiation of negotiations by the U. N., as provided for in article 59.[4]

For the most part the specialized agencies are organized in a similar fashion. Each, however, is an independent international legal entity; each has its own membership similar to but not the same as that of the United Nations. Spain, for example, is a member of the FAO, UNESCO, WHO, and several others but not of the United Nations itself. The Soviet Union, on the other hand, has membership in the United Nations but is not a member of IBRD or the IMF and most other specialized agencies.

Each agency has its own governing body and secretariat. With two exceptions the agencies are supported by assessments on member States.[5] Their principal functions include the gathering and publishing of technical information and the furnishing of expert advice, assistance, and other services to members. They also make recommendations and develop conventions with a view to facilitating international cooperation among member states on various social, economic, and cultural matters.

The purposes of the specialized agencies are indicated by their titles and are generally spelled out in some detail in the constitutions of the organizations. The purpose of the ITU, for example, is to maintain and extend international cooperation in telecommunications and to develop the efficient operation of technical facilities. The UPU is concerned with the efficient exchange of international mails. FAO seeks to provide increased supplies of food and other agricultural products and improve the living conditions of rural peoples.

There has been some criticism of the specialized agencies in this country and in others, notably in the Soviet Union, for engaging in activities which are regarded as not properly the concern of international organizations and for duplication of functions among themselves and with the United Nations. On the other hand, many observers have pointed out that some of the functions which they perform are of great importance in the modern world. This is readily apparent and is generally recognized in the case of the UPU, which makes possible a reliable international mail service, or ICAO, which contributes to safety and efficiency of international air travel. It is less evident, and less generally accepted, in the case of some of the other specialized agencies. Nevertheless, the agencies operating in the fields of health, labor, education, agriculture, and others undoubtedly have a value to many countries. That this is the case is suggested by the extent of the membership in the agencies and by the widespread use of their facilities, particularly by the underdeveloped countries.

[4] For text of the constitutions of these organizations, see U. S. Senate Committee on Foreign Relations. A Decade of American Foreign Policy: Basic Documents, 1941–49. S. Doc. 123, 81st Cong., 1st sess., U. S. Government Printing Office, Washington, D. C., 1950.
[5] See table of specialized agencies below.

The specialized agencies

Agency	When organized	Date of United States participation	Number of members (March 1955)	Assessments on members, 1955	United States assessment	United States percent
United Nations Educational, Scientific, and Cultural Organization (UNESCO)	1945	1945	72	$9, 491, 420	$2, 847, 426	30. 00
World Health Organization (WHO)	1946	1948	84	10, 049, 360	3, 349, 790	33. 33
Food and Agriculture Organization (FAO)	1945	1945	71	5, 890, 000	1, 767, 000	30. 00
International Labor Organization (ILO)	1919	1934	70	6, 990, 913	1, 747, 729	25. 00
World Meteorological Organization (WMO)	1950	1950	87	314, 809	33, 881	10. 76
International Civil Aviation Organization (ICAO) [1]	1944	1945	65	2, 530, 260	824, 539	32. 60
International Telecommunications Union (ITU)	1934	1934	90	5, 403, 200	484, 000	8. 96
Universal Postal Union (UPU) [2]	1874	1874	93	408, 543	17, 820	4. 36
International Bank for Reconstruction and Development (IBRD)	1945	1945	56	[3]		
International Monetary Fund (IMF)	1945	1945	56	[3]		

[1] Stated in Canadian dollars.
[2] Estimate based on previous year's experience.
[3] No assessments; financed by capital subscriptions from member governments and income from operations.

The agreements entered into between the specialized agencies and the U. N. are negotiated agreements, not unilateral expressions of the U. N.'s conception of what the relationship between it and the specialized agencies ought to be.   They are essentially agreements to cooperate, and there are few instances of the surrender of any rights of decision on the part of the specialized agency to the United Nations.[6]

The agreements between the U. N. and ILO, ICAO, and FAO contain relatively more detailed provisions for cooperation than do the others, especially in administrative, technical, and financial matters.   However, with the exception of the Bank and the Fund agreements, the content in all cases is fairly similar.

In general, the provisions of the agreements fall into three categories.   One category is made up of articles providing for reciprocal arrangements, including reciprocal representation, without voting power, at meetings concerned with matters that are of interest to either organization; reciprocal proposal of agenda items; the fullest and promptest exchange of information and documents; and the furnishing of information requested by the International Court, with the right of the agencies in turn to call on the Court for advisory opinions under specified conditions.[7]

A second category of provisions in these agreements includes articles which obligate the specialized agency to take unilateral action. The agencies agree to transmit to the U. N. annual reports on their activities; to consult with the U. N. in the preparation of their budgets; to consider any recommendations made to them by the General Assembly and the Council; and to notify the U. N. of action taken on its

[6] In the case of the ICAO agreement, the General Assembly is given a veto power over an application for membership in this agency by a state that is not a signatory of the 1944 convention, a member of the U. N., or a neutral in World War II.   A similar veto is given the Economic and Social Council as to applications for membership in UNESCO by states not members of the U. N.
[7] See art. 96 (2) of the United Nations Charter.

recommendations; to cooperate with and "render assistance to" organs and suborgans of the U. N. in facilitating coordination; and to inform the Economic and Social Council of any formal interagency agreements.

A third category of articles in these agreements provides for administrative and financial cooperation. The specialized agencies "recognize that the eventual development of a unified international civil service is desirable from the standpoint of effective administrative coordination." In the meantime they agree to consult together in order to avoid competitive recruitment, and to achieve as much uniformity as possible in administrative matters. They also agree to cooperate in regard to statistical services so as to eliminate duplication. They recognize "the desirability of establishing close budgetary and financial relationships," and "shall consult together concerning the desirability of the inclusion of the budget within a general budget of the U. N." Any arrangement to this effect, however, is to be the subject of a supplementary agreement.[8]

The agreements with the two older agencies—the Universal Postal Union and the International Telecommunications Union—are briefer and more general in their terms than the others. This applies especially to the articles dealing with assistance to the organs of the U. N., personnel arrangements, administrative and technical services, and financial and budgetary arrangements. For example, in regard to financial arrangements the older organizations simply agree to transmit their budgets to the General Assembly for recommendations thereon. No mention is made of the desirability of an international civil-service board.

The agreements with the Bank and the Fund differ in significant respects from the other agreements. It is emphasized that each must function as an independent international organization. The agencies are not to be required to furnish the U. N. any information which they regard as confidential. Representation of the United Nations in the operations of the two agencies is limited to meetings of the Board of Governors, and the agencies agree merely to give due consideration to the inclusion in their agenda of items proposed by the U. N. It is reciprocally agreed not to present recommendations "without reasonable prior consultation." Furthermore, "the U. N. recognizes that the action to be taken by the Bank on any loan is a matter to be determined by the independent exercise of the Bank's own judgment," and the U. N. agrees to refrain from making recommendations with respect to any particular loan. Also, the Bank and the Fund consent to transmit quarterly financial statements, but the U. N. agrees to take into consideration that these agencies do not depend on annual contributions for their budgets, and each is to enjoy full autonomy in deciding the form and content of its budget. As regards administrative and personnel matters, the Bank and the Fund agree to consult with the U. N. in order to insure the most effective use of the services and facilities of the two organizations.

D. United Nations Structures and Procedures

The organs chiefly concerned with the coordination of the United Nations and the specialized agencies are the General Assembly, the

---

[8] There is also provision for amendment of the agreement and for authority for the Secretary-General and the director of an agency to enter into supplementary arrangements.

Economic and Social Council, and the Secretariat. The charter specifies that primary responsibility for coordination shall be vested in the Economic and Social Council, which may make recommendations to the General Assembly, the organ with ultimate responsibility. With respect to examination of the budgets of the agencies, however, the General Assembly assumes primary responsibility. The Secretariat is involved through the assistance it renders to the General Assembly and the Council in the performance of their coordinating functions, as well as in direct relationships with the secretariats of the specialized agencies.

The organization of each of these U. N. organs for the performance of its coordinating functions is given here only in barest outline.

THE GENERAL ASSEMBLY

The reports of the Economic and Social Council respecting the specialized agencies are referred to the General Assembly.[9] Generally speaking, these reports are concerned with policies and programs, although these often overlap with budgetary and administrative questions.

In carrying out its responsibility for examining the budgets of the specialized agencies, the General Assembly is assisted by an Advisory Committee on Administrative and Budgetary Questions, consisting of nine specialists serving as individuals and not as representatives of governments. The Advisory Committee examines the budgets and fiscal practices of the U. N. and the specialized agencies and makes reports and recommendations thereon at each regular session of the Assembly.

THE ECONOMIC AND SOCIAL COUNCIL

The Economic and Social Council, as previously noted, has a dual responsibility. It initiates and supervises the carrying out of social, economic, and cultural programs of the United Nations itself and it coordinates the programs and activities of the specialized agencies. In connection with the first function, it has established a large number of commissions and subcommissions, regular and temporary committees, and various other bodies.[10] Even though the chief concern of these bodies is with the U. N.'s own social and economic programs, many of them are necessarily involved to some extent in coordination with the specialized agencies. The Economic and Social Council has a Committee of the Whole to deal with questions concerning coordination with the specialized agencies.

In 1949 the Economic and Social Council made provision for what has come to be called the United Nations Expanded Technical Assistance Program.[11] This was a joint U. N.-specialized agency program, financed not out of regular assessments but from voluntary contributions. The program actually got underway in 1950.

[9] The Assembly's Second (Economic) and Third (Social, Humanitarian, and Cultural) Committees consider such reports. These Committees have at times held joint meetings because of the close inter-relationship of the social and economic problems dealt with in the Economic and Social Council reports.

[10] In 1951 an ad hoc committee made a thorough examination of the organization and operation of the Council and its commissions (United Nations, Economic and Social Council, 13th sess., U. N. Doc. E/1995). At its 13th session (1951), the Council also made several organizational changes in regard to its own agenda and the regional commissions (United Nations Bulletin, vol. 11, pp. 334, 348).

[11] U. S. Senate Committee on Foreign Relations. Subcommittee on the United Nations Charter. Review of the United Nations Charter: A Collection of Documents. S. Doc. 87, 83d Cong., 2d sess. U. S. Government Printing Office, Washington, D. C. 1954, pp. 756–764. (Hereafter referred to as Collection of Documents.)

Special coordinating machinery for this program was established in the form of a Technical Assistance Committee. This Committee was composed of the countries constituting the Economic and Social Council. Its function was to coordinate general policy. A Technical Assistance Board (TAB), composed of representatives of the participating agencies, was set up to review all project requests made by the underdeveloped countries either to the U. N. or to the specialized agencies. The TAB was also to have authority to allocate a portion of the funds voluntarily contributed to the program. Resident representatives of the Board were to act as field coordinators, but were given no authority over the staff of the participating agencies.

In the early stages the Technical Assistance Board acted on agreement of the members. Later, provision was made for an Executive Chairman of the Board, to be appointed by the Secretary-General of the United Nations. The TAB could take action through agreement between the majority of the Board and the Executive Chairman. In case of a disagreement between a majority of the Board members and the Executive Chairman, either one could refer the matter to the Technical Assistance Committee.

The influence of the Technical Assistance Committee and Technical Assistance Board goes beyond the mere making of recommendations. While operations remain the responsibility of the participating agencies, the creation of the position of resident representative, as a coordinator and spokesman in various situations, is an important experiment in closer working relations between the U. N. itself and the specialized agencies in the field.

THE SECRETARIAT

The Secretary-General is called upon from time to time by the General Assembly and the Economic and Social Council to prepare reports on problems relating to the work of the specialized agencies, and to the coordination of their policies and operations with U. N. social and economic activities. Moreover, various units of the Secretariat are continuously engaged in cooperative and consultative relationships with the secretariats of the specialized agencies.

THE ADMINISTRATIVE COMMITTEE ON COORDINATION

At its third session, the Economic and Social Council requested the Secretary-General to establish a standing committee composed of the directors of the specialized agencies and the Secretary-General of the United Nations, under the latter's chairmanship, in order to ensure implementation of the agreements entered into between the United Nations and the specialized agencies. First referred to as the Secretary-General's Committee on Coordination, this body became known in 1947 as the Administrative Committee on Coordination. It submits regular reports twice a year to the Economic and Social Council, dealing with a wide range of coordination problems. It confers on occasion with the General Assembly's Advisory Committee on Administrative and Budgetary Questions.

E. PROBLEMS AND PROPOSALS

GENERAL CONSIDERATIONS

The charter framed at San Francisco, while providing machinery for the achievement of coordination and unity of purpose between the United Nations and the specialized agencies, at the same time allows a large measure of flexibility and decentralization of responsibilities. Developments since 1945 have led to demands in some quarters for greater integration of the activities of the United Nations and the agencies. Those who hold this point of view charge that present arrangements are wasteful and duplicative. Others point out, however, that the present loose system has advantages.

It is held by some that to increase the power of the United Nations over the agencies would subject the latter to the cold war political environment of the United Nations and make more difficult the fulfillment of international economic and social objectives. The fact that the U. S. S. R. and many of the satellite nations are not members of most of the specialized agencies has made it possible to conduct programs of international social and economic development in a nonpolitical atmosphere which does not exist in the U. N. proper. It should be noted, however, that the U. S. S. R. and the satellites have now joined some of the specialized agencies and may join others at any time.

The lack of uniformity in the memberships of the United Nations and the specialized agencies, it is pointed out, is in itself an obstacle to complete integration. If the United Nations were given more power in the coordination of agency programs, nations which now do not belong to some of the agencies could nevertheless influence the policies adopted in relation to them. On the other hand, nations which are not members of the United Nations but belong to one or more of the specialized agencies would be precluded from contributing to the formulation of U. N. policies with respect thereto.

The functions and powers of the various specialized agencies, it is further contended, are defined and limited by the agreements under which they are established. It is doubtful if much support could be found for a system under which the United Nations would be given the major responsibility for directing the development of these agencies by majority or even a special vote of some kind. Then, too, not all states are interested in belonging to all agencies and it would be inequitable to compel members of the United Nations to share in the expenses attendant upon the financing of each specialized activity in a centralized system. In addition, the argument is made that the independence of the agencies tends to encourage the broadest possible participation of states in each one.

Aside from these considerations, a further argument advanced is that the administrative task of organizing under the United Nations the great variety of technical, social, and economic programs now carried on by the specialized agencies would be an extremely complex one. It is doubtful, the argument runs, that closer integration would bring with it any appreciable increase in administrative efficiency; and, even if it did, there might be a counterbalancing loss in initiative and vitality in the agencies.

Other objections to a more centralized system point to the unsuitability of the Economic and Social Council as a coordinating body. The Council is composed of a varying membership of 18 governments elected by and responsible to the General Assembly, whereas the agencies all have much larger memberships and are themselves responsible to member governments. If further integration is desired, it is argued, the Council is not the proper body through which to achieve it. That end would be better served by the creation of some autonomous agency, perhaps on the order of the Administrative Committee on Coordination.

Doubts have also been expressed about the political feasibility of tying the specialized agencies too closely with the United Nations for fear that if that organization ceased to obtain widespread support, great harm would be done to the agencies. A loose system permits the agencies to grow or decrease in importance on the basis of their own merits and usefulness in the international community.

On the other hand, it is held that the present decentralization does not sufficiently tie the specialized agencies to considerations of general U. N. policy. There may be instances where the activities of an agency operate to the detriment of the United Nations. The makers of general international policy, it is contended, should be able to exercise overall supervision of the specialized agencies since the latter do not exist in a political vacuum; they are, rather, part and parcel of the political process of international relations. Experience has shown that a general breakdown in international collaboration severely circumscribes the work of all international agencies.

The opinion is also advanced that close integration of the agencies and the United Nations would promote a more realistic appraisal of their work. The agencies depend for their effectiveness upon support of governments and such support is largely contingent upon political considerations, which find their focus in the United Nations. In practice, it is true that international politics inevitably influence the work of the agencies. It should be noted that requirements for membership do not in any instance exclude states on the basis of ideology. Communist states are free to join any of the agencies and the Soviet Union has applied for membership in the International Labor Organization and UNESCO.

Perhaps the principal argument in favor of greater centralization is that effective administration and budgetary control are difficult, if not impossible, under the present loose system of coordination. To be efficient, it is contended, international organization should represent a comprehensive, unified structure with a central authority where the power of decision resides. Under the present general organization, when gaps in activities or conflicting policies or overlapping are discovered, there is no sure process whereby issues can be resolved. Furthermore, the United Nations does not have the authority to assign to the agencies any particular task since each decides upon its own activities. Not only should the United Nations be given such authority, but the organization should also be allowed to determine the fields of responsibility of the agencies and to outline the broad programs which they carry out. If the activities or policies of the agencies conflict, the United Nations should be able to take the necessary remedial action.

Another administrative difficulty which is cited in support of centralized control lies in the perpetual temptation for each agency to seek exclusive control of all matters which could be interpreted as falling within its jurisdiction, and to be in jealous rivalry of other agencies or of the United Nations itself. In the absence of any overall control, there is the tendency for each to extend its functions and responsibilities and magnify the value and importance of its work in relation to the others.

Insofar as financial expenditures are concerned, the total budgets of the specialized agencies, which have a tendency toward expansion, present a serious problem to the smaller states, as well as to the United States. Economy, in some instances, may be the most important element upon which the survival of an agency depends. And there cannot be strict economy in a system under which administrative costs are duplicated many times over in different agencies. A strong case for unitary budgetary control is presented by the argument that the total expenses for member countries must be kept within reasonable bounds.

Much of the argument over decentralization versus centralization of the U. N. and the specialized agencies may actually be somewhat academic. The more fundamental problem may be that of national coordination and control of representatives in these various bodies. If each nation followed consistent and integrated policies in the U. N. and in the specialized agencies, the problem of coordination would in many ways solve itself. What apparently happens, instead, is that bureaucratic jurisdictional squabbles and struggles for power within the governments of the participating nations are often transferred to the international scene. On the other hand, it may be that the lack of coordination between the U. N. and the specialized agencies may itself stimulate jurisdictional dissension in the national governments.

REORGANIZATION OF THE ECONOMIC AND SOCIAL COUNCIL AS A COORDINATING BODY

As previously pointed out, the Economic and Social Council has primary responsibility both for coordinating the policies and activities of the specialized agencies and for initiating programs in economic, social, cultural, health, and related matters, fields in which some of the specialized agencies are active. Ultimate responsibility for the coordinating function, as well as for the U. N.'s own social and economic program, is vested in the General Assembly, but the charter clearly intends the Council to be the active coordinating body.

A former official of the League of Nations, who asserts that—

it is * * * generally agreed that the work of the Council and its attendant commissions has been disappointing—

believes that the Council's dual responsibility, that is, of unilateral action and coordination, is an insurmountable handicap and—

as a result ECOSOC [the Economic and Social Council] has been rendered amorphous. It is at once the cupola of 11 autonomous specialized agencies and the cupola of its own structure of committees, functional commissions, regional commissions, special boards and funds. In this shapelessness lies, I believe, a major remediable cause of its weakness.[12]

Mr. Loveday notes that in 1952—notwithstanding the fact that during the preceding year some of the Council's commissions had been

---

[12] Loveday, A. "Suggestions for the Reform of the United Nations Economic and Social Machinery," International Organization, vol. VII, pp. 325-341, at p. 326 (August 1953).

suspended—there reported to the Council 14 subcommissions and working bodies, 11 functional commissions and subcommissions, 3 regional commissions, 11 specialized agencies, and a miscellaneous group of 8 other bodies, making a grand total of 47 altogether (in addition to reports of the Secretary-General). The Council and its subcommittees held 172 meetings during the year and the Council adopted 104 resolutions. Mr. Loveday further observes that the Council was occupied most of the time with its own social and economic programs, and with the discussion of human rights. It was able to give attention only to one or two major matters of coordination, and most of its resolutions relating to the specialized agencies merely acknowledged receipt of reports. Mr. Loveday contends:

> The truth of the matter is that ECOSOC cannot reduce its agenda to reasonable proportions and become an effective body unless it sloughs altogether one or another of its functions.[13]

His proposal is that the Council should be made exclusively a coordinating body. Its social and economic functions would be transferred to a new specialized agency, to be located in Geneva, near the ILO and WHO. Some of the functions of the United Nations Secretariat with relation to social and economic affairs would also be transferred to the new agency, as would the United Nations Technical Assistance Administration. (The TAB would not be transferred.) The new agency would absorb the Council's Economic Commission for Europe and Economic Commission for Asia and the Far East, while the Economic Commission for Latin America would be brought more or less under its wing.

The proposal also would have the Human Rights Commission detached from the Council and report directly to the General Assembly. The sole remaining function of the Council, in brief, would be to coordinate the specialized agencies.

Mr. Loveday also suggests that while this proposal would not actually require any change in the United Nations Charter, it might be desirable to consider the deletion or modification of article 68 and the second section of article 62, both of which deal with the Council's functions in the field of human rights.

Other observers—though inclined to agree that the Council's mixture of functions complicates its organization, overcrowds its agenda, and results in some relative neglect of coordination problems—believe that the above proposal is too drastic. In the first place, they consider it highly unlikely that such a change would receive substantial support within the U. N. Further, they question the desirability of concentrating in a single new agency as conglomerate a group of social and economic functions as the Council is now responsible for. It would be even more difficult than it is now, it is argued, to coordinate these programs with those of the existing specialized agencies if they were to be removed bodily from the U. N. From this point of view, it is argued that it would be more desirable if some of the U. N. social and economic functions are to be transferred, to transfer a given group of functions to an agency established with a fairly specific mission.

As for the major issue, it is contended that the Council would function less well, rather than better, as a coordinating body if its own program were transferred to a new specialized agency. It is no doubt

---

[13] Ibid., p. 328.

difficult to act as the coordinator and the coordinated, as the Council now does. On the other hand, it is argued, the Council's familiarity with international economic and social cooperation derived from its own programs gives it a firmer background—and a greater leverage—for coordination than it could have if it acted solely as a coordinator. The United Nations Secretariat, too, without the experience and controls growing out of its role in administering U. N. programs would be in a less advantageous position to assist the Council and the Assembly on coordination matters. In short, it is argued, the shifting of the U. N.'s entire social and economic program out of the organization might result, not in more effective coordination, but in a marked accentuation of the tendency toward independence of action on the part of the specialized agencies.

Mr. Loveday also makes the point, as others have done, that the Council might well consider having its advisory committees composed of individuals serving in a personal capacity (not as national representatives) meeting in executive session, rather than in public. In this connection he calls attention to the Assembly's Advisory Committee on Administrative and Budgetary Questions, which appears to have performed an independent and technical service in reviewing the U. N. and specialized agency budgets.

It may be said, in concluding discussion on the appropriateness of the Economic and Social Council's present powers and the performance of its coordinating functions, that the Council itself has given consideration to its own reorganization. A 1951 reorganization, providing for the suspension of some of the functional commissions and the establishing of a Committee on Coordination, appears to have resulted in somewhat more attention being given to matters of coordination. Whether or not there is to be a drastic change in the Council's own social and economic activities, the need for further strengthening of its coordinating role is widely recognized.

SUPERVISION OF SPECIALIZED AGENCY BUDGETS

The United Nations Charter provides that the General Assembly shall examine the administrative budgets of the specialized agencies with a view to making recommendations to the agencies concerned, but gives the Assembly no actual control. The agencies (except in the case of the Bank and the Fund) have agreed to consult with the U. N. in the preparation of their budgets, and to transmit their prepared budgets to the General Assembly. In turn, representatives of the specialized agencies are permitted to participate without vote in meetings of the Assembly and any of its committees when administrative or financial questions directly involving them are being discussed. Finally, the U. N.-specialized agency agreements (except as otherwise noted) provide for consultation—

concerning the desirability of the inclusion of the budget within a general budget of the United Nations.

The General Assembly's Advisory Committee on Administrative and Budgetary Questions has conducted thorough examinations of the budgets of the specialized agencies. Although considerable progress has been made in working out uniform financial regulations and standard methods of reporting, the Advisory Committee's examinations are handicapped in many ways. The Committee has pointed out, for example, the need for more effective work by the U. N. and the secretariats of the agencies in arranging for a more uniform presentation of budgets:

> At present, a number of different budgetary conceptions prevail: While some agencies go into minute detail in explanation of their estimates, others register only titles of expenditure with little, if any, explanatory information. In consequence, the size of budget documents and the type of material contained therein is strikingly varied.[14]

The Committee is handicapped also by the fact that the governing bodies of the specialized agencies convene at different times, resulting in many instances in the submission to the U. N. of preliminary estimates rather than actual budgets at the time the General Assembly considers these matters. In most cases agency budgets have already been adopted before being considered by the U. N., so that the General Assembly's recommendations can be considered only with reference to the next budget to be adopted. The budgets of the Bank and the Fund, in accordance with the agreements with these agencies, are not even subject to examination by the Assembly.

Notwithstanding these obstacles, the examination of the budgets by the Advisory Committee of the Economic and Social Council has served a useful purpose. The Committee has not adhered to a narrow policy of examining merely the form of presentation of the budget or the adequacy of budgetary and financial procedures. It has not hesitated to examine and make comments and recommendations upon a great variety of expenditure items.[15]

The effect of the Advisory Committee's examination and the General Assembly's recommendations on administrative and budgetary matters is difficult to assess. The Committee, composed of individual experts, is apt to look at the specialized agency budgets, and at the entire problem of specialized agency coordination, with a somewhat more critical eye than, say, the Economic and Social Council, or the Secretariat. In the last analysis, however, control rests with the agencies and their only actual obligation is to report back to the Assembly what, if any, action has been taken on recommendations.

PROPOSAL FOR A CONSOLIDATED U. N.-SPECIALIZED AGENCY BUDGET

The General Assembly in its early sessions discussed the possibility of establishing a consolidated U. N.-specialized agency budget. This would involve approval of agency budgets by the General Assembly. The matter was studied in 1948 by the Administrative Committee on Coordination, which made inquiries of the agencies as to their views, and issued a report.[16] The replies of the agencies were negative. The Committee itself expressed the opinion that there would be no advantage in continuing to explore the idea of a consolidated U. N.-

[14] United Nations General Assembly, Twenty-fifth Report of the Advisory Committee on Administrative and Budgetary Questions, U. N. Doc. A/2287, December 4, 1952, p. 14.

[15] In its report to the 7th session of the General Assembly, for example, the Committee commented, often critically, on these matters among others, with reference to one or more of the agencies: agency budgeting and budget presentation of extrabudgetary (especially expanded Technical Assistance Program) funds; travel items and the need for strict agency control over them; arrears of contributions and the practice of adding to the estimates an amount equivalent to the anticipated arrears; the need for greater uniformity in the presentation of budgets; the proposal for a consolidated budget (see below); application of the Council's priority criteria (see below); administrative practice regarding cost of living adjustments; coordination of services and the Secretary-General's report thereon; conference schedules and places of meeting; location of permanent agency headquarters; uniformity in the form of the annual reports; and the use of the U. N. telecommunications system.

[16] United Nations, Economic and Social Council, First Report of the Coordination Committee, U. N. Doc. E/614, January 29, 1948, Annex V.

specialized agency budget.   It recommended instead the development of alternative methods and techniques of coordination.   It pointed out that a consolidated budget would require amendment of the constitutions of the specialized agencies; changes in the character of General Assembly delegations so as to include specialists competent to discuss specialized agency programs; the lengthening of General Assembly sessions; and the devising of arrangements to meet the difficulty that the U. N. and the specialized agencies do not have the same membership.   It appeared to the Committee that it would be more practicable to try to achieve coordination without going to these lengths.[17]

Strong disagreement with the 1948 stand of the Administrative Committee on Coordination was expressed in a report prepared by the Senate Expenditures Committee's Subcommittee on Relations with International Organizations:

The subcommittee cannot agree with the conclusions of the Administrative Committee on Coordination.   It is true that there are obstacles.   However, given the will to cure existing weaknesses and achieve substantial economy, efficiency, and conservation of resources, a consolidated budget system can be adopted. Since the majority of the member governments of the agencies are also members of the United Nations, no sound reason appears to exist for their failure to amend the constitutions of these agencies.   With respect to program coordination being basic to budgetary coordination, the subcommittee is of the opinion they are intertwined inseparably, with one dependent upon the other.   If effective budgetary coordination is achieved, effective program and project coordination will follow.   There appears to be no good reason why necessary changes could not be made in the character of General Assembly delegations and provision could easily be made for lengthening the session of the Assembly.   With respect to the problems presented by divergent membership in the United Nations and the specialized agencies, procedures could easily be worked out whereby the section of the budget relating to each specialized agency would be initially voted in the General Assembly only by those member governments which are members of that agency.   Thus, when the Fifth Committee of the General Assembly is dealing with the budgets of the specialized agencies, members of the United Nations which are not members of a particular agency would not participate in the consideration of the budget of that agency.   Arrangements can also be worked out whereby members of specialized agencies which are not members of the United Nations would be able to debate and vote on the budgets of those specialized agencies to which they belong.   Arrangements of this kind between the International Labor Organization and the League of Nations have proved to be satisfactory.   Finally, following such initial action on the budget of each agency, the consolidated budget of the United Nations and the agencies included therein could then be approved by the General Assembly in plenary session.[18]

The adequacy of U. N. supervision of budgets of the specialized agencies under article 17 (3) of the charter and under the provisions of the existing agency agreements will no doubt continue to be debated.   The issue is crucial to the status of the agencies, which are well aware of the implications of budgetary control not merely for form and adequacy of budgetary presentation, and for provision of administrative services, but also for control of their programs.   In

---

[17] The issue was raised again by the General Assembly at its sixth session, when the Secretary-General and the Advisory Committee on Administrative and Budgetary Questions were asked to give attention to the matter.   The Advisory Committee reported that the Administrative Committee on Coordination was still of its earlier opinion, and that after consultation with the Secretary-General it had come to the conclusion that it would be premature to place the matter before the seventh session of the General Assembly for discussion.   The Advisory Committee added that it—
"proposes to keep the question under continuous review and, after consulting with the Secretary-General, it will at an appropriate time make recommendations to the Assembly."
Finally, the Committee sounded this note:
"* * * the long-term view of member states on the advantages of comprehensive budgeting will be largely influenced, and indeed may be determined, by the position taken by the executive heads of the United Nations and the specialized agencies in respect to common services and the coordination of services."
United Nations, General Assembly, Twenty-fifth Report of the Advisory Committee on Administrative and Budgetary Questions (cited in note 14), p. 16.
[18] U. S. Senate Committee on Expenditures in the Executive Departments, Subcommittee on Relations With International Organizations.   S. Rept. 90, pt. V, 1951, pp. 55-56.

fact, one of the chief arguments for a consolidated budget is that it would be one way of effecting, or at least of encouraging, coordination and central control of the policies and programs of the agencies.   Any proposal to strengthen article 17 (3) of the United Nations Charter, whether by formal amendment or by U. N.-specialized agency agreement, must expect to meet with firm resistance from advocates of a highly decentralized system.

U. N. COORDINATION OF POLICIES AND PROGRAMS OF SPECIALIZED AGENCIES

The problem of coordinating the policies and programs of the specialized agencies is in part that of preventing overlapping and duplication.   More positively, however, it is the problem of so relating programs from year to year that the total effort of the U. N. and the agencies in the social and economic fields yields maximum results toward the achievement of goals set by the charter.   It is not enough that the U. N. and the agencies do not carry on the same programs or projects; it would seem equally essential that the programs of each agency be designed to fit into a general pattern, in accordance with a carefully worked out system of priorities.   It is also partly a problem of fixing responsibility.   Ambassador Lodge, for example, has pointed out that—

* * * speaking frankly and realistically, the specialized agencies are, for practical purposes, independent.   In past years, for example, the publicity coming from one specialized agency had a significant and understandably irritating effect on a sizable number of Americans, with reactions which damaged the United Nations proper and which prejudiced some of the fine work actually being done by the specialized agencies * * *.   That is the principal objection.   It isn't to the United Nations itself.   It is notably to ill-advised publicity which has come out of one of these specialized agencies in previous years.[19]

For the elimination of duplicating programs, the U. N. and the specialized agencies have adopted a number of devices and arrangements, including an annual catalog of projects, agreements concerning distribution of responsibilities, and numerous working agreements and consultations.

At its 11th session (1950) the Economic and Social Council adopted a set of criteria intended to provide for the U. N. and its agencies a common approach to the valuation of priorities between programs within a particular field of work and between projects within those programs.   In 1952, at its 14th session, the Council drew up a list of six major social and economic programs, and of contributory programs, upon which it suggested that the U. N. and the agencies might concentrate their efforts.[20]   The Council simply listed these subjects; no attempt was made to indicate an order of importance among the six fields, or among the contributory programs.

The General Assembly has several times considered the possibility of the establishment of an overall system of priorities, including an order of relative importance.   No generally accepted solution has been reached.   In the meantime, the Advisory Committee has notified the specialized agencies that in examining their budgets it would give special attention to seeing whether their programs are properly integrated for work of primary importance, and whether due regard has been given to relative priorities within programs, and to the application of the criteria of the Council and Advisory Committee.   The

[19] U. S. Senate Committee on Foreign Relations, Subcommittee on the United Nations Charter, Review of the United Nations Charter.   Hearings, pt. 1, 1954, p. 39.
[20] Collection of Documents, pp. 769–777.

Committee interprets its own jurisdiction as regards program matters and priorities in the following words:

> The Committee emphasized that, while not claiming authority to deal with matters of policy as such, in connection with the substance of proposed programmes, it does regard itself as competent to deal with the financial implications of such matters and with possible repercussions on the total expenditure of the United Nations and the specialized agencies.[21]

The report of the Senate Expenditures Subcommittee on International Organizations expresses the view that the U. N. should have at least enforcement powers with respect to the application by the agencies of U. N. priority criteria, unless a consolidated budget should be adopted:

> Although it would require amendment of the constitutions of the specialized agencies to empower the United Nations to enforce criteria with respect to their projects, such action should ultimately be taken, if coordinated work programs are to be used for the greatest good of the greatest number.[22]

While it may be expected that increasing attention will be paid to the development of a system of priorities with an order of importance indicated, it is altogether likely that any proposal to confer enforcement authority on the U. N. will meet with strong opposition, as in the case of the proposal for a consolidated budget.

PROPOSALS AFFECTING THE EXPANDED TECHNICAL ASSISTANCE PROGRAM

The expanded Technical Assistance Program furnishes at once the most striking illustration of U. N.-specialized agency coordination on a large scale, and the difficulties involved in effecting such coordination. The centralizing features of the program have met with considerable resistance. This is illustrated by recent developments concerning the allocation of funds. Funds for the program come from voluntary contributions of United Nations member states and other states as well. Under the original resolution setting up the program, the first $10 million of these funds was to be allocated to the participating agencies on the basis of specified ratios. The second $10 million was to be divided in the following way: 70 percent was to be allocated automatically in the same ratios as the first $10 million, while the remaining 30 percent was to be allocated in such manner as the Technical Assistance Board of the Economic and Social Council might decide. Later the method of allocation was changed so that the first $10 million was to be allocated on an automatic basis, the balance being subject to allocation by TAB.

At the 16th session of the Council in the summer of 1953, the decision was made to allocate 75 percent of the funds automatically according to the established ratios, leaving only 25 percent to be allocated by the TAB. In a major reversal the Council decided (in July 1954) that from 1955 on funds would no longer be allocated in accordance with percentages fixed in advance but would be distributed on the basis of requests submitted by governments and established priorities. The Technical Assistance Committee will authorize the allocations, after review of an overall program drawn up by the Technical Assistance Board. In order to avoid major fluctuations in the total amounts earmarked for each of the participating organizations from year to year,

---

[21] United Nations, General Assembly, Twenty-fifth Report of the Advisory Committee on Administrative and Budgetary Questions (cited in note 14), p. 17.

[22] U. S. Senate Committee on Expenditures in the Executive Departments, Subcommittee on Relations With International Organizations (cited in note 18), p. 42.

the allocations to each will be not less than 85 percent of what it was for the preceding year, or proportional amounts depending on the funds available.

The agencies have objected to TAB review of programs, especially since institution of provision for an Executive Chairman and for the majority principle in decision-making. Moreover, they have shown considerable concern over the appointment of resident representatives of the U. N. in the field.

The arguments against a centralized program are chiefly that the technical agencies are the best judges of their own programs and that a nontechnical TAB review is not useful; that the resident represent-atives may create unfortunate barriers between technical agency personnel and officials of the underdeveloped nations being assisted; that the administrative costs of TAB and the resident representatives absorb an undue proportion of the program's funds (approximately 5½ percent of a total of $25,300,000 during the last fiscal period); that TAB allocation involves delays and uncertainties, thereby impairing essential planning; and that the distinction between technical assist-ance performed as part of the agency's regular work and the expanded program prevents the full integration by the participating agencies of their technical assistance programs.

Those who support the TAB position, on the other hand, insist that a centralized review is essential to a balanced program including health, agricultural, educational, and other aspects; that resident representa-tives are needed in the field to act as points of contact with officials of the countries being assisted, as well as with officials in charge of the United States and other bilateral technical assistance programs; that the proportion of funds devoted to administrative costs can be greatly reduced if the total funds for the program are enlarged, since the exist-ing arrangement could administer a much larger program; and that such delays and other disadvantages as may result from TAB review of programs or allocations of funds are of minor consequence as com-pared to the benefits of centralized planning and control. To the argument that the distinction between regular and expanded agency technical assistance work is in part an unreal and awkward arrange-ment, the advocates of centralized control reply that the expanded program should not be turned over to the agencies because it would reduce the desired U. N. emphasis on the development of under-developed areas and eliminate the gains that have resulted from voluntary financing, unified direction, and interagency coordination.

Criticism of the plan is not confined to those who dislike its central-ized features. It is generally considered that the administrative costs are high and that proper field coordination is difficult to obtain. The smaller specialized agencies especially do not find it easy to delegate planning responsibility to field officers, and yet the resident repre-sentatives have no line authority, being able only to coordinate and negotiate. Finally, even those sympathetic with central control of programing are not altogether satisfied with TAB as a control body. It has been proposed, for example, that an intergovernmental com-mittee should replace TAB, on the grounds that control should be vested in the governments rather than in representatives of the agencies.

F. Concluding Comments

Secretary of State Dulles has spoken of the "inadequate control" exercised by the United Nations over the specialized agencies. Ambassador Lodge supported this position by noting that for practical purposes the specialized agencies are "independent."

These tentative conclusions are consistent with those reached by a Senate subcommittee in 1951 which spoke of agreements between the United Nations and the specialized agencies as "merely agreements to cooperate and nothing more," and urged closer integration as among the agencies themselves and between the agencies and the United Nations.[23]

Despite these criticisms, it should be recognized that the specialized agencies were intentionally given a considerable degree of autonomy. The existence of that status has enabled many of them to carry on operations in spite of the cold war stalemate which has hampered United Nations operations in some fields. It should also be recognized that the United Nations as an organization, and the United Nations acting through its individual members, has within it the means of remedying many of the shortcomings that have developed in recent years with respect to coordination of activities and the planning of specialized agency budgets.

Two opposing tendencies are at work with respect to the relations of the United Nations organization and the specialized agencies. One leads in the direction of greater centralization of programing, administrative, and budgetary responsibilities. The other seeks to maintain the independence of the agencies in all essential respects. Although efforts have been made to develop effective coordination, results so far have left much to be desired.

Suggestions have been advanced for important changes in United Nations-specialized agencies coordinating machinery, either with or without charter amendment. At the same time it has been pointed out that more adequate coordination could in all probability be achieved if members of the United Nations, which form a majority in all specialized agencies, followed consistent policies to advance this end.

Exploration of the possibilities of establishing a consolidated budget for the United Nations and the specialized agencies leads to the conclusion held more or less generally that control of the budget would mean in large measure control of policies and programing—in effect, a centralized authority with all its advantages and disadvantages. Advocates of a decentralized system can be expected to resist any moves to strengthen United Nations' power over agency budgets, by amendment of the charter or the constitutions of the specialized agencies, or by changes in the U. N.-specialized agencies agreements. Similarly, proposals that the United Nations be empowered to enforce criteria leading to the coordination of programs would meet with opposition from the same sources.

In general, the United Nations and the agencies have taken some steps to develop cooperation through interagency consultations and agreements rather than seeking improvement through organizational changes. It is evident that much more still can be done in this direction within the existing framework. In fact, solution of many of the problems of coordination of the specialized agencies with the United Nations may be primarily dependent on the insistence of the participating nations that their representatives in the various specialized agencies and in the United Nations support coordinated national policies, rather than on the more drastic remedy of charter revision.

---

[23] U. S. Senate Committee on Expenditures in the Executive Departments, Subcommittee on Relations With International Organizations (cited in note 18).

HUMAN RIGHTS, DOMESTIC JURISDICTION, AND THE UNITED NATIONS CHARTER

STAFF STUDY NO. 11

OCTOBER 24, 1955

PREFACE

By Walter F. George, *Chairman*

This staff study concerns one of the most controversial areas of
United Nations' activities. It sets forth in an objective manner the
principles and practices of the United Nations in dealing with the
subject of human rights, describes some of the questions that have
arisen in the United States with respect to this subject, and presents
some of the proposals that have been made for charter changes.

The charter affirms the faith of the peoples of the United Nations
in—

fundamental human rights, in the dignity and worth of the human person, in the
equal rights of men and women and of nations large and small * * *.

Few would disagree with this statement. Difficulties have arisen,
however, relating to the extent to which the United Nations might
encourage the promotion of these principles within member states.
The fact that members of the United Nations differ so greatly in
custom, history, religion, and their attitudes toward the individual
raises profound questions as to the degree to which there can be
fundamental agreement on what is encompassed by the subject of
human rights. Indeed, in a country such as our own, whose Constitution embodies concepts of individual freedom which go far beyond
those that exist in many countries of the world, the very suggestion
that there is an international obligation to promote human rights
arouses certain fears; for if human rights are inalienable rights of
people as we believe, then responsibilities assumed by international
organizations must be clearly defined to avoid any implication of
international authority to impair those rights.

This study was prepared by Mary Shepard, Foreign Affairs Division,
Legislative Reference Service, Library of Congress, under the direction of the subcommittee staff. It does not necessarily reflect the
views of the Subcommittee on the United Nations Charter.

OCTOBER 24, 1955.   305

CONTENTS

HUMAN RIGHTS, DOMESTIC JURISDICTION, AND THE UNITED NATIONS CHARTER

A. Introduction

On January 1, 1942, the Allied Nations issued a declaration of unity which expressed the conviction that victory was essential—

to defend life, liberty, independence, and religious freedom, and to preserve human rights and justice in their own lands as well as in other lands * * *.[1]

After the war the common policy of the Western Allied Governments was to promote observance of these rights, seeking where possible to incorporate guaranties in binding instruments, national and international. The Constitution of Japan and constitutions of the constituent states of Western Germany, for example, bear the imprint of this policy. The peace treaties with the ex-enemy states in Europe contain clauses on human rights, inserted at the instance of the Allies. For example, under the Rumanian treaty that state undertakes:

* * * to secure to all persons * * * the enjoyment of human rights and of fundamental freedoms, including freedom of expression, of press and publication, of religious worship, of political opinion, and of public meeting.[2]

Increasing doubts as to the wisdom of imposed obligations, caused in part by violation of the treaties by the Communist satellite countries, resulted in the omission of a similar clause from the Japanese Peace Treaty, and the substitution instead of a pledge by Japan—

to strive to realize the objectives of the Universal Declaration of Human Rights.

Indicative of this change in attitude were the remarks of John Foster Dulles, the principal negotiator of the treaty for the United States: [3]

Human rights should have their primary sanction in community will and when treaties ignore that, and try to substitute an alien will, the treaties themselves usually collapse through disrespect, dragging down the whole structure of international law, order, and justice.

Embodied in the United Nations Charter is the concept that observance of human rights is a proper subject of international concern. Under the charter, the United Nations is authorized to promote such observance. No attempt is made to spell out the meaning of fundamental human rights in the charter [4] aside from what may be deduced from the qualification that they shall be promoted without discriminations relating to "race, sex, language, or religion." Nor is any distinction made between those rights whose repression would result in a threat to the peace and others whose observance

---

[1] U. S. Congress. Senate. Review of the United Nations Charter: A Collection of Documents. Doc. No. 87, Jan. 7, 1954, p. 38. Hereinafter referred to as Collection of Documents.
[2] U. S. Department of State. Treaty of Peace With Rumania. Publication No. 2769, 1947, p. 45.
[3] Quoted in U. S. Congress. Senate. Committee on the Judiciary. Treaties and Executive Agreements. Hearings, 1953, p. 863. Hereinafter referred to as 1953 Hearings.
[4] At one time the United States considered inserting specific mention of freedom of information and of religion in the proposed charter. See U. S. Department of State. Postwar Foreign Policy Preparation, 1949, p. 386.

may be necessary for the full development of the human personality but are not necessarily essential to the preservation of peace.[5]

In giving effect to the human rights provisions of the charter, the United Nations has engaged in a wide range of activities. It has, for example, set up commissions to give special attention to human rights and the status of women, and subcommissions on freedom of information and of the press, and the prevention of discrimination and protection of minorities. It has issued reviews and reports and initiated studies of forced labor, slavery, and trade-union rights. Moreover, the General Assembly has passed resolutions calling attention to conditions which have allegedly involved violations of human rights.

The charter contains no provisions, however, giving the United Nations authority to take positive action in this field in the absence of a breach of, or threat to, international peace. On the contrary, it specifies that the Organization shall not intervene in matters essentially within the domestic jurisdiction of any state unless there is a threat to the peace. This has meant that those who want to move beyond the recommendatory realm in the promotion of human rights have sought either to interpret existing charter provisions as having compulsive legal force within member states, or to encourage the negotiation and conclusion of treaties which might have that effect. It is these attempts to interpret the charter broadly or to negotiate conventions relating to human rights that have given rise in the United States to concern that internationally determined human rights may have an impact on the United States Constitution that would go beyond the intent of the United States Government in approving the charter.

It is the purpose of this study to examine the provisions of the charter relating to human rights, to see how those provisions have been given effect, to review the impact of United Nations human rights activities upon the domestic jurisdiction clause of the charter and upon attitudes in the United States toward the United Nations, and to consider proposals to change the charter provisions concerning human rights.

B. Human Rights Provisions of the Charter

Various articles of the charter authorize the United Nations to study, debate, establish subsidiary organs, recommend, draft conventions, and call conferences for various objectives, including the promotion of the observance of human rights. The member states are pledged to act in cooperation with the Organization in achieving this purpose. There is the general limitation on the Organization, however, that it cannot "intervene" in matters "essentially within the domestic jurisdiction" of any state although it may take action to enforce the peace regardless of considerations of domestic jurisdiction.

The first reference to human rights in the charter is in the preamble. Then in the main body of the document one of the purposes of the Organization is stated to be (art. 1, par. 3):

* * * To achieve international cooperation * * * in promoting and encouraging respect for human rights and for fundamental freedoms for all without distinction as to race, sex, language, or religion.

[5] Marian Neal. The United Nations and Human Rights, 1953, p. 116.

The General Assembly is made responsible for initiating studies and making recommendations to assist—

in the realization of human rights and fundamental freedoms for all without distinction as to race, sex, language, or religion (art. 13, par. 1).

As part of a program for international economic and social cooperation, the United Nations is charged with promoting observance of human rights and freedoms, in order to create conditions "necessary for peaceful and friendly relations among nations." Article 55, which sets out this program, reads:

With a view to the creation of conditions of stability and well-being which are necessary for peaceful and friendly relations among nations based on respect for the principle of equal rights and self-determination of peoples, the United Nations shall promote:
> (a) higher standards of living, full employment, and conditions of economic and social progress and development;
> (b) solutions of international economic, social, health, and related problems; and international cultural and educational cooperation; and
> (c) universal respect for, and observance of, human rights and fundamental freedoms for all without distinction as to race, sex, language, or religion.

Article 56, whose interpretation has aroused much conflicting opinion, reads as follows:

All members pledge themselves to take joint and separate action in cooperation with the Organization for the achievement of the purposes set forth in article 55.

Responsibility for discharging the functions outlined in articles 55 and 56 is vested in the General Assembly, and, under the authority of the Assembly, in the Economic and Social Council (art. 60). The Council is empowered to—

make recommendations for promoting respect for, and observance of, human rights and fundamental freedoms for all (art. 62, par. 2).

The charter specifically provides for the establishment of a Commission on Human Rights under the Council (art. 68) and also calls for the encouraging of respect for human rights and fundamental freedoms as a basic objective of the trusteeship system (art. 76).

Various proposals were made at the San Francisco Conference to provide for guaranties of human rights, both by the Organization itself and by the member states, but none was adopted. A Panamanian proposal, for example, to amend article 1, paragraph 3 (above p. 2) to read—

promotion and *protection* of human rights and fundamental freedoms—

was resisted with the objection that this would raise the—

question as to whether or not the Organization should actively impose human rights and fundamental freedoms within individual countries and that this would lead many people to expect more of the Organization that it could successfully accomplish.[6]

The prevalent view in 1945, as brought out in one report, seemed to be that assuring or protecting human rights was primarily the concern of each state

unless such rights and freedoms were grievously outraged so as to create conditions which threaten peace, or obstruct the application of the provisions of the charter, then they cease to be the sole concern of each state.[7]

[6] Quoted in Jacob Robinson. Human Rights and Fundamental Freedoms in the Charter of the United Nations. 1946, p. 36.
[7] United Nations Conference on International Organization: Selected Documents. Department of State Publication 2490, 1946, p. 483.

It was also anticipated at the time that after the Organization was established steps would be taken to draft an international bill of rights.[8]

Although there is no definition of human rights and freedoms in the charter beyond the qualification of nondiscriminatory treatment, it is argued by some that the concept to some extent has been made explicit by the Universal Declaration of Human Rights, drafted in the United Nations and approved by the General Assembly in 1948.[9] But the declaration was not formulated as an amendment of the charter and has no legal validity as a definition. It does indicate something of a consensus among nations as to what those rights are. This is not to imply that the expression, "human rights," is without meaning. But the concept is elastic and can mean many things to many people.[10]

Sharp differences of opinion have arisen over the extent of obligations imposed by the charter and on the limiting effect of the domestic jurisdiction clause on activities by the Organization in this field. The Assembly has upon occasion held that specific actions, such as systems of forced labor, or unfavorable treatment of wives of foreign nationals (by the Soviet Union) were in contravention of the human rights provisions of the charter.[11] The Union of South Africa, subjected to charges of violations of human rights for its racial policies and to resolutions of criticism, has repeatedly protested that the United Nations has no proper concern in these matters of domestic jurisdiction.[12] Despite Communist-bloc protests alleging intervention in internal affairs, the United States has joined with other nations in the U. N. in accusing Bulgaria, Hungary, and Rumania of suppressing human rights.

C. HUMAN RIGHTS ARTICLES AND THE UNITED STATES CONSTITUTION

The view has been advanced in the United States that certain charter provisions relating to human rights have the effect of changing national laws which may be inconsistent with those provisions. This issue was given impetus by a court action in California which related to the alien land law of that State. In *Sei Fujii* v. *California* [13] a California district court of appeals held in 1950 that the California alien land law was invalid under the United Nations Charter. Two years later the Supreme Court of California, on appeal, affirmed the decision holding the land law invalid. In so doing, however, the court relied on the equal protection clause of the 14th amendment of the United States Constitution instead of on the provisions of the charter.[14] In other words, although the California Supreme Court rejected the argument of the district court as to the applicability of the United Nations Charter, it reached the same conclusion by basing its decision on a provision that had been in the United States Constitution for 80 years.

The interest generated by the Sei Fujii case was due not so much to the substance of the decisions, however, as it was to the constitutional

---

[8] Ibid., pp. 483 and 496.
[9] For text, see Collection of Documents, p. 247.
[10] In this connection see UNESCO. Human Rights: Comments and Interpretations, A Symposium. Allan Wingate. New York, 1950.
[11] Collection of Documents, p. 285.
[12] Ibid., pp. 283, 285. See also pp. 532, 533.
[13] Collection of Documents, p. 288.
[14] This clause reads: "No state shall make or enforce any law which shall abridge the privileges or immunities of citizens of the United States; nor shall any state deprive any person of life, liberty, or property without due process of law; nor deny to any person within its jurisdiction the equal protection of the laws."

and charter issues involved.   The California district court of appeals had reasoned that:

The charter has become "the supreme law of the land, and the judges in every State shall be bound thereby, anything in the constitution or laws of any State to the contrary notwithstanding." (United States Constitution, art. VI, sec. 2.) * * * This Nation can be true to its pledge to the other signatories to the charter only by cooperating in the purposes that are so plainly expressed in it and by removing every obstacle to the fulfillment of such purposes * * *. A perusal of the charter renders it manifest that restrictions contained in the alien land law are in direct conflict with the plain terms of the charter * * * and with the purposes announced therein by its framers. * * * Clearly such a discrimination against a people of one race is contrary both to the letter and to the spirit of the charter, which, as a treaty, is paramount to every law of every State in conflict with it. The alien land law must therefore yield to the treaty as the superior authority.

In contradicting this argument, the California Supreme Court held that a treaty does not automatically supersede local laws which are inconsistent with it unless the treaty provisions are self-executing. The court found that none of the relevant provisions of the charter were self-executing. The preamble and article 1, the court held—

* * * state general purposes and objectives of the United Nations organizations and do not purport to impose legal obligations on the individual member nations or to create rights in private persons.

As for articles 55 and 56 of the charter, the court reasoned that—

* * * although the member nations have obligated themselves to cooperate with the international organization in promoting respect for, and observance of, human rights, it is plain that it was contemplated that future legislative action by the several nations would be required to accomplish the declared objectives, and there is nothing to indicate that these provisions were intended to become rules of law for the courts of this country upon the ratification of the charter * * *. The provisions of the charter pledging cooperation in promoting observance of fundamental freedoms lack the mandatory quality and definiteness which would indicate an intent to create justiciable rights in private persons immediately upon ratification.   Instead, they are framed as a promise of future action by the member nations * * *.   The charter represents a moral commitment of foremost importance, and we must not permit the spirit of our pledge to be compromised or disparaged in either our domestic or foreign affairs.   We are satisfied, however, that the charter provisions relied on by plaintiff were not intended to supersede existing domestic legislation, and we cannot hold that they operate to invalidate the alien land law.

In a more recent instance, where a plaintiff in Iowa complained of a violation of the Iowa and United States Constitutions, as well as the United Nations Charter, in being denied rights of burial because of race, the Iowa courts ruled that the provisions of the United Nations Charter had no bearing on the case.[15]

The differences revolved around the meaning of the charter articles.[16] Article 55 provides that—

* * * the United Nations shall promote * * * universal respect for, and observance of, human rights and fundamental freedoms. * * *

and so does not impose any specific obligations on a member of the organization.   A number of interpretations, however, can be placed upon the language of article 56 in which member nations have—

* * * pledged themselves to take joint and separate action in cooperation with the Organization for the achievement of the purposes set forth in article 55.

[15] 349 U. S. 70.
[16] For references to these articles in the debate on constitutional amendment, see Collection of Documents, pp. 308–310, 314.

At the San Francisco Conference there was no generally agreed-upon explanation of the meaning of article 56. In view of this fact, it would seem that considerable latitude is left to each member state to follow its own interpretation, particularly insofar as its own domestic law is concerned. Of relevance in these circumstances is the official commentary of the Secretary of State contained in the report transmitted to the Senate at the time the charter was submitted for approval: [17]

* * * The United States delegation deemed it perfectly appropriate for the member states to pledge themselves to cooperate with the Organization for the achievement of these (economic and social) purposes.

On the other hand, the view was advanced that the further element in the Australian proposal [18] calling for national action separate from the international organization went beyond the proper scope of the charter of an international organization and possibly even infringed on the domestic jurisdiction of member states in committing them to a particular philosophy of the relationship between the government and the individual.

The pledge as finally adopted was worded to eliminate such possible interpretation. It pledges the various countries to cooperate with the Organization by joint and separate action in the achievement of the economic and social objectives of the Organization without infringing upon their right to order their national affairs according to their own best ability, in their own way, and in accordance with their own political and economic institutions and processes.

In an earlier case in the United States Supreme Court [19] four Justices expressed the view that account should be taken in decisions on human rights of the policy affirmed in the United Nations Charter. It should be noted, however, that the charter provisions were not controlling in that opinion.

The present United States Attorney General has advanced the view that although there is an obligation on members of the United Nations to "promote" the economic and social purposes of the charter and "to take joint and separate action" for their achievement, there are doubts as to whether articles 55 and 56 could have internal effect, and, at any rate, their terms prevent them from being self-executing. In commenting on the domestic implementation of treaties he has stated that in some cases:

* * * the treaty as drafted, may stipulate or require that it be regarded as not self-executing. If its implementation requires appropriations or criminal sanctions or similar domestic legislation, it will necessarily depend on legislation passed by both Houses. In other situations, where the treaty might have internal effect, its terms may prevent it from being self-executing. A notable example is articles 55 and 56 of the United Nations Charter, obligating the parties to "promote" stated social and economic objectives and pledging themselves "to take joint and separate action" for the achievement of these purposes. Recently, the California Supreme Court held these provisions were non-self-executing.[20]

Writers on the subject have advanced varying interpretations. An analysis made by Goodrich and Hambro weighs most of the relevant factors: [21]

The phraseology agreed to [in art. 56] was a compromise and like most compromises is capable of more than one interpretation. The question arises with respect to the significance of the qualifying words. "In cooperation with the Organiza-

[17] Report to the President on the Results of the San Francisco Conference. Department of State Publication 2349, June 26, 1945, p. 115. Hereinafter referred to as Report to the President.

[18] At the San Francisco conference Australia had wanted article 56 to pledge all members to undertake "to take separate and joint action and to cooperate with the Organization and with each other" to achieve the purposes of acticle 55.

[19] *Oyama* v. *California* (1948), 332 U. S. 633, 673 (1948).

[20] 1953 hearings, p. 922.

[21] Goodrich and Hambro. The Charter of the United Nations. Boston, World Peace Foundation, 1949, pp. 323–324.

tion" presumably refers to the Organization as a separate entity functioning through the appropriate organs and not to its individual members; otherwise "joint and separate action in cooperation with the Organization" becomes repetitious. If this is the proper interpretation, it would then appear that members pledge themselves not only to cooperate with each other, but also to cooperate with the appropriate organs of the United Nations with a view to achieving the purposes in question. It does not mean that recommendations of those organs become binding, but it does obligate members to refrain from obstructionist acts and to cooperate in good faith in the achievement of the purposes of article 55.

D. DRAFTING HUMAN RIGHTS TREATIES

As has been noted, the promotion of human rights by the United Nations has taken a variety of forms such as the adoption of the declaration on human rights, and the creation of special study groups. In addition, the Organization has engaged in the preparation of draft treaties on genocide, civil and political rights, economic, social and cultural rights, freedom of information, the political rights of women, and other subjects. For the past several years there has been concern in the United States not only over the possible impact of human rights charter provisions on domestic law, but also over the activities of the United Nations in drafting human rights treaties and United States participation in the process. The negotiation of these treaties probably has aroused greater apprehension among Members of Congress and various legal and other circles in this country than other types of United Nations activities in the human rights field. It is held in some quarters that the United Nations has gone beyond the proper limits of its authority in drafting treaties on human rights.

A number of these treaties, it is further contended, contain clauses which would, if they were ratified by the United States, be in conflict with the constitutional provisions safeguarding human rights. Moreover, it is asserted, they would transform some matters now solely within the national jurisdiction into matters of international concern; would move in the direction of transferring some national powers to international authorities; and would result in the sharing of some powers traditionally reserved to the States with the Federal Government or with international authorities.

The problems which have been brought into focus by the drafting of the human rights treaties go beyond the treaties themselves. As the debate on a United States constitutional amendment during the 83d Congress revealed, they involve the larger issue of the relationship between the Constitution and an evolving international legal system, represented principally by the United Nations and its related agencies.

The functions of the United Nations in the economic and social field, including the drafting of human rights treaties as previously pointed out, are exercised by the General Assembly, and under its authority by the 18-nation Economic and Social Council which it elects. Not only does the charter authorize the General Assembly to make—

recommendations for the purpose of * * * encouraging the progressive development of international law and its codification (art. 13)—

but the Economic and Social Council may—

prepare draft conventions for submission to the General Assembly, with respect to matters within its competence * * * call, in accordance with the rules prescribed by the United Nations, international conferences on matters falling within its competence (art. 62, pars. 3, 4).

These provisions relating to economic and social activity are more extensive than those provided in the Covenant of the League of Nations. In the League, members were called on to secure fair conditions of labor and to entrust the League with supervision over the execution of agreements with regard to the narcotics traffic. The broad aims found in the United Nations Charter, however, such as the promotion of human rights and the attainment of higher standards of living, were not mentioned in the covenant.[22]

Nevertheless, under the League there was considerable international cooperation in the economic and social fields. Nearly 100 international agreements were concluded under League auspices in its first 15 years.[23] Included among these were several conventions on such matters as the status of refugees and the manufacture, regulation, and distribution of narcotic drugs.

Although the Charter of the United Nations does not specifically authorize the General Assembly to propose conventions for ratification by member states, the Assembly under article 10 can make recommendations to the members of the United Nations on any matter within the scope of the charter.[24] Furthermore, article 13 authorizes the Assembly to make recommendations for the purpose of promoting international cooperation in the economic and social fields.[25] In practice, the Assembly has proposed conventions for ratification. No obligation rests on member states to ratify such conventions although as members they may participate in the drafting initiated in the appropriate organs.

A number of procedures may be used in preparing draft conventions. The International Law Commission was established by the Assembly to help in codifying and developing international law and it may submit drafts to the Assembly. The Economic and Social Council and its subsidiary bodies can also prepare drafts for General Assembly consideration. International conferences may be called, either to draft conventions for further consideration by the United Nations, to draft and consider conventions independently, or to consider conventions already drafted in the United Nations. Such conferences need not, and often do not, include the entire membership of the United Nations (and may include nonmembers); nor is it necessary for the draft treaties agreed upon at them to be forwarded to the General Assembly.

In practice, the International Law Commission of the United Nations has drafted few conventions. The principal human rights treaties have been drafted by the Assembly and the Economic and Social Council working together, in one instance with the help of a U. N. sponsored international conference. At least two of the lesser treaties have been drafted in final form and opened for signature by

[22] Cheever, Daniel S., and H. Field Haviland, Jr. Organizing for Peace. Boston, Houghton Mifflin, 1954, p. 69.
[23] Myers, Denys P. Handbook of the League of Nations. Boston, World Peace Foundation, 1935, p. 249.
[24] With one exception, relating to peace and security functions.
[25] At the San Francisco Conference the Belgian and Australian delegations wanted to insert in the charter a provision which would have authorized the General Assembly to "submit general conventions for the consideration of states * * * with a view to securing their approval with appropriate constitutional procedures." Later the amendment was withdrawn with the explanation by the Australian delegate that since the powers of the Assembly had been expanded under art. 10 so that it could make recommendations directly to the members of the United Nations in relation to anything covered by the charter, he was satisfied that the problem had been properly taken care of.

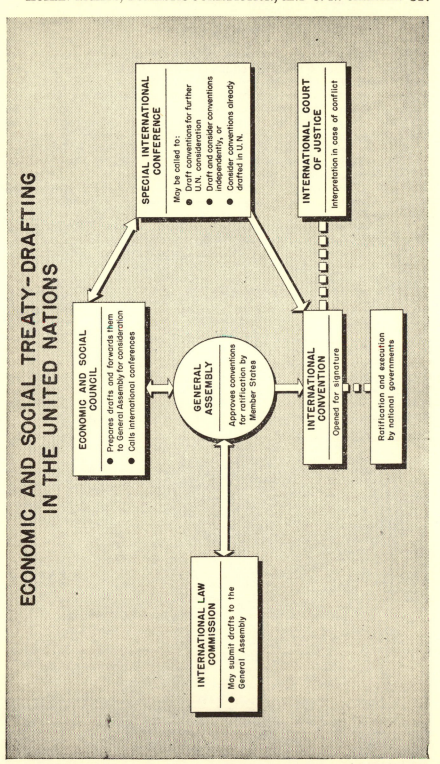

U. N. sponsored conferences after preliminary work in the United Nations.[26]

The charter does not list approval of international conventions as among important questions requiring a two-thirds vote in the General Assembly. Although the Genocide Convention was approved and proposed for ratification by unanimous vote of the Assembly, the Right of Correction Convention (discussed below) was approved by 25 votes, a bare majority of the members voting and less than an absolute majority. The conventions themselves specify the number of ratifications which must take place before they enter into effect among the ratifying parties thereto. This may range, for example, from 20 ratifications, as in the Genocide Convention, to 6, as in the Right of Correction Convention. If a convention does not receive the required number of ratifications, it does not become effective, even among those ratifying and, in any event, no state may be bound by a convention which it has not ratified. Similar provisions govern the abrogation of a convention. For example, if the parties to the Genocide Convention should be reduced by withdrawals to less than 16 it will cease to be in effect.

E. HUMAN RIGHTS TREATIES DRAFTED IN THE UNITED NATIONS

Since its inception the United Nations has been engaged in the drafting of a number of treaties dealing with the general subject of human rights. Six of these treaties have been opened for signature: none of them has been ratified by the United States. The effect of some of these, at least among nations ratifying them, would be to define, to some extent, the concept of human rights in the charter and to supplement the efforts of the United Nations to promote them. The treaties raise in sharpened form the general issue of domestic jurisdiction and of the proper scope of international authority.

Conventions on human rights completed under the auspices of the United Nations, or under consideration by the United Nations

1. COMPLETED

Conventions	Source of draft and date opened for signature		Entered into effect among nations ratifying	Total number of ratifications and accessions to date	United States ratifications
	U. N. General assembly	International conference			
Genocide Convention	Dec. 9, 1948		Jan. 12, 1951	50	
Convention on Prostitution	Mar. 21, 1950		July 25, 1951	14	
Convention Relating to the Status of Refugees		July 28, 1951	Apr. 22, 1954	15	
Convention on the Political Rights of Women	Mar. 31, 1953		July 7, 1954	22	
Right of Correction Convention	do			2	
Convention on the Status of Stateless Persons		Sept. 28, 1954			

2. UNDER PREPARATION OR DRAFTED BUT NOT APPROVED

Draft Convention on the Gathering and International Transmission of News.
Draft Covenant on Political and Civil Rights.
Draft Covenant on Economic, Social, and Cultural Rights.
Draft Convention on Freedom of Information.
Draft Convention on Nationality of Married Persons.
Draft Convention on the Elimination of Future Statelessness.
Draft Convention on the Reduction of Future Statelessness.
Draft Supplementary Convention on Slavery.

[26] A chronology of the Genocide Convention provides an example of the procedures followed. By resolution of the General Assembly at its 1946 session the Economic and Social Council was instructed to undertake preparatory studies for a draft convention. These studies were initiated early in 1947 when, at the request of the Council, the U. N. Secretariat drew up a preliminary draft, which was circulated to member states for their comments. In March 1948, the Council established an ad hoc committee of seven member-states which completed its own draft. After a general review by the Council, the draft was forwarded to the Assembly where it was debated in the Legal Committee. The revised text was discussed again in full Assembly and finally, on December 9, 1948, the Convention on Genocide was approved for the consideration of member states.

1. THE GENOCIDE CONVENTION

Only one treaty, the Genocide Convention, has so far gained substantial worldwide acceptance. The United States has not ratified it and is therefore not bound by it. This convention offers an illustration of some of the major constitutional and international problems which are involved in treaty drafting by the United Nations or by other international organizations.[27]

At its first session in December 1946, the U. N. General Assembly declared in a resolution that genocide, "a denial of the right to existence of entire human groups," was a crime under international law. Besides inviting member states to enact legislation for the prevention and punishment of the crime, the resolution called for the drafting of a convention to facilitate international cooperation to the same end. The convention as drafted was approved unanimously by the General Assembly in December 1948 and proposed for the signature and ratification or accession of member states.[28] It is now in effect as between some 50 ratifying states.

The United States signed the convention and it was sent by the President to the Senate for its consent to ratification in June 1949. Early the following year public hearings were held by a subcommittee of the Committee on Foreign Relations. On May 23, 1950, the subcommittee reported the convention to the full committee with 4 specific understandings and 1 declaration designed to clarify its meaning. Since misgivings continued, the understandings were redrafted as reservations by the full committee. The committee, however, did not recommend the convention to the Senate and no further action has been taken.[29]

In general terms, arguments in favor of the convention presented to the Foreign Relations Committee were to the effect that collective action by the nations in this matter was called for to prevent and suppress the lawlessness represented by genocide. Genocide aroused resentment among peoples everywhere and destroyed the friendly relations between states. Moreover, mass destruction of human groups was a concomitant of aggression against other nations and a threat to the peace. From the viewpoint of international interests, ruthless action of this nature caused wholesale dislocations of peoples and created the problem of caring for them by neighboring states.

Arguments against ratification, although generally condemning genocide, stressed that the proposed convention "raises important fundamental questions but does not resolve them in a manner consistent with our form of government."[30] Since genocide had never occurred in the United States, action of any kind was unnecessary.

---

[27] See U. S. Congress. Senate. Committee on Foreign Relations. The Genocide Convention. Hearings, January 1950. 555 pages. Hereinafter referred to as Genocide Convention Hearings.
[28] For text, see Collection of Documents, p. 253.
[29] U. S. Congress. Senate. Committee on Foreign Relations. Legislative History, 81st Cong., 2d sess. Doc. No. 247, December 22, 1950, p. 28.
[30] Genocide Convention Hearings, p. 158.

The convention might afford a vehicle whereby nations could intervene in each others' domestic affairs and far from contributing to peaceful relations, could be a cause of unfriendly relations. Criticism was also directed at the convention for being ineffectual for the purpose it was designed to serve.

The Senate Foreign Relations Committee has not considered the convention since 1950. In May 1954, a committee memorandum stated that—

there are no plans to do so at this time.

and that—

the present administration has indicated that it does not expect to seek action on the convention. The Genocide Convention, therefore, is still pending before the Committee on Foreign Relations. It could not become effective for the United States unless * * * the Senate gave its advice and consent to ratification, and the President proceeded to ratify it.[31]

2. THE DRAFT COVENANTS ON HUMAN RIGHTS

At the San Francisco Conference several states advanced the idea that a bill of rights should be attached to, or included in, the United Nations Charter. However, the conclusion was reached that—

* * * the present Conference, if only for lack of time, could not proceed to realize such a draft in an international contract. The Organization, once formed, could better proceed to consider the suggestion and to deal effectively with it through a special commission, or by some other method.[32]

The State Department commentary which accompanied the U. N. Charter when it was before the Senate for approval contained the observation that the proposed United Nations Commission on Human Rights would—

have the opportunity to work out an international bill of rights which can be submitted to member nations with a view to incorporation in their fundamental law, just as there is a Bill of Rights in the American Constitution.[33]

Apparently, the United States view at that time was for the United Nations to propose a bill which the member states, acting individually, could embody in their domestic law in whatever form they saw fit.

Following this line of policy, the United States representatives proposed in the Human Rights Commission that a bill of rights should take the form of a declaration which, while not binding the members, would give, it was contended, tremendous impetus to the advancement of human rights throughout the world. The United Kingdom, on the other hand, pressed for the conclusion of a general convention, confined to a limited number of fundamental rights but enforceable under international law. The decision was taken by the Commission to prepare drafts of both a declaration and a convention.

The Universal Declaration of Human Rights, as finally adopted by the United Nations in 1948, reflects the views of many nations and differs in a number of respects from the United States conception of essential rights. It received the approval of the United States representative, however, on the grounds that it gave expression to many of the traditional American liberties and because "we believe in the

---

[31] U. S. Senate. Committee on Foreign Relations. Memorandum on Status of the Genocide Convention. May 1954.
[32] Department of State. United Nations Conference on International Organization Publication 2490, 1946, p. 496.
[33] Report to the President, p. 118.

overall pattern of this document." In indicating this approval the representative emphasized that the declaration was not a legally binding instrument:

In taking up the consideration of the declaration it is of primary importance that we keep clearly in mind the basic character of the document. It is not a treaty; it is not an international agreement. It is not and does not purport to be a statement of law or of legal obligation. It is a declaration of basic principles of human rights and freedoms, to be stamped with the approval of the General Assembly by formal vote of its Members.[34]

At first the draft of a convention on human rights (as distinct from the declaration) covered only civil and political rights. Principally at the instance of Australia, France, and the Soviet Union, economic, social, and cultural rights were later included. In 1952, the United States and several other nations succeeded in having the draft separated into two covenants, one consisting of political and civil rights and the other of economic, social and cultural rights.[35]

The attempt to draft these covenants has brought into sharp focus, even more than the declaration, all of the divergencies of political, legal, philosophical, economic, and social concepts that prevail in the United Nations membership. As the covenants were being developed in the United Nations, concern was expressed in the United States over the effect ratification might have with respect to the Bill of Rights in the United States Constitution, Federal-State relationships and domestic laws on human rights. The drafts represent an effort to regulate internationally by treaty important questions hitherto considered uniquely of domestic interest. In addition, they deal with the fundamental relationships between the state and the individual, relationships with regard to which there are wide divergencies among the nations.

Aside from these issues, critics of the draft treaty on political and civil rights point out that one of the fundamental concepts of the Bill of Rights, which is protection of the individual against possible government despotism, has been obscured, if not largely lost, in the United Nations draft.[36] The treaty, they point out, allows serious limitations on certain rights which, in effect, would go far toward nullifying the proclamation of the rights. Although the draft provides that there would be no derogation of rights in any contracting state by virtue of ratification of the treaty, this would not obviate the fact that the draft would propagate a faulty conception of liberty among member nations, and wide ratification would have the effect of giving international sanction to the permissible limitations. Moreover, they argue that some of the economic, social and cultural rights in the draft on these subjects are in essence aspirations and are not suitable for legal implementation or government guarantee.

In the spring of 1953 Secretary of State Dulles announced that the United States would not become a party to covenants such as the ones being drafted. The drafts are not in final form and are still under consideration by the United Nations.

---

[34] Collection of documents, p. 252.
[35] For texts of recent drafts, see Collection of Documents, pp. 267, 271.
[36] See Senator John Bricker's comments along this line. In U. S. Congress. Senate Committee on Foreign Relations. Review of the United Nations Charter. Hearings, 1955, p. 1656. See also remarks of ex-President Truman, ibid., p. 1630.

3. FREEDOM OF INFORMATION

In 1948 a conference on freedom of information was convened by the United Nations Economic and Social Council and three draft conventions were approved: one on the gathering and international transmission of news (the Newsgathering Convention), sponsored by the United States; another on an international right of correction, submitted by France; and a third, on freedom of information, proposed by the United Kingdom.

As originally conceived, the proposed convention on freedom of information would have guaranteed to the nationals of every contracting state, and nationals of other contracting states lawfully residing within its territory, freedom to impart and receive information without governmental interference. In addition, governments would agree not to control the use or availability of the facilities of mass communications in a discriminating manner.

As work proceeded on the draft, a sharp cleavage developed between those who sought to insert provisions to control the press through governmental legislation and those who opposed such interference. So many proposals for restrictive controls were advanced that many delegations, including United States representatives, began to fear that far from guaranteeing freedom of information the convention would have the opposite effect of giving international sanction to governmental restrictions. A 1951 revised draft was viewed as suffering from the same defects.[37]

In the United States, objections were raised to the convention on the grounds that it was contrary to the first amendment of the Constitution safeguarding freedom of the press from encroachment by the Government. The United Nations was also said to be intervening, in infringement of the charter, in the essential domestic jurisdiction of member states in drafting treaty law on basic human rights, including freedom of the press.[38]

No final action has been taken in the United Nations on the 1951 draft. It has long been apparent, however, that the United States would not approve a convention based on this draft and that the President would not submit it to the Senate for its consent to ratification.[39]

The Newsgathering Convention, amalgamated with the Right of Correction Convention, was approved by the General Assembly in 1949 but not opened for signature pending completion of the Convention of Freedom of Information. At the Assembly's 1952 session several countries, including France, urged adoption of a Right of Correction Convention. The United States had opposed such a convention on grounds that it could become a source of distorted propaganda as it offered governments the right to require other governments, parties to the convention, to issue "corrections" of news stories which they did not approve. A version somewhat different from that of 1949 was nevertheless approved by a vote of 25 to 22. Since the executive branch does not favor the draft, it has not been submitted to the Senate for consent to ratification.

---

[37] For text of this draft, see Collection of Documents, p. 256.
[38] Elisha Hanson. Freedom of the Press: Is It Threatened in the United Nations? American Bar Association Journal, June 1951, p. 417. See also, Frank Holman. The Convention on Freedom of Information: A Threat to Freedom of Speech in America. American Bar Association Journal, August 1951, p. 567.
[39] For a review of developments which have taken place and difficulties encountered in the United Nations, see Carroll Binder's "Freedom of Information and the United Nations," International Organization, May 1952, p. 210.

4. OTHER CONVENTIONS

A Convention on the Political Rights of Women, providing for the right of women to vote and to be eligible for election, was approved and opened for signature by the General Assembly at its 1952 session. The Secretary of State has indicated that the United States will not sign the convention partly because it does not constitute "a proper field for exercise of the treatymaking power." [40]

Other conventions on the general subject of human rights drafted under the aegis of the United Nations relate to prostitution, refugees, and stateless persons. In addition, various amendments and protocols to conventions antedating the United Nations have been adopted and opened for signature, including a number relating to slavery, traffic in women and children, and traffic in obscene publications.

F. DOMESTIC JURISDICTION AND HUMAN RIGHTS

Two principal points of view prevail in the United States as to whether the domestic jurisdiction clause of the charter (art. 2, par. 7) is applicable to treaty drafting in the United Nations particularly as it involves human rights. This article reads:

Nothing contained in the present charter shall authorize the United Nations to intervene in matters which are essentially within the domestic jurisdiction of any state or shall require the Members to submit such matters to settlement under the present Charter; but this principle shall not prejudice the application of enforcement measures under chapter VII.

Some emphasize that when conventions are drafted and proposed by the United Nations, the organization is merely acting as a conference of 60 nations and that each nation has inherent national powers to act which need not necessarily be derived from its adherence to the charter. When meeting as the General Assembly, the argument runs, member states do not lose the legal capacity which they otherwise possess to negotiate treaties. From this point of view it is contended that article 2, paragraph 7, does not apply to prevent the drafting of conventions, whatever their subject. [41]

Others hold that article 2, paragraph 7, applies to all the activities of the Organization, including treaty drafting, and that it operates to prevent the United Nations, as an organization, from drafting or proposing treaties whose substance is considered to be within the essential domestic jurisdiction of states. [42] Thus, even discussion of certain subjects might be viewed in some quarters as intervention in domestic matters, and has been so considered at various times by the Soviet-bloc nations, France, and South Africa.

It was brought out at San Francisco that one purpose for including the domestic jurisdiction clause in the charter was to make clear that in carrying out its functions the United Nations would deal "with and through" governments and there would be no direct interference in the economic or social affairs of member states. The purpose was to establish a general principle, not a "technical and legalistic" formula. The principle was sufficiently flexible, it was thought, to permit of

[40] Collection of Documents, p. 296.
[41] See Myers McDougal and Gertrude C. K. Leighton. The Rights of Man in the World Community: Constitutional Illusions Versus Rational Action. Yale Law Journal, December 1949, p. 78.
[42] See, for example, George Finch. The Need To Restrain the Treatymaking Power of the United States Within Constitutional Limits. American Journal of International Law, January 1954, p. 63. See also U. S. Congress. Senate. Committee on the Judiciary. Treaties and Executive Agreements. Hearings, 1955, pp. 492–497.

evolution according to the "changing conditions of the world community." In the last analysis, the United States delegate contended—

there can be no successful intervention into the domestic life of any member state without that state's consent or acquiescence.[43]

It was proposed in San Francisco that a reference to international law be included in the nonintervention clause as a test to determine what was domestic. This did not gain general acceptance, largely because of the view that the body of international law and traditional conceptions were inadequate and "not of a character which ought to be frozen into the new organization."[44] It was also pointed out that—

the charter itself being international law, it could be argued that all of the matters referred to in the charter are now no longer "domestic."[45]

On the other hand, the view was advanced that the reference was unnecessary since the clause was part of an international agreement and would naturally be interpreted in terms of international law.[46]

In practice the United Nations has largely followed the traditional rule of international law that if the substance of a matter is controlled by an international agreement, or other provisions of international law, then it ceases to be solely within the domestic jurisdiction of the states concerned. According to this rule, the effect of ratification of treaties on human rights would be to make the matters covered of international concern and to remove them from the exclusive realm of domestic jurisdiction, at least among those states ratifying or accepting the treaties.

Since most of the members of the United Nations, including the United States, have in general not objected to the drafting of treaties in the economic and social field, they have evidently not considered the mere drafting or United Nations approval as a form of intervention in matters essentially within domestic jurisdiction. Only the Soviet Union and Czechoslovakia appear to have invoked the principle in protest against the drafting of certain treaties on human rights. At one point in the drafting of measures for carrying out a human rights convention, the Soviet representative declared that this constituted "an attempted gross infringement" of the domestic jurisdiction clause of the charter.[47] The Soviet Union has also alleged violation of the clause in the drafting of the convention on the nationality of married women and together with Czechoslovakia has invoked article 2, paragraph 7 as a bar to the drafting of the protocol on the status of stateless persons.[48]

One author expresses the view that the—

root of the difficulty lies in the lack of demarcation between domestic and international legislation—

and that—

A line must be drawn beyond which the international organizations know they cannot pass. The United Nations should draw the line in a resolution of the

[43] Quoted in Jacob Robinson. Human Rights and Fundamental Freedoms in the Charter of the United Nations. New York, the International Press, 1946, p. 46.
[44] Report to the President, pp. 44–45.
[45] Robinson, op. cit., p. 45.
[46] For proposals to make the International Court the official organ for the interpretation of the charter, see U. S. Congress, Senate, Committee on Foreign Relations, The International Court of Justice, Staff Study No. 8, May, 1955. 29 pages.
[47] United Nations. Economic and Social Council. Commission on Human Rights. Summary Record. December 15, 1947. Document E/CN.4/SR 38, p. 9.
[48] United Nations. Economic and Social Council. Documents E/AC.7/SR 101, pp. 15–17; E/AC.7/SR 102, p. 5; and E/AC.7/SR 267, p. 9. See also United Nations. General Assembly. Seventh Session. Third Committee. Summary record, 421st meeting, paragraph 4

General Assembly and should facilitate a judgment on the question by the International Court. The United States should draw the line by amendment in the Federal Constitution.[49]

A proposal to draw the line in the Constitution was contained in the Bricker amendment and similar proposals considered by the Senate in 1953 and later. Senator Bricker explained that section 2 of one proposed amendment (S. J. Res. 1, 83d Congress, 1st session)—

makes article 2, paragraph 7, of the U. N. Charter effective insofar as the United States is concerned.[50]

This section reads:

No treaty shall authorize or permit any foreign power or any international organization to supervise, control, or adjudicate rights of citizens of the United States within the United States enumerated in this Constitution or any other matter essentially within the domestic jurisdiction of the United States.[51]

In the final version approved by the Judiciary Committee in 1953, section 2 was eliminated and section 1 appeared as follows: [52]

A provision of a treaty which conflicts with this Constitution shall not be of any force or effect.

It has been argued that recognition of the supremacy of the Constitution over treaties is the only "dividing line" necessary for safeguarding the human rights of American citizens as against possibly harmful treaties. Senator Bricker and others have contended that this supremacy should be clearly expressed in the Constitution, while others hold the view that precedent and judicial dicta have already established it in fact.

The General Assembly has never adopted a resolution specifically attempting to define the area which is essentially within the domestic jurisdiction of member states, nor has the International Court been asked for an advisory opinion on the matter.[53]

G. The Federal-State Question

As the hearings in the Senate on the Genocide Convention brought out,[54] the general problem of domestic jurisdiction in relation to treaties includes, in the United States, the problem of safeguarding State powers as against those of the Federal Government. Under the United States Constitution, Congress has the power to enact legislation "necessary and proper" to put a ratified treaty into effect internally, if such action is required. There are grounds, therefore, for the belief that a treaty requiring implementation by domestic law may provide a basis for enhancing federal powers at the expense of powers traditionally exercised by the states.

The problem of giving full domestic effect to proposed covenants on human rights in federal-type nations which may ratify them has been debated during the course of the drafting of the covenants in the United Nations. A number of nations, including India and Australia, have sought to insert federal-state clauses in the draft treaties which

[49] Florence E. Allen. The Treaty as an Instrument of Legislation. New York. MacMillan, 1952, p. 105.
[50] 1953 hearings, p. 9.
[51] 1953 hearings, p. 1.
[52] Collection of Documents, p. 301.
[53] For a review of recent Court action which bears on the question of domestic jurisdiction see Henri Rolin's The International Court of Justice and Domestic Jurisdiction. International Organization, vol. 8, February 1954, pp. 36–44.
[54] Genocide Convention. Hearings, pp. 45–47, 57–59, 67–69, 101–102, 168–169, 195, 199, 208–210, 232, 251, 235, 531–533.

would relieve federal-type states of treaty obligations for matters under state control in their federal constitutional systems.

It has been proposed, for example, that a federal-state clause be inserted in the draft covenants which would provide that: [55]

This covenant shall not operate so as to bring within the jurisdiction of the federal authority of a federal state * * * any of the matters referred to in this covenant which, independently of the covenant, would not be within the jurisdiction of the federal authority.

Subject to this stipulation, the obligations of a federal government would be the same as those of other ratifying states to the extent that the matters dealt with were within the federal jurisdiction under its constitution. However, in other respects, the only obligation of the federal government would be to recommend favorably the provisions to the appropriate authorities of its states or other constituent units and to report to the U. N. Secretary-General on their relevant laws or other action in reference thereto. With the aim of safeguarding the principle of equality of contracting parties an additional paragraph would provide that—

A contracting state shall not be entitled to avail itself of the present covenant against other contracting states except to the extent that it is bound by the covenant.

In 1952, when the Department of State was actively concerned with such treaties, its view was that a qualification of this kind would appropriately safeguard the federal-state division of powers in the United States and that Federal powers would not be increased if the covenants were ratified.[56] Under this qualification the obligations undertaken, it was held, would be limited to matters which under the Constitution were within the delegated federal powers.

In the United Nations, member states which did not wish to see a federal-state clause included in the covenants stressed that such an insertion would result in federal states enjoying a privileged position. A general rule of international law, they argued, was that states were responsible for the fulfillment of their international obligations with respect to their territories as a whole and this rule should not be violated. A qualifying clause would have the effect of a reservation which would nullify a large part of the covenants as far as federal states were concerned. It was contended that when states become parties to treaties they must all be equally bound. On the other hand, the view was advanced that reservations could be made by federal states, should they require them, to deal with internal matters.

Arguments in favor of the qualifying clause were to the effect that to attempt to settle present-day problems from the point of view of traditional doctrine would be to frustrate the organic growth of international law. Some accommodations would have to be made to the special position of federal states. As international cooperation developed, the question was bound to arise with increasing frequency. Moreover, the general rule of international law only applied in the absence of any specific provision to the contrary. As for reservations, if a federal government could not undertake commitments for its constituent units, it would not be proper for the government to ratify

---

[55] United Nations. Economic and Social Council. Commission on Human Rights. Report of the Tenth Session. Document E/2573, April 1954, pp. 25-28.
[56] 1953 hearings, p. 325.

the covenants, and then to make reservations on certain matters involving the power of states or other constituent units.

Doubts as to the effectiveness of safeguarding state powers, either by the insertion of a clause in a treaty or by reservation, have been raised by legal experts in the United States. A subsidiary body of the American Bar Association came to the conclusion, as stated in a 1951 report, that: [57]

1. An international treaty cannot be safeguarded by a clause in the treaty or by reservation or understanding against the expansion of the limited power of the Federal Congress in the United States to such extent as necessary to fulfill the obligation under the treaty if Congress determines to exercise such power * * *.

No action of the parties or of the Senate and the President at the time of ratification of a treaty can take away the constitutional power of Congress to execute the treaty and to fulfill the national obligation under the treaty if Congress decides to do so.

2. Without affecting the *power* of Congress * * * the *duty* of the Federal Government toward other contracting nations for the fulfillment of United States obligations under a treaty and the intent of the United States at the time of execution of the treaty can be restricted by a clause in a treaty such as the following:

It is expressly stipulated (1) that federal states are not bound by the treaty to cause their legislative authorities to enact any legislation which they could not constitutionally enact in the absence of the treaty; and

(2) it is the intention of the parties that the respective constitutional powers of state and federal authorities in federal states shall not be deemed to have been affected in any way by the coming into force of this instrument as an international agreement.

This view is not shared by others who argue that the balance between federal and state powers can be maintained by means of federal-state clauses in treaties, as well as by reservations. With regard to reservations Senator Wiley, for example, has stated: [58]

A reservation or understanding attached to a duly concluded treaty and accepted by the other party or parties is an integral part of the whole instrument agreed upon. No rights can arise from the instrument which are prohibited by one of its parts. If the reservation or understanding precludes legislative action by the National Government in an area otherwise reserved to the States, the treaty itself necessarily precludes such action.

The right of Congress under the necessary and proper clause to implement a treaty is coextensive with the treaty itself including any of its reservations or understandings.

In the United Nations the International Law Commission was asked to report in 1950 on the effect of reservations in international law "both from the point of view of codification and from that of progressive development of international law." Partly on the basis of its report, the General Assembly adopted a resolution on January 12, 1952, recommending that [59]—

* * * organs of the United Nations, specialized agencies, and states should, in the course of preparing multilateral conventions, consider the insertion therein of provisions relating to the admissibility or nonadmissibility of reservations and to the effect to be attributed to them.

The effect of this recommendation would be that the drafters of multilateral conventions would attempt to regulate reservations to the con-

---

[57] American Bar Association. Joint report (February 1, 1951) on progress in the study of the constitutional aspects of international treaties to the house of delegates of the American Bar Association by the Committee for Peace and Law Through United Nations and the Section of International and Comparative Law. (In Report of Standing Committee on Peace and Law Through United Nations, September 1, 1951)

[58] Statement by Senator Alexander Wiley, Congressional Record, vol. 100, pt. 1, 83d Cong., 2d sess., January 22, 1954, p. 668.

[59] United Nations. General Assembly. Official Records: Sixth session. Resolutions. Supplement No. 20 (A2119), 1952, p. 84.

ventions, possibly including federal-state reservations, by provisions inserted in the treaties themselves.[60]

One approach to the federal-state problem has been taken by the International Labor Organization. In its constitution there is a clause relating to federal states which automatically applies to all conventions approved by the Organization. Similar in intent to the paragraphs proposed for insertion in the covenants, the clause lays down procedures to be followed in bringing conventions to the attention of the appropriate legislative authorities. Under this clause a federal-type government may distinguish between conventions. Those which it regards as appropriate for federal action can be considered by the federal authority. Those which it regards as appropriate for action by the constituent provinces, states, or other governmental units can be transmitted to them for "the enactment of legislation or other action." There is no obligation, however, to enact such legislation.

The same subsidiary body of the American Bar Association referred to above has indicated that in its view this kind of procedure should be applied in the United Nations. A 1951 report stated: [61]

If the subject of human rights and freedoms in the world under the United Nations Charter is to be pressed in the current state of conflicting and confused ideologies, the best approach would be by way of the procedure followed by the International Labor Organization, rather than by way of legally binding multipartite treaties. The International Labor Organization proceeds in an advisory way formulating standards which are embodied in recommendations for legislative action by the members of the Organization or in conventions for ratifications in the usual course, except as specifically provided with respect to federal states which, where an International Labor Convention is wholly or partly within the sphere of state action, have the duty to make effective arrangements for reference of the convention to the proper federal or state authorities for the enactment of legislation or other action, and to report from time to time what has been done.

H. HUMAN RIGHTS AND CHARTER REVISION

As previously pointed out, the United Nations has drafted a number of treaties on the general subject of human rights, only one of which has so far gained wide international acceptance. Proposals have also been made which would modify the charter's human rights articles themselves or which would regulate treaty drafting on economic and social subjects in the United Nations.

The following outline of proposals affecting human rights and the United Nations makes no attempt to be comprehensive but is merely suggestive of the different lines of thought which have been advanced on this subject.

1. SHOULD THE HUMAN RIGHTS CLAUSES OF THE CHARTER BE ELIMINATED OR CHANGED?

In some quarters objections have been raised to the human rights provisions in the charter on the grounds that the relationship of an individual to his own government is peculiarly a matter of domestic concern to a state. The human rights clauses in the charter give the

[60] In its consent to ratification of the charter of the Organization of American States, the Senate attached a reservation relating to federal-state powers. See Collection of Documents, pp. 175–178. The latest drafts of the covenants on human rights contain the following clause: "The provisions of the Covenant shall extend to all parts of federal states without any limitations or exceptions." This clause, if finally adopted, presumably would preclude any reservations relating to federal-state powers by federal-type states.
[61] American Bar Association. Joint report by the Standing Committee on Peace and Law Through United Nations and the Section of International and Comparative Law. In report of Standing Committee on Peace and Law Through United Nations, February 1, 1952, p. 71.

United Nations authority to concern itself with these relationships, within the limits of the domestic jurisdiction clause. International law, it is contended, should be confined to the relationships between states and not be concerned with relationships between a state and its nationals. The philosophy of this point of view has been stated by one author: [62]

In a world of sovereign nations there will always be differences in forms of government. Forms of government arise from social conditions and customs. And an essential characteristic of a nation's form of government is the relation of the individual to the government * * *.

The very essence of sovereignty is the right of a nation to decide its form of government, which means its own conceptions of the rights of its citizens.

On the other hand, there are some persons who maintain that to strike out the human rights clauses of the charter would eliminate one of the principal purposes for the existence of the United Nations. [63] In the ideological struggle between free and totalitarian concepts an essential difference, they contend, is in attitudes toward the rights of the individual. Fundamental human rights, the argument runs, are and always have been a matter of international concern: the articles in the charter have not made them so but have merely registered the fact. [64] Moreover, it is contended, the observance of human rights bears a direct relationship to the maintenance of peace. As Secretary of State, Gen. George C. Marshall stated: [65]

The charter of the United Nations reflects these (human rights) concepts and expressly provides for the promotion and protection of the rights of man, as well as for the rights of nations. This is no accident. For in the modern world, the association of free men within a free state is based upon the obligation of citizens to respect the rights of their fellow citizens. And the association of free nations in a free world is based upon the obligation of all states to respect the rights of other nations.

Systematic and deliberate denials of basic human rights lie at the root of most of our troubles and threaten the work of the United Nations. It is not only fundamentally wrong that millions of men and women live in daily terror of secret police, subject to seizure, imprisonment, or forced labor without just cause and without fair trial, but these wrongs have repercussions in the community of nations. Governments which systematically disregard the rights of their own people are not likely to respect the rights of other nations and other people and are likely to seek their objectives by coercion and force in the international field

2. SHOULD THERE BE A DEFINITION OF HUMAN RIGHTS IN THE CHARTER?

The authorization given the United Nations to promote the observance of human rights, since it is general and undefined, would seem to permit the organization to concern itself with any right whose suppression may arouse international repercussions, subject to the domestic jurisdiction limitation. From one viewpoint, the lack of definition may be an advantage since it allows adaptability to developments in the international field. Too narrow a definition would tend to restrict the United Nations whereas too wide a definition, such as the universal declaration, if it were an integral part of the charter, would broaden the jurisdiction of the United Nations beyond the area in which it has operated and permit, to a greater degree than heretofore, what many states would consider intervention in domestic affairs.

[62] Raymond Moley. Chicago Journal of Commerce, June 7, 1950, editorial.
[63] See testimony of Ernest A. Gross. In U. S. Senate, Committee on Foreign Relations, Review of the United Nations Charter. Hearings, 1955, p. 1661.
[64] See statement by Secretary of State Dulles, 1953 hearings, p. 898.
[65] U. S. Department of State. Report on the United Nations, 1948, publication 3437, p. 175.

A possible reconciliation of these views may lie in the proposal that the United Nations be limited to promoting observance of those rights deemed essential to the maintenance of peace, or manifestly of international interest, with or without an accompanying definition. A variation of this approach would be to try to distinguish between fundamental rights and others not so basic. The same result might be obtained by a suitable application of the domestic jurisdiction clause.

Still another proposal has been for the universal declaration of human rights to be incorporated in the charter as a definition. The declaration defines the rights, briefly, as the right to life, liberty, and security of person; freedom of religion; freedom of opinion and expression; freedom of assembly; self-government through free elections; freedom from slavery and torture; the right to a fair trial and to equality before the law; presumption of innocence until proved guilty; the right not to be subjected to retroactive laws; freedom of movement within one's state and freedom to leave or return to it; the right of asylum; the right to a nationality; the right to found a family; the right to privacy; the right to own property, to social security and to work; the right to form and join trade unions; the right to an adequate standard of living, to education, and to rest and leisure; and the right to participation in the cultural life of the community.

In United Nations practice the declaration has often been cited in resolutions of the General Assembly as a standard to be observed, sometimes with the inference that it enjoys almost an equal status with the charter.[66] To attach it to the charter as a definition, however, would make it a part of the international law of the charter. If the declaration were merely incorporated as a definition, it would impose an obligation on the United Nations to promote observance of the rights without necessarily imposing a corresponding duty on the part of member states to implement them in their domestic law. Conflicts between national standards and the international standard, not emphasized at the present time, might cause dissension in the United Nations and make its work more difficult.

Moreover, in spite of the fact that the declaration was approved by a large vote in the United Nations General Assembly in 1948, the measure of universal consensus on the nature of fundamental human rights is probably not as substantial as this vote would seem to indicate. In the first place, all of the Soviet bloc, as well as Yugoslavia, the Union of South Africa, and Saudi Arabia, abstained from voting on the declaration. The United States itself, although voting in favor, indicated that it did so with reservations as to certain rights. For example, it was stressed during the course of the preparatory work that the United States did not consider language relating to the economic, social, and cultural rights as implying an obligation on the part of governments to assure enjoyment of these rights.

Further, as already noted, for a number of years efforts have been directed in the United Nations toward the drafting of human rights covenants, which have not yet been completed and on which there are serious disagreements.

It has proved possible for at least one group of nations in western Europe to agree on a definition of fundamental human rights. This was so principally because of their like-mindedness and the fact that

66 Collection of Documents, pp. 283–286.

there is already a relatively high standard for the protection of the rights in most of these countries. In 1950 a European Convention on Human Rights was drafted and is now in effect between 11 countries. The convention, based largely on the universal declaration, is confined to the minimum of those traditional civil and political rights on which there was substantial consensus.[67]

Insertion of a definition in the charter would give the United Nations a mandate to promote observance of the defined rights. Whether such action would represent a broadening or a restriction of the present practice of the United Nations would depend on the phraseology of the definition as well as on other changes which might be made in the charter.

3. SHOULD THE CHARTER OBLIGATE MEMBER STATES TO PROMOTE OR GUARANTEE OBSERVANCE OF HUMAN RIGHTS?

Some quarters in the United Nations interpret the charter articles as imposing on member nations an obligation parallel to that of the United Nations in promoting the observance of human rights, at least with regard to those rights whose suppression may disturb peaceful and friendly relations among nations. For example, there has been an inclination to interpret the provision that human rights shall be promoted "without distinction as to race, sex, language, or religion" as a human right in itself, particularly insofar as racial discrimination is concerned, and that there is an obligation on nations to eliminate discrimination.

Indeed, for the United Nations to fulfill its obligation presumes some parallel efforts on the part of member states to the same end. Otherwise, there would be a confusing conflict of objectives. The assumption of member states of an obligation which would make this parallelism clear, it is urged, might promote greater harmony of purpose. On the other hand, it has been suggested that since there is not even a minimum standard of respect for human rights among member states, an obligation not based on some expectation of fulfillment would do little to advance the cause of human rights, and might do positive harm by fostering disrespect for international obligations.

Proposals for member nations to guarantee observance of human rights were rejected at San Francisco. As already noted, however, since that time some Western European nations have found it possible to agree on a bill of political and civil rights and have jointly agreed to safeguard them.[68] A different situation prevails in the United Nations. There, sharp differences make it doubtful that the requisite majority could agree on a definition or that they would go further and obligate themselves to implement the rights in their domestic law.

In the United States, a charter change of this nature would have to be viewed in relation to its effect on domestic human rights law and federal-state powers.

---

[67] Convention for the Protection of Human Rights and Fundamental Freedoms. In United Nations Yearbook on Human Rights for 1950. New York, 1952. P. 418–426. A protocol to the convention was adopted in 1952. A clause in the convention (article 60) precludes it from being construed to limit any right or freedom enjoyed under the laws of a contracting state.

[68] It should be pointed out that the European Convention on Human Rights allows some of the same limitations which have been criticized in the United Nations Draft Covenant.

4. SHOULD THE UNITED NATIONS BE A GUARANTOR OF THE OBSERVANCE OF HUMAN RIGHTS?

At the present time the United Nations is only authorized to promote observance of human rights within the limits of its general authority. Agreement on a bill of rights to be implemented in domestic law would presumably have to be a part of any United Nations guaranty of observance, with the difficulties already noted. In addition, some international interpretative and enforcement procedures would have to be provided if the guaranty were to mean anything in practice.

The latest United Nations draft of a covenant on political and civil rights provides for a Human Rights Committee which would act as a factfinding and good-offices agency to adjust complaints of violations made by states parties to the covenants. Disputes could also be taken to the International Court of Justice. The present draft of a covenant on economic and social rights outlines a system whereby ratifying states would report "in stages" to the United Nations under a program to be agreed upon.

Many proposals have been examined during the course of drafting such measures. The most vehement conflict of opinion has centered on whether only states should be permitted to make complaints of violations of human rights to an international agency or whether individuals and groups should also have access to it. One suggestion was for the creation of an International Court of Human Rights to which not only states but nongovernmental organizations, groups, and individuals could apply, and whose judgments would be final and binding. A milder procedure for creation of conciliation or negotiation committees open to individuals and groups as well as states has also been suggested. Another alternative, supported by several representatives, called for setting up the office of a United Nations Attorney General where complaints could be received from any source. Negotiations for a friendly settlement with the states concerned could be undertaken and if unsuccessful the matter could be brought by the Attorney General before the Human Rights Committee. Yet another proposal was that the Human Rights Committee itself should be permitted to investigate serious violations of human rights.[69]

None of these proposals has found substantial support mainly because governments have been unwilling to permit their citizens to have access to an international agency with respect to matters that may involve the relationship between the individual and his own government. Furthermore, there has been in some quarters doubt of the wisdom of permitting an organization, some, if not a majority, of whose members do not enjoy a high standard of human rights, to create or control agencies of the kind suggested.

In the European Convention on Human Rights, the obligation for safeguarding the rights listed in the convention rests primarily on the governments of the ratifying states. A violation of rights which finds no redress in national courts may, however, by request of any ratifying state, be brought before the European Commission on Human Rights, elected by the Council of Europe's Committee on Ministers. If settlement is not reached through the Commission, the Committee

[69] For a more detailed discussion of these proposals, see Marian Neal. The United Nations and Human Rights, 1953. p. 135.

of Ministers itself may decide by a two-thirds vote on measures to be taken. The ratifying states undertake to regard as binding any decision of the Committee of Ministers, or of a European Court of Human Rights, if they have accepted its jurisdiction. The convention stipulates that means of settlement other than those provided in the convention will not be used except by special agreement among the disputants.

Various plans for world government include a bill of rights in the proposed constitutions with alternative suggestions as to the rights to be reserved to the peoples, safeguarded by the national state, or placed under the jurisdiction of the international authority. In the United States, one of the serious criticisms of the draft covenant on civil and political rights has been that it is based on the theory that substantive civil and political rights are granted to the people by the government instead of being rights which are inherent and inalienable in the people.

One group which has proposed a world constitution has sought to incorporate into it the idea of inherent individual rights. In the "Preliminary Draft of a World Constitution" [70] a bill of rights, modeled somewhat after that of the United States, is included. It stipulates that no law could be passed or held valid in a world republic or any of its component units which was in conflict with the provisions of the bill. The proposed bill would reserve such rights to the people.

Other proposals for world government would limit international jurisdiction over human rights to those which might be threatened by the exercise of limited powers delegated to the world government. In the Clark-Sohn plan,[71] for example, the international government would not—

purport or attempt to safeguard the individual against violation of fundamental rights by his own national or local government.

The United World Federalists would prohibit interference by the world organization with rights and liberties guaranteed to persons by their own national and state institutions.[72]

There would seem to be little support in the United Nations for changing the terms of the charter to provide that the Organization be given power to protect the human rights of nationals of member states beyond the potential power it now has to suppress threats to, or breaches of, the peace.

5. SHOULD THE CONCEPT OF DOMESTIC JURISDICTION BE FURTHER DEFINED OR DEVELOPED?

As previously pointed out, there is disagreement as to whether the domestic jurisdiction clause of the charter could be applied to limit the treaty-drafting operations of the United Nations in the field of human rights. It has been suggested that before draft treaties are submitted to member states for signature, they should first be approved by a two-thirds or three-fourths vote of the Assembly. Such a vote would, in effect, serve as a judgment that the subject matter of the

[70] Committee to Frame a World Constitution. Preliminary Draft of a World Constitution. Chicago, 1947. 32 p.
[71] Grenville Clark and Louis B. Sohn. Peace Through Disarmament and Charter Revision. July 1953, Foreword, p. v.
[72] United World Federalists. World Government Highlights. April 1951, p. 13.

treaty was one of legitimate and substantial international concern and not essentially a matter of domestic jurisdiction. A change of this kind could be brought about without charter amendment. Even then, however, the action of the Assembly would be only of a recommendatory nature and individual states would be free to accept or reject the treaty recommendation or could refuse to act at all on the grounds that the subject matter was essentially within their domestic jurisdiction.

While there would probably be great difficulty in redefining the concept of domestic jurisdiction, it might be possible for organs of the United Nations to agree that when domestic jurisdiction is raised in a substantial fashion as a bar to treaty drafting in the human rights or other fields, the matter of jurisdiction could be settled by seeking an advisory opinion from the International Court of Justice.

Thus the Court might be asked to judge whether the subject matter of a convention was essentially within the domestic jurisdiction of any state. Under the Court statute it could apply tests such as international custom and the general principles of international law.[73]

Another suggestion which has been advanced is to insert into the charter a clause similar to the one in the constitution of the International Labor Organization whereby economic and social treaties approved by the United Nations, including any on human rights, would be forwarded to the appropriate federal or state legislative authorities in a federal state for whatever action they might care to take. In the United States, this would have the effect of permitting the 48 States to consider international agreements on matters involving State jurisdiction.

I. Concluding Summary

Since early in United Nations history, members have been trying to define the rather imprecise human rights language of the charter. They have attempted to promote those rights by a variety of methods ranging from the creation of study groups and the adoption of general resolutions on the subject to the negotiation of treaties which have been submitted to states with the recommendation of the United Nations that they be approved.

So far as the United States is concerned, strong emotions have been aroused in connection with United Nations activities relating to human rights. There is a tendency in some quarters, at least, to resent even the assumption that any governmental agency or international organization might bestow or guarantee rights which are inherently and inalienably characteristics of freemen. As a result, attempts to construe certain charter provisions in such a way as to invalidate domestic law, while not successful, have nevertheless created apprehension that the United Nations charter may affect internal United States constitutional relationships including the relationships between American citizens and their state or national government in such a way as to impair important elements of national sovereignty. Even the process of negotiating conventions in the field of human rights has raised questions as to the legitimate area in which international activities may be undertaken without conflicting with

---

[73] For an analysis of the idea of making the International Court the official organ for the interpretation of the charter, see Staff Study No. 8 on the International Court, op. cit.

the domestic jurisdiction clause of the charter. That there may be some area for such activity, however, is indicated by the fact that there has been little, if any, opposition in this country to treaties such as those relating to the slave trade, refugees, and stateless persons.

That there has been concern about the scope of the human rights provisions of the charter and the activities of the United Nations in negotiating human rights treaties should not obscure the fact that the interest of the Organization in the subject has had salutary effects in some areas of the world. The rights which Americans view as inherent and inalienable such as the right to life, to liberty, to freedom of speech and the press, are virtually nonexistent in some parts of the world. They are goals to which many peoples aspire. The interest of the United Nations in these matters has served to focus attention upon them.

The United States has not ratified any of the human rights conventions noted above, not because it does not sympathize with the aspirations of the peoples to have and assert many of these rights, but largely because such treaties might have an effect on internal constitutional relationships, because of a concern lest they could limit rights now exercised by the American people, or because the conventions are viewed as unnecessary in this country.

Recent policy statements have indicated that while the United States is interested in raising the level of practice in the observance of human rights throughout the world, it believes that the problem can best be approached by methods other than the conclusion of treaties on the subject. Secretary of State Dulles, in an instruction to the United States representative at the ninth session of the United Nations Commission on Human Rights, wrote:

There is a grave question whether the completion, signing, and ratification of the Covenants at this time is the most desirable method of contributing to human betterment particularly in areas of greatest need. * * *

The Secretary suggested that in place of trying to develop an acceptable treaty on human rights, the United States delegate should put forward other suggestions of method, based on American experience, for developing throughout the world a human rights conscience which will bring nearer the goals in the charter. He added:

In making such suggestions, I am sure you will want to give special weight to the value of bringing the facts to the light of day, to the value of common discussion of problems in the international forum of the Commission on Human Rights, and to the value of each country drawing on the experience of other countries for inspiration and practical guidance in solving its own problems.[74]

In line with this policy the United States representative on the Commission on Human Rights has proposed a U. N. human rights action program which may be summarized as follows:

(1) Each member of the United Nations would transmit annually for consideration by the Commission on Human Rights a report on developments and progress achieved in the field of human rights and measures taken to safeguard human liberty; and the Commission would submit to the Economic and Social Council such comments and conclusions on the report and other relevant information as it deemed appropriate. The Commission would call the attention of member

[74] Collection of Documents, p. 263.

states to the advisability of setting up advisory bodies, composed of competent persons, to assist their governments in the preparation of their reports.

(2) The Commission would initiate studies of specific aspects of human rights on a worldwide basis stressing in these studies general developments, progress achieved and measures taken to safeguard human liberty, with such recommendations as would be necessary. Specific subjects would be selected for study and an adviser, chosen by the Secretary-General, would prepare a report on the subject and assist the Commission in its consideration of the report.

(3) The United Nations would provide technical assistance at the request of governments, without duplication of the existing activities of the specialized agencies, in the form of advisory services of experts, fellowships and scholarships, and seminars. The assistance would be applicable to any subject in the field of human rights, provided the subject was one for which adequate advisory assistance was not available through a specialized agency and which did not fall within the scope of existing technical assistance programs.

The Commission on Human Rights has recommended that the General Assembly approve a program of technical assistance, but has not yet come to any final decisions on the other two proposals advanced by the United States.

THE STATUS AND ROLE OF THE SECRETARIAT OF THE UNITED NATIONS

STAFF STUDY NO. 12
NOVEMBER 1, 1955

PREFACE

By Walter F. George, *Chairman*

This staff study explores some of the problems that have arisen as a result of the activities of the Secretary General of the United Nations and his staff, the location of the headquarters of the Organization in the United States, and the privileges and immunities that have been accorded to officials in connection with their United Nations activities.

The United States has had comparatively little experience with these problems inasmuch as the United Nations is the first worldwide organization for the promotion of peace to which we have belonged. It is the first such organization to have had its headquarters in the United States. Despite some lack of prior experience, this country took the initiative, however, in inviting the United Nations by concurrent resolution of the Congress to establish its headquarters here. Furthermore, the United States was one of the first nations to confer certain privileges and immunities upon the Organization. Moreover, as this study indicates, the United States has a far greater number of its citizens employed by the United Nations than does any other country.

So long as our national interest requires our participation in the United Nations, it is incumbent upon us to assist in providing conditions in which the Organization may effectively discharge its functions. By reason of our position as the host nation and the site of the headquarters, we have one of the principal responsibilities for the effective functioning of the machinery of the Organization. By the same token, as the guest, the United Nations has special responsibilities toward this country to see that its hospitality is not abused.

While I recognize that the location of the United Nations in the United States has given rise to some special problems, there is no fundamental conflict of interest which cannot be solved by the exercise of restraint and good sense on both sides.

This staff study, No. 12 in the series issued by the subcommittee, was prepared by Francis R. Valeo and Mrs. Ellen C. Collier, Foreign Affairs Division, Legislative Reference Service, Library of Congress. It does not necessarily reflect the views of the subcommittee or any of its members.

CONTENTS

THE STATUS AND ROLE OF THE SECRETARIAT OF THE UNITED NATIONS

A. INTRODUCTION

The United Nations is a voluntary organization of sovereign states. Normally, therefore, virtually all important proposals that the United Nations take a particular course of action are initiated by one or several of the member states. If a sufficient number of members agree to the proposals, and through the instrumentality of the United Nations indicate their approval, the states carry them out. In short, whether the United Nations fulfills its various purposes depends to a very large extent on the good faith and agreement of the member states and only incidentally upon the international institution and its secretariat—the "machinery"—most of which is physically housed on New York's East River.

However, the existence of this machinery does create certain questions as to the international juridical status of the United Nations. The Organization carries on important activities throughout the year when the Security Council or General Assembly are not in session. It has its own headquarters and some 4,000 employees. These employees make up the Secretariat, the one principal organ of the United Nations, excluding the International Court, which is not actually composed of member states as such. The Secretariat, like the Court, acts for all the members of the United Nations, not any particular member. Provisions of the charter dealing with the Secretariat were designed primarily to assure the maintenance of a capable and impartial staff in an organization with sufficient independence to serve in that fashion.

This study reviews some of the problems which have been encountered and examines various proposals relating to this aspect of the United Nations system. It does not cover in detail the internal administration of the Secretariat. Under the charter, changes in that connection can be made by the Secretary General alone or with the authorization of the General Assembly. The study also deals with the legal status of the United Nations in the United States, where its headquarters are located, and in other countries in which offices are maintained.

In the past decade a number of questions have arisen concerning the role of the Secretary General, the degree of control he may exercise over the staff, and the precise juridical nature of the Secretariat. These questions, technical in themselves, have a broader significance. They involve the fundamental nature of the United Nations Organization and its capacity to serve the interests of member states.

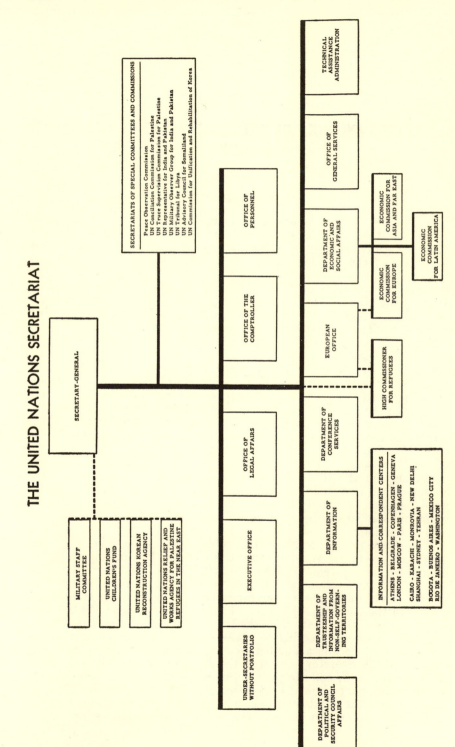

THE UNITED NATIONS SECRETARIAT

B. BACKGROUND

The charter provisions relating to the Secretariat and status of the Organization

The charter establishes the Secretariat as one of the principal organs of the United Nations, along with General Assembly, the Security Council, the Economic and Social Council, the Trusteeship Council, and the International Court of Justice. Articles 97, 98, and 99 of the charter outline the principal functions of the Secretary General and the Secretariat.[1] Article 97 makes the Secretary General the chief administrative officer of the Organization. Under article 98 he is given the duty of acting in that capacity at all meetings of the General Assembly, the Security Council, the Economic and Social Council, and the Trusteeship Council, and of performing other functions entrusted to him by these organs. In addition, he is required to make an annual report to the General Assembly on the work of the Organization.

The role of the Secretary General of the United Nations as described in the charter differs somewhat from that of the comparable official in the League of Nations. The Covenant of the League assigned only functions of an administrative nature to the Secretary General of that organization. As a result, Sir Eric Drummond, the first Secretary General of the League, confined his political activity, as distinct from his administrative functions, to discreet suggestions and mediation. Some observers believe this to be inadequate. One student of the League Secretariat has written:

[In] the nearly unanimous opinion of students of international administration [the Secretary General's] constitutional powers were too restricted * * * a greater leeway for the action of the head of the international administration would have profited the organization as a whole and might have contributed to more effective political action on the part of the League.[2]

Article 99 of the United Nations Charter was designed to meet this criticism and broaden the functions of the U. N. Secretary General. It provides that—

The Secretary General may bring to the attention of the Security Council any matter which in his opinion may threaten the maintenance of international peace and security.

What this means, in effect, is that in many major matters the Secretary General can take the initiative in dealing with member states. In his official capacity, he is the only individual, as an individual, who can do so. With this one principal exception, major activities of the United Nations must ordinarily be initiated by a member state. At San Francisco a proposal to broaden even further the powers of the office by allowing the Secretary General to bring matters before the

---

[1] A few other functions are mentioned in the charter. Under art. 102 the Secretariat is to register and publish all treaties. Under art. 12 the Secretary General has explicit responsibilities to notify the General Assembly, with the consent of the Security Council, what matters relating to peace are being dealt with, or have ceased to be dealt with, by the Council. See also arts. 15, 20, and 73.

[2] Ranshofen-Wertheimer, Egon F. The International Secretariat, A Great Experiment in International Administration. Washington. Carnegie Endowment for International Peace, 1945, p. 37. Supporting this view was the contrasting example of Albert Thomas, the first Director General of the International Labor Organization. He had assumed an active, open, and forceful leadership in the International Labor Organization, and his Organization survived although the League of Nations died. Some attributed the difference in the vitality of the League and ILO to the differing political roles of their first administrators.

General Assembly as well as the Security Council was rejected. An amendment to permit him on his own initiative to bring possible violations of the charter before the Council was also rejected.[3]

Under the charter the Secretary General is appointed by the General Assembly following a recommendation by the Security Council. At the San Francisco Conference the sponsoring powers insisted on retaining the veto in the nomination of the Secretary General. The smaller states were opposed to this special position of the great powers because of the fear that the Secretary General might be subject to the control of the permanent powers, or that he might become a source of contention among them. However, the permanent members remained adamant on this matter, on the grounds that the Secretary General had to enjoy their confidence if he were to be able effectively to discharge his duties. Consequently, the smaller nations redirected their efforts and sought to prevent the adoption of a 3-year term for the Secretary General which, they felt, was so short that it would have the effect of making him too conscious of the imminence of reelection and hence subject to excessive pressures. To that extent their views prevailed and, in consequence, the length of term for the Secretary General is not stated in the charter. Later there was informal agreement that he should serve a term of 5 years, subject to extension. It was made clear, however, that since a term was not specified in the charter, this procedure could be altered in the light of experience.

The United Nations Secretariat under the Secretary General is patterned after that of the League of Nations. Prior to the League, international conferences and organizations had been staffed, as a rule, by national delegations. During the League experience, however, the concept of an international civil service evolved.

The Secretary General has responsibility for appointment of the staff under regulations established by the General Assembly.[4] Article 101 of the charter stipulates:

> The paramount consideration in the employment of the staff and in the determination of the conditions of service shall be the necessity of securing the highest standards of efficiency, competence, and integrity. Due regard shall be paid to the importance of recruiting the staff on as wide a geographical basis as possible.[5]

Article 100 sought to provide for the independence of the Secretariat in these terms:

> 1. In the performance of their duties the Secretary General and the staff shall not seek or receive instructions from any government or from any other authority external to the Organization. They shall refrain from any action which might reflect on their position as international officials responsible only to the Organization.
> 2. Each Member of the United Nations undertakes to respect the exclusively international character of the responsibilities of the Secretary General and the staff and not to seek to influence them in the discharge of their responsibilities.

---

[3] Masland, John W. The Secretariat of the United Nations. Public Administration Review, vol. 5. Autumn 1945, p. 365.

[4] There was considerable discussion of incorporating a provision in the charter establishing 4 or 5 deputies to be appointed in the same manner as the Secretary General. However, the small powers at the San Francisco Conference feared that this would result in the control of these offices, and the whole Secretariat, by the five permanent members of Council. They also feared that deputies selected in this manner would not be sufficiently responsible to the Secretary General. As a result, all amendments in this connection were defeated.

[5] The provisions on geographical distribution and independence of the Secretariat had not been incorporated in the Covenant of the League.

Articles 104 and 105 set forth the legal status and immunities of the Organization and its staff: [6]

ARTICLE 104

The Organization shall enjoy in the territory of each of its Members such legal capacity as may be necessary for the exercise of its functions and the fulfillment of its purposes.

ARTICLE 105

1. The Organization shall enjoy in the territory of each of its Members such privileges and immunities as are necessary for the fulfillment of its purposes.

2. Representatives of the Members of the United Nations and officials of the Organization shall similarly enjoy such privileges and immunities as are necessary for the independent exercise of their functions in connection with the Organization.

3. The General Assembly may make recommendations with a view to determining the details of the application of paragraphs 1 and 2 of this Article or may propose conventions to the Members of the United Nations for this purpose.

Regular diplomatic privileges and immunities normally extended to personnel accredited to a nation are not conferred by these articles. Rather the emphasis seems to be to assure officials and the representatives of the Organization of a status enabling them to serve the purposes of the United Nations without undue interference. This arrangement differs from the League Covenant which did provide full diplomatic privileges and immunities to the officials of the Organization when engaged in official business.

C. THE SECRETARY GENERAL

From the beginning it was recognized that the quality of the Secretariat would depend largely on the individual who occupied the position of Secretary General. His authority to appoint the staff, his interpretation of his duty, his initiative, and his relationship with the member governments would have a profound influence on the role which he and the Secretariat would be accorded in practice.

The Preparatory Commission, which was established in 1945 to prepare in more detail for the new organization, recommended defining the terms of the office of the Secretary General in a manner which would enable a man of "eminence and high attainment" to accept the position. It was the opinion of this group that—

* * * [The] Secretary General, more than anyone else, will stand for the United Nations as a whole. In the eyes of the world, no less than in the eyes of his own staff, he must embody the principles and ideals of the charter to which the Organization seeks to give effect.[7]

Trygve Lie, then Foreign Minister of Norway, a candidate advanced by both the United States and the Soviet Union, was appointed

---

[6] Prior to the League of Nations the granting of diplomatic privileges and immunities to international organizations and their staffs was not usual. During the League period the practice was greatly extended. Although the Covenant of the League of Nations had no explicit provisions on the juridical status of the organization, it did give diplomatic privileges and immunities to the representatives of the member states and to officials of the League when engaged on business. Kunz, Josef L. Privileges and Immunities of International Organizations. American Journal of International Law, vol. 41. October 1947, p. 829.

[7] Report of the Preparatory Commission, Document PC/20, p. 87. The importance attached to the position by many is demonstrated by the fact that names such as Anthony Eden and General Dwight D. Eisenhower were mentioned as possible candidates. For various reasons, however, it was agreed that the Secretary General should be a citizen of one of the smaller powers rather than of the permanent members of the Security Council.

the first Secretary General on February 1, 1946. He was succeeded on April 7, 1953, by Dag Hammarskjold, then a Minister without portfolio in the Swedish Government.

The veto and the Secretary General

After the initial appointment of Mr. Lie, the cleavage between the Soviet Union and the western powers made agreement upon a Secretary General as difficult as agreement on other major questions. When Mr. Lie's first term expired in 1950, the Soviet Union vetoed his reappointment.[8] Although originally a stanch supporter of Lie, the U. S. S. R. opposed the Secretary General because of his stand against the aggression in Korea. The seriousness with which the matter was viewed is shown by the fact that the United States, which has never invoked the veto, threatened its use to prevent any other appointment on the ground that failure to reappoint Lie would in effect penalize him for an action of the Organization which was disapproved by a permanent member. The step proved unnecessary since no other candidate received the necessary seven votes and when the Council could not agree on a recommendation, the Assembly voted to extend Mr. Lie's term for an additional three years.

Some contended that this procedure was a violation of the charter. Chief among them was the Soviet bloc, which refused to recognize Lie as Secretary General for the rest of his stay in office. Credentials and correspondence from the Soviet bloc were addressed to the Secretariat, not the Secretary General. Lie said in regard to the Soviet Union's policy of nonrecognition:

* * * this action, in my opinion, is by far the most serious violation of article 100 of the charter that has occurred. The policy of the Soviet Government and its allies has been, and continues to be, a policy of the crudest form of pressure, not only against me but against any future Secretary General who may incur the displeasure of the Soviet Union for doing his duty as he sees it under the charter.[9]

Lie considered that his insistence on the independence of the Secretary General was vindicated when his appointment was extended in 1950 against the strong opposition of the Soviet Union. However, the Secretary General acknowledged that the Soviet boycott had limited his activities "to a small part of the political role intended for the Secretary General by the charter." [10] He attributed his resignation largely to the fact that the influence of the United Nations for peace was impaired because he could not exercise the full powers of the office of Secretary General when some of the members, particularly one of the permanent powers, would not deal with him. In resigning, he said:

* * * The influence of the United Nations for peace was weakened when its Secretary General could not exercise the full influence of his office as the universally recognized spokesman of the whole Organization. Above all, I desired that my continued presence in the office of Secretary General should not reduce even by the smallest margin the chance of preventing war and preserving peace.[11]

---

[8] The veto was invoked by the Soviet Union a second time in this regard in March 1953 to prevent the appointment of Lester Pearson of Canada.
[9] Lie, Trygve. In the Cause of Peace. New York, Macmillan, 1954, pp. 12–13.
[10] Ibid., p. 385.
[11] Ibid., p. 409.

The political role of the Secretary General to date

The first Secretary General of the United Nations took an active political part in the operations of the Organization. During his incumbency the Security Council, the General Assembly, the Economic and Social Council, and the Trusteeship Council adopted rules of procedure which permitted the Secretary General to make statements in these various organs on questions under consideration.

Lie took a clear-cut position on several controversial issues before the United Nations. He advocated, for example, the dropping of the Iranian question from the Security Council agenda after the Soviet Union had removed its troops from that country. He urged action by the Council to stop Arab intervention after Israel proclaimed itself a state in May 1948. He circulated a memorandum seeking to bring about the seating of the Chinese Communist representative as the representative of China,[12] and traveled to the major capitals urging a 20-year United Nations peace program. After the North Korean invasion of South Korea on June 25, 1950, the Secretary General invoked article 99 and called the attention of the Security Council to the matter as a threat to peace and urged appropriate action.

In taking these positions, however, Lie lost the support of some member states—the Arab countries for his Palestine stand, Nationalist China for his advocacy of the seating of Communist China, and the Soviet Union for his position on the Korean conflict. Before his stand on Korea he was frequently criticized in the United States for taking the same side as the Soviet Union on certain issues, such as the seating of Communist China.

The second Secretary General, Dag Hammarskjold, has given a somewhat different interpretation to his role than his predecessor. He has discussed his position in these terms:

I do not conceive the role of the Secretary General and the Secretariat as representing what has been called a "third line" in the international debate. Nor is it for him to initiate "compromises" that might encroach upon areas that should be exclusively within the sphere of responsibility of the respective national governments.

* * * [The] relationship of the Secretary General to the governments should be one of a trusted consultant on those considerations following from adherence to the charter and membership in the United Nations that should be taken into account by the governments in coming to their own policy decisions.[13]

How that approach has worked out in practice is illustrated in one major political question. Mr. Hammarskjold made a trip to Communist China after the General Assembly resolution of December 10, 1954, had requested the Secretary General to seek the release of United States airmen and other United Nations personnel imprisoned in Communist China and to make—

by the means most appropriate in his judgment, continuing and unremitting efforts to this end.[14]

The initiative, in other words, came from the General Assembly rather than the Secretary General. Once he had been instructed, however, Hammarskjold exercised his own initiative in dealing with

---

[12] U. S. Congress, Senate Committee on Foreign Relations, Subcommittee on the United Nations Charter. Review of the United Nations Charter. A Collection of Documents. Washington, U. S. Government Printing Office, 1954 (83d Cong., 2d sess., S. Doc. No. 87), p. 419. Hereinafter referred to as Collection of Documents.
[13] U. N. Press Release SG/336, September 14, 1953, p. 7. Quoted from F. R. Scott, The World's Civil Service. International Conciliation, January 1954, p. 274.
[14] U. N. Document A/L/182.

the Peking government.   At the end of May 1955 four American prisoners held by the Chinese Communists were released, and some, including United States Ambassador Henry Cabot Lodge, Jr., gave credit to the Secretary General for this development.   In August, when the Peking regime freed the other airmen referred to in the above-mentioned resolution, President Eisenhower extended thanks to—

all who have contributed to this humanitarian result, particularly the United Nations and its Secretary General.[15]

In October 1955, on the other hand, Secretary General Hammarskjold was criticized by several delegates for urging that the question of including a clause calling for self-determination in the draft covenant of human rights be referred to a temporary subcommittee.   The Saudi Arabian delegate said, "Never, in 5 years in office, did his predecessors take such a stand on such a vital issue." [16]

D. THE STAFF OF THE SECRETARIAT

The Secretary General is aided in his work by the staff of the Secretariat.   Members of the staff make all the preparations necessary for the conduct and recording of the many multilingual meetings held under United Nations auspices.   They collect statistics, prepare reports, publish numerous documents, service a variety of programs in the economic, social, and humanitarian fields, publish information about United Nations activities, and perform a myriad of other tasks.

The only guidance to staff appointments given by the charter to the Secretary General is that—

the highest standards of efficiency, competency, and integrity—

should be the paramount consideration in the employment of the staff, and that—

due regard shall be paid to the importance of recruiting the staff on as wide a geographical basis as possible.

The clause calling for due regard to recruitment on a geographical basis has been interpreted to mean that every member of the United Nations should be represented on the staff.   A "desirable range of posts" is calculated for each country by a formula connected with each member's financial contribution.[17]

The provision on geographic distribution has caused some criticism.   Objection has been raised to linking the quota of employees with financial contribution.   Some underrepresented countries have also charged that there has not been sufficient effort to secure as wide

[15] Department of State Bulletin, August 15, 1955, p. 262.
[16] New York Times, October 13, 1955, p. 7.
[17] The appendix contains a chart showing the "desirable range of posts" and the number of positions actually held by nationals of the various countries.   This does not include posts of a lower level, which are locally recruited, or positions which have special language requirements.   "As a rough guide, it shall be assumed that the numerical representation of a country on the Secretariat is reasonable if its percentage of total staff does not deviate more than 25 percent from its percentage of total contribution to the budget of the United Nations save that this deviation should not apply in an upward direction to countries whose contribution is more than 10 percent and that no country shall be regarded as overrepresented if the number of its nationals employed in the Secretariat is less than four." * * * Bulletin of the Secretary General, No. 77, April 21, 1948, A/652, p. 7, . For a discussion of the financial contributions of members, see Staff Study No. 6, Budgetary and Financial Problems of the United Nations.

a geographical distribution as possible.[18]   On the other hand, others have complained that considerations of efficiency, competence, and integrity have been relegated to the background by the effort to obtain wide geographic representation.   It is held further that such a system of appointments and promotions necessarily involves considerations other than merit.[19]

Without a conscious effort to secure geographic distribution, most positions would probably gravitate to citizens of the United States and the Western European countries since there are many applicants from these sources.   Other countries, particularly underdeveloped countries, frequently have a shortage of trained personnel.

Control of the staff of the Secretariat

Member states undertake in the charter to respect the "exclusively international character" of the responsibilities of the staff of the Secretariat and not to seek to influence it in the discharge of these responsibilities.   The Preparatory Commission wrote in 1945:

> Such a Secretariat cannot be composed, even in part, of national representatives responsible to governments.   For the duration of their appointments, the Secretary General and the staff will not be the servants of the state of which they are nationals, but the servants only of the United Nations. * * *[20]

The Commission also contended that one could serve the highest interests of his nation by serving the purpose of the United Nations, which is international peace.

Some have argued that loyalty to one's nation is incompatible with the requirements of an international civil service.   Others, however, hold that loyalty to one's nation is not only not in conflict with employment in the Secretariat but essential to effective performance in that body.   Thus, one author has written:

> * * * As long as international administration is not world government, demanding an integral transformation of one's national loyalty into a global loyalty, the person most useful for international service is one combining the best characteristics of his national origins with belief in and devotion to the international agency in which he is employed.   This synthesis is possible, as the practice of more than 20 years [in the League of Nations] has proved beyond doubt, and can be achieved even under the system of sovereign states.[21]

The question of the relationship between a United Nations employee and his national government was raised in an acute form after a Federal grand jury in New York in late 1952 returned a presentment that there was "infiltration into the United Nations of an overwhelmingly large group of disloyal United States citizens," which constituted a menace to the security of the United States.[22]

[18] Behanan, K. T.   Realities and Make-Believe, Personnel Policy in the United Nations Secretariat.   New York.   William-Frederick Press, 1952, p. 6.
[19] Crocker, Walter R.   Some Notes on the United Nations Secretariat.   International Organization.   November 1950, p. 609.
[20] Report of Preparatory Commission, op. cit., p. 85.
[21] Ranshofen-Wertheimer, op. cit., p. 244.
[22] At that time there were more than 2,000 Americans employed in the Secretariat, of whom 377 were in professional positions.   In making an investigation of the subject, a Senate subcommittee questioned 33 concerning whom they had received information that they were or had been involved with the Communist Party.   Activities of United States Citizens Employed by the United Nations.   Report of the Subcommittee To Investigate the Administration of the Internal Security Act and Other Internal Security Laws, January 2, 1953, p. 3.

The United States representative to the United Nations, Henry Cabot Lodge, Jr., has stated:

The prime consideration, as regards employment of United States citizens by the U. N. * * * is one of justice and of a sense of the general fitness of things. It boils down to this fact, that it is clearly wrong for any United States Communist to be employed at the United Nations when there are so many good Americans from which to choose.[23]

Aside from the question of whether American Communists should be employed in the Secretariat, another aspect of the problem is whether any employees of the United Nations can harm the national interests of the United States.

Ambassador Lodge stated:

* * * [In] the United Nations there is no secret or classified information. The only information which the United Nations ever received about the war in Korea, for example, was mimeographed material which I transmitted, after the Pentagon had released it to the press. There is, therefore, nothing to spy on in the United Nations. No United States citizen working there has ever been indicted for spying.[24]

The clause of the charter requiring that due regard be given to geographic distribution of staff has brought into the Secretariat nationals from Eastern Europe—the Soviet Union, Byelorussia, Poland, and Czechoslovakia, along with those of other nations. In actual practice, however, these countries have not filled their quotas of employees. The Soviet Union for example, has a quota of 131 to 175 but the number of Soviet citizens employed is 19.

Personnel from the Eastern European countries, unless emigres, presumably would be Communists or acceptable to the Communist regimes. While they may not have access to data of any security significance in the United Nations itself, it has been contended that their presence in this country in itself constitutes a danger of espionage. The same argument of course would apply to personnel in the embassies of the Eastern European countries in the United States.

Independence of the Secretary General in choosing staff

A fundamental problem involved in the status of employees from Eastern European countries and Communists in general is the degree of independent control that the Secretary General may exercise over his staff. It has already become a fixed practice to allocate to all the permanent members of the Security Council representation at the highest echelon of the Secretariat.

The rest of the appointments are supposed to be made in compliance with requirements of the charter and at the discretion of the Secretary General. In practice he has often requested help from the member governments in recruitment or selection. In the early years when large numbers of positions were being filled, the Secretary General sought information about American nationals from the United States Government, but this country refrained from giving advice on appointments in an effort to avoid the appearance of attempting to influence the Secretary General or of infringing his independence. Finally, in the fall of 1949, when loyalty issues had assumed major proportions in this country, the Secretary General made an arrange-

---

[23] U. S. Congress. House Committee on Foreign Affairs, Subcommittee on International Organizations and Movements. Hearings, February 2, 1954 (83d Cong., 2d sess.), p. 3.
[24] Ibid., p. 2.

ment with the Secretary of State whereby the Department of State would examine United States records on American personnel employed or seeking employment in the United Nations. However, according to Secretary General Lie, the only judgments which the Department rendered were usually in a single word such as "reject" or "incomplete," and the Secretary General did not feel this was sufficient grounds on which to act against any particular employee or applicant.[25]

In the fall of 1952, the Senate Internal Security Subcommittee conducted an investigation of the activities of United States citizens employed by the United Nations, and 26 witnesses invoked the fifth amendment on various questions related to communism.[26] Secretary General Lie, with the advice of a committee of jurists, discharged these persons principally on the grounds that refusal to answer the questions of the subcommittee constituted a breach of staff regulations concerning the conduct required of staff members.

Lie was criticized in the General Assembly by many non-Communist countries as well as by the Soviet block for the dismissals. Some charged he had yielded to "pressures" from the United States. The criticism was linked with the fact that the Secretary General previously had declined to discharge employees from eastern European countries in the Secretariat whose retention had been protested by the present Communist governments of those countries.

This apparent difference of approach is supported by those who believe that since the United States is the host country, the Organization has special obligations toward it, as well as practical need to maintain good relations with the people of this country. Others, however, contend that the Organization has equal obligations to all members, and that therefore discharging Americans disapproved by the United States Government, when similar action affecting nationals of other states was not taken, constitutes an undesirable precedent.

In 1953 President Eisenhower established an International Organizations Employees Loyalty Board. His order provided for loyalty investigations of such employees and the transmission of advisory opinions on individuals from the Secretary of State to the Secretary General.

The General Assembly in November 1949 established an Administrative Tribunal as the highest board of appeal open to employees of the United Nations Secretariat who felt that their rights might be infringed by action of the Secretary General. Several Americans who had been discharged for invoking the fifth amendment were ordered by the Tribunal to be reinstated or to receive substantial indemnities.

The United States had initially opposed the establishment of the Tribunal, arguing that such a tribunal would weaken the position of the Secretary General as principal administrator of the United Nations. Western European countries and others, however, held that it was essential to protect the individual employee from politically inspired dismissal.[27]

[25] Lie, op. cit., p. 389.
[26] Activities of United States Citizens Employed by the United Nations, op. cit., p. 3.
[27] Wriggins, Howard. Status of the United Nations Secretariat, Role of the Administrative Tribunal. New York, Woodrow Wilson Foundation, 1954, p. 6.

After the ruling, the United States argued in the General Assembly that—

* * * the Tribunal has gone about as far as it is possible to go in assuming for itself the function the charter placed in the hands of the Secretary General.[28]

The United States called upon the General Assembly to annul the awards. Others, however, held the view that the Tribunal had powers of a judicial nature which should not be subject to review by political organs.[29]

In an advisory opinion the International Court of Justice ruled that the General Assembly could not withhold indemnities awarded by the Tribunal.[30] The United States, nevertheless, was able to secure the enactment of a resolution which provided that in the future the awards of the Tribunal would be subject to judicial review and established a committee to study procedures for this purpose.[31]

E. STATUS OF THE ORGANIZATION

The United Nations Organization envisioned in the charter a decade ago now has a staff of more than 4,000 employees and provides facilities for the meetings of delegates who come from all over the world and who are representatives of many different ideologies. To ensure that the United Nations can operate in the United States, this country has conferred on the Organization certain privileges as well as limited immunities from national jurisdiction. Thus, representatives of other nations or those in the Secretariat who come from abroad are permitted to enter the United States even if they would not in other circumstances qualify for admission under quotas or other immigration restrictions. Similarly, this country has granted certain immunities, as have other countries, to enable U. N. officials to carry out legitimate assignments.

A Convention on the Privileges and Immunities of the United Nations was approved by the General Assembly on February 13, 1946, to become effective in each member state upon that state's acceptance. The object of this convention is to define the legal capacity and immunities which member nations agreed were necessary for the effective functioning of the Organization.[32] The convention provides that the United Nations, as an organization, is to have the capacity to enter into contractual arrangements, to acquire and dispose of property, and to institute legal proceedings. It also provides certain privileges and immunities to official representatives of member states, the chief purpose of which is to avoid interference with their attendance at United Nations meetings.[33]

Only the Secretary General and his immediate assistants have the privileges and immunities normally accorded diplomatic envoys. For the rest of the staff of the Secretariat the immunities and privileges

---

[28] James P. Richards, United States Representative to the General Assembly, November 19, 1953. Department of State Bulletin, December 21, 1953, p. 875.
[29] Wriggins, op. cit., p. 19.
[30] H. Con. Res. 262 of the 83d Cong. expressed the view that the awards should not be paid out of funds to which the United States contributes. They are being paid out of the staff assessment fund, described below.
[31] For report, see U. N. Document A/2909. The subject will be debated in the 10th session of the Assembly.
[32] For text, see Collection of Documents, p. 191.
[33] These also include representatives of nongovernmental organizations recognized under art. 71, and private individuals invited on official business.

which are established by the convention include immunity from legal process in respect to words spoken and written and acts performed in their official United Nations capacity; exemption from taxation on salaries paid by the United Nations; immunity from national service obligations; and immunity from immigration restrictions and alien registration. These immunities cover an employee in his own country as well as in the state in which he is serving. Secretariat personnel also are to receive the same currency exchange facilities and the same repatriation facilities in time of international crisis as are accorded to officials of comparable ranks forming part of the diplomatic missions to the country.

The treaty recognizes that immunity is not conferred for the benefit of the individual, but for the benefit of the Organization. The Secretary General is expected to waive it for any employee if he feels the immunity impedes the course of justice and can be waived without damage to the interests of the United Nations. The Security Council has the right to waive the immunity of the Secretary General.

As of June 1954, 43 members had acceded to this convention, which is in force among those who have accepted it. The United States has not ratified the convention.

Inasmuch as the convention has not come into force so far as the United States is concerned, relations between this Government and the United Nations are governed by the headquarters agreement signed on June 26, 1947, and subsequently approved by Congress and the General Assembly.[34]

Under the headquarters agreement the United Nations has the right to make regulations operative within the headquarters district in New York in order to establish therein conditions necessary for the Organization to carry on its functions. These regulations prevail in the district over any contrary Federal or local laws, although these laws otherwise apply. The United Nations may operate its own postal system, radio broadcasting, and other communications facilities in accordance with supplementary agreements with the United States. Freedom of access to the headquarters area is guaranteed, and principal permanent representatives to the United Nations are given the diplomatic privileges which the United States extends to that Nation's diplomatic envoys. In the case of members whose governments are not recognized by the United States, such immunities apply only within the headquarters district, at their residences, and in transit on official business.

The principal differences between the headquarters agreement and the general convention are that under the former the Secretary General and Assistant Secretaries General are not guaranteed diplomatic privileges and immunities; United States citizens employed by the Secretariat are not exempt from income taxation on their salaries or from national service obligations; and no provisions are made for special exchange facilities or for special repatriation facilities in time of international crisis.[35]

Problems concerning immunities of United Nations employees when they have been charged with violation of national law have been few.[36]

[34] Collection of Documents, p. 197.
[35] Scott, op. cit., p. 308.
[36] See Crosswell, Carol McCormick. **Protection of International Personnel. New York,** Oceana Publications, 1952, pp. 57–69.

Probably the best-known incident is that of Valentin Gubitchev, a Soviet national employed by the Secretariat, who was convicted in the United States of violation of United States law by receiving certain secret documents. When he was arrested, the Soviet Union claimed Gubitchev was entitled to diplomatic status and therefore immune from arrest for any act. The United States and the Secretary General, however, held that a Secretariat official had immunity only in connection with official United Nations acts, and that since Gubitchev was arrested in connection with a private act he was not immune from United States jurisdiction in this instance.[37] The case served to highlight the fact that immunities and privileges recognized for employees of the United Nations Organizations are less sweeping than those normally granted to diplomatic representatives under traditional practice.

Problems in connection with the privileges and immunities of the United Nations have arisen largely in the United States. Although there are numerous information centers throughout the world, a branch office in Geneva, small special missions, and headquarters of the Specialized Agencies elsewhere, the largest concentration of United Nations employees and delegates is in the United States. Since headquarters are in this country, moreover, United States citizens constitute the largest single national block of employees.

A difficulty has arisen over the unwillingness of the United States to exempt its nationals and aliens resident in this country (unless of nonimmigrant status) from Federal income tax on their emoluments from the United Nations. To meet this situation the Organization adopted a tax equalization staff assessment plan.[38] Under this plan, salaries are placed on a gross basis and all employees are assessed a percentage of the gross according to an agreed formula. Employees who pay a national income tax on their salaries, as do Americans, are then reimbursed for that amount from the fund so raised. Any excess in the fund has been credited to miscellaneous revenue. If some such arrangement had not been adopted, many non-American employees whose governments do not levy taxes on income from international organizations would have received higher take-home pay than Americans doing comparable work.[39] Other members of the United Nations, however, have considered the method inequitable since, in effect, they have been required to contribute the major part of the annual cost of this tax reimbursement to one member state.

Another difficulty between the United States and the Organization has arisen over the question of freedom of access to the U. N. headquarters. Since 1950 there have been occasional complaints that persons entitled by the headquarters agreement to access to the United Nations have been denied such access.[40]

---

[37] In early 1950 Mr. Gubitchev was tried, convicted, and deported.
[38] Collection of Documents, p. 215.
[39] Some states, such as Canada, do not exempt their citizens from taxation, but do credit the amount they pay in United Nations staff assessments against their income tax.
[40] Obligations of the United States to United Nations persons. American Society of International Law. Report of Committee To Study Legal Problems of the United Nations. Proceedings of the American Society of International Law, 1954, p. 174. In March 1954 the United States restricted a woman observer, Mrs. Dora Grace, representing the Women's International Democratic Federation [an organization with semiofficial status in Communist countries] on the roll of consultative agencies, to a 70-block mid-Manhattan area. New York Times, March 27, 1954, p. 1.

Finally, a conflict on the scope of U. N. immunities arose over the questioning of certain United States citizens employed by the Secretariat by a Senate subcommittee. Such employees were instructed by the Secretary General that they did not have immunity from legal process in regard to their private activities. However, they were instructed not to answer questions concerning official activities of the United Nations. They were authorized to answer questions relating to their positions as staff members when the answers were matters of public record.[41]

One witness invoked this immunity on a particular question on the grounds that the answer would involve disclosing the operations of an official body of the United Nations. The subcommittee objected to this interpretation of the Secretary General's instructions, and held that it would be contemptuous of the Senate for a witness to use "any such excuse" for refusing to disclose pertinent information.[42]

In comparison with the centuries through which international law defining immunities and privileges for diplomatic officials has evolved, experience with officials of international organizations is limited. The only regular arrangement of the League of Nations regarding immunities, for example, was with the host government, Switzerland, and even then much of the practice was based on informal agreements.[43] Problems were ironed out gradually, as they arose. The same process, to some extent, appears to be operating as between the United Nations and the United States at the present time.

F. PROPOSED REVISIONS OF THE CHARTER

Selection of the Secretary General

Out of a decade of experience have come several proposals for basic changes in the juridical status of the United Nations Organization and of the Secretary General. Former Secretary General Lie has recommended that the selection of the Secretary General should be a matter not subject to the veto.[44] This effect might be achieved through amendment of article 97, which deals with the Security Council's role in the selection of a Secretary General, or by modification of article 27 on voting procedures in general in the Security Council. The same effect might also be obtained without charter amendment. The permanent members, for example, might agree among themselves not to use the veto in the selection of the Secretary General.[45] Actually, Trygve Lie's term was extended by the General Assembly after the Soviet Union had vetoed his renomination when the Security Council could not agree on a successor. As noted earlier, however, the Soviet Union refused to recognize Lie after his term had been extended in this manner.

Changes in the veto involving the selection of the Secretary General would carry significant implications as to the type of person who might be selected for the post. Under the present system the candi-

---

[41] U. S. Congress, Senate Committee on the Judiciary, Subcommittee To Investigate the Administration of Internal Security Act and Other Internal Security Laws. Report on Activities of United States Citizens Employed in the United Nations, January 2, 1953 (82d Cong., 2d sess.), p. 2.
[42] Ibid., p. 2.   The witness then invoked the fifth amendment.
[43] Ranshofen-Wertheimer, op. cit., p. 267.
[44] Lie, op. cit., p. 428.
[45] For a fuller discussion of veto changes see Staff Study No. 1 of this subcommittee.

date must be in the first instance a man deemed politically neutral, or at least acceptable to both the Communist and free nations. If the veto were eliminated presumably an outspoken anti-Communist could be selected, if the majority approved him. However, the chance would always exist that a person unacceptable to the United States might also be elected at some time.

To some extent, the advisability of removing the veto from the Secretary-General's selection is related to the role that he is expected to play in the Organization as well as to what the functions of the United Nations are conceived to be. If the Secretary General is to be regarded as an independent political force in the United Nations he would obviously have greater freedom of action if his selection were not dependent on the acquiescence of all five permanent members. In such circumstances, the Secretary General might more readily be able to take vigorous positions on threats to world peace and other issues.

In effect, the first Secretary General did precisely that in calling attention to and urging action with respect to the aggression in Korea as well as the question of seating Communist China in the United Nations. These actions cost him a loss of support and confidence. While his actions may have had considerable influence on world opinion, they also had the effect of reducing his capacity to serve the permanent members in a conciliatory role.

If the Secretary General is to play a major role in mediation and conciliation, then, his acceptability to the permanent members is not only valuable but perhaps essential. Had Secretary General Hammarskjold for example, lacked such acceptability, it is questionable whether he could have exerted any helpful influence in regard to the question of the American prisoners held by the Chinese Communists. Similarly, it is unlikely that he would have been asked to make arrangements for the Four Power Geneva Conference in July 1955.

Strengthening the role of the Secretary General

Proposals have been advanced which would redefine the role of the Secretary General in the operations of the United Nations. Several of these would strengthen the basis in the Charter for his independent political activity. Such proposals would have the effect of—

* * * removing ambiguities, in the charter and in the precedents, concerning the political leadership responsibilities of the Secretary General. They would tend to make such responsibilities clear and of first importance.[46]

As expressed by one writer on the subject:

Unquestionably, the definition in the charter of the political powers which a liberal interpretation would give to articles 97, 98, and 99 would greatly strengthen the Secretary General's hand. Such clarification could prove of particular value in time of challenge of the Secretary General's initiative. What Mr. Lie has won through practice could be spelled out in the charter, promoting a continued vitality and growth of the Secretary General's political activity.[47]

It has been suggested that article 99 be broadened so as to allow the Secretary General to call to the attention of the General Assembly, as well as the Security Council, threats to the peace.[48] This change

---

[46] Sayre, Wallace S. Annals of the American Academy of Political and Social Science, November 1954, p. 139.
[47] Schwebel, Stephen M. The Secretary General of the United Nations, His Political Powers and Practice. Cambridge, Harvard University Press, 1952, p. 206.
[48] Grenville Clark and Louis B. Sohn. Peace Through Disarmament and Charter Revision. Detailed proposals for revision of the United Nations Charter, July 1953, p. 128.

would be in keeping with the trend toward greater concentration of activity in the General Assembly which has resulted from the extensive use of the veto in the Security Council.

As pointed out earlier, this proposal was rejected at the San Francisco Conference. Under present conditions, however, it may be more important for the Secretary General to be able to work through the General Assembly. Even now, under the present rules of procedure, the Secretary General can include items on the provisional agenda of the Assembly, or submit written or oral statements to that organ. If necessary, he might use these methods without charter amendment to call the attention of the Assembly to threats to the peace.

Moving in the other direction, it would be possible to remove article 99 altogether and restrict the functions of the Secretary General to those of an administrative nature. In this connection, it might be argued that there is more to be gained than lost in eliminating the formal political functions of the Secretary General. In the one case when article 99 was invoked, the Korean aggression, the matter had already come to the attention of the Security Council as the result of a request by the United States for an emergency session. By his intervention in the matter, the Secretary General, in the opinion of some people at least, impaired his subsequent usefulness as a conciliator. This argument, however, ignores one important factor. By entering formally into the matter of the Korean aggression, the Secretary General may well have to serve to influence many of the smaller states in alining themselves with the enforcement action.

Experience has shown that the present provisions of the charter allow the Secretary General considerable latitude. If his duties and powers were significantly extended by charter amendment, it might be considered a mandate for the Secretary General to assume a greater role of political leadership in the Organization. Such a trend would be favored by those who hold that the Secretary General can contribute most to the maintenance of peace by taking an international view of world problems and openly working for whatever course he thought would best serve the cause of peace. Others, however, believe that the leadership of the Organization should continue to be vested primarily in the member states which command the majorities in the voting of the United Nations.

National control of staff of Secretariat

Undoubtedly, any members recruited for the staff of the Secretariat in Communist countries have the approval of the governments of those countries. At the present time, as noted earlier, the United States is consulted by the Secretary General with respect to the loyalty of American applicants for employment with the United Nations.[49]

The effect of such action, of course, is to increase the influence of individual nations over the personnel of the Secretariat. If the practice were to become widespread, and the advice of member states binding, it would be equivalent to including in the charter a clause stipulating that each applicant should have the approval of his national government before being employed by the United Nations.

---

[49] The late Senator McCarran introduced a bill (S. 3, 83d Cong.) in the Senate which provided that any American citizen taking or already holding a position with the United Nations would first have to receive a security clearance from the Attorney General, or be subject to a fine of $10,000 or imprisonment up to 5 years. While this bill passed the Senate, it was not acted on by the House.

Some contend that the present tendency to assert national control over Secretariat employees is incompatible with article 100, which calls for the Secretariat's independence from the influence of national governments.

One view is that—

* * * attempts [to require employees to have the prior approval of their national governments] are in flagrant violation of the charter. They not only violate the express stipulation of the charter that the Secretary General shall not receive instructions "from any government or from any other authority external to the organization" (art. 100/1) but they are also in flagrant violation of the undertaking solemnly accepted by all member states "not to seek to influence" the Secretary General and the staff "in the discharge of their responsibilities" (art. 100/2).[50]

Apart from the question of whether or not it is a violation of the charter, certain practical difficulties do arise. National governments change, and a person who has the approval of one government might not have the approval of its successor. This issue arose in regard to Czechoslovakia. After the Communist coup of 1948, Czech nationals employed by the United Nations were denounced by the new Communist regime and their dismissal was demanded. This demand was resisted by the Secretary General. If the Secretary General were bound by the charter to accept the dictates of the national governments with respect to the employment or dismissal of their nationals, changes in governments would in all likelihood often be accompanied by changes in the Secretariat. The prospects of developing an effective and efficient staff in these circumstances would be affected accordingly.

Privileges and immunities

There have been proposals that international officials should have a clearly recognized and guaranteed status which would be of a nature to enable them to perform their duties without interference. One method of accomplishing this objective would be to spell out the privileges and immunities of the officials of the United Nations in an annex to the charter.[51] This would have the effect of making the immunities consistent among all the member states. Under this proposal acceptance of a minimum standard of immunities for U. N. officials would be a requisite for membership in the organization.

Much the same effect might be achieved if all states were to accede to the General Convention on Privileges and Immunities as has been urged by both Secretaries General. The United States is the principal nation which has thus far not done so. A joint resolution authorizing accession was passed by the Senate in 1947 but action was not completed in the House of Representatives. The request for authority to accede to the convention has not been resubmitted by the executive branch since 1949.

The increasingly common practice of granting immunities to employees of international organizations is viewed with concern in some quarters as is the growing number of persons who are exempt from national jurisdiction in varying degrees. A committee of the International Bar Association, for example, has stated:

[50] Honig, F. The International Civil Service. Basic Problems and Contemporary Difficulties. International Affairs, April 1954, p. 177.
[51] John Pinder. U. N. Reform. Proposals for Charter Amendment. London, Federal Union, 1953, p. 24, and Grenville Clark and Louis B. Sohn, op. cit., p. 148.

While this committee does not question the desirability of that practice [of granting privileges and immunities] in the interest of developing an independent international civil service, nevertheless it does not believe that such personnel— running now into thousands of persons—should be immune to the extent which they now are from all law. It therefore suggests jurisdiction over them by courts of the United Nations.[52]

Changing the location of headquarters

In 1945 and 1946 there was considerable pressure to select a small European country as the site for the headquarters of the United Nations. The primary reason appears to have been the feeling that the Organization would develop more independently outside the atmosphere of one of the most powerful of the permanent members of the Security Council.

However, those who favored locating the headquarters in the United States prevailed. They argued that in the United States the integrity of the Organization would be assured and that its presence on American soil would encourage the United States, which had not been a member of the League of Nations, to become a firm supporter of the new international organization.[53] Now, 10 years later, there are some who still believe that many of the problems which have arisen concerning the Secretariat and the Organization are attributable to the location of the Organization in this country. One commentator has suggested:

The clash between the concept of an international institution, run by an international service whose standards and loyalties are detached from that of any other member nations, and the claim of member nations to control the activities and opinions of their nationals, even though they are international civil servants, has now occurred in a most acute form. It would hardly have arisen if the United Nations—as many wanted it—had established its headquarters, in accordance with tradition, in one of the smaller and highly respected states, such as Switzerland or the Netherlands, instead of being located in the territory of its most powerful member.[54]

Those who hold this view believe that many of the problems involving the independence of the Secretariat and the status of the Organization would be solved by moving the headquarters from the United States.

One observer goes so far as to say that—

removal to the milder political climate of a small neutral country is essential to [the] survival of the United Nations.[55]

The view is also expressed that, in case of a general war, the United Nations would be in the midst of a belligerent state and could, therefore, not serve a useful purpose even if it were not destroyed by an atomic bomb.

[52] International Bar Association Committee on the Constitutional Structure of the United Nations report, January 1, 1954, p. 37. For a discussion of some of the proposals to establish additional courts under the United Nations system with jurisdiction over individuals, see Staff Study No. 8, the International Court of Justice. See also, Kunz, Josef L. Privileges and Immunities of International Organizations, American Journal of International Law, October 1947, p. 862.
[53] Even after the decision for the United Nations had been made, the exact locality had to be decided. A gift of $8,500,000 by John D. Rockefeller, Jr., for the purchase of the East River property in New York City where the headquarters is now located, was influential in the selection of this location.
[54] W. G. Friedmann. The United Nations and National Loyalties. International Journal, Winter, 1952–53, p. 19.
[55] Berlitz, Jean. "Jean Berlitz is the pseudonym of a member of the U. N. Secretariat now stationed abroad." Move the U. N. ? The Neutral-Host Concept. The Nation, March 28, 1953, p. 264.

If the United Nations were moved outside the United States, it might have the effect of separating the Organization from questions of our own national security. Any move, however, would be costly, and there would be no guaranty that similar problems of status would not arise in another country.

The proposal, moreover, has implications beyond mere physical location. If the suggestion for removal were made by any other member state but the United States a decision to move might be considered a rebuff to this country. If it were suggested by the United States, it could be taken as a sign that the Organization was not wanted in this country and could be interpreted as a prelude to United States withdrawal from the Organization.

Some feel that the important element in the question of the location of the United Nations is that, wherever established, it should be in territory under the exclusive sovereignty of the Organization.[56] This would provide greater independence for the United Nations but it would also give it something of the characteristics of a government, at least to the extent of giving it jurisdiction over specific territory.

One student of the League of Nations has reached the following conclusion:

> The headquarters of the international administration must be established at a place where its full and unimpaired functioning not only in normal times but also in times of crisis is safe from all interference on the part of the particular government on whose territory the agency operates. Experience has proved conclusively that mere inviolability of premises and grounds is insufficient protection in times of emergency. The situs on which the agency is operating must not only enjoy exterritoriality but should be "international territory" * * *[57]

There does not seem to be much possibility of obtaining international territory as a site for the U. N. headquarters. The idea of establishing such a site for the League of Nations in Switzerland had to be abandoned "in view of the practical impossibility of achieving such a concession from Switzerland."[58]

CONCLUDING COMMENTS

Former Secretary General Lie once said:

> In an international organization that in most respects faithfully reflects the world as it is—a world of sovereign nations, the Secretariat has exclusively international responsibilities. The Secretary General and his staff have in some respects been placed by the charter in an advance—and correspondingly exposed—position.[59]

That statement presents the dilemma of the Secretary General and the United Nations. While the organization is one of sovereign equal states, the needs of those states for continuing international services places a special burden on the Secretary General and his staff. The Secretariat requires sufficient independence so as to be able to serve all

---

[56] Pinder, John, op. cit., p. 24.
[57] Ranshofen-Wertheimer, op. cit., p. 435.
[58] Ibid., p. 232. Similarly, the original plan of establishing a "self-contained international enclave of up to 40 square miles" in Westchester County, N. Y., or Fairfield County, Conn., was abandoned after vigorous protest from groups of citizens in the area concerned. Lie, op. cit., p. 63.
[59] Lie, op. cit., p. 386.

the member states. On the other hand, the Secretariat has little utility independent of the system of sovereign states which it services.

States want an impartial, efficient Secretariat of high standards. At the same time, they also want recruitment on a geographical basis. The two may not always be compatible. States will applaud a Secretary General who displays initiative when his initiative happens to coincide with their national views. They may be inclined to criticize him for the same characteristics when it runs counter to their views.

The provisions of the charter relating to the Secretary General and the Secretariat permit some latitude in operations at the present time. Thus, the Secretary General can be given political tasks by the Security Council and by the General Assembly. By the same token, those organs can take action which would result in restricting the freedom of the Secretary General to operate in the international political realm or he himself may decide that it is desirable to restrict his activity in this respect. In the final analysis, the discharge of the functions of the Secretary General in a manner most likely to contribute to the effective operations of the organization and to peace would appear to depend largely on the perceptiveness and the ability of the individual who serves as Secretary General.

APPENDIX

COMPOSITION OF SECRETARIAT

NATIONALITY STATISTICS

Staff appointed on nationality basis at New York and overseas offices, nationality by category, Aug. 31, 1955

Nationality	Principal Officer, Director, and Under Secretary categories	Professional	Principal level, general-service category[1]	Total	Percent	Special category[2]	Desirable range of posts
Afghanistan		3		3	0.26		1–3
Argentina	1	17	1	19	1.64	1	11–19
Australia	1	14	1	16	1.38		16–26
Austria (nonmember)		2		2	.17		
Belgium	1	23	2	26	2.24		12–20
Bolivia		4		4	.34		1–3
Brazil	1	9	1	11	.95		11–19
Bulgaria (nonmember)		1		1	.09		
Burma		5		5	.43		2–3
Byelorussian S. S. R							4–8
Canada	4	29	4	37	3.19	3	31–51
Ceylon (nonmember)		2		2	.17		
Chile	1	10		11	.95	1	2–4
China	5	43	5	53	4.57		48–80
Colombia		7		7	.60		4–6
Costa Rica							1–3
Cuba		7		7	.60		2–4
Czechoslovakia	2	11		13	1.12	5	8–14
Denmark		19		19	1.64		7–11
Dominican Republic		1		1	.09		1–3
Ecuador		5		5	.43	2	1–3
Egypt		10		10	.86	1	4–6
El Salvador		1		1	.09		1–3
Ethiopia		1		1	.09		1–3
Finland (nonmember)		2		2	.17		
France	8	84	6	98	8.44	7	51–85
Germany (nonmember)		1		1	.09		
Greece	1	9		10	.86		2–3
Guatemala							1–3
Haiti		4	2	6	.52		1–3
Honduras							1–3
Hungary (nonmember)		3		3	.26		
Iceland			1	1	.09		1–3
India	3	43	1	47	4.05		28–48
Indonesia		3		3	.26		5–9
Iran	1	8		9	.78	1	2–4
Iraq		2		2	.17		1–3
Israel		4		4	.34		2–3
Japan (nonmember)		3		3	.26		
Jordan (nonmember)		1		1	.09		
Lebanon		4		4	.34	1	1–3
Liberia							1–3
Luxembourg		1	1	2	.17	1	1–3
Mexico	3	7		10	.86		7–11
Netherlands	2	23		25	2.15	1	11–19
New Zealand	1	8		9	.78		4–8
Nicaragua		2		2	.17		1–3
Norway		20	1	21	1.81	1	4–8
Pakistan	1	13		14	1.21		6–10
Panama		1		1	.09		1–3
Paraguay		1		1	.09		1–3
Peru		6		6	.52		2–3
Philippine Republic		6		6	.52		2–4
Poland	2	17		19	1.64	3	15–25
Saudi Arabia		1		1	.09		1–3

See footnotes at end of table.

Staff appointed on nationality basis at New York and overseas offices, nationality by category, Aug. 31, 1955—Continued

Nationality	Principal Officer, Director, and Under Secretary categories	Professional	Principal level, general-service category [1]	Total	Percent	Special category [2]	Desirable range of posts
Spain (nonmember)		2		2	.17		
Sweden	6	9	3	18	1.55		13–23
Switzerland (nonmember)	1	19		20	1.72		
Syria		6		6	.52		1–3
Thailand		4		4	.34		2–3
Turkey		6		6	.52		6–10
Ukrainian S. S. R							17–29
Union of South Africa	1	8		9	.78		7–11
Union of Soviet Socialist Republics	3	16		19	1.64		131–175
United Kingdom	16	116	21	153	13.18	6	77–129
United States of America	22	245	72	339	29.20		290–387
Uruguay		5		5	.43		2–3
Venezuela		3	1	4	.34		4–6
Yemen		1		1	.09		1–3
Yugoslavia	2	6		8	.69	1	4–6
Stateless and undetermined		2		2	.17	3	
Total [3]	89	949	123	1,161			

[1] At headquarters.
[2] Staff members who have permanent residence status in the host country, and who would otherwise be counted for purposes of nationality statistics.
[3] Not included in above totals:

Total of special category	38
General service category under principal level	2,174
Posts with language requirements	471
Manual workers	210
Field service	118
Special appointments	19
Special internes	15
Total	4,206

Percentage figures represent percentage of total staff appointed on a nationality basis.

NOTE.—Persons on short-term appointments, which do not in any case exceed 6 months, are not included in this report. There are 58 such appointments.

Source: Staff of the United Nations Secretariat, Report of the Secretary General. United Nation Document a/C.5/L.331, September 23, 1955, Annex II.

O